The Crescent Arises over the Banyan Tree

The **Institute of Southeast Asian Studies (ISEAS)** was established as an autonomous organization in 1968. It is a regional research centre dedicated to the study of socio-political, security and economic trends and developments in Southeast Asia and its wider geostrategic and economic environment. The Institute's research programmes are the Regional Economic Studies (RES, including ASEAN and APEC), Regional Strategic and Political Studies (RSPS), and Regional Social and Cultural Studies (RSCS).

ISEAS Publishing, an established academic press, has issued more than 2,000 books and journals. It is the largest scholarly publisher of research about Southeast Asia from within the region. ISEAS Publishing works with many other academic and trade publishers and distributors to disseminate important research and analyses from and about Southeast Asia to the rest of the world.

The Crescent Arises over the Banyan Tree

A Study of the Muhammadiyah Movement in a Central Javanese Town, c.1910–2010

2nd Enlarged Edition

Mitsuo Nakamura

Institute of Southeast Asian Studies
Singapore

First published in Singapore in 2012 by
ISEAS Publishing
Institute of Southeast Asian Studies
30 Heng Mui Keng Terrace
Pasir Panjang
Singapore 119614
E-mail: publish@iseas.edu.sg
Website: <http://bookshop.iseas.edu.sg>

All rights reserved. No part of this publication may be reproduced, stored in a retrieval system, or transmitted in any form or by any means, electronic, mechanical, photocopying, recording or otherwise, without the prior permission of the Institute of Southeast Asian Studies.

© 2012 Institute of Southeast Asian Studies, Singapore.

The responsibility for facts and opinions in this publication rests exclusively with the author and his interpretations do not necessarily reflect the views of the policy of the publishers or their supporters.

ISEAS Library Cataloguing-in-Publication Data

Nakamura, Mitsuo, 1933–
   Crescent arises over the banyan tree : a study of the Muhammadiyah movement in a central Javanese town, c.1910s–2010. 2nd enlarged ed.
   1. Muhammadiyah (Organization)—History.
   2. Islam—Indonesia—Kotagede—History, anthropology.
   I. Title.
BP10 M9N16 2012   2012

ISBN 978-981-4311-91-5 (soft cover)
ISBN 978-981-4279-86-1 (e-book, PDF)

Copyright of all photographs in this book belongs to the author except where otherwise mentioned.

Cover photo: Old Banyan Tree (Waringin Sepuh) in the entrance yard of the Great Mosque of Kotagede (photographed c.1900).
Courtesy of van Bevervoorde Collection, KITLV.

Typeset by Superskill Graphics Pte Ltd
Printed in Singapore by Mainland Press Pte Ltd

*In memory of Gus Dur (1940–2009)
who has widened my view on humanity.*

Religion is sociologically interesting not because, as vulgar positivism would have it, it describes the social order (which, insofar as it does, it does not only very obliquely but very incompletely), but because, like environment, political power, wealth, jural obligation, personal affection, and a sense of beauty, it shapes it.
Clifford Geertz (1966, pp. 35–36).

The vain task of trying to find out in what precise way certain symbols found in the ritual, poetry, or iconography of a given society 'reflect' or 'express' its social or political structure can then be abandoned. Symbols may well reflect not structure, but anti-structure, and not only reflect it but contribute to creating it.
Victor Turner (1974, p. 270).

CONTENTS

List of Figures and Maps ... xi
List of Tables ... xvii
List of Boxes ... xix
Foreword to the Second Edition by Professor Merle C. Ricklefs ... xxi
Preface to the Second Edition ... xxv
Foreword to the First Edition by Professor H.A. Mukti Ali ... xxxiii
Preface to the First Edition ... xxxix
Notes ... xlv

PART I: DEVELOPMENT OF THE MUHAMMADIYAH IN KOTAGEDE, c.1910s–1972 ... 1

1. **Introduction: The Islamization of Java** ... 3
   The Muhammadiyah in the Islamization of Java ... 3
   Approaches and Sources of Study ... 9
   The Paradoxes of the Muhammadiyah in Kotagede ... 13
   Abangan, Santri, Priyayi: The Problem of Conceptualization ... 16

2. **Kotagede under the Banyan Tree: Traditional Society and Religion** ... 18
   Royal Cemetery and Market ... 18
   Traditional Administration in Kotagede ... 26
   Traditional Economy in Kotagede ... 40
   The Impact of Administrative Reforms on Kotagede ... 46

3. **The Beginning of the Muhammadiyah: Court Religious Officials and the Urban Middle Class** ... 51
   Abdi Dalem Santri in Kauman, Yogyakarta ... 51
   The Growth of the Middle Class in Kotagede ... 57
   The Beginning of the Muhammadiyah in Kotagede ... 62
   Confrontation with the PKI (1924) ... 71

4. **The Development of the Muhammadiyah: Religion and Social Action** — 78
   Muhammadiyah Founders in Kotagede — 79
   Schools and Clinics: The Social Activism of the Muhammadiyah — 93
   "Silver Period" and "Silver Mosque" — 103

5. **The Sociology of Ummat Islam: Structure and Anti-Structure** — 119
   The Post-War Political Development — 120
   The Post-War Economic Impoverishment — 125
   Who are the Muhammadiyah Members? — 134
   Geographic Distribution — 135
   Age and Sex — 136
   Education — 137
   Year of Muhammadiyah Affiliation — 139
   Occupational Composition — 139
   Hard Work, Simple Life, and Children's Education — 143
   Rezeki: "Luck" or "Livelihood"? — 151
   Ummat Islam — 154

6. **The Ideology of the Muhammadiyah: Tradition and Transformation** — 165
   Religious Communications among Javanese Muslims — 165
   Gadho-Gadho vs. True Muslims — 168
   Javanese Speech Levels — 180
   Lahir vs. *Batin* — 183
   Kasar vs. *Alus* — 186
   Hawa Nafsu vs. *Ikhlas* — 191
   Ikhlas vs. *Pamri* — 198

7. **Conclusion: Re-Islamization of Java** — 208

Postscript to Part I — 212

PART II: KOTAGEDE REVISITED, 1972–2010 — 215
"Coming Home" by Nur Atika — 216
Introduction to Part II — 219

8. **Social Changes in Kotagede, 1972–2010** — 221
   Administrative Re-designation — 221

	Urbanization	224
	Growing Diversity in Ethnicity and Religion	234
	Diversity in Political Choice	237
	Globalization	245
9.	**The Achievements of the Muhammadiyah**	253
	Background: A Black Hole in History	253
	Religious Propagation (*Dakwah*)	254
	The Muhammadiyah Schools	263
	Iqro' and Qur'anic Kindergarten	271
	PKU vs. PUSKESMAS: Competition and Complement in Health Care	277
	Wakaf: The Foundation for the Muhammadiyah's Institutional Strength	278
10.	**Internal Dynamics of the Muhammadiyah Movement**	283
	Three Generations of Leadership	283
	The Second Generation of the Muhammadiyah Leadership	284
	Pak Bashori: A Typical Second Generation Leader	285
	An Opposition Nipped in the Bud	286
	Ibu Umanah and Ibu Mardi: Typical 'Aisyiyah Leaders	287
	Criticism against Complacency and Stagnation	290
	Leadership Change	296
	Social Dimensions of the New Leadership	302
	The General Membership of Muhammadiyah	303
	Reforming Reformists: Life History of Bachrun Nawawi	304
	Kaharuddin Noor: A Younger Leader	306
	Facing Common Societal Problems	307
	Prospects for New Leadership	308
11.	**Challenges Facing the Muhammadiyah**	311
	The Challenge of Pluralism and Democracy	311
	The Problem of Poverty	315
	Overcoming the "Culture of Poverty"	324
	Overcoming the "Poverty of Culture"	331
12.	**Festival Kotagede: Conflict and Integration**	341
	The Beginning: Success of Festival Kotagede 99	341
	FK 2000: Democracy, Schism and Harmony	346
	FK 2002: Divided Again	350
	Implications of "*Kotagede Ewuh*"	351

13.	The May 2006 Earthquake and Reconstruction of Kotagede	355
14.	**Concluding Remarks: Future of the Muhammadiyah**	361
	Background for the Success of the Muhammadiyah	361
	The Muhammadiyah and the Soeharto Government	362
	Stagnation of the Muhammadiyah Leadership	364
	Criticism from the Younger Generation	364
	Reformasi, Politics, and the Muhammadiyah	365
	Festival Kotagede: Jubilation and Frustration	367
	The Challenge of the "Common Good"	368
	Love for Kotagede	369
	Concern for the Poor	370
	The Future of the Muhammadiyah	371

Postscript to Part II	372
Bibliography	381
Glossary	397
Appendices	403
Index	407
About the Author	429

LIST OF FIGURES AND MAPS

Map 1	Java, Yogyakarta and Kotagede	xlvi
1.1	Bird's eye view of the Royal Cemetery complex (Pasareyan) in Kotagede	10
1.2	Graves of Senapati and other royal family members of Later Mataram	11
1.3	Front gate of the Great Mosque of Mataram	12
2.1	Map of Kotagede	23
2.2	Kotagede: *kota* vs. *desa*	25
2.3	Mausoleums for royal graves	29
2.4	Front view of Royal Cemetery complex in Kotagede during the 1971 general election	30
2.5	*Abdi Dalem Jurukunci* on duty	30
2.6	Requesting the help of the spirit of Senapati at the inner gate of the Royal Cemetery	37
2.7	Bathing in Siliran Spring (women's section)	38
2.8	Boys gathered at the Great Mosque for prayer before group circumcision	38
2.9	Boys leaving the Great Mosque for group circumcision	39
3.1	Friday prayer in the inner hall of the Great Mosque (*minbar* dates back to Sultan Agung's time)	55
3.2	Religious lecture meeting (*pengajian*) on the front porch (*srambi*) of the Great Mosque	55
3.3	Main road (northern route) from Kotagede to Yogyakarta — Mt. Merapi in the background	59
3.4	Front view of Kotagede market	59
3.5	Inside scene of Kotagede market	60
3.6	Main road (eastern route) from Kotagede to Plered	60
3.7	Open reception hall (*pendopo*) of Sopingin, Chief Key-Keeper (*Lurah Jurukunci*)	72
3.8	Palace-like house of a Kalang family (used for R.K. head's election meeting)	72

4.1	House of the "merchant king" Atmosudigdo	81
4.2	Cemetery of the "merchant king" Bahuwinangun	81
4.3	Portrait of Kyai Haji Amir (c.1892–1948)	87
4.4	Kinship and marriage relationships among Muhammadiyah founders in Kotagede	90
4.5	Indonesian students in Cairo, at the front gate of Al-Azhar University, 1928	96
4.6	Kotagede youths in Holland, 1930	100
4.7	*Tukang perak* (silver craftsmen) pounding out silver trays	104
4.8	Engraving motifs on silver trays	105
4.9	Smoothening and polishing silverware	105
4.10	Extending and thinning silver threads	106
4.11	Pak Dullah Siddiq, an entrepreneur with craftsmen at his tortoise-shell workshop *(kerajinan penyu)*	106
4.12	*Buruh jahit* (sewers) at *konfeksi* (ready-made clothes) workshop	107
4.13	H. Humam Siradj with a cutter at *konfeksi* workshop	107
4.14	Workers at *imitasi* (imitation accessories) workshop	108
4.15	Haji Masjhudi, founder of Kotagede Muhammadiyah, in front of his general store	114
4.16	Haji Masjhudi and Professor Mukti Ali at Bani Mukmin's annual Syawalan meeting	114
4.17	Syawalan meeting of Bani Mukmin — descendants of Haji Muchsin and spouses	115
4.18	Syawalan meeting of Bani Mukmin — descendants of Haji Masduki and spouses	115
4.19	Haji Masjhudi in prayer *(do'a)*	116
4.20	People paying last tribute to Haji Masjhudi's body	116
4.21	Haji Masjhudi's body carried to cemetery in Alun-Alun for burial	117
4.22	Haji Masjhudi's body placed in his grave facing west	117
5.1	Exhibition by the Publications Division of the Muhammadiyah at the Sekaten Festival of Yogyakarta, 1932	138
5.2	K.H. Pringgo Hastono (b. 1884), retired *penghulu* (chief religious official) of Kotagede Surakarta	144
5.3	Muhammadiyah leaders in Kotagede	144
5.4	Pak Mudjono, Parmusi (Indonesian Muslim Party) politician in Kotagede	145

List of Figures and Maps   xiii

5.5	Nizar Chirzin, Muhammadiyah youth leader	145
5.6	*Takbiran* on the last night of Ramadhan	155
5.7	Girls gathered for *takbiran*	156
5.8	Collection of *zakat fitrah* (religious tax) in rice on the eve of Idul Fitri	156
5.9	Distribution of *zakat fitrah* on the eve of Idul Fitri	157
5.10	Procession to *sholat ied* (festive prayer) on Idul Adha	157
5.11	Men and boys in *sholat ied* (festive prayer) on Idul Adha	158
5.12	Women and girls in *sholat ied* (festive prayer) on Idul Adha	158
5.13	*Khutbah* (sermon) after *sholat ied* (festive prayer) on Idul Adha	159
5.14	*Korban* (sacrificial animals) led to the slaughter on Idul Adha	159
5.15	Cow being sacrificed	160
5.16	Goat being sacrificed	160
5.17	Slaughtered animals taken for distribution of meat	161
6.1	Syawalan meeting of R.K. Prenggan (speaker is the sub-district military commander, Pak Rasjidin)	187
6.2	Syawalan meeting of Kotagede Muhammadiyah (speaker is Pak A.R. Fakhruddin, national chairman of Muhammadiyah)	188
6.3	Pak A.R. and his audience	193
6.4	Visit of General Nasution to Silver Mosque in Kotagede	193
6.5	(From left) Professor Abdul Kahar Muzakkir, Pak Wardi, Pak Jamhari, Pak S.K. Hardjono, and the author in Alun-Alun, Kotagede	194
6.6	Pak M. Asrofie speaking at a *pengajian* (religious lecture meeting) in Purbayan	202
6.7	Professional *dhagelan* troupe performing at Independence Day celebration	202
6.8	Amateur *kethoprak* group performing in Purbayan	203
6.9	Commercial *kethoprak* troupe performing in Gedongan	203
6.10	Gambling near *kethoprak* show	204
6.11	1971 general election posters in front of Kotagede market	204
6.12	Parmusi (Indonesian Muslim Party) campaign posters	205
Map 2	Kotagede Region	217
Map 3	Yogyakarta City and Kotagede Region	218
8.1	Front view of the village office of Jagalan	222
8.2	Village office of Jagalan with multi-purpose hall constructed after the 2006 earthquake	223

8.3	Sign of "Kawasan Kotagede" at the western end of the bridge over Gajah Wong River	223
8.4	Mt. Merapi seen from Ring Road	225
8.5	Remains of *pendopo* Sopingin	226
8.6	Two-storeyed buildings on Jl. Kemasan	228
8.7	Front entrance of Kotagede market on Legi day	231
8.8	Traffic jam in front of Kotagede market on Legi day	231
8.9	Traffic on Jl. Karanglo looking to the east	232
8.10	Muhammadiyah elementary school at Bodon — reconstructed after the 2006 earthquake	233
8.11	PUSKESMAS, community health care centre	234
8.12	A man of Chinese descent living on the outskirts of Kotagede	235
8.13	A standard house built with aid from the World Bank after the 2006 earthquake	246
8.14	Outer wall of Rumah Pesik	247
8.15	Rumah Pesik seen from a narrow alley	248
8.16	Front of Monggo chocolate firm	250
8.17	Inside view of Monggo chocolate firm	251
8.18	Factory floor of Monggo chocolate firm	251
9.1	Al-Huda Mosque in Bodon for the central *pengajian* of Kotagede Muhammadiyah	256
9.2	A neighbourhood mosque, Masjid Baiturrahman, in Kampong Selokraman	257
9.3	*Sholat ied* during Idul Adha at Karang	259
9.4	PDHI Building — a pengajian in session	260
9.5	PDHI Hall — former pilgrims association conducting a regular *pengajian*	261
9.6	*Pengajian* at PDHI Hall	261
9.7	Dr Amien Rais in a *pengajian* at the Great Mosque	263
9.8	Inner yard of SMP Muhammadiyah Yogyakarta 7	265
9.9	Students and a teacher at SMK Muhammadiyah Yogyakarta 3	268
9.10	Qur'an kindergarten — a teacher tutoring children to recite the Qur'an	272
9.11	Iqro' textbook by K.H. As'ad Humam	273
9.12	Iqro' textbooks in the printing plant of Team Tadarus AMM	274
9.13	Front view of AMM Meeting Hall	275
9.14	Pak Jazir speaking at a *pengajian* in the AMM Meeting	

	Hall. Photograph of AMM's founder, As'ad Humam, is on the wall	276
9.15	A *pengajian* in session at AMM Meeting Hall	276
9.16	Drs. Mardjuki with a bundle of *wakaf* documents in Kotagede	280
10.1	Pak Bashori and wife showing their little fingers after voting at the 2004 presidential election	284
10.2	Ibu Hj. Umanah Rofi'ie, an 'Aisyiyah leader	288
10.3	Front covers of *Brosur Lebaran* 1991, 2006 and 2009	291
10.4	Pak Kaharuddin (front left) and Pak Natsir (right) in a *pengajian* at the Great Mosque	299
10.5	2009 annual conference of Kotagede branch of Muhammadiyah at Yogyakarta City Hall	302
10.6	Pak Bachrun Nawawi (left) at 2009 annual conference of Kotagede branch of Muhammadiyah	305
10.7	Drs. Habib Chirzin speaking at a discussion on epistemology in April 2011	309
11.1	Free medical check-up of the aged by PKU Muhammadiyah	316
11.2	An advertisement for RASKIN	317
11.3	A vegetable vendor (*bakul*) in Kotagede market	320
11.4	Drs. Asngari Jakfar, a leader for micro-financing	327
11.5	PPHQ Market for Sacrificial Animals	329
11.6	Sacrificial animals at PPHQ	330
11.7	Inner yard of the Royal Cemetery	334
11.8	Still asking for help from the spirit of Senapati in 2008	337
11.9	Drs. Charris Zubair and the PUSDOK panel; a two-storeyed *langgar* behind him	339
12.1	The Plight of Handicraft Workers in Kotagede	347
12.2	*Jaelangkung* (straw men) at Festival Kotagede 2000	349
13.1	Professor A. Kahar Mudzakkir's house damaged by the 2006 earthquake	356
13.2	A silver shop damaged by the 2006 earthquake	357
13.3	The left wing of the Silver Mosque damaged by the 2006 earthquake	358
13.4	Pamphlets of Kanthil Foundation	359

LIST OF TABLES

2.1	Economic Specialization in Kotagede, 1903	42
3.1	Occupations of House-Compound Holders in Kotagede, 1922	57
5.1	Comparison of Occupational Composition of House-Compound Holders in 1922 and Household Heads in 1971	126
5.2	Silverwork Industry in Kotagede, 1935–71	129
5.3	Distribution of Muhammadiyah Members in Kotagede Kota	136
5.4	Age Distribution of Muhammadiyah Members	137
5.5	Terminal Education of Muhammadiyah Members and Kotagede Adults	137
5.6	Years of Affiliation with Muhammadiyah	139
5.7	Occupational Composition of Muhammadiyah Members and Household Heads in Kotagede, 1971	140
5.8	Descendants of Haji Mukmin by Occupation	143
8.1	Population Growth in Kotagede by Kelurahan/Desa, 1970–2007	225
8.2	Religious Affiliation in Kotagede, 2006–07	237
8.3	Results of 2004 Election for Yogyakarta City Council in Kecamatan Kotagede	242
8.4	Results of 2009 Election for City Council of Yogyakarta in Kecamatan Kotagede by Kelurahan	242
9.1	Mosques and *Langgar* in Kemantren Kotagede, 1978	255
9.2	Muhammadiyah Schools in Kotagede, 2004–07	264
9.3	Schools in Kecamatan Kotagede, 2007	269
9.4	Patients Visiting PKU and PUSKESMAS, January–June 2007	277
9.5	List of Major Wakaf Lands managed by the Muhammadiyah Kotagede	279
10.1	List of Major Topics of *Brosur Lebaran*, 1980–95	292
10.2	List of Major Topics of *Brosur Lebaran*, 2000–08	297
10.3	Personal Background of Candidates for the Branch Leadership of the Muhammadiyah, Kotagede, 2005–10	297

10.4 Personal Background of Candidates for the Branch Leadership
of the 'Aisyiyah, Kotagede, 2005–10   301

11.1 Poor People and Poor Household Heads (HH) in Kotagede   318
11.2 Population by Occupation, Kecamatan Kotagede, 2007   319
11.3 Business Enterprises (*Perusahaan/Usaha*) and their Employees
in Kecamatan Kotagede, 2007   322

13.1 Damage and Victims of 2006 Earthquake in Kotagede   355

LIST OF BOXES

1. "Over" vs. "From Behind" the Banyan Tree	xxxvii
2. The Test of Professor Sartono	xli
3. Prayer for Snouck Hurgronje	92
4. Kaum Rois: Baseline of Javanese Islam	102
5. On a Certain Morning in 1970	127
6. Protest of *Orang Halus* (Ghosts)	175
7. The Beatles in Kotagede	207
8. Mobile Phones Spared Tsunami Panic	229
9. Ex-Tapol (Political Prisoners)	239
10. The Enshrined Turtle	333
11. The Fall of a Banyan Tree	340

FOREWORD TO THE SECOND EDITION

A CHANGING SOCIETY AND A CHANGING MUHAMMADIYAH

The first edition of this book, published by Gadjah Mada University Press in 1983, was a significant landmark in the study of Indonesian — especially Javanese — society. This was originally a Ph.D. thesis in anthropology submitted to Cornell University, one that had been inspired to a considerable degree by Clifford Geertz's path-breaking work *The Religion of Java*. That was based on fieldwork done in 1953–54 and was published in 1960. Nakamura's fieldwork was done nearly two decades later and, whereas Geertz and his colleagues had worked in the East Javanese town of Pare (dubbed "Modjokuto" in their publications), Nakamura turned to the town of Kotagede, on the edge of the royal capitol of Yogyakarta. This was the site of the Mataram dynasty's earliest royal graves (from the late sixteenth and early seventeenth centuries) and an important base for the Islamic Modernist movement Muhammadiyah. It was, in other words, a very different place from Geertz's East Javanese site — an area only settled about a century before, without high royal traditions and far from the centre of Islamic reformism. Moreover, Geertz and his colleagues worked in the first post-Revolutionary years of newly independent Indonesia, whereas Nakamura was at work early in the New Order period of Soeharto. So a different view of the religious and cultural life of the Javanese emerged. Nakamura's work lacked the rhetorical flourishes and institutional fire-power of Geertz's, but it was at least as important as — some would say more important than — Geertz's as a study of social realities in much of Java. Nakamura's work was deeply researched, sympathetic and sensible, challenging many stereotypes and assumptions. But its publication by an Indonesian press with poor distribution networks meant that it was never as widely read or as influential as the work of Geertz, except in specialist circles.

Mitsuo Nakamura's return to this subject to produce an updated account is thus immensely welcome and should be widely read. We know that social, political, economic and religious realities have changed dramatically in Java since the times of Geertz and of Nakamura's own earlier research. To illustrate how dramatic those changes are, we may note that, according to data cited by

B.J. Boland, in Javanese villages from 0 to a mere 15 per cent of the people prayed in the 1960s, in 1967 only 14 per cent of the people of Yogyakarta paid the alms (*zakat*) and in Central Java only 2 per cent observed the fast.[1] By contrast, in surveys done in 2006–10 for my own book on the deepening Islamization of the Javanese from the 1930s to the present, around 90 per cent of respondents claimed that they observed the five daily prayers and fasted during Ramadan.[2] This may not tell us that 90 per cent of Javanese in fact do pray or fast during Ramadan, but it certainly tells us that, for the vast majority of people, this has become the only acceptable answer to social surveys in a much more deeply religionized society. Figures for observance of the pilgrimage tell a similar story. From 1950 to 1958, only around 2,500–4,000 people went on the *hajj* each year from Javanese-speaking areas. In fact, in 1958 the available statistics report that the number of departing *hajis* was just 2,037. This was, remarkably enough, fewer than colonial-era statistics report as departing a century before, in 1858 — when 2,283 reportedly set off for Mecca — even though during the intervening century the Javanese population had increased something like six- or eight-fold. By late in the first decade of the present century down to the present, however, the queue of Javanese waiting to go on the *hajj* (a queue made necessary by Saudi Arabia's quotas for pilgrims) was hundreds of thousands of people long and stretched years in advance. For example, in 2010, Central Java's quota of 29,435 was full and the waiting list had nearly 80,000 people on it.[3]

This new edition of *The Crescent Arises over the Banyan Tree* is a formidable work of scholarship, reflecting the transformations adumbrated in the previous paragraph. That crescent — the Modernist movement of Muhammadiyah — seemed to be rising inexorably in the early 1970s, assisted in large part by the Soeharto government's promotion of religion as a social-control and anti-Communist tool. The banyan tree — older forms of spirituality in Java, in which objects such as banyan trees had supernatural potency — seemed

---

1. B.J. Boland, *The Struggle of Islam in Modern Indonesia*, Verhan-delingen van het Koninklijk Institute voor Taal-, Land- en Volken-kunde, no. 59 (The Hague: Martinus Nijhoff, 1971), p. 186.
2. M.C. Ricklefs, *Islamisation and Its Opponents in Java: A Political, Social, Cultural and Religious History, c. 1930 to the Present* (Singapore: NUS Press; Honolulu: University of Hawai'i Press, 2012), pp. 270–71.
3. Ibid., pp. 86, 272–73. The 1858 figures are from M.C. Ricklefs, *Polarising Javanese Society: Islamic and Other Visions c. 1830–1930* (Singapore: Singapore University Press; Honolulu: University of Hawai'i Press; Leiden: KITLV Press, 2007), p. 59.

to be progressively overshadowed. But forty years later the scene is different. While the banyan tree still languishes (and, indeed, one of the actual banyan trees at Kotagede's royal graves has been uprooted), there is probably more performance of older style art forms than was true during Nakamura's first field work there, when many such arts were suspect because of their association with Communist propaganda programmes. That crescent moon has changed, too, for it now shines in a much wider variety of styles, as religion strengthens its hold on local society. Nakamura notes below (pp. 255–56) the increase in the number of mosques in Kotagede, from the two he counted in the 1970s to the fifty-one he counted in 2010. This increase in the number of mosques is replicated across the rest of the Javanese-speaking heartland and, indeed, across Indonesia.

While Kotagede remains overwhelmingly Javanese in ethnicity, its religious life is now marked by much greater plurality than in the 1970s. There are Catholics and Protestants there now, but even more significantly there is a wider variety of Islamic styles represented. Traditionalist Islam as represented by Nahdlatul Ulama is to be seen and some Traditionalist practices are evidently increasing in popularity. Other, more radical styles have also arrived. Muhammadiyah in Kotagede, as across the rest of Indonesia, has felt itself directly threatened by infiltration and subversion from Partai Keadilan Sejahtera (PKS), a semi-Islamist political party modelled to a considerable extent on Egypt's Muslim Brotherhood. So it has had to take steps to defend itself from this threat by disallowing PKS activists using Muhammadiyah properties to promote their views. Other more radical activists, including those rejecting the Indonesian nation and promoting an international caliphate at one quixotic extreme, are also present locally.

The link between politics and religious life is always crucial and here Nakamura notes a phenomenon that is more generally observable across Indonesia: the religionizing of all politics. He writes (p. 244) that all political parties — including those that some scholars prefer to call "nationalist" or even "secular" — "have emphasized the image that their candidates are pious Muslims. So, the nationalist parties are not exclusively 'nationalistic' … [and] the Islamic parties … are no longer exclusively Islamic."

Kotagede is no longer a Muhammadiyah-dominated town. In fact, it may never have been so dominated by Muhammadiyah as Muhammadiyah leaders had thought. The organization faces challenges in many directions. Simple opposition to older Javanese traditions — many with roots in non-Modernist and even pre-Islamic ideas — is no longer adequate and new approaches need to be found. Some of this is encapsulated in the idea of "cultural proselytization" (*dakwah kultural*), a concept hotly debated and very differently interpreted by many Muhammadiyah leaders. It is remarkable that nowadays a Muhammadiyah meeting might open with a performance of *gamelan* or *wayang*. Nakamura perceives that, alongside Muhammadiyah's long-standing Islamization and purification agenda, "a new counter or parallel trend of Javanization has been developing within Muhammadiyah itself" (p. 308). Older Javanese art forms must, however, be purged of any supernatural aspects in the minds of Modernists; they are, in effect, demoted to being "just culture". Traditionalist believers, on the other hand, retain many ideas that, to Modernists, smack of ignorance and superstition. This accommodative trend remains controversial within Modernist ranks and Nakamura tells us that there are Kotagede Muhammadiyah members, particularly of the older generation, who remain opposed to much of it (pp. 332, 338).

Persistent poverty and an evidently increasing gap between the rich and the poor in Kotagede remain a major issue for Muhammadiyah. It is, after all, not only a religious purifying organization, but a social welfare organization as well. It has long been seen as a model for non-governmental and religiously inspired social activism. But it finds poverty an intractable issue and has been accused even from within its own ranks of becoming elitist, particularly in its widespread educational institutions.

By pursuing all of these issues at the level of the town of Kotagede, Mitsuo Nakamura brings to life what, in the hands of other writers, may sometimes seem rather abstract and generalized, even stereotypical. Here is a major religious institution, one of the largest and most impressive in the Islamic world, facing a complex and messy local reality of plurality, social problems and poverty. This is a world of real people and real issues, dealt with on a daily basis in the heat and humidity of tropical Java.

This is a fine book by an outstanding, determinedly interrogative scholar, accustomed to leaving no stone unturned. As I noted at the beginning of this Foreword, in its 1983 version, *The Crescent Arises over the Banyan Tree* was an important landmark. In its 2012 greatly expanded and updated edition, it is so again.

Merle C. Ricklefs
Professor Emeritus, The Australian National University
June 2012

PREFACE TO THE SECOND EDITION

The book before the reader is a study on the development of the Muhammadiyah movement in Kotagede, a small town in the Special Region of Yogyakarta, Republic of Indonesia, over a period of approximately one hundred years from the early twentieth to the beginning of the twenty-first century. The Muhammadiyah, a modernist Islamic social and educational organization, was established in 1912 (1330 AH) by Kyai Haji Ahmad Dahlan (1868–1923), a preacher (*khatib*) of the Great Mosque of the Sultanate of Yogyakarta. The organization is celebrating its centennial anniversary in 2010 (1430 AH) according to the Islamic calendar.

In 1890, Dahlan went to Mecca for pilgrimage and was deeply impressed by the ideas of such modernist Islamic thinkers as Jamaladdin Al Afghani, Muhammad 'Abduh and Muhammad Rashid Rida. He felt that the backwardness of the Javanese Muslims and their suffering under the Dutch colonial rule were rooted in the sorry state of Islam in Java, contaminated by syncretism and deviations (*bid'ah*). So, he began to advocate a return to the pristine teachings of the Qur'an and Hadith, and purification and re-invigoration of Islam through *ijtihad* (independent reasoning) over *taqlid* (blind obedience). He brought *tajdid* (reform) into a number of religious practices including the use of vernacular languages rather than Arabic in Friday sermons and religious propagation (*pengajian*) to make the teachings of Islam understandable to ordinary Muslims. He also introduced a modern school system for the education of Muslim children, for both boys and girls, in which religious and secular subjects were taught side-by-side. He urged the pious actions in Islamic philanthropy towards the poor and the needy of payment of religious taxes (*zakat*), contribution of sacrificial animals (*qurban* or *korban*), voluntary donations of money (*infaq* or *infak* and *sadaqa* or *sadaka, sedakah*), and institution building for educational and social welfare through permanent donation of property (*waqaf* or *wakaf*).

Over the past 100 years, the Muhammadiyah has grown nationally to be the second largest Islamic civil society organization in Indonesia, claiming some 30 million members and supporters. The largest is Nahdlatul Ulama (NU), a traditionalist organization, which claims around 40 million followers.

The major sphere of Muhammadiyah's activities is in institution building (*amal usaha*) for education and social welfare. According to its recent official statistics, it runs more than 10,000 schools from kindergartens to universities; also, more than 900 social welfare institutions including hospitals, clinics, delivery houses, orphanages, elderly houses, rehabilitation centres, houses for the handicapped, cooperatives, and numerous microfinance unions. These institutions are spread throughout the country and managed by the branches of Muhammadiyah: those branches are found in 419, or 84.30 per cent, of all districts and municipalities (*kabupaten* and *kota*) totaling at 497 in the country.[1]

Part I of this volume, The Development of the Muhammadiyah in Kotagede, ca. 1910s–1972, is an almost exact reproduction of my earlier work, *The Crescent Arises over the Banyan Tree: A Study of the Development of Muhammadiyah in a Central Javanese Town* (Yogyakarta: Gadjah Mada University Press, 1983). The book traced the development of the movement in the town of Kotagede from its very beginning to the year 1972, employing both historical as well as ethnographic approaches. The study was based mainly upon data collected through fieldwork in Kotagede between October 1970 and May 1972, with some additional material from archival work in the Netherlands. It was originally submitted as a Ph.D. dissertation to Cornell University in 1976.

The book presented a local case in which the Muhammadiyah movement had transformed the religious life of the townspeople from the one deeply imbued with *kejawen* (Javanese syncretic Islam mixed with pre-Islamic and local beliefs and practices: *kejawén*) to that of reformism — purified and adapted to modernity — over decades. The town is one of the oldest in Islamized Java with a history of at least 400 years going back to the late sixteenth century when it was built as the first capital of the Mataram Kingdom. So, the case of "re-Islamization" from *kejawen* to reformist one in this town had a particular significance in understanding contemporary religious transformation of traditional Javanese society.

I then asserted on the basis of my observation in Kotagede as follows: "The reformist version of orthodox Islam [= Muhammadiyah] is a vigorously proselytizing religious ideology, and has, is, and will bring profound changes to the social, cultural, economic and political aspects of Javanese life in the town." (p. 208 below) This statement was rather bold since it was made in 1976 before the outbreak of the Iranian Islamic Revolution in 1979, which for the first time raised public concern over the "Resurgence of Islam" in the Western world after World War II. My statement was bold, too, in an

---

1. See more details for those figures in the official website of the Muhammadiyah <http://www.muhammadiyah.or.id>, "Jaringan Amal Usaha".

environment where the dominant view among Western scholars assumed that modernization would promote secularization, i.e., continuous weakening of religion in public life which was a common observation worldwide including in the Islamic world. After my field experience, I became in particular, rather critical of Clifford Geertz's compartmentalization of Javanese population into a rather inconsistent but rigid trichotomy of *abangan-santri-priyayi*.[2] (See Part I, pp. 16–17 below.) I was also beginning to question the excessive emphasis on the cultural uniqueness of the Javanese concept of power claimed by Benedict Anderson at the expense of well-rooted Islamic legitimatization of Javanese sovereignty. (Cf. also Part I, pp. 28–40 below.) I was, however, almost a "minority of one", especially among American colleagues in the 1970s. As William Roff pointed out as late as 1985, there was indeed "an extraordinary desire on the part of Western social science observers to diminish, conceptually, the place and the role of the religion and culture of Islam, now and in the past in Southeast Asian societies."[3]

More than a generation has passed since my original study in Kotagede. Empirical as well as theoretical works on Islam in Indonesia have mushroomed during this period and have made my work obsolete.[4] In recent years, however, I have come to feel that a republication of my 1983 book might be worthwhile for several reasons. Firstly, with the passing of time, it has become imbued

---

2. *Abangan* = nominal/non-practising Muslims, *santri* = practising Muslims or Islamic students, *priyayi* = aristocrats and court/government officials.
3. William R. Roff, "Islam Obscured? Some Reflections on Studies of Islam and Society in Southeast Asia". *ARCHIPEL* 29 (1985): 7–34. In this general atmosphere, Prof. Roff called me "maverick" — personal communication.
4. The recent increase of academic works on the development of Islam in Indonesia, especially in Java, is overwhelming indeed. Readers of my old book would remember the fact that I had appealed then to my colleagues to break "intellectual stagnation" in the study of Islam in Indonesia in its preface (see p. xl below). However, the subsequent development was something like: "Asked for rain and got a flood". Since there have appeared indeed a large number of significant works by Indonesian and foreign scholars, I feel it difficult to selectively list them up here. So, I would mention just a minimum that has made me learn most. It includes Merle C. Ricklefs' three volume series on the modern history of Java, in which Islam has been treated as an inseparable factor in societal formations: *War, Culture and Economy in Java 1677–1726* (Allen & Unwin, 1993); *The Seen and Unseen Worlds in Java 1726–1749* (Allen & Unwin, 1998); and *Polarising Javanese Society: Islamic and other visions* (c. 1830–1930). Professor Ricklefs has made the unseen spiritual world of Java, often mystified by scholars themselves, visible and understandable for us who are equipped with modern common

with a sort of historic value as a piece of contemporaneous documentation on the Muhammadiyah movement in the early 1970s. Secondly, the book has been out of print for a long time, and I have received frequent requests from various sources for additional copies. Thirdly, the original publication contained a number of rather disturbing errors in typescript, photographs, paging, and so forth, and required revision. And fourthly, reprinting this book would be my humble way of joining in the commemorations of the centennial anniversary of the Muhammadiyah. I therefore decided to republish the old book as Part I of the present volume. In order to keep the original version intact as a historical document, revisions for inclusions in this volume have been limited to a minimum — mostly correction of minor factual and typographic errors, addition of some footnotes, and rearrangement of photographs.

Besides that, I have inserted a number of Boxes in Parts I and II of this second edition. They contain excerpts from my field-notes and additional information intended to supplement data in the text.

Part II of this book, Kotagede Revisited, 1972–2010, is written entirely anew for the current publication. It is based mainly on recent fieldwork undertaken in the three months period between December 2007 and February 2008. It also incorporates information accumulated over a number of visits to Kotagede after the period of my initial fieldwork. Thus, the coverage of Part II extends from 1972 to the mid-year of 2010. I was also fortunate to be in the field of July–August 2010, when the entire city of Yogyakarta was enlivened with the centennial anniversary of the birth of Muhammadiyah, which also coincided with the forty-sixth National Congress held there.

The field research for Part II was aimed, in part, to continued the documentation of the Muhammadiyah movement in the town of Kotagede, and also, in part, to examine the validity of my prediction, i.e., deepening Islamization in Javanese society that I had presented in the original book. The Muhammadiyah has in fact achieved an amazing degree of progress in religious propagation and institution building through the subsequent decades

---

sense. I add to this list the work of Azyumardi Azra, *The Origins of Islamic Reformism in Southeast Asia: Networks of Malay-Indonesian and Middle Eastern 'Ulamā' in the Seventeenth and Eighteenth Centuries* (Allen & Unwin and University of Hawaii, 2004). Professor Azyumardi's book has made us possible to appreciate the dynamics of Islamic globalism prior to the deeper penetration of the Western powers in the region and the contemporary significance of its history. Those are from my minimum "must" readings as historical background in order to understand the development of Islam in Java and Indonesia in the twentieth and twenty-first centuries.

of Soeharto's rule. This is indicated by the simple but persuasive fact that, whereas there were only two mosques in the town when I visited there for the first time in 1970, the number of mosques under the management of the Muhammadiyah grew to fifty-one by 2010. Muhammadiyah's achievements are also significant in the area of institution building for public services, i.e., education and social welfare, as Part II below describes in detail.

The advancement of the Muhammadiyah was also quite remarkable in such neighbourhoods known to be former strongholds of PKI (Partai Komunis Indonesia or Indonesian Communist Party) in addition to the neighbourhoods of its traditional strongholds since the time prior to the G30S/PKI Affairs. The local population in the former was regarded mostly as *abangan*, which meant that a significant portion of the *abangan* population has become *santri* in recent decades. They came and prayed in the newly built neighbourhood mosques. Kotagede had become known as a "*santri* town" or even as a "Muhammadiyah town" by the end of the 1980s.

Yet, more recent developments do not paint a simple success story for the Muhammadiyah. From the 1980s, significant criticisms started rising from within the Muhammadiyah movement that it had failed in the continuous transmission of religious values to younger generations and that its leadership had become less responsive to ongoing social changes and stagnant without proper generational change.

Indeed, enormous social changes had already been beginning in the 1970s and accelerated through the 1980s and 1990s in almost all fields of the towns' life, bringing about new challenges to the Muhammadiyah. First of all, urbanization was engulfing the town: an absolute increase in population had occurred. Residential areas were spreading into former farmlands, and there was easier access to the city of Yogyakarta due to new roads and the increasing number of automobiles and motorcycles. Secondly, newcomers of various ethnic and religious backgrounds brought significant heterogeneity to the town. And thirdly, globalization in terms of transnational flow of goods, money, information and people was entering the town.

The fall of the Soeharto regime and the onslaught of *Reformasi* movement in 1998–99 lifted the lid of Pandora's box nationally, and also in Kotagede. The post-*Reformasi* situation further pushed forward the above-mentioned social changes. A number of socio-cultural elements, which until then were regarded as alien or antagonistic to the Muhammadiyah movement, surfaced openly, enjoying the freedom of expression and association. As a result, the dominance, if not monopoly, of the Muhammadiyah in the public sphere came to an end. One of the consequences is the resurgence of *kejawén*, especially that of traditional repertoires of Javanese culture and performing arts.

The guarantee of freedom for popular participation in politics through a series of parliamentary and presidential elections has made the political constellation of the town even more complicated than ever. Political diversification has become the order of the day even within the Islamic forces. Militant Islamist organizations, unknown until recently, have appeared in public. This was followed by the increased visibility of non-Islamic political forces.

On the top of all this, extensive damages, physical and non-physical, caused by the earthquake of May 2006 introduced a number of new dimensions to the social and cultural landscape of the town including the appearance of domestic and overseas NGOs.

The Muhammadiyah in the post-*Reformasi* situation is operating in a new social contexts of democracy, pluralism, and globalization. Meanwhile, continuous poverty among the local population presents a persistent social problem, if not a factor for social instability. The problem of poverty seems to be inhibiting the progress of the local population towards further economic prosperity and social justice.

Part II of this book describes and discusses those changes and challenges, which the Muhammadiyah has recently faced and is facing now. The enormity of the task Muhammadiyah is tackling at present is unprecedented. A number of contrasting, sometimes, contradicting trends are working in the ongoing social dynamics, making the direction of the Muhammadiyah uncertain.

In terms of ideology and value orientation of the townspeople in which the Muhammadiyah operates, an extreme diversification is developing. In addition to the reformism of the Muhammadiyah as an establishment and the revived NU and independent Muslim activism as alternatives to it, Islamism — violent as well as non-violent, *kejawén*, purer Javanism, Christianization, secularization, the flooding of "metropolitan pop-culture", and commercialism and consumerism — to mention only the conspicuous trends are now all jostling each other openly in this tiny old town.

Politically, the Muhammadiyah endured the dictatorship of Soeharto successfully and contributed to the establishment of a parliamentary democracy nationally. Precisely because of this victory of democratic reform, the Muhammadiyah is, however, no longer an oppositional banner bearer vis-à-vis an authoritarian regime. Many of its activists have joined the post-Soeharto governments nationally as well as locally. The Muhammadiyah is now one of the pillars of moderate mainstream Islam in a democratic Indonesia. It is asked to be proactive in terms of policy formulation and implementation, rather than reactive to the powers-that-be.

Yet, it is difficult to deny an impression that the basic strategy being pursued by the Muhammadiyah for a new Indonesia still remains too general and abstract. The stated vision of "superior civilization" (*peradaban unggul*), "excellent religious community" (*ummat utama*), or "truly Islamic society" (*masyarakat Islam sebenar-benarnya*) — all in the terminology of the current Muhammadiyah movement — remain vague, need to be defined, and further to be operationalized to become attainable goals.

In principle, the Muhammadiyah also supports democracy and pluralism rooted in Pancasila. Ideologically or theologically, however, it is still not clear yet how the Muhammadiyah will be restraining its own puritanical urge — sometimes pushing it to go along with self-righteous, exclusivist demands of Islamists. It is not clear yet either how it will contribute to the creation and maintenance of genuine tolerance, harmony and cooperation with communities of other faiths. All this is still vague and unclear especially at the local branch level.

Socially, the pioneering role in the past of the Muhammadiyah in promoting modernity in education and social welfare is no longer tenable now. Government services in those areas have improved to a great degree and expanded widely. They have even become serious competitors of the Muhammadiyah, if not they have already surpassed Muhammadiyah's past advantages. For example, Muhammadiyah's PKUs (hospitals and clinics) are overtaken by government's PUSKESMAS (Community Health Service Center) in terms of the quality and cost of medical and health services. Also, now many government schools in primary and secondary education excel in their service to the Muhammadiyah ones at a lesser monetary burden upon parents.

Economically, a number of large businesspeople, who once supported the Muhammadiyah, have almost all disappeared now except a few. They have either declined or moved out from Kotagede. As mentioned before, in their place, a new middle class, achieving upward social mobility via higher education and securing employment in bureaucracy and modern sectors of society, have become the main social agent of the Muhammadiyah movement along with a still significant number of small to medium businesspeople, male and female. Meanwhile, its constituency has been widened to lower middle classes, and even to the lower classes, partly thanks to the progress of its propagation (*dakwah*) and welfare activities among the poorer segments of society. Yet, the Muhammadiyah has not been able to offer an effective strategy for structural transformation to eradicate deep-rooted poverty still prevailing among a significant portion of the local populace.

These are complicated and compelling challenges, indeed, and require a huge amount of effort to formulate and implement effective responses. So, I can make no simple statement to predict the course of further development of the Muhammadiyah in the next few decades, let alone that for another century. However, one thing seems to be clear — Muhammadiyah will require a great degree of vitality, innovativeness, and dedication in order to keep up with the increasingly rapid pace of social change.

I will be satisfied if the reader shares with me the appreciation of this complexity and enormity of challenges that the Muhammadiyah faces after reading this book. I hope that the reader will also recognize the practical and theoretical significance of research on Indonesian Islamic social movements like the Muhammadiyah for their direct roles and relevance in shaping of Indonesia's future. Extrapolating, the fortune of the Muhammadiyah and other Islamic social movements may be closely related to the future shape of mankind, too, since the total Muslim population is almost one quarter of the world population, and Indonesian Muslims form the largest group therein.

With the present work, I am happy to join again an increasing number of Indonesian as well as foreign scholars who are undertaking research on Indonesian Islam. I sincerely invite comments on this work from colleagues in academia as well as from the general reader. Your honest criticisms are welcome in terms of empirical data, analysis or interpretation presented here so that not only the shortcomings to be found in this book can be corrected, but also our common storehouse of knowledge and understanding on contemporary Indonesian Islam can be enriched further.

Mitsuo Nakamura
Ito, Japan
February 2011

FOREWORD TO THE FIRST EDITION

It is a great honour indeed for me to be requested both by Dr Mitsuo Nakamura, the author of this book, and Drs H.J. Koesoemanto, the Executive Director of Gadjah Mada University Press, to write a few lines as foreword to this book.

This book, *The Crescent Arises over the Banyan Tree, A Study of the Muhammadiyah Movement in a Central Javanese Town,* is originally a dissertation submitted to Cornell University, U.S.A. in 1976. The "town" is "Kotagede" in Yogyakarta. The study covers a period of approximately 70 years, from 1900 to 1970. His approach is historical and ethnological.

Kotagede was chosen as his field of study due to various considerations. The development of Muhammadiyah in Kotagede presents a number of paradoxes in view of the various opinions so far presented by the Western students on the history of modern Islamic movement in Indonesia in general and of Muhammadiyah in particular.

The first paradox is that Muhammadiyah, as an organized effort to cleanse Javanese Islam from admixtures of heterodox local customs and beliefs, gained strong support in the midst of a local community where these heterodox elements had long been deeply rooted in the form of the cult of royal glorification. Strong aspirations for orthodox Islamic reform emerged from among the population, which had been thoroughly imbued with extremely syncretic religious traditions.

The second paradox is the existence of a number of rich Javanese traders and craftmen in Kotagede prior to 1900, whose wealth, entrepreneurial skills and business networks were very much impressive. It has been a common assumption among the students of modern Javanese society that, as a result of the Dutch encroachment in the field of international and domestic trade activities in Java since the day of the Dutch East Indian Company and its employment of the Chinese as middlemen between the indigenous sector and European sector of the economy, indigenous Javanese trade and industry were stifled or at least reduced to the level of petty peddling and casual handicraft (D.H. Burger, *The Structural Changes in Javanese Society: The Supra-Village Sphere,* Ithaca, 1956). It has further been assumed that a social class based upon trade and industry is something antithetical to the official social philosophy in Javanese society in which two classes — the rulers with the nobility and court officials (*priyayi*) on the one hand and the peasantry on the other — have constituted the only legitimate positions in society, leaving no place in it for a commercial class (Lance Castles, *Religion, Politics, and Economic Behavior in Java: The Kudus Cigarettes Industry*, New Haven, 1967). Kotagede is located in the heartland of south Central Java where this presumably non-mercantile Javanese tradition has been pervasive. Yet the wealth, vigor and the tightness of the networks of these Kotagede traders and craftmen had been well-known in the region for a long time.

These two paradoxes lead to a third one: Kotagede traders and craftmen are not *santri,* devout Muslims, prior to the Muhammadiyah. Most of them are *abangan,* nominal Muslims. This phenomenon is quite different to the observation of Western writer, like Clifford Geertz, *(Islam observed: Religious development in Morocco and Indonesia,* New Haven, 1968) who maintains the historical and functional connections between Islam and trade. Islam came to Indonesia through the route of trade and later on when trade was turned inward by the Dutch dominance along the costs, there was an elective effinity between the itinerant and small traders, who moved from one place to another along with their commercial commidities, and hostels for their temporary sojourn and prayer. So mosque and market have been a natural pair. As far as the traders and craftmen of Kotagede prior to the first decade of this century are concerned, they were *abangan*. If there existed any element of Islamic orthodoxy in Kotagede at that time, it was to be found among the group of local court officials *(abdi dalem)* who, as part of their official duties, were obliged to andhere to at least the outward ritual orthodoxy of Islam.

In other world, as far as pre-Muhammadiyah Islam in Kotagede is concerned, Geertz's thesis of the historical and functional connections between Islam and trade does not seem particularly apt. On the one hand it underrates the significance of Islamic elements (albeit in syncretic forms) in the traditional polity of the principality court and on the other it overlooks the fact that not all commercial elements were Islamically devout.

A fourth paradox arises from the observation of more recent development in Kotagede. In spite of some qualifications made above, it is undoubted that there was once a paralleling and mutually stimulating process of the growth of the indigineous entrepreneurship on the one hand and reformist Islam on the other in the pre-War history of Muhammadiyah in Kotagede. But the process seems to have ended with the collapse of Dutch colonial rule in 1942. The War, the revolution and the subsequent political and economic turmoils have deprived Kotagede entrepreneurs of opportunities to recover their pre-War levels of economic strength with a few exception.

This observation implies that the conventional assumption of congruence between modern entrepreneurship and reformist Islam is only partially appropriate to apply to the pre-War history of Kotagede and is much less adequate in reference to the current situation.

This does not mean that Muhammadiyah does not make any progress in its movement after the second World War. On the contrary, the current social basis of the Muhammadiyah movement has become much wider than before and is drawing a considerable portion of its strength from the lower middle stratum and even from some of the lowest stratum of the town's populace. Also, the teaching of the Muhammadiyah in this changing social environment seems to have acquired a new relevance.

It seems that Dr Nakamura would like to prove that the views expressed by several Western writers on modern Islam in Indonesia are inapt. Here, in his book, he demonstrates the existential conditions as observed in Kotagede.

After discussing at length Kotagede and the Muhammadiyah, he draws the conclusion that orthodox Islam in the form of a reform movement, Muhammadiyah, has arisen from within the traditional Javanese Islam as its internal transformation rather than as an outright import of a new ideology and has brought, is bringing, and will bring about profound changes in social, cultural, economic and political aspects of Javanese life.

The view expressed here may appear to come into direct conflict with an assumption widely held among students of contemporary Indonesia that Islam, especially its reformist version, is losing political strength. For example, George Kahin has recently expressed such a view in his preface to Ken Ward's, *The Foundation of the Partai Muslimin Indonesia,* 1970.

Another observer of Indonesian politics studying the result of the 1971 general election noted surprisingly poor show of the electoral support Parmusi obtained (Masashi Nishihara, *Golkar and the Indonesian Election of 1971,* Ithaca, 1972).

On the contrary, Nakamura insists that the Muslims in Indonesia are still strong politically. He notes the persistence of Nahdlatul Ulama in the rural areas of Central and East Java in the 1971 elections and a more recent event of the passage of the Marriage Law with numerous amendments to appease Muslim critics despite Muslim political parties' numerical weakness in the post election parliament.

To support his contention, he points out the observation mady by G.W.J. Drewes, "Indonesian Mysticims and Activism" in Gustave von Grunebaum (ed). *Unity and Variety in Muslim Civilization* (Chicago, 1955), Hoesein Djajadiningrat, "Islam in Indonesia, in Kenneth W.Morgan (ed.), *Islam the*

Straight Path (New York, 1958), and Daniel S. Lev, *Islamic Court in Indonesia: A Study in the Political Bases of Islamic Institution* (Berkeley, 1972). All of them stress the view on the strenght of Islam in Indonesia.

To be exact, however, the two groups of observers are not differing in opinion on the assesment of the same phenomenon. The first one is focussing on the weakening of the political strength of Muslims. The second one, however, is concerned about the growth of the number of serious believers in socio-religious terms. Their opinions are not mutually exclusive and both can be right. Yet, there remains a problem of how to account for the relationships between the waning of Muslim political strength and the waxing of Muslim social reform.

In addressing this problem Nakamura has stood by an obvious but often forgotten truism that Islam is a religion, a faith for the believers and not a marker for political grouping. Politics in fact forms only a peripheral concern for most Muslims' daily lives. Instead of merely looking Islam as a symbol of political solidarity, he has tried to understand the intellectual content, ethical relevance and significance of ritual actions of Islam as they are practiced in real-life context of Kotagede. After living amidst Javanese Muslims for a prolonged period of time he started gradually to feel and realize that there is nothing peculiar about being a pious Muslim in that given environment and it also makes sense to be a more devout one, too.

Furthermore, in his evaluation of Muhammadiyah, Dr Nakamura said that Muhammadiyah is a multi-faced movement. It looks doctrinair at a distance. Yet at a closer examination, we realize that there is little theological systematization. What is there is rather an array of moral admonitions taken direct from the Qur'an and Hadith. It looks exclusivistic when viewed from outside, but in fact it is extremely open when you are within. It looks organizationally imposing, but, actually, it is an aggregate of individuals who value personal devotion most. It looks an organization of high discipline, but in fact there is no effective disciplinary device other than individual's conscience. It looks agressive and fanatic, but in fact its way of propagation are gradualist and tolerant. And finally but perhaps most importantly, it looks anti-Javanese, but actually it embodies Javanese virtues in many ways. Perhaps we can say here we have a case of a universal religion like Islam having become a living religious tradition in the Javanese environment.

This is the assessment of Dr Nakamura on Muhammadiyah as observed in Kotagede.

I think the reader might obtain a much more comprehensive picture of Muhammadiyah should Dr Nakamura explain the reasons for the emergence of this organization in Indonesia in the first decade of the twentieth century followed by its process and growth as to be able to assess its success and failure during the period as observed by the writer in Kotagede. Then the history of Islamic intellectual movement in Indonesia in the twentieth century, as represented by Muhammadiyah, is revealed.

I hope the reader might agree with me that this book is worthy to be read as to know another view of foreign observer on Muhammadiyah which is not parallel to that of many Western observers on the same phenomenon.

H.A. Mukti Ali
Yogyakarta
April 1983

BOX 1
"Over" vs. "From Behind" the Banyan Tree

When I asked the late Professor Mukti Ali to write a foreword to my original book, he questioned me about its title in the Indonesian version. I answered that it might just be translated literally from the English original into Indonesian, "Bulan Sabit menerbit di atas Pohon Bringin." He was pondering for a while and then suggested that "menerbit di atas (= arises over)" would better be replaced by "muncul dari balik (= emerges from behind)". He added that I should avoid unnecessary suspicion or misunderstanding for the fact that banyan tree was the symbol of the Golkar Party in power whereas crescent (and star) was that of the banned Masyumi Party. I felt that Pak Mukti's version did not make much difference as far as the graphic image I was intending by the English title was concerned. So, I followed his advice. The Indonesian version, translated by Yusron Asrofie, was published as *Bulan Sabit Muncul dari Balik Pohon Bringin: Studi tentang Pergerakan Muhammadiyah di Kotagede, Yogyakarta* (Yogyakarta: Gadjah Mada University Press, 1983). Surely, nobody made fuss about the Indonesian title.

PREFACE TO THE FIRST EDITION

The original version of this book is my doctoral dissertation in anthropology submitted to Cornell University in 1976. Data for the dissertation was obtained through fieldwork and archival research. The fieldwork was conducted in the town of Kotagede in the Special Region of Yogyakarta, Central Java, Indonesia, for a period of nineteen months between October 1970 and April 1972. The archival research of two and a half months was carried out in the Netherlands between June and August 1972.

In this book I attempt to present a history and an ethnography of a local branch of the Muhammadiyah movement, one of the most influential Islamic movements in contemporary Javanese society. My perception of Islam in Java in general, and of the Muhammadiyah movement in particular, changed markedly through my field experience. Before fieldwork, I thought that Islam in Java was a losing religion: Javanese Muslims were politically divided and weak, economically stagnant, ideologically conservative, and culturally dull in spite of their numerical strength; Islam as a religion concerned only a small proportion of the Javanese population, a particular segment which was commonly referred to as *santri* in recent social science literature. Personal encounter with Islam and Muslims through fieldwork has changed my perception: Islam in Java is by no means a waning religion but a vital living faith providing guidelines for ethics and inspiration for aesthetics; the Islamization of Java is not a completed historical event but an ongoing process; the Muhammadiyah represents part of this process of continuing Islamization; Islam concerns not a particular segment of Javanese society but its entire population in that it constitutes an integral part of Javanese religious traditions. This book is thus, in a sense, a testimony for the 'conversion' of my view on the significance of Islam in Javanese society. But, at the same time, it is my hope that this book will also contribute to providing some empirical answers to questions often asked about Islam in Java: To what extent and in what ways are the Javanese Muslims? And why is it that Islam still persists in Java?

In revising the original dissertation for publication, I have tried not to be tempted to produce an entirely new work. The "ethnographic present" of this book remains at 1970–1972 as it is in the original dissertation. Certainly, there have been many developments in the town since then. Also, a number of important academic works on Islam in Java have appeared and my own knowledge and understanding of the subject has increased further in more recent years. However, I have resisted the desire to incorporate these factual and intellectual developments into the present work. Instead, I intend to write another monograph in the near future in which the period subsequent to the original fieldwork will be covered and new theoretical dimensions expounded.[1] On this occasion, therefore, the revision has been kept to a minimum: the correction of errors in fact and interpretation; the elimination of redundancy and premature arguments; improvements in language and style; the adoption of the new official spelling for Indonesian and Javanese words; and selective updating of references. No new substantial information has been added.

Many people have contributed to the research on which the writing of this book was based. I would like to thank, first of all, those individuals in the town of Kotagede, especially the local leaders and ordinary members of the Muhammadiyah, who helped my fieldwork in various ways. They are too many to be mentioned individually. My particular appreciation goes to the following four local students who worked as my research assistants for almost the entire period of my fieldwork: Muhadjir Darwin, Effa Djumairy, Dahrowy Hasjim, and Wahzary Wardojo. I also acknowledge the assistance of the Indonesian government authorities, including the Indonesian Institute of Sciences (LIPI), who sponsored my research. I am also grateful to Professor Selosoemardjan and Professor Sartono Kartodirdjo whose advice was helpful in designing fieldwork and to Drs. Tedjo Susilo who introduced me to the town of Kotagede. I also thank Drs. R.S. Kami of the Royal Institute of Anthropology and Linguistics, Leiden, who helped my archival research in Holland. I also acknowledge the help of Akira Nagazumi, Kenji Tsuchiya, Masashi and Suzuko Nishihara, Ken'ichi Goto and Yoshitaka Masuko. I am also grateful to Bapak and Ibu R.M. Tjokrodiprodjo who made my family and me feel at home in Yogyakarta.

A number of teachers helped my graduate study at Cornell University. Professors James T. Siegel, Robert J. Smith, and Oliver W. Wolters were my immediate supervisors. Professor Siegel was instrumental in shaping my studies in anthropology and on Southeast Asia and in completing my doctoral work. Professor Smith read critically the early versions of my dissertation and helped tirelessly in improving my writing. Professor Wolters encouraged me to challenge some conventional assumptions concerning the history of modern Indonesia. Three other professors joined in my supervision at different times: Lauriston Sharp, Benedict R. O'G. Anderson, and Milton Barnett. For the generous help of all of them, I express my sincere appreciation. I would like

---

1. "Another monograph" did not materialize.

> **BOX 2**
> **The Test of Professor Sartono**
>
> On Friday, 15 December 1970, I went to see Professor Sartono Kartodirdjo at his house. Pak Sartono was the "Godfather" of the post-independence generation of historians of Indonesia. I had met him before in Ithaca during the preparation of my research. He welcomed me and told me to take a seat in his study. As soon as I did, he took up a big, thick book from his bookshelves, and handed it to me. It was a hard cover copy of Clifford Geertz's *The Religion of Java*. Then, he asked me: "There is a big mistake in that book. Have you noticed it?" In fact, I had been bothered by the mistake for some time since I had started to learn Javanese at Cornell. The mistake was contained in the acknowledgement, which was placed at the very beginning of the book: "*Nuwun pangestunipun sedaya kalepatan kula.*" And the words were dedicated, among others, to his "*Abangan*" landlord."
>
> Although I was still a beginner in Javanese language then and have never succeeded in mastering it since, Geertz's words sounded odd to me. What he has written literally meant "Please celebrate (*nuwun pangestunipun*) all my mistakes". I did not think that was what he meant. Instead, he must have wanted to say, "*Nyuwun pangapunten sedaya kalepatan kula* (Please forgive all my mistakes)" — a standard expression for greeting at the end of Fasting Month. Also, addressing his landlord "*Abangan*" sounded improper to me since the term implied not so much the neutral nuance of "non-practising Muslim" but rather that of "impious person". The word was rather pejorative as I understood.
>
> Somewhat hesitantly, I answered to Professor Sartono: "Isn't it in the opening page of the book?" He nodded and smiled broadly. I seemed to have passed his test which, according to him, a number of American Ph.D. students failed. Since then, he became very helpful to me suggesting this and that for my fieldwork including introducing me to one of his students who originated from Kotagede. He also often invited me to seminars and conferences held on the Bulaksumur campus of Gadjah Mada University while I was in Kotagede. I owe him a great deal of academic debt. However, I am still very much afraid that my present work is not up to his expectation. (Cf. "Is Geertz's mistake to be celebrated? A Note on Truth and Ethics in Ethnography (In Japanese), *The Japanese Journal of Ethnography* 56, no. 1 (1991): 92–94.)

to add my special thanks to Professor George McT. Kahin for his general guidance as the Director of the Cornell Modern Indonesia Project.

Institutionally, the Fulbright-Hays Graduate Study Program of the U.S. Government, East-West Center of the University of Hawaii, Syracuse

University, Yale University Language Institute, and Cornell University helped me by providing either opportunities, or financial support, or both, for graduate study in the U.S.A. My field work was assisted by a grant from the London-Cornell Project financed by the Carnegie Corporation of New York. My stay in the Netherlands for archival research was supported by a scholarship from the Netherlands Ministry of Education and Science. I would like to express my deep gratitude to those institutions (and key individuals therein) for their support. Without it my study in the U.S.A., Indonesia, and the Netherlands would not have been possible.

Many people helped me directly in the production of my dissertation and thanks are due to them: Willa Appel, Bob Love, Joyce Nakahara, Bernice De Young and Alice Cook, in Ithaca, New York: and Jacki Gray, Bev Jones, Judy Gill and Judy Herman in Adelaide, South Australia. More recently a number of people have assisted me in the revision of my dissertation. I thank Professor John D. Legge of Monash University, Melbourne, for encouraging me to publish it and for his suggestions for its revision; my deep appreciation also goes to Dr. S. Soebardi of the Australian National University, Canberra, and Drs M. Yusron Asrofie of the State Institute of Islamic Studies, Sunan Kalijaga, Yogyakarta, who read and commented on my dissertation, and helped to eliminate many primitive mistakes from this book; Ann Kumar, Barbara Andaya, Christine Dobbin and Judith Pead have also earned my gratitude for reading and commenting on my dissertation. Henny Fokker-Bakker typed part of the dissertation into a computer for revision and checked my Dutch translations, and Judith Wilson and Lois Carrington helped to improve my English: their assistance has been valuable and I thank them all. I acknowledge with thanks a grant from the Toyota Foundation, Japan, which enabled me to stay at the Australian National University for a research project and provided me with the opportunity to complete the revision of my dissertation for publication. I also thank the Department of Anthropology and the Department of Social and Political Change, Research School of Pacific Studies, the Australian National University who hosted me as Visiting Fellow. My special thanks go to Professor H. Mukti Ali who has provided the foreword to this book. I am also grateful to Drs H.J. Koesoemanto, Executive Director of the Gadjah Mada University Press, for publishing this book, first in English and later in its Indonesian translation.

Finally, I would like to acknowledge the help of members of my family. My wife, Hisako, pushed me through graduate study and was my closest co-worker in the field, sharing the experience emotionally and intellectually. Her observation of marriage and divorce among Javanese Muslims (which now has resulted in her M. A. thesis in anthropology at the Australian National

University) has been helpful in developing my understanding on Islam and Muslims in Java. She has also given me substantial comments as well as technical assistance in revising my dissertation for this book. My gratitude to her is simply beyond expression. Our three children, Yuko, Taro and Jiro, also assisted my work in various ways. Their presence as small children in Kotagede (especially the birth of Jiro there) helped Hisako and me to establish a closer rapport and a wider contact with the townspeople. Yuko and Taro who are now in their mid-teens have prepared a portion of the typescript of this revision. This book is to a great degree a product of family enterprise.

In spite of all the help given to me in the preparation of this book, errors of fact, interpretation, and other kind of shortcomings may still be found. I alone should be held responsible for them. I ask the forgiveness of the reader for such shortcomings and would like to receive his or her corrections, criticisms or comments. I am presenting this book to the public not because I am convinced of the value of my contribution in the study of modern Islam in Indonesia. Rather I am doing so because I am deeply concerned with the intellectual stagnation in the field over the recent years and would like to join in the efforts of my colleagues to break this stagnation. I would therefore be very happy if my present work could be used as material to stimulate discussion or as a stepping-stone for better research by others.

Mitsuo Nakamura
The Australian National University
Canberra, Australia
July 1981

A NOTE ON PROPER NAMES

Place names in this book are all real: the uniqueness of the research site has precluded the use of fictitious geographic names. Personal names in the original edition of this book were sometimes real but sometimes were pseudonyms since there was a necessity to protect their privacy under the New Order. However, those individuals quoted in pseudonyms previously are now almost all reverted into, or referred to, their real ones throughout in this edition.

A NOTE ON THE SPELLING OF JAVANESE AND INDONESIAN WORDS

In the spelling of Javanese and Indonesian words including derivatives from Arabic, I have followed the local practices which are generally in compliance with the government guidelines of 1972 and 1974. Consonants in Javanese and Indonesian are pronounced mostly in similar ways as in English except *c* to be pronounced as *ch* in *chair* and *sy* as *sh* in *ship*. Javanese retroflexes, *dh* and *th* are so spelled in this book in contrast to *d* and *t*, with the exception of place names including Kotagede. The name of the town in which this study has been done should be written and pronounced as *Kutha Gĕdhé* if the linguistically correct orthography is to be followed. However, the spelling of Kotagede has become official and so prevalent among Indonesian public nowadays so that it seems unnecessary to resort to the "correct" one. Vowels in Javanese and Indonesian are also pronounced almost the same way as in English except *e* and *a*. The *e* can be *ĕ, è,* or *é*. I have ignored those differences except for some direct quotes in Javanese expression. The *a* in the Javanese penultimate and final syllables without consonants is pronounced as *o* as in *often* in English. So, the same Javanese word (or the word of Javanese origin) may be spelled differently according to contexts, e.g., Panembahan Senapati vs. Pasukan Senopati, and *pendhapa* vs. *pendopo*.

A NOTE ON THE QUOTATION FROM THE QUR'AN

The numbering of the Qur'anic verses in this book follows the Egyptian edition. The first number indicates the number of a chapter and the second, that of a verse. I have relied mostly on Arberry (1955) in the English rendering of the Qur'anic verses.

MAP 1
Java, Yogyakarta and Kotagede

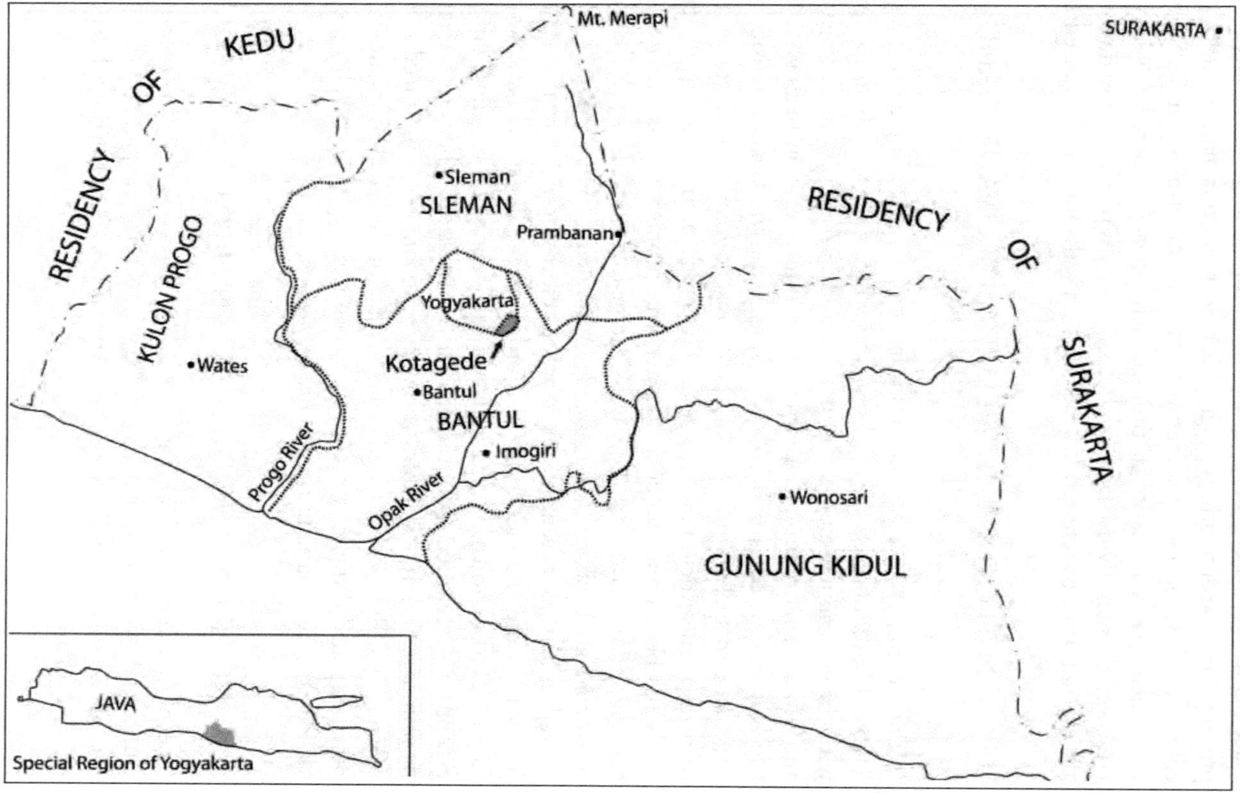

PART I

The Development of the Muhammadiyah in Kotagede, c.1910s–1972

1

INTRODUCTION
The Islamization of Java

> But it should be clear ... that the blanket use of the word "Islam" conceals the fact that one is not coming to terms with an abstraction, but with people; that the term is complex; it cannot meaningfully be discussed as a tide, but rather as a web of dynamisms and tensions. (Johns 1975, p. 36)

This is a study of ongoing Islamization in urban south Central Java focused on the case of a local branch of the Muhammadiyah movement in the town of Kotagede, the Special Region of Yogyakarta. (See Map 1.) This study attempts to present the argument that the Muhammadiyah movement in the town is a contemporary manifestation of the historically continuing process of Islamization, that its development has been related to changes in the social, economic, political aspects of the town, that it is transmitting and yet transforming local religious traditions so that they approach more closely to the orthodoxy of Islam, and that this process of Islamization in the town is likely to progress in the future.

THE MUHAMMADIYAH IN THE ISLAMIZATION OF JAVA

The Islamization of Java, especially its early history, has been a subject debated by generations of historians of Java. Ramified arguments and counter-arguments have developed among them concerning such questions as when, where, how, and why the Javanese population started to accept Islam as their professed religion and who played what role in the historical process. In spite of considerable scholarly efforts so far devoted to answering these questions, comprehensive and definitive works have yet to appear.[1] Although I have no intention of participating in these arguments, nor do I have expertise to do so, my field observation in the town of Kotagede and my inquiry into its local history have led me to question some of the premises underlying the previous studies on the historical Islamization of Java, as shall be discussed later in this Introduction.

The primary concern of this study is not with the historical Islamization of Java in general, but more specifically with the current state of Islam and its immediate past in the town under study. The subject has been approached as a process, i.e. as something going on. The concept of Islamization should be applicable not only to an event of the historical past but also to a recurring process including the one going on at present. By "ongoing Islamization" I mean a process in which a substantial number of Muslims regard prevailing religious situations (often including themselves) as unsatisfactory and, as a corrective measure, strive to live up to what they conceive of as the standard of the orthodox teaching of Islam. In other words, the process can be regarded as a self-conscious re-Islamization of Muslims by themselves. What is emphasized in the process is not merely the necessity to conform to the ritual orthodoxy of Islam but also the genuine devotion to fulfilling the moral and ethical teaching of Islam.

The religious upsurge of this kind seems to have occurred in various organizational expressions through the history of Islam in Java, and it has certainly taken the form of a number of organizations based upon the principles of modern voluntary association since the turn of the twentieth century. One

---

1. For summary descriptions of the history of Islam in Southeast Asia (including the Indonesian archipelago), see de Graaf, Roff, and Benda in *The Cambridge History of Islam* (1970). For a survey of debates on the Islamization of the region among the historians of Southeast Asia, see Legge's *Indonesia* (1980, Chapter Three, "The Influence of Islam," especially note 9, page 53). For the most recent state of the scholarship on this subject, note Johns (1980). It should also be remarked that a number of philological works on historical religious texts are gradually widening the basis of our inquiry into this subject in terms of primary sources. Those which are directly relevant to the Islamization of Java include: Drewes (1969, 1978), Johns (1965), and Soebardi (1971, 1975). See also Kumar (1980*a* and 1980*b*).

of the largest and most influential among them has been the Muhammadiyah movement, first established in 1912 in the City of Yogyakarta. The name of the organization means literally the "followers of Muhammad". By the end of the 1920s, its branches were found in almost all major cities and towns in Java. From the late 1920s, the movement spread into a number of places in the outer islands of the Netherlands East Indies. The Muhammadiyah adopted, from the beginning, the stance of political non-involvement vis-a-vis the colonial authorities and concentrated on the areas of education and social welfare, establishing a number of schools, clinics, hospitals, orphanages, and the like. Within a quarter of a century after its establishment, the Muhammadiyah became one of the largest religious organizations in the Dutch colony.[2] It survived the period of the Japanese occupation (1942–1945) and the Independence Revolution (1945–1949) and grew larger through the 1950s and 1960s. Under the current condition of the New Order since 1966, it continues to grow further organizationally.[3]

Being one of the most representative Islamic organizations in the modern history of Indonesia, the Muhammadiyah has been the subject of a number of studies by Indonesian as well as foreign scholars.[4] The present study has

---

2. According to one source, there were 1,271 branches with well over 100.000 individual members of Muhammadiyah in 1942 (see Alfian 1969, p. 496).
3. A recent official publication from the Muhammadiyah enumerates 12,400 schools (various kinds at various levels from kindergarten to university), 833 social welfare institutions (polyclinics, hospitals, orphanages, and the like), and approximately 600,000 individual members registered at its headquarters (Muhammadiyah 1979).
4. There are a number of scholarly works in English on the Muhammadiyah movement in particular and on the modern Islamic movements of Indonesia in general. First, to enumerate works on Muhammadiyah: Mukti Ali (1957) provides a useful bibliographical introduction to the study of the Muhammadiyah. Alfian (1969) is a detailed monograph on its pre-War politics. Deliar Noer (1973) surveys modern Islamic movements including the Muhammadiyah up to the end of Dutch period. Palmier (1954) reports on the Muhammadiyah at an early stage of its post-Independence reconstruction. Federspiel (1970) is a convenient summary of the Muhammadiyah ideology. My own previous work (1977) sketches the life of a Muhammadiyah leader from Kotagede. Peacock's recent works (1978*a*, 1978*b*, 1979) approach the Muhammadiyah from a Weberian viewpoint. On the early Masyumi Party, in which Muhammadiyah held the position of a special member, Deliar Noer (1960) contains rich primary information.

benefited from these preceding works, and attempts to build upon them and shed new light on one aspect of the movement which has not received sufficient attention thus far: local realities of the Muhammadiyah movement.

The research for this study was conducted in the town of Kotagede in the Special Region of Yogyakarta, Central Java. The town possessed various advantages for the observation of a local development of the Muhammadiyah. The town has been an ethnically pure Javanese town,[5] set in the heartland of Javanese civilization. It appeared in history for the first time in the latter half of the sixteenth century as the original location of the court *(kraton)* of the Kingdom of Later Mataram, one of the earliest Islamized kingdoms in the interior of south Central Java. The early rulers of the Later Mataram Kingdom achieved what turned out to be the final phase in the ascendancy of Javanese civilization over the entire Indonesian archipelago in its pre-colonial history, combining the agricultural basis of riceland in Central Java and the seafaring power based upon trading centers on the north coast of the island. The Kingdom also embodied a refined syncretization of indigenous,

---

More generally on modern Islam in Indonesia: Benda's study (1958) on Islamic politics during the Japanese occupation provides a broad overview on the position of Islam under Dutch colonial rule. The many works of Geertz (1960, 1963*b*, 1965 and 1968) have been most influential in shaping the post-War Western understanding of religious situations in Java. Jay (1963) and Castles (1967) document interactions between religion and politics or economy in certain communities in Java. Federspiel's work on the Persatuan Islam (1970) is a useful introduction to this distinctive reformist movement In West Java. Seigel (1969) analyses the relationship between local social structure and Islam in the modern Acehnese society. Taufik Abdullah (1971) focuses on the politics of reformist movements in Minangkabau during the late 1920s and the early 1930s. Lev's work (1972) is on the Islamic judicial system but also contains information on the relationship with it of various Islamic movements. Boland (1971) covers Islamic politics since Independence up to the late 1960s. Ward (1970) deals with the formation of the Partai Muslimin Indonesia (Parmusi) by the New Order and Samson (1973) compares it with the Masyumi Party. Intellectual developments under the New Order up to the early 1970s are examined by Muhammad Kamal Hassan (1980).

5. According to the 1930 Volkstelling (population census), the town consisted of 9,862 souls, 99.49 per cent of whom were Javanese, the second highest rate of *inlanders* (natives) among all the urban centres in Java (the highest being the town of Kedawung in West Java with 99.60 per cent) and the highest in the Principalities, Central and East Java. (Cf. Milone 1966, pp. 116, 124, and *passim*).

Hindu-Buddhist, and Islamic religious elements in its court life (Berg 1932). The seat of the court of the Later Mataram moved out from Kotagede early in the seventeenth century. The Kingdom itself was then dismembered and reduced to four principalities (Surakarta, Yogyakarta, Mangkunegaran and Pakualaman) through continuous internal strife and Dutch intervention over the next two centuries. However, Kotagede has survived all these turmoils and maintained its identity as a distinct Javanese urban centre to this day largely owing to its particular religious and economic features. The town, as a place where the founders and some of the decendants of the royal family of the Later Mataram were buried, received special care and protection from the principality courts as a joint *tanah pusaka*, ancestral land. Kotagede became a center of the cult of royal glorification. The town also developed from its early days as a center of indigenous trade and industry serving a wide area in central and east Java.

Developments leading to the establishment of the Muhammadiyah in the town took place in this milieu. As early as the mid-1910s, a local religious association named Syarekatul Mubtadi (lit, "Association of Beginners" in Arabic) was founded by some Kotagede Muslims. The purpose of the association was to promote a better understanding of the Islamic teaching. The association aimed at direct learning from the Qur'an and the Hadith (the record of the deeds and the sayings of the prophet Muhammad). It also included both sexes in its membership and audience. In 1923, after several years' existence as an independent local organization, the Syarekatul Mubtadi in Kotagede decided to incorporate itself as a local branch belonging to the Muhammadiyah organization, which had by then started to spread from Yogyakarta city itself to other parts of Java.

The Muhammadiyah in Kotagede has grown steadily since then to this day. Its membership has increased from a few score people when the local branch was first organized in 1923 to almost one thousand individuals at present (1972) of the total population of approximately 15,000 in the town. Its accomplishments in Kotagede over the period of some fifty years have been enormous. The most conspicuous achievements are visible in the fields of general education and social welfare. By 1972 the Muhammadiyah had a number of kindergartens, three public grade schools, two public high schools and another religious high school, a polyclinic and a maternity clinic, a new community mosque (in addition to the old one possessed by the principality courts), a *musholla* (a mosque for women),[6] a number of *langgar* (a small

---

6. See new explanation in Chapter 9, note 4.

neighbourhood prayer house for daily prayers), and a shortwave radio station. It organizes regularly many courses of informal religious education *(pengajian)* for adults and children in various parts of the town and in its vicinity. It has initiated numerous changes in religious beliefs and practices among the townspeople: Islamic annual rituals, weekly and daily prayers, community rites, rites of passage for individuals and families, all have undergone significant changes because of the initiative or influence of the Muhammadiyah. To a substantial number of people in Kotagede who have joined or who have been closely associated with the Muhammadiyah, the meaning of Islam has altered profoundly from what it had been to their ancestors a few generations ago. The subsequent history and the present state of the town of Kotagede, including even those aspects which are only indirectly related to religion, have been influenced to a significant degree by the presence and the development of the Muhammadiyah there.

Besides strictly local achievements, the Muhammadiyah in Kotagede has also made a number of contributions to the advancement of the Islamic cause on the regional and even national scale. In the early years of the post-colonial government of Indonesia, a Kotagedean was appointed to the cabinet portfolio in charge of religious affairs,[7] and a person, who is affinally related to a Kotagede family, was the incumbent when this study was conducted in 1970–72.[8] The first head of the Yogyakarta regional office of the Department of Religious Affairs, was a founder of the Muhammadiyah branch in Kotagede.[9] Numerous positions in the offices of the same Department at the regional, municipal, and ward levels in Yogyakarta have been occupied by many Kotagede Muhammadiyah members. In many parts of the Indonesian archipelago, the Muhammadiyah and other Islamic schools have received a number of teachers originating from the Muhammadiyah circles in Kotagede. Kotagede also has produced a large number of professionals including medical doctors, engineers, lawyers, university professors and college teachers — many of them from Muhammadiyah families. The Kotagede branch of the Muhammadiyah has been one of the most active and influential in the

---

7. H.M. Rasjidi in the first Sjahrir Cabinet, November 1945–March 1946, as a State Minister without portfolio and then in the second Sjahrir Cabinet, March–October 1946, as the Minister of Religious Affairs.
8. Prof. H.A. Mukti Ali in the second Development Cabinet under President Suharto, 1971–1978.
9. Kyai Haji Amir (ca. 1892–1948). For his life history, see Chapter 4, pp. 86–92.

organization located close to its headquarters in Yogyakarta, which renders immediate support to it in time of need.

One is almost tempted to regard this phenomenon of the Muhammadiyah development in Kotagede as a social and intellectual explosion of a sort. Indeed, a local intellectual has employed the term "Islamic revolution" to describe this upsurge of religious energy which has occurred in this small Javanese town over the past few generations (Hardjono 1969, p. 27).[10] Yet the Kotagede phenomenon does not seem unique. There are a number of signs suggesting that there were numerous parallel developments reflecting religious and social fermentation occurring independently but simultaneously in a large number of urban centers across the island of Java (and in the outer islands) during the first decades of this century. The case of Kotagede seems to be only one of these developments.[11] It is hoped therefore that this examination of local Muhammadiyah development in Kotagede will contribute to an understanding of general patterns of modern Islamic transformation in Javanese society.

APPROACHES AND SOURCES OF STUDY

In concrete terms, this study attempts to describe and analyse the process of Muhammadiyah development in Kotagede, and to discuss its implications for various aspects of the lives of the townspeople. The study is historical as well as ethnographic in its approach, covering a period of some seventy years between ca. 1900 and 1972. This rather long time-span in covering the history of the Muhammadiyah development in the town was made possible by the availability of two documents left by two contemporary Dutch observers. One is a monograph written in 1905 by van Bevervoorde, the then

---

10. The same local intellectual has likened the role of Kotagede to that of Kota Gedang in Minangkabau, Sumatra, in terms of their contribution to the Islamic as well as the nationalist movement of Indonesia: Kota Gedang is connected with such prominent figures as Haji Agus Salim, Mohammad Hatta, and Sutan Sjahrir. *Masa Kini* (23 September 1972, Yogyakarta).
11. Solichin Salam (1963*b*, pp. 41f; 1965, pp. 55, 63f) reports that prior to the establishment of the Muhammadiyah in Yogyakarta, there already existed various independent organizations in the Yogyakarta Residency including "Ichwanul Muslimin, Taqwimiddin, Walfadjri, Hambudi Sutji, Chajatul Qulub, Ta'awanul alal birri, Prijo Utomo." In 1921 these organizations finally dissolved themselves in order to join the Muhammadiyah.

Assistant Resident of Yogyakarta, on the general state of affairs in Imogiri (another Royal Cemetery complex of the Later Mataram) and Kotagede (van Bevervoorde 1905). The monograph has enabled me to set the baseline for historical inquiry in this study at around the year 1900, a decade before the formation of the above-mentioned Syarekatul Mubtadi. This monograph is valuable in that it provides detailed descriptions of the relationship between the principality courts and the townspeople of Kotagede, including religious and administrative regulations centring around the Royal Cemetery complex. In other words, the monograph gives us a glimpse of the actual working of what is termed above the cult of royal glorification practised by the principality courts. In addition, van Bevervoorde reports extensively on the population, administration, trade and industry of the town, which is useful as general background information.

The other document is a set of two articles originally published in 1926 by van Mook, the then Controller of Agricultural Affairs in Yogyakarta (1926*a* and 1926*b* in Dutch original; 1958 in abridged English translation;

FIGURE 1.1

Bird's eye view of the Royal Cemetery complex (Pasareyan) in Kotagede (drawn in the late nineteenth century).
Source: Courtesy of van Bevervoorde Collection, KITLV.

Introduction

FIGURE 1.2

Graves of Senapati and other royal family members of Later Mataram (photographed ca. 1900).
Source: Courtesy of van Bevervoorde Collection KITLV.

and 1972 as an Indonesian translation of 1926*a*). The work by van Mook is a monograph in urban sociology with a particular emphasis on the consequences of administrative reforms undertaken in the town during the late 1910s and the early 1920s. The Muhammadiyah movement in the town is mentioned by van Mook as an indication of the hopeful development of the healthy middle-class who he expected to carry on the tasks of administrative reform — rationalization and modernization in government. Like van Bevervoorde's, van Mook's report is also rich in information on the trade and industry of the town and permits us to compare developments in these fields over a period of more than two decades between 1900 and the early 1920s.

Information on the subsequent periods of the Muhammadiyah development in Kotagede has been obtained from various sources: documents of the Muhammadiyah movement itself, documents of Dutch authorities, and memories of the Muhammadiyah's past leaders and non-Muhammadiyah elders in the town. Detailed life-histories have been taken from a number of key persons. For an ethnography of Muhammadiyah at present, ordinary

FIGURE 1.3

Front gate of the Great Mosque of Mataram (photographed ca. 1900).
Source: Courtesy of van Bevervoorde Collection, KITLV.

anthropological methods of data collection have been employed: participant observation, informal interview, household survey, the examination of Muhammadiyah publications, local government statistics, and local newspapers. Efforts have been made to document a number of religious meetings sponsored by the Muhammadiyah and other organizations in order to obtain information on the contents of religious communications in local contexts utilizing the vernacular language (Javanese).

THE PARADOXES OF THE MUHAMMADIYAH IN KOTAGEDE

The picture of the Muhammadiyah in Kotagede which has developed from this study presents a number of paradoxes in view of what has been known so far among Western scholars about the history of modern Islamic movements in general and of the Muhammadiyah in particular.

The first paradox is that the Muhammadiyah movement, as an organized effort to cleanse Javanese Islam from admixtures of heterodox local customs and beliefs, gained strong support in the midst of local community where these heterodox elements had long been deeply rooted in the form of the cult of royal glorification. Strong aspirations for orthodox Islamic reforms emerged from among the population, which had been thoroughly imbued with extremely syncretic religious traditions. To borrow the expression of the local intellectual mentioned above, "the existence of the Muhammadiyah organization and its progress [has taken place] in the atmosphere of traditions which not long ago had been filled with the smell of incense and the smoke of opium" (Hardjono 1969, p. 27). Incense-burning, of course, refers to pre-Islamic ritual practices, and opium-smoking was symptomatic of moral decay among the powerful and the rich; both practices became the target of vehement attack by the early Muhammadiyah movement.[12] (The traditional environment from which the Muhammadiyah movement emerged shall be described in Chapter 2.)

The second paradox is the existence of a number of rich Javanese traders and craftsmen in Kotagede well prior to 1900 whose wealth, entrepreneurial

---

12. The extensiveness of opium-smoking among the well-to-do of the Yogyakarta Residency can be indicated by the following statistics: There existed 83 licensed opium-sale places in 1903 (including one in Kotagede) and 24 in 1924; in the latter year a total of 22,653 thail (1 thail = 38,601 gram) of opium costing ƒ679, 596.60 was sold to 2,679 licensed opium smokers there (Dingemans 1925, p. 49; 1926a, p. 29). As a result of anti-opium campaigns waged simultaneously but independently by the Dutch authorities and by various reformist Muslim movements this practice was virtually wiped out from the principality by the end of Dutch rule according to local sources.

skills and business networks in the general area of south Central Java were comparable to those of the Chinese in the rest of Java: those Kotagedeans had even acquired a derogatory name, *Pecina Jawa* (Javanese Chinese). It has been a common assumption among the students of modern Javanese society that, as a result of the Dutch encroachment in the field of international and domestic trade activities in Java since the days of the Dutch East Indies Company and its employment of the Chinese as middlemen between the indigenous sector and European sector of the economy, indigenous Javanese trade and industry were stifled or at best reduced to the level of petty peddling and casual handicraft (Burger 1956).[13] It has further been assumed that a social class based upon trade and industry is something antithetical to the official social philosophy of Javanese society in which two classes — the rulers with the nobility and court officials *(priyayi)* on the one hand and the peasantry on the other — have constituted the only legitimate positions in society, leaving no place in it for a commercial class (Castles 1967, p. 4). Kotagede is located in the heartland of south Central Java where this presumably non-mercantile Javanese tradition has been pervasive. Yet the wealth, vigour, and the tightness of the networks of these Kotagede traders and craftsmen had been well known in the region for a long time. (Aspects of these traders and craftsmen shall also be discussed in Chapter 2.)

These two paradoxes lead to a third one: Kotagede traders and craftsment were not *santri,* devout Muslims, prior to the Muhammadiyah. If they had been so, it would be another case of what Clifford Geertz has observed as historical and functional connections between Islam and trade. According to Geertz, the connections are partly historical in that "Islam was drawn to Indonesia by a trade expansion [up to the fifteenth century] which two centuries later was turned inward by the Dutch dominance along the coasts," and partly functional in that "there was an elective affinity ... between itinerant, small-scale, catch-as-catch-can trading and an assortment of informal, independent, freely accessible, virtually costless religious hostels scattered broadly over the countryside" (Geertz 1968, pp. 67–68). So "mosque and market have been a natural pair *(ibid.)*". Geertz's thesis, however, seems to rely too heavily on the historical experience of the north coastal regions of Central and East Java while the relationship among Islam, political authorities, and trade in South Central Java seems to present a different pattern (see Sutherland 1975). As far as the traders and craftsmen of Kotagede prior to the first decade of this century are concerned, they were as much *abangan* (peripheral, nominal Muslims) as the bulk of the people in the town. If there existed any elements

---

13. For a refutation of this view, see Dewey (1962, pp. 190–203).

of Islamic orthodoxy in Kotagede at that time, they were to be found among the group of local court officials, *abdi dalem* (royal servants), who, as part of their official duties, were obliged to adhere to at least the outward ritual orthodoxy of Islam. Of such officials, those who were especially responsible for the upkeep of the Royal Cemetery complex and the performance of court rituals there, were known as *abdi dalem jurukunci* (royal key-keepers). They formed part of the *abdi dalem santri*, or *abdi dalem putihan* (court religious officials) of the Javanese principalities.

In other words, as far as pre-Muhammadiyah Islam in Kotagede is concerned, the thesis of Geertz for the historical and functional connections between Islam and trade does not seem particularly apt: on the one hand it underrates the significance of Islamic elements (albeit in syncretic forms) in the traditional polity of the principality courts while on the other it overlooks the fact that not all commercial elements were Islamically devout. It is true that since the 1910s the development of the Muhammadiyah has drawn many members from among wealthy traders and craftsmen in the town (as Chapter 3 shall present). Yet it is also true, as shall be examined later, not all wealthy Kotagedeans became Muhammadiyah supporters. There was a particular group of rich people known as "Wong Kalang" (lit., "Kalang People") who, with their peculiar Hindu-Javanese traditions, stayed aloof for a long time from the advancement of Islam in the town. One thing that emerges from this study is the fact that the process of Islamization in the town has not been a uniform and faceless social event but the result of numerous choices made by a large number of actual individuals. (These choices shall be highlighted through some life histories in Chapter 4.)

A fourth paradox arises from the observation of more recent developments in Kotagede. In spite of some qualifications made above, it is undoubted that there was once a paralleling and mutually stimulating process of the growth of indigenous entrepreneurship on the one hand and reformist Islam on the other in the pre-war history of the Muhammadiyah in Kotagede. But the process seems to have ended with the collapse of the Dutch colonial rule in 1942. The War, the Revolution and the subsequent political and economic turmoils have deprived Kotagede enterpreneurs of opportunities to recover their pre-war levels of economic strength (as shall be described in Chapter 5). For the majority of Kotagedeans, who are small traders, artisans, unskilled workers, and day labourers, the days of economic comforts seem to have gone for good with the end of the Dutch period: the standards of living for the bulk of the population in Kotagede have been pushed downwards over the past thirty years. The establishment of the New Order in 1966 certainly put an end to the preceding period of economic chaos, but its programmes of economic development have not necessarily been beneficial to the majority of people in Kotagede in that they must cope with a new situation in which the flood of foreign capital, technology and commodities threatens their traditional sources of livelihood. Yet, the Muhammadiyah movement has, according to the field observation for this study, kept growing over the same period, and is unlikely to lose its elan in the foreseeable future.

This observation implies that the conventional assumption of congruence between modern entrepreneurship and reformist Islam is only partially appropriate to apply to the pre-war history of Kotagede and is much less adequate in reference to the current situation. As shall be examined later (Chapter 5), the current social basis of the Muhammadiyah movement has become much wider than before and is drawing a considerable portion of its strength from the lower middle stratum and even from some of the lowest stratum of the town's population. Also, the teaching of the Muhammadiyah in this changing social environment seems to have acquired a new relevance (as shall be discussed in Chapter 6).

ABANGAN, SANTRI, PRIYAYI: THE PROBLEM OF CONCEPTUALIZATION

It should be noted that these paradoxes have derived not so much from the history of the Muhammadiyah in Kotagede itself but rather from certain ways of looking at it. This is where the problem of conceptualization comes in. A number of Indonesian scholars have already criticized an arbitrariness in the way of looking at Javanese society in terms of a trichotomy of *abangan, santri* and *priyayi* which has been developed by Clifford Geertz (1960) and followed by a large number of Western observers. The Indonesian scholars have argued that the *abangan-santri* dichotomy is a valid categorization based upon religious differentition while *priyayi* is a status category not to be contrasted properly to *abangan* or *santri,* but to *wong cilik,* the "little people" (Koentjaraningrat 1960, 1967; Sartono 1966, 1972; Harsya 1973; Deliar 1973). For example, Deliar Noer maintains:

> Geertz' division of the Javanese into *putihan* [= *santri*], *abangan* and *prijaji* [*priyayi*] is, however, quite misleading, because such a division is not based on the same criteria. The proper division into *putihan* and *abangan* is based on one's devotion to Islam. *Prijaji* [*priyayi*] denotes nobility, in traditional Java those connected with the administration, and can thus be contrasted to the common people. The basis for the division into *putihan* and *abangan* can also be applied to the *prijaji* [*priyayi*] group, so that in this group too

the presence of *ulama* or *kijahi* [*kyai*] is not an impossibility. (Deliar 1973, p. 19, n. 33).

The presence of "royal key-keepers" *(abdi dalem jurukunci)*, a sub-category of the court religious officials *(abdi dalem santri* or *putihan)*, as the pivot of local society in Kotagede and as an integral part of the *priyayi* officialdom of the Javanese principalities supports such Indonesian criticism of Geertz. *Abdi dalem santri* or *priyayi santri* was not an "anomaly" as a social category nor a term of linguistic "barbarism", as Geertz has suggested (1956, p. 140).[14]

On the basis of the concept of Islamization and the revision of the categorization of Javanese society mentioned above, this book suggests that the current process of Islamization in Kotagede should not be regarded merely as a matter of change in the ideological orientation of a certain segment of the local society, i.e. from traditionalism to modernism within the *santri* group, but rather as a matter relevant to the religious outlook of the entire local population: an increasingly large number of individuals in the *abangan* category have moved and are still moving towards the category of *santri*, becoming more orthodox in their thought and deed as Muslims. Hence the title of this book, *The Crescent Arises over the Banyan Tree*, in the sense that *santri* elements represented by the crescent have grown out of *abangan* elements represented by the banyan tree. This title is simply intended to be a graphic summation of the local historical process without having any of the political implications which it might evoke among certain individuals.

---

14. For the case of traditional social categorization in Surakarta, see Soejatno (1974, pp. 99–101).

2

KOTAGEDE UNDER THE BANYAN TREE
Traditional Society and Religion

'YELLOW, THREE LEGGED TURTLE TO KOTAGEDE.' A yellow turtle having only three legs, found recently on the Samas seashore (22 km south of Yogya city) by a boatman, has been handed over by the Bantul Regional Chief to the guard of the Siliran bathing complex near the Kotagede royal cemetery to be further kept there as an extraordinary pet turtle by order of the Yogyakarta kraton [court]. A yellow or white turtle is rare and considered as a sacred beast by some people here. *Kedaulatan Rakyat*, 11 December 1973, "Latest News in Brief" (English original).

ROYAL CEMETERY AND MARKET

The town of Kotagede was founded in the middle of the sixteenth century by Pamanahan Ki Gede Mataram, a captain of the king of Pajang, the first Islamized kingdom in south Central Java.[1] Raffles narrates the beginning of

---

1. The beginning of the Kingdom of the Later Mataram is still clouded with legends. The description here follows the authority of de Graaf (1954, 1958, 1961 and 1962) and Pigeaud/de Graaf (1976).

the town, on the basis of indigenous chronicles available to him in the early nineteenth century, as follows:

> to *Panambahan* [Ki Gede Mataram] was assigned a population of eighteen hundred working men in the district of Mentauk, afterwards called *Matarem* ... The province of *Mentauk* or *Matarem* at that period did not contain more than three hundred villages, scattered in different parts of the country. On the arrival of *Panambahan* near *Brambanan* [Prambanan], he was received by the *Sunan Adi Jaga* [Sunan Kalijaga], who would not allow him to perform the usual ceremony of kissing his feet, thus by implication predicting the future greatness of his descendants. At Pasar Gede [Kotagede], then a wilderness, *Panambahan* was duly installed, under the title of *Kiai Gede Matarem*. (Raffles 1817 [1965] vol. II, p. 142)

Ki Gede Mataram died in 1584 and was buried in the courtyard of the mosque of the town. His son, who later became known by the title Panembahan Senapati Ingalaga, succeeded him. Senapati was called "Prince to the north of the market" (Ngabehi-lor-ing-pasar) while he was still young residing in the capital of Pajang. Senapati destroyed the kingdom of Pajang, established his own kingdom, Mataram, and made Kotagede the seat of his court *(kraton)* in 1587. A chronogram for this year of his triumph is inscribed on the stone gate of the mosque of the town. Senapati, after a number of military expeditions to various parts of Java, died in 1601 and was buried beside his father in the graveyard of the mosque in which by this time a number of members of the royal family and high officials of the kingdom were buried. During the reign of his successor, who later became known as Seda-ing-Krapyak (r. 1601–13), the graves of the royal ancestors of the Later Mataram were housed in three mausoleums, enclosed by walls, and made a special compound, *pasareyan* ("cemetery" in High Javanese), the royal cemetery of Later Mataram. Sultan Agung (r. 1613–46), the most powerful king of the Later Mataram, moved the seat of his court from Kotagede to Karta. He constructed another royal cemetery on the hill-top of Imogiri in which he was buried in 1646. Thereafter both Kotagede and Imogiri have been used by the descendants of the House of the Later Mataram as their official burial grounds.

The Royal Cemetery in Kotagede seems to have acquired special significance for the well-being of the Kingdom of the Later Mataram as the following anecdote in a local tradition indicates:

> Once during the time when Sinuhun [Susuhunan] Amangkurat Amral [Amangkurat II, 1677–1703] was governing the Kingdom of the Mataram in Kartasura [as the capital], the land suffered a shortage of food and many people were unable to eat. The Sinuhun was extremely disheartened and

summoned his brother, Pangeran Puger. Pangeran Puger faced the Sinuhun, who said: "If this situation goes on for long, I want to withdraw and kill myself. I am not strong enough to tolerate this. I cannot govern the land. I ought not to be respected by the people in the kingdom because I am an ignoble king." Pangeran Puger answered: "Please be patient. I will excuse myself from you and will ask Allah for His help. I want to visit the Pasareyan Mataram [in Kotagede] ..." (Martohastono n.d., pp. 12–13).

Pangeran Puger, according to the tradition, then changed into the clothes of a rustic santri, *santri dhusun*, and visited the Royal Cemetery in Kotagede with offerings. He bathed in the Gajah Wong River, meditated under the Old Banyan Tree and prayed in the Great Mosque, where he remained awake all night. Next day, he went back to Kartasura and found on his way home that all the markets were full of inexpensive rice (ibid.).

Already by the end of the seventeenth century the town of Kotagede seems to have acquired two major enduring features: the location of a royal cemetery and a center for indigenous industry and trade. In addition to its initial generic name, Mataram, the town became known by the name of "Kutha Gedhe" in Low Javanese *(Ngoko)* or "Kitha Ageng" in High Javanese *(Krama)*, both meaning "big town", or by its alternative name, "Pasar Gedhe" (big market) in Low Javanese, often abbreviated further as "Sargedhe".[2]

After a bitter war of succession in the middle of the eighteenth century, in 1755 the Kingdom of the Later Mataram was split into two parts of equal size and population between the Susuhunate of Surakarta and the Sultanate of Yogyakarta. Generally, the eastern half of the territory went to Surakarta and the western half, to Yogyakarta. However, the royal cemeteries of Kotagede and Imogiri were retained as common "ancestral land" *(tanah pusaka)* and placed under the joint administration of the two groups of local officials from the two courts. (The two minor principalities of Mangkunegaran and

---

2. This statement was true in the middle of the nineteenth century and also in the early decades of this century (*Aardrijkskundig...* 1869 and van Mook 1926*a* and 1926*b*). The present official designation of the town is "Kotagede", a combination of the Indonesian word "kota" (town) and the Low Javanese word "gedhe" (big). This practice is also widely observable in the daily conversations among the townspeople. The alternative name of the town, "Pasar Gede" or "Sargedhe", continues to be used commonly. These may be regarded as a reflection of the socio-linguistic situation of the town in which Indonesian is making an inroad into the Javanese world. For the sake of convenience, the name of the town shall be spelt as "Kotagede" throughout this book.

Pakualaman did not participate in the administration of the town.) Besides a small number of ordinary officials for general administration, there were a number of special officials, "key-keepers" *(jurukunci)* of the royal cemetery, who were awarded appanages *(lungguh)* by the respective kings of Surakarta and Yogyakarta in the form of a number of people, a certain amount of land, and other privileges. As a result, there were created enclaves belonging to the Susuhunate of Surakarta in the territory of the Sultanate of Yogyakarta. In these common ancestral territories the inhabitans and the land were divided between the two courts in such a manner that even a single *kampung* (neighbourhood) and its people were split into two parts.[3]

Between 1825 and 1830, most parts of Central Java were devastated by the War of Dipanegara.[4] However, according to local traditions, the war spared Kotagede; rather, the town received new impetus during the war in that a large number of craftsmen and traders from the central market of Yogyakarta took refuge in the town and many of them settled down and stayed on there after the war.

As shall be described in detail later, the town continued to grow as a prosperous Javanese town through the rest of the nineteenth century. In the early decades of the twentieth century, the four central Javanese principalities of Surakarta, Yogyakarta, Mangkunegaran, and Pakualaman underwent reforms in land system and administration. The old system of *patuh* (appanage-holder) and *bekel* (agent of appanage-holder) was based on the premise that all land and people belonged to the king and he apportioned them among the nobles and officials as appanages whose day-to-day management became the responsibility of *bekel*.[5] The new system of *kalurahan* was based upon the principles that individual villagers possess rights to land and jointly form a village community as a legal personality. Kotagede (and Imogiri) experienced these reforms a couple of years later than the rest of the principalities because of the difficulty of exchanging and merging people and land to produce new village communities.[6]

---

3. On the division of the Kingdom of the Later Mataram, see Ricklefs (1974*a*).
4. On the War of Dipanegara, see Kumar (1972), Ricklefs (1974*b*), and Carey (1974*a*, 1974*b*).
5. On the pre-reform land system and the administration of the Sultanate of Yogyakarta, see Rouffaer (1932), Selosoemardjan (1962) and O'Malley (1977).
6. For the reforms and their outcome in Kotagede, see van Mook (1958 [1926*a* and 1926*b*]); for Yogyakarta in general, see O'Malley (1977).

After World War II, with the abolition of the Susuhunate of Surakarta by the Republic of Indonesia, the former Surakarta enclaves in Kotagede and Imogiri were absorbed into the Special Region of Yogyakarta (a new region made by the merging of the Sultanate of Yogyakarta and the principality of Pakualaman). Those former Surakarta enclaves in the Region are only known today by the name of Surakarta attached to their new appellations. Hence there are found administrative units called Kotagede Surakarta (Kotagede Sk) and Imogiri Surakarta (Imogiri Sk) in the Special Region of Yogyakarta.

At present (1972), most parts of the town of Kotagede belong administratively to the City of Yogyakarta as the Ward (Kemantren) of Kotagede and the rest to the Regency (Kabupaten) of Bantul. The Gajah Wong River, a tributary of the Opak River, makes a natural boundary between the old city of Yogyakarta and the town of Kotagede and supplies abundant water for the irrigation of the rice and sugarcane fields which cover most of the flat lands in this area. (See Figure 2.1.)

The layout of the town reflects its beginning in the sixteenth century. Nowadays, however, the geographic centre of the town is not the place where the court used to be but the market. The market is not only physically large for a local town of Kotagede's size but is also a busy place visited by hundreds of people every day and by thousands on every Legi day in the Javanese week which cycles in five days.

To the south of the market lies a neighborhood which bears the name, Alun-Alun. Alun-Alun usually refers to an open square adjacent to the royal palace in the traditional plan of a Javanese court town. In Kotagede today, however, Alun-Alun is no longer an open space but a crowded residential area. Further south of the neighbourhood of Alun-Alun, there are a few remnants of the Later Mataram palace. In a neighbourhood which bears the name of Kedaton (*Kedhaton* a synonym of kraton, palace, in archaic Javanese), there is an uninhabitet patch of land which is believed to have been the former palace site. There is a small building in the space which contains a massive, glossy rock, Watu Gilang (Shining Stone) and three stone balls, Watu Canteng (lit., Felon). The large rock is said to have been the seat of Senapati, the founder of the Later Mataram, and the small balls, the ones Senapati used to play with as marbles.

To the southwest of the market, still in the central area of the town, is an extensive graveyard compound, Pasareyan, for the royal family of the Later Mataram. The Royal Cemetery consists of eight quarters, separated from each other by high brick walls pierced by gates of Hindu-Javanese style. The first quarter is a front entrance yard, in which is a pair of very old banyan trees. The older one, Waringin Sepuh (High Javanese) or Ringin Tua (Low

FIGURE 2.1
Map of Kotagede

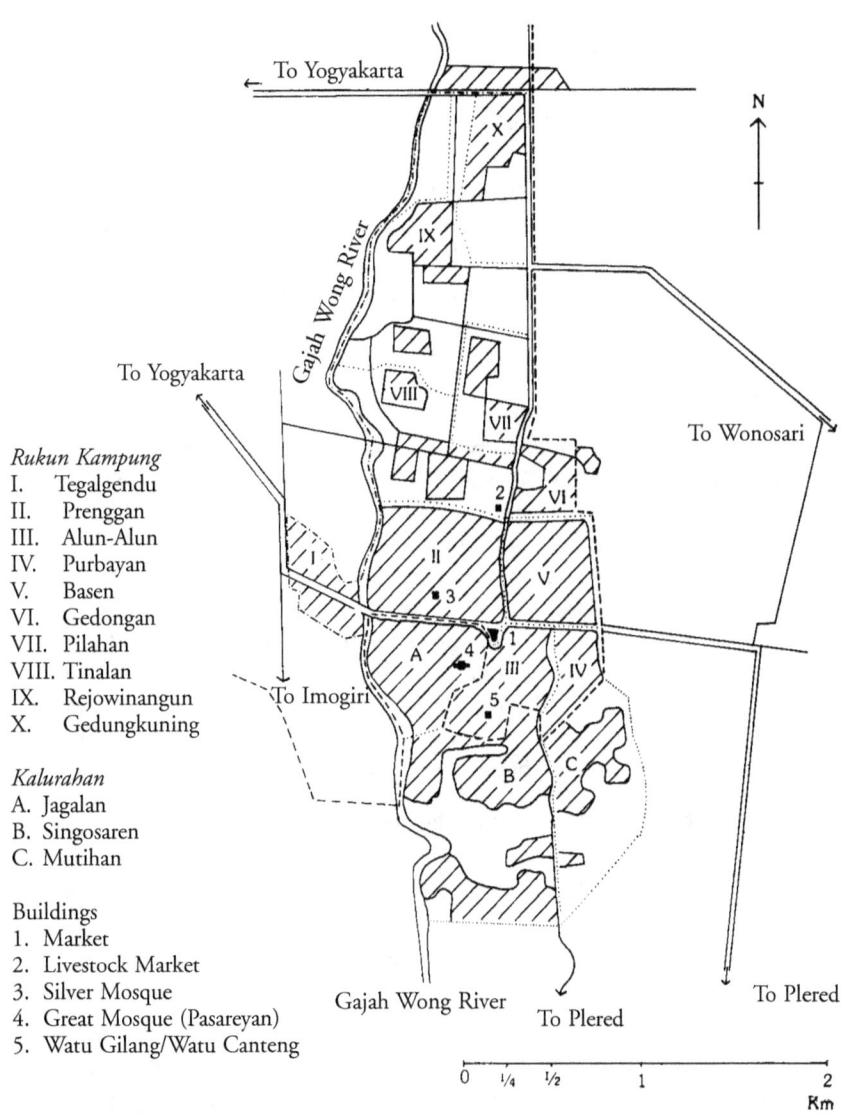

Javanese), meaning "The Old Banyan Tree", is said to have been planted by Sunan Kalijaga, one of the nine legendary Islamic saints, to whom the early Islamization of Javanese kingdoms in attributed.

The second quarter of the Royal Cemetery contains Mesjid Ageng Mataram, or "The Great Mosque of Mataram", a large wooden structure with an extensive yard. The third quarter is a reception area: those who intend to visit the Royal Cemetery are received here by the key-keeper officials. In the fourth quarter there is a pair of small waiting halls for the key-keepers from the two courts. The fifth quarter is the Royal Cemetery itself. The last three quarters constitute a bathing complex named Siliran, and contain a spring, two ponds, and two separate bathing places for men and women.

The entire complex of the Royal Cemetery maintains an atmosphere of sanctity and solemnity as aptly depicted by van Mook half-a-century ago in the following passage:

> The restful mood of the clean-swept, shadowy court is continued in the dusky interior of the mosque, while the melodious tones of the Koran and the religious formulas being recited and the clear voices of the children playing under the trees divest it of any deadness. The shadows of the roof sloping down at a more and more gradual incline and those of the spreading foliage reach out towards each other across the quiet gleam of the water in the water trough, and the coming and going faithful glide like colorful ghosts through the spot of sunlight in between. Here the Javanese have been able to unite the works of man and the works of nature to create the atmosphere of dreamy meditation and refreshing consolation characteristic of all their sanctuaries and burial places (van Mook 1958, p. 281).

To return to the town itself, along the three main roads running from the market to the north, east and west, and also in the neighbourhoods behind these roads, there are shops, workshops and residential buildings, which make up the core of the town. This core area of about 1 square kilometre, which extends roughly 500m in each cardinal direction from the market, is locally referred to as Kotagede *raja* or Kotagede *kota*, "central" or "urban Kotagede", in contrast to Kotagede *desa*, "rural Kotagede", which lies outside the core. At present, core Kotagede comprises four neighbourhood associations (*rukun kampung*, abbreviated as R.K.), the smallest administrative unit in the municipality of Yogyakarta (Kota Madya Yogyakarta): R.K. Prenggan, R.K. Basen, R.K. Purbayan, and R.K. Alun-Alun. Core Kotagede also comprises the *kalurahan* (the rural administrative village) of Jagalan, and the hamlet (*kedukuhan*) of Joyopranan in the village of Singosaren, both belonging to the Regency (*Kabupaten*) of Bantul (see Figure 2.2). The two latter areas are thoroughly urban in terms of land use pattern and in the lifestyle of

FIGURE 2.2
Kotagede: kota vs. desa

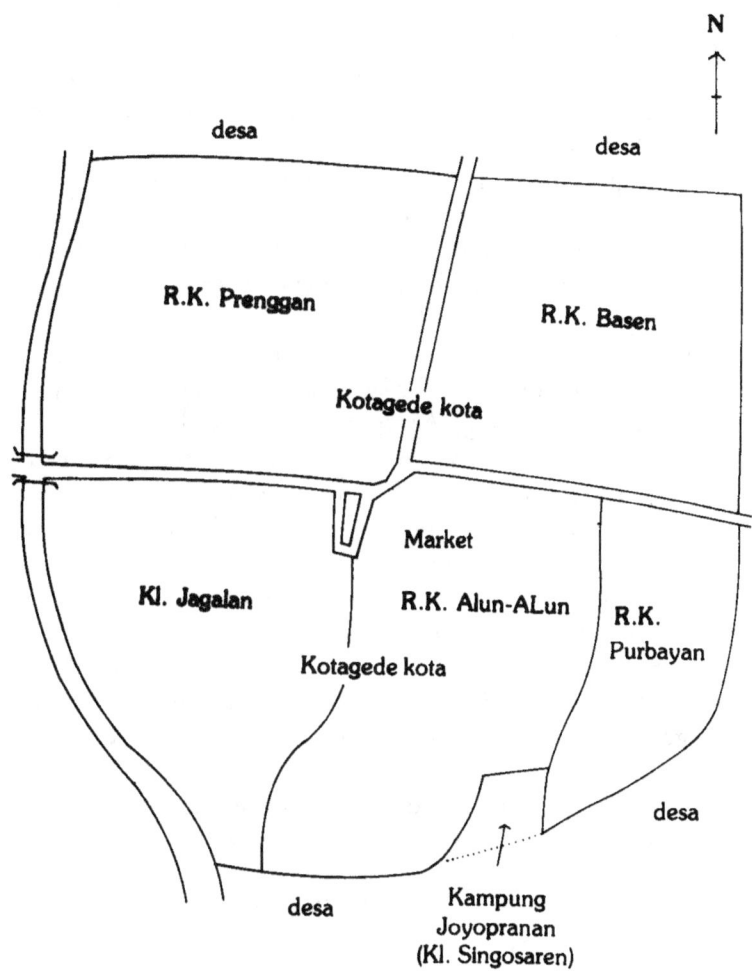

the inhabitants but are nevertheless administratively categorized as rural. In spite of these administrative divisions, the complex of core Kotagede, or Kotagede *kota*, is conceived of by the townspeople of Kotagede themselves as one single social and geographic entity. It is in this Kotagede *kota* that the Muhammadiyah movement was born and found the strongest support, in contrast to Kotagede *desa*.

TRADITIONAL ADMINISTRATION IN KOTAGEDE

The administration by the appanage system including key-keeper *(jurukunci)* officials was in effect in Kotagede until 1920 when the new village *(kalurahan)* system was introduced. (The following descriptions are based upon van Mook 1926*a*, 1926*b*, and 1958 unless otherwise indicated.) The key-keeper official was appointed by the *adipati*, or grand vizier, of the court in the name of the Susuhunan of Surakarta or the Sultan of Yogyakarta. The appointment to the office of key-keeper during the nineteenth century seems to have been mostly hereditary, i.e., from father to son. The number of key-keeper officials seems to have varied from six to eight for each of the Yogyakarta and Surakarta territories in Kotagede. Among the key-keeper corps, two for each of the two territories occupied the position of chief key-keeper, or *lurah jurukunci*. The chief key-keeper was ranked as *panewu* in the Javanese officialdom and was given the title of *Raden* or *Mas* in the Javanese aristocracy. All the key-keepers were awarded appanages *(lungguh)*: the amount of land and the number of personal followers awarded were specified in the letter of appointment. The key-keeper as appanage-holder *(patuh)* was entitled to levy taxes on the people in his appanage. The taxes took the forms of agricultural products, money, and labour. The kinds and amounts of the revenues which the appanage-holder owed directly to the court were fixed by the court regulations, but the appanage-holder was free to extract further revenues from the people under him to finance his office and household, and feed and clothe his personal followers. The business of tax collection and labour conscription of an appanage-holder was usually contracted out to the agent *(bekel)*, who was chosen from among the common people in the appanage by the appanage-holder. The *bekel* was responsible for delivering fixed amounts of the various kinds of taxes to his master but he was, in turn, free to exploit further the people under him.

The people in an appanage were classified into *kuli kenceng, magersari,* and *pengindung* in terms of the status of landholding. The *kuli kenceng,* or *kuli pokok,* who had hereditary rights to the use of house, house-compound, and agricultural land if he was a farmer, formed the bulk of the population (*erfbezitter* in Dutch and "house-compound holder" as its English equivalent). The house-compound holder was liable for the payment of head tax and the performance of various labour services. The *magersari*, who had his own house built on land belonging to someone else (most often an appanage-holder's or a *bekel's*), became a personal follower of the latter. The *pengindung*, who had neither his own house-site nor house but lived in someone else's house (most often that of an appanage-holder's or *bekel's*), also became the latter's personal servant.

In order to illustrate the rights and obligations of the key-keeper official in Kotagede, a translation of the letter of appointment to the position of chief key-keeper *(lurah jurukunci)* in the Surakarta territory dated 1866 AD is presented below:[7]

> Our Majesty Susuhunan Paku Buwana Senapati Ingalaga Ngabdurrahrnan Sayidin Panatagama IX grants a letter of appointment to Jimat Ahmad Dalem Resadipa as follows:
>
> We [*Ingsun* the first person pronoun only to be used by king or God], by Issuing this letter, raise and make him the chief *(lurah)* of Our subjects *(kawula)*, the key-keepers *(jurukunci)*, in the tax-free land *(perdikan)* of Kotagede and grant him a revocable transfer of rights to Our royal properties in the village of Katitang in the amount of one *jung*, one *bau*, and one *lupit*[8] of *sawah* (rice fields) and rights to retain personal followers and coconut trees in Kotagede in the amount of 112 *magersari*, 17 *pengindung* and 400 trees in eight *kampung* [their names omitted] in Kotagede and further rights to some plots of land in the villages of Dodogan and Dringo. A certain portion of the market dues is also due to him. He is also entitled to wear official uniforms which are restricted to the office holder of the chief key-keeper. In return he is obliged to perform the services of providing ritual meals and mats for prayer meetings at the Mosque on Thursday evenings and Fridays. He is also obliged to perform the services of repairing the Mausoleums, the Mosque, the waiting halls, and the gates in the royal graveyard complex if damage occurs to any of these. It is also his obligation to provide food and drink when the royal messenger or other court dignitaries visit the Royal Cemetery.
>
> He, Mas Jimat Amad Dalem Resadipa, as well as the key-keepers and the Mosque officials, should recite the Qur'an on the eve of every Friday [Thursday evening] under the leadership of the *penghulu* [head of Mosque officials]. They all should strictly observe the religion and correct any negligence of religion among their subjects in Kotagede.
>
> Now that he is appointed to the position of the chief key-keeper he should always be dedicated to the duties of his office, observe earnestly religious obligations, avoid anything prohibited, and pray sincerely to Allah for the firmness of the magnificence and glory of Us, the Susuhunan, for the

---

7. The following is my free translation of one of the letters of appointment appended to van Mook (1926*a*, pp. 395–96 and 1972, pp. 57–59). In translating the Javanese text, Dr Soepomo Poedjosoedarmo's help was invaluable but he should not be held responsible for any mistakes in my translation.
8. One *jung* (= 4 *bau*, 28,386 m^2), one *bau* (7,096.5 m^2), and one *lupit* (= half *bau*, 3,548.25 m^2).

well-being of the court, and for the security of the State of the Susuhunan. He should always conform to the proper standard for the conduct of the *perdikan* people and should not indulge in wrongdoing such as gambling, opium-smoking, deceiving, or having connections with criminals. Should any violation occur, his office shall certainly be revoked and calamity shall befall him. All the subjects under Mas Jimat Amad Dalem Resadipa shall also comply with the prohibitions made known to him in this letter of appointment. Those who violate them shall be promptly arrested and punished. We, the Susuhunan, also make it known to all the subjects in Kotagede that should any of them be maltreated by local officials, he shall be authorized directly to appeal to Us by personally appearing in the front square *(alun-alun)* of the court in Surakarta.

A fact that stands out clearly from this letter of appointment is that the community of Kotagede, as a *perdikan desa* (tax-free village) centring around the institution of the Royal Cemetery, was to serve for the glorification of the Javanese ruler and his state. On the position and the function of these "tax-free villages" in the Javanese polity, Moertono states as follows:

> Protection and encouragement of religious life from older times on took the form of granting special rights to religious groups and communities. Usually gifts of land were distributed by the king to religious communities, not merely as a means of subsistence, but primarily so that they would be financially strong enough to perform their religious services satisfactorily for the welfare of the king and so of his realm. (Moertono 1968, p. 83)

Islam in this version was inseparable from the cult of royal glorification. The key-keepers, Mosque officials, their personal followers, and indeed the entire population in Kotagede under them, all had an obligation to pray to Allah "for the firmness of the magnificence and glory" of the ruler, the well-being of his court, and the security of his state.

Through this local administrative system, the entire population of Kotagede was mobilized to take part in the cult of royal glorification. This fact becomes clearer when one looks at the obligations which the *bekel* and the ordinary people *(wong cilik)* under him had to perform for the key-keepers. The report of van Bevervoorde's written in 1905 gives pertinent information on these obligations (van Bevervoorde 1905, Chapter 6). These obligations consisted of two kinds: (a) annual and (b) intermittent or occasional.

To the first category belonged three annual occasions of Garebeg.

Pigeaud observed that Garebeg was a composite of "national *slametan* [ritual communal feast], periodical ceremony for the prosperity of the court, and extension of well-known village *slametan*" formed out of the "combination of three national *slametan* with the ceremonies of Islamic holidays and the

FIGURE 2.3

Mausoleums for royal graves (photographed ca. 1900).
Source: Courtesy of van Bevervoorde Collection, KITLV.

FIGURE 2.4

Front view of the Royal Cemetery complex in Kotagede during the 1971 general election.

FIGURE 2.5

Abdi Dalem Jurukunci on duty.

practise of the charity of the king [free food distribution]" (Pigeaud 1932, p. 27).

The Garebeg was held three times a year according to the Islamic calendar, first, on the twelfth day of the third month of Maulud (Rabingulawal), second, on the first day of the tenth month of Syawal following the fasting month of Ramadhan, and, third, on the tenth day of the eleventh month of Besar (Dulkijah). Garebeg Maulud was to commemorate the Prophet Muhammad's birthday: a pair of royal *gamelan* (instruments for Javanese gong orchestra) named Kyai Sekati was played at the Central Mosque of the court from the sixth of Maulud for six continuous days and nights, giving the occasion its alternate name, Sekaten. From the 1920s the annual fair of the Yogyakarta principality started to be held concurrently with Sekaten on Alun-Alun Lor (the main public square to the north of the royal palace) and Garebeg Maulud became the largest of the three court ceremonies. The second Garebeg, known as Garebeg Puasa, started in the month of Puasa (Ramadhan), the Muslim fasting month, culminated in the festival of Idul Fitri on the first day of the month of Syawal. The third Garebeg was to commemorate the Islamic festival of Hajj (Pilgrimage) or Idul Adha (Sacrifice).

On all three occasions, the entire corps of local officials of the court had to gather in the capital in order to participate in various ceremonies and rituals. The local officials travelled to the capital from the place of their appointment, accompanied by a procession consisting of their *bekel*, personal followers and conscripts. The occasion of Garebeg included a royal audience given to court officials, the ruler's appearance before the public, a parade of royal palace troops, an exhibition of royal heirlooms, royal prayers at the Central Mosque, and the distribution of ritual meals provided by the ruler to the public (see Groneman 1895, R. Soedjono 1931, Pigeaud 1932). During the earlier years of the Later Mataram, *bupati* (regents) in the *manca negara* (outer territories) were required to pay personal homage to the ruler in the court, with their retinues and conscripts carrying tributes due to him, at least once a year, on one of the three occasions of Garebeg, most often on Maulud (Selosoemardjan 1962, p. 29).

For the *bekel* and the ordinary people *(wong cilik)*, the Garebeg was a period of burdensome labour service to the appanage-holder. The monograph of van Bevervoorde meticulously lists up the obligations imposed upon the *bekel* and the people on these occasions (1905, pp. 101–109). For example, on the Garebeg Maulud and the Garebeg Besar, all the *bekel*, each with a fixed number of conscript selected from among the ordinary people, accompanied the appanage-holder to the capital and stayed there until the ceremonies were over. The Garebeg Puasa was the most prolonged of all: starting with the eve of the 21st day of the month of Puasa, on the eves of odd-numbered days of the last ten days of the month, the *bekel* and conscripts accompanied their master to the Great Mosque in Kotagede for the *maleman* (lit., night thing). The *maleman* was the evening prayer with a ritual meal after sunset which signalled the end of the daytime fasting obligation. The preparation of the ritual meals and drinks for the master (as mentioned in the letter of appointment) was also the responsibility of the conscripts. On the early days of the Syawal, the *bekel* was given an audience by the king, the crown prince, the grand vizier of the court and by the Dutch Governor-General.

During the eighth month of Ruwah (Saban), preceding the month of Puasa, the king sent his messengers to the Royal Cemetery in Kotagede for the ceremony of *nyadranan*, offerings to the deceased ancestors. On this occasion, the *bekel* and the conscripts also had to participate in the ceremony with their master. Another special ceremony with prayers was performed in the Great Mosque of Kotagede on the 26th day of the seventh month of Rejeb: it was called *mikradan* commemorating the Prophet Muhammad's journey to Heaven, Mi'raj. The key-keeper officials were accompanied by the *bekel* and conscripts on this occasion as well.

On the birthdays and accession days of the king and the crown prince, *labuhan* offerings were made by the courts to Nyai Loro Kidul, the Goddess of the South Ocean, the guardian of the Kingdom of the Later Mataram. The *bekel* and the conscripts were to join the procession led by the court officials to the mouth of the Progo River to throw the offerings for the Goddess into the ocean.

These were the annual occasions on which the *bekel* and the conscripts had to accompany the key-keepers in the performance of their duties according to van Bevervoorde's documentation around the turn of the century.

There were also a number of intermittent occasions which required the services of the *bekel* and the conscripts. These occasions included the death of the king or the crown prince, the marriage and the circumcision of the sons and daughters of the appanage-holder, the upkeep and repair of the buildings in the Royal Cemetery complex and the appanage-holder's own residence. The appanage-holder was also entitled to make use of the labour services of the ordinary people under him on other occasions broadly defined as "whenever he felt it necessary" (van Bevervoorde 1905, p. 112).

According to the report of van Bevervoorde on the local administration at the year-end of 1903, there were in Kotagede altogether 16 key-keeper officials, all appanage-holders, and 30 mosque officials, some of whom were appanage-holders but most of whom were not. Their appanages were managed by 76 *bekel*, and there were 1,736 house-compound holders *(kuli kenceng)* in the total population of 10,173 people in the town (van Bevervoorde 1905, Appendix 0).[9]

Some elderly people in the town still remember the days when the royal key-keepers *(abdi dalem jurukunci)* performed their religious duties in the Royal Cemetery complex. The following, is an exerpt from such a reminiscence written by Prof. M. Rasjidi (see Chapter 1, note 7 above):

> On Fridays the *[jurukunci]* officials, whose costumes looked like those of the people in Mecca, performed prayers in the Mosque and then went into the royal grave compound and offered another prayer there.
>
> During the month of Puasa, the Mosque of Kotagede was an extraordinarily active place. Before sunset, there were already many people present on the porch *(srambi)* waiting for breaking of the fast, performed by eating a bit of rice porridge together. Then the time for the Isya' prayer came and the *taraweh* [joint prayer at night in the month of Puasa] was visited by an unusually large number of people. When *the taraweh* prayer was over, scores of children struck the large drum *(bedhug)* so that its cannon-like sounds could be heard throughout the neighborhood.
>
> On Fridays [during the month of Puasa], the Mosque was so full of people that there was no longer room for any more visitors. The porch was already crowded, and the pious and children wore new, clean clothes. There were always some people from nearby villages who came fully dressed with metal buckles and jewelry, too.
>
> Before the sermon, I would always see some people who brought *kampil*, that is, a small bag made of palm leaves, containing copper or silver coins. These people walked around and bowed here and there among those who sat in lines and placed the coins on their prayer mats. The coins were of many kinds: half guilders, quarters, ten cents, five cents, two-and-a-half cents, and one cent. Among small children who gathered behind the adults, there were some who got seven-and-a-half cents or even fifteen cents. There were even one or two naughty ones who switched places to get the coins again.
>
> On the days of the 21st, 23rd, 25th, 27th and 29th, *maleman* was held in the front yard of the Mosque. At five-thirty in the evening, the notables in Kotagede came in solemnity bringing with them their own mats, lamps, spittoons, dishes of rice with side dishes, and their official parasols. When

---

9. This figure of the total population of the town in 1903 and that of the 1930 census (see Chapter 1, note 5 above) are not exactly comparable because of some changes in the boundary of the town as a result of the 1920 administrative reforms.

the time came to break the fast, they ate their meal by the light of kerosene lamps whose glass globes were clearly polished.

As a small child, I roamed among the dishes of food which were spread around in the front yard of the Mosque. This was the religious situation around the Mosque and the graveyard of Panembahan Senopati. (Rasjidi 1967, pp. 10–11).

Court ceremonies performed in the complex of the Great Mosque of Mataram and Royal Cemetery helped enhance the authority of the ruler. Also various local customs, *adat-isti-adat*, were an integral part of this version of Islam encompassing both the ruler and the ruled. The following statement by another local elder points up this aspect:

Religion in Kotagede was very traditional. There were very few who actually took the religion earnestly. But customs, *adat-isti-adat*, were also part of the religion and people simply followed them. For example, it was a tradition to perform a *slametan kekah*, on the seventh day after a baby was born. This was already a deeply rooted tradition in Kotagede and everybody did it although nobody knew that the religion in fact taught us what to do on such an occasion. Marriage was the same. A marriage had to be officiated by a *kaum* or *lebai*. Now it is done through the KUA, Office of Religious Affairs, as you know. At that time, however, everything had to be legitimized (*disyahkan*) by *kaum*. Prayers were performed only by *kaum*. Ordinary people (*orang kampung*) did not have to pray. It was also enough if the fasting was done by *kaum* only. Ordinary people did not have to fast. Then *zakat fitrah* (religious taxes) were presented to *kaum* and to religious teachers as tokens of appreciation.

At that time those who controlled the government here were the key-keepers and Islamic traditions [among them] were quite strong. For example, when people wanted to play *gamelan*, they were not allowed to do so on Fridays. From four o'clock on Thursday afternoon to the time until the noon prayer on Friday was over, nobody was allowed to play *gamelan*. This was a tradition which was not written down but which was certainly in effect. Anyone who violated it would surely be prosecuted. In addition, every day between six o'clock in the evening, that is the time for *Maghrib* prayer, and eight o'clock, the time for *Isya'*, no *gamelan* should be played. So, for my parents' and my own generation, there was no such word as, *Isya'*, but only "after *Isya'*" (*bakda Isya'*) indicating that the drum (*bedhug*) was struck to announce the time when the *Isya'* prayer was over, but not the time for *Isya'* as you know now. In the old days in Kotagede, thus the drum was struck when the *Isya'* prayer was over. It was to signal that people could start playing *gamelan* and perform other entertainments. The drum was struck to make people observe the custom and if anyone dared to violate the tradition, he would surely be punished *(kuwalat)* by the spirit of the dead *(semare)* [i.e. the spirit of Senapati].

Still another old man who was active in the formative period of the Muhammadiyah in Kotagede relates his experience about how things were in the early decades of this century before the advent of the Muhammadiyah:

> In the month of Maulud, ritual dishes were prepared and neighbours were invited to come join a *kenduren (slametan)* with the intention of sending prayers together to our leader, Nabi Muhammad. For the month of Maulud, the ritual dish was *sega wudhuk* [rice cooked with coconut milk] and a whole fried chicken called *ingkung*. In the month of Ruwah or Saban, a round cake, *apem*, was made and offered to the ancestors. On the nights of the 21st, 23rd, 25th, 27th and 29th of the month of Ramadhan, which were called *maleman*, we made ritual dishes and distributed them among neighbours.
>
> People obseved all of these *adat* Islam until Muhammadiyah became active. In addition to these *adat*, there were many *upacara* (ceremonies) performed in the Royal Cemetery. When a member of the Royal family of Surakarta died, the body was brought to Kotagede for a night and was then carried to Imogiri for burial. It was believed that if the body did not stay in Kotagede for a night, there would be another death in the Kraton. *Abdi dalem*, high as well as low, all joined the funeral procession. It was really *rame* (crowded and lively) on this kind of occasion.

There were many other customs and legends which directly contributed to the aura of awe around the Royal Cemetery as the repository of mystical powers *(kasekten)* and around the corps of *abdi dalem jurukunci* who were in charge of maintaining this awe-inspiring institution.[10]

As mentioned above, in the front court of the Royal Cemetery complex is the Old Banyan Tree (Waringin Sepuh), which is believed to have been planted by Sunan Kalijaga before the rise of the Later Mataram kingdom to indicate the future location of its court. The tree is a source of many legends. It was believed that the tree could portend an approaching death in the royal family of Surakarta or Yogyakarta by shedding one of its branches. The leaves of the tree are also used as charms: two of them being put together back to back with a piece of its air-root, and a bottle of water taken from the Siliran Spring were used as *jimat*, or charms, in order to protect a Kotagedean travelling far from his native town (see van Mook 1958, p. 28).

---

10. For a general exposition of the Javanese concept of *kasekten*, *see* Anderson (1972*a*).

The royal key-keepers who sat on guard duty in the Royal Cemetery complex told me a number of mysterious incidents they witnesssed there. They often saw ghosts of the deceased royal family members of Mataram passing freely through the high, thick walls that surround the cemetery. One of the *raja* buried in the cemetery even appeared once in the form of a wild tiger. The three adjoining mausoleums in the cemetery which shelter the graves of the earliest members of the Later Mataram royalty were particularly mystical. Shortly after these buildings were first built in the early seventeenth century, they were burned down by fire in spite of the fact that there was no source of fire there. The cause of the fire was popularly attributed to the very presence of the royal corpses buried there which, as a locus of mystical powers, self-heated and finally started a fire (see Kusudyarsono 1970, p. 2). One of the three mausoleums, named *witana*, houses the grave of the founder of the Later Mataram, Panembahan Senapati. The building was believed to have the mystical capacity to give predictions for impending misfortunes in the kingdom of the Later Mataram by discharging reddish-yellow smoke and flames from top.[11]

In one of the ponds of the bathing quarters (Siliran), whose water comes from a spring located at the foot of a cliff on which the royal graveyard is situated and which is therefore thought by some to have mystical powers to cure various diseases, there continued to live a pair of yellow turtles. The older one, named *ati kang wening* or "pure heart" is thought to be a messenger of Panembahan Senapati. Those who come to bathe in the water for curing often bring a piece of meat for the turtle; if it eats the meat with good appetite, it is thought that the feeder had done a favour for the royal messenger and that the chances of his or her receiving a favour in return from the turtle's master, Senapati, are thus enhanced.[12]

At the foot of the same cliff, there is a stone altar on which people offer incense, petals of jasmine flowers, and sometimes a dish of ritual food before addressing their request to the spirit of the deceased royalty. Until very recently,

---

11. The most recent occurrence of this mystery is said to have been witnessed on the eve of 1 October 1965, the night before the eruption of the abortive G30S coup. Some *jurukunci* on night duty saw reddish smoke and flames coming from the top of the mausoleum of Senapati and on the next day learned that one of the most tragic events in the history of post-Independence Indonesia had taken place (Kusudyarsono, *ibid.*).
12. As the newspaper excerpt quoted at the beginning of this chapter indicates, this tradition of regarding a yellow turtle, especially a deformed one such as one with three legs, as a mystically potent creature still continues to this day.

there was a woman *dhukun* (magical healer) who was living for many years in a neighbourhood named Dondongan situated in the front court of the Royal Cemetery complex. She was often called upon by the people to help in communicating with Senapati et al. for a small fee. She is believed to be almost 100 years old (1972) and is too old and too weak to continue in the role of a *dhukun*. I only saw her once or twice officiating a ritual at the altar mentioned above. Nobody else has come forward to replace her.

There were also many unwritten regulations and restrictions on the conduct of the townspeople which were carefully observed, partly because they were followed as *adat-isti-adat* and partly because their violation was sanctioned by the local authorities.

For example, no vehicles except those from the court were allowed to enter Kotagede across the bridge over the Gajah Wong River. Those who came to Kotagede to visit the Royal Cemetery or for private business had to abandon their vehicles at the neighbourhood of Tegalgendu located right across the river to the west of it and walk another 700 meters on foot to reach the center of the town. This regulation was strictly enforced until 1925 (see van Mook 1958, p. 278).

FIGURE 2.6

Requesting the help of the spirit of Senapati at the inner gate of the Royal Cemetery.

FIGURE 2.7

Bathing in Siliran Spring (women's section).

FIGURE 2.8

Boys gathered at the Great Mosque for prayer before group circumcision.

FIGURE 2.9

Boys leaving the Great Mosque for group circumcision.

Another regulation concerned the height of buildings in the town. No inhabitants in the town were allowed to construct two-storeyed buildings lest they be able to look down into the Royal Cemetery from these buildings. This regulation remained in effect until the end of Dutch era in spite of the fact that wealthy people in the town were quite capable of constructing such buildings and might well have done so in view of the land shortage in residential areas. A few of the rich, in fact, cunningly evaded the regulation by digging downward to build part of their houses underground for utilitarian as well as prestige purposes.

Still another restriction, which is in effect even at present as *adat* and practised by many, is that the townspeople should not place their feet in the direction of the Royal Cemetery when they lie down to sleep for to do so would be to show disrespect to the Mataram royalty in the graves.

The key-keeper officials were responsible for the maintenance of law and order as well as for the morals of the local people as indicated in the letter of appointment quoted above (pp. 27–28). The key-keeper officials took every opportunity to remind the townspeople under their jurisdiction that they should not indulge in *ma-lima* or "five vices". The five vices usually referred to *main* or "playing (gambling)", *madat* or "smoking (opium)", *maling* or "stealing", *madon* or "womanizing", and *minum* or "drinking (alcohol)".

All in all, the Royal Cemetery loaded with mystical powers *(kasekten)* constituted the nucleus of the local society of Kotagede. The bulk of the population was directly involved in the functioning of this institution under the authority of the key-keeper officials. The traditional attitude of the local people to the Royal Cemetery and its personnel was that of fear and obedience. Professor Abdul Kahar Mudzakkir, one of the national leaders of the Muhammadiyah movement that the town of Kotagede has produced, put it as follows:

> People here in Kotagede were afraid of the powers of the living as well as the dead. They feared the Dutch Governor and Resident in Yogyakarta, the Sultan of Yogyakarta and his Bupati, Wedana, and other officials, Field Police, local key-keeper officials and even *bekel*. They feared Senapati and his family who were all already dead but who they believed to have mystical powers influencing the living. They feared certain trees, graves, stones, old houses, and even such a man-made thing as a bronze statue in front of the Governor's Residence in Yogyakarta. They feared various sorts of ghosts who make noise, eat leftovers, appear at crossroads, or who roam in the market after dark, and many others. As a matter of fact, however, true Islamic teachings tell us that no one should be afraid of anything or anybody except Allah, the Almighty.

Changes in the religious outlook of the townspeople did take place as we shall see later. Before examining that, let us take a brief look at changes in the socio-economic environment of Kotagede around the turn of the century.

TRADITIONAL ECONOMY IN KOTAGEDE

Many of the townspeople in Kotagede claim that the mode of their livelihood has been non-agricultural for many generations; some even say since time immemorial. The majority conceive that their ancestors' position in Later Mataram society was that of *abdi dalem karya*, "craftsmen in royal service" or court artisans (see Tedjo 1970, p. 14). These craftsmen seem to have been gathered to Kotagede when the court of the Later Mataram kingdom was set up there. Certain names of the neighbourhoods of Kotagede suggest the variety of specialization which must have existed since the early period of the town's history. To cite a few examples, Mranggen derives its name from *mranggi* or "sheath making", Pandéyan from *pandhé* or "ironsmith", Sayangan from *sayang* or "copperware", Samakan from *samak* or "leatherwork", Kemasan from *kemasan* or "goldsmith", and Jagalan from *jagal* or "slaughtering".

There are a number of local legends about those craftsmen who were endowed with extraordinary skills in handicraft often inherited from their mystical ancestors or acquired by themselves through miracles or tricks. A number of early traders were also said to have possessed extraordinary intelligence and knowledge in trade whose origin was also attributed to supernatural sources. In this regard, too, Kotagede has been a highly potent place for mystical powers.

During the earlier periods of the town's history, the largest patrons of the Kotagede craftsmen and traders were obviously the principality courts and their officials who needed artefacts of extraordinary value: Javanese daggers *(kris)*, swords, spears, gold and silver ornaments, jewels, fine furniture, musical instruments, carriages, and the like as attributes of their rank and power. Kotagede was one of the places in which these goods were traditionally produced. The production and distribution of commodities for popular consumption seems to have been of secondary importance for the economy of the town until the latter half of the nineteenth century.

The regional economy of the four principalities in South Central Java started to change after the War of Dipanegara (1825–30). At least three processes seem to have been of great significance: (a) the deeper penetration of European plantations, first in indigo and later in sugar cultivation;[13] (b) the development of transportation networks by railroads directly connecting this hitherto isolated region with the parts on the north coast of Java, Semarang and Surabaya, among others; and (c) the rapid increase in population which, according to one estimate, experienced a four-fold growth between 1830 and 1900.[14] The upshot of these developments seems to have been an absolute increase in demands for commodities of popular consumption among the peasantry of the region.

The local economy of Kotagede started to grow in response to this altered situation in the regional economy. Among others, two remarkable developments took place in the late nineteenth century. One was the emergence of a number of industrialists and merchants who specialized in the production and distribution of daily essentials for the peasantry. The other was the enhancement of the position of a particular group of people called

---

13. For an overview of the penetration of European plantations into the Javanese principalities in the nineteenth century, see Selosoemardjan (1962, Ch. VIII) and O'Malley (1977, pp. 168–78).
14. Geertz (1963*b*, p. 69). For a more recent and more modest estimate, see Widjojo (1970).

"Wong Kalang" or the Kalang People, who had been playing specialized roles in the services of the principality courts as we shall see later. The fact that the principality courts looked with disfavour on the entry of Chinese and other foreign Orientals into their territories in the latter decades of the nineteenth century might have encouraged the growth of these indigenous entrepreneurial groups (see E.N.O.I., IV, 1921, pp. 627–28).

The report of van Bevervoorde includes an enumeration of the number of traders and craftsmen in Kotagede providing an overview of economic activities developed in the town by the end of the nineteenth century. According to van Bevervoorde, among the total of 1,773 "house-compound holders" (*kuli kenceng*, or *erfbezitters*) registered in Kotagede at the year-end of 1903, economic specialization has been observed as shown in Table 2.1.

TABLE 2.1
Economic Specialization in Kotagede, 1903

I. Trade	
1. Trade in cotton goods	24
2. Jewelry and gold work	13
3. Batik trade (wholesale and large retailing)	13
4. Trade in ornaments and wares	6
5. Wax and dyewood trade	6
6. Rice and foodstuff trade (wholesale and large retailing)	3
Total	65
II. Handicraft	
1. Gold and silver workshop	82
2. Jewelry workshop	39
3. Batik workshop	38
4. Tinsmith	23
5. Ironsmith	7
Total	189

Source: van Bevervoorde (1905, pp. 93–95).

Since these figures represent the number of enterprises or workshops, the total number of people actually involved in these economic activities must have been much larger. What is remarkable about these figures is the fact that the number of enterprises apparently serving the needs of the peasant masses rather than those of the royal courts occupied almost one half of the total number of enterprises in trade and handicraft: at least 40 enterprises

(37 in batik and cotton goods trade and 3 in foodstuffs) out of the total of 65 in trade were engaged in the distribution of popular goods. Also at least 68 enterprises (30 in tin and ironwork and 38 in batikking) out of the total of 189 in handicraft produced commodities for popular consumption. Obviously, Kotagede was changing from a town of court artisans *(abdi dalem karya)* to a centre of indigenous industry and trade for the peasantry of the region as symbolized by its colloquial name, Pasargede, or Great Market. The report of van Bevervoorde contains some descriptions on the magnitude of the economic activities carried out in Kotagede and their significance for the region of Yogyakarta and for Java in general. Some excerpts are as follows:

> In Pasargede, as already suggested by its name "great market," a very renowned market is indeed held on every Legi day; also *warung* (small stalls) in the market are selling things every day but it is on Legi days that the market is most crowded by people visiting there. In the market of Pasargede, every day people buy and sell such ordinary goods as agricultural products, prepared foods, drugs, fish, tobacco and salt; besides these, on Legi days, stamped *kain* (batik cloths), iron and copper ware, especially copper *dandang* (rice cooker), *kendil* (another type of rice cooker), sickles, hoes, birds, charcoal, limes, and flowers for the Royal Cemetery are on sale ...
>
> In Pasargede a great amount of trade is carried on in cotton goods, batik, rice, gold and silverware, copperware, jewelry, wax, and dyewood for batikking. All these goods are daily changing hands in great amounts and one can say that Pasargede is the largest trading place in the entire region of the Residency of Yogyakarta ... Merchants from all over Java visit there every day and the town is extremely lively ... If one wants to go to Yogyakarta city [from Kotagede], the means of transportation are always available in the desa of Tegalgendu just across the Gajah Wong River. There, a horse-cart for extremely low tariff is found at any time ...
>
> The industry of Pasargede is well known beyond the limits of Yogyakarta region and, above all, its gold and silverware has an extraordinary reputation all over Java. The work is alive with extreme refinement of form and original designs but some influence of European designs is recognizable. Representative articles include kris, kris heads, kris sheaths, kris rings, buckles, chains, earrings, rings, small dishes, lids, figurines, waist belts, rattles and the like ... (van Bevervoorde 1905, pp. 88, 91, 94).

The report of van Bevervoorde also remarks on the wealth of some of these merchants and craftsmen whose large stone and brick houses crowded the core neighbourhoods of Kotagede. He mentions an interesting episode which he personally experienced. In the early days of his tenure in Yogyakarta, there was an incident in which counterfeit five-guilder bank bills were circulated in Central Java. In his capacity as the Assistant Resident of Yogyakarta, he accompanied an investigating team of the Field Police to Kotagede for a house-to-house checking to see if the counterfeit bills had entered the town. In a rich merchant's house, he came across a total of 35,000 guilders in bank bills stored in a tin box. Besides, there were also several thousand coins in rix-dollars (ibid., p. 92). In view of the fact that the annual salary of the *lurah jurukunci*, or the chief key-keeper of Kotagede, was only 618 guilders in 1903 (ibid.), it can be appreciated that an extraordinary accumulation of wealth was made by some Kotagede merchants.[15]

The emergence of these wealthy merchants occurred from within the mainstream of the economy of the town. In contrast, there was a group of marginal people in terms of the social relations and economy of the town, who nevertheless took an enormous advantage of the changing regional economy. They were the Kalang People.[16]

Local legends say that the Kalang People were originally war captives brought back by Sultan Agung from his unsuccessful expedition to Bali in the early seventeenth century. They were also believed to be descendants of a union between an ape and a princess so that they possessed ape-like tails. Until the 1920s they were concentrated in the neighbourhood of Tegalgendu on the west bank of the Gajah Wong River and were not allowed to reside in Kotagede proper. Their name, "Wong Kalang", probably derived from their peculiar, Hindu-Balinese type ritual, *obong kalang*. *Obong kalang* was a funeral ritual in which a paper figure representing the deceased person was "cremated" at intervals indicated by the Hindu-Balinese calendar while the actual corpse was buried in the ground following Muslim practice. As their professed religion, they followed Islam but the Wong Kalang practised many other customs which looked quite strange to "native" Kotagedeans. For generations, a strong we-they consciousness existed between the Kalang People and the mainstream of the townspeople in Kotagede. The Kalang People were also noted for endogamy. Many marriages were between cousins, including

---

15. Except for a few years in the early 1930s, the value of the Dutch guilder (*f*, or *rupiah* in the East Indies) was stable at the rate of $2\frac{1}{2}$ guilders for one American or Mexican dollar until 1942.
16. For what might the earliest account of the Kalang People in Western literature, see Raffles (1817 [1965], vol. II, pp. 327–29). For more recent references, see Stutterheim (1935) and Adam (1938). The description here is, however, mostly based on local information obtained in Kotagede.

first cousins. Sometimes the Kalang People in Tegalgendu exchanged marriage partners with other Kalang groups living in similar ghetto-like settlements in various places of Central and East Java.

Before the administrative reform of the early 1920s there were two sub-groups among the Kalang People in Tegalgendu: one belonging to the Surakarta Susuhunate and the other to the Yogyakarta Sultanate. The head of the Surakarta sub-group of the Kalang People was given the title of *mantri kalang*. His duty was to provide and supervise carpentry services from his group for the repair of buildings in the Royal Cemetery complex. The Yogyakarta sub-group traditionally specialized in transportation by horses. The transportation of goods between the port town of Semarang on the north coast and the city of Yogyakarta was a monopoly of this group granted by the Yogyakarta court.

The Kalang People derived great advantages from the monetarization of the rural economy and the improvement of transportation. Sometime around the turn of the century, the Surakarta sub-group obtained a licence from the court to open pawnshops throughout the territory. Within a short period, they developed an extensive network of pawnshops bringing in a huge amount of profit.[17] The Yogyakarta sub-group was no less successful. They continued to specialize in the transportation of goods utilizing all available means — trains, motor vehicles, and horses. They were remembered to have been the first "natives" in Java to have acquired a number of Rolls Royces when they were imported to Java.

The enormity of the wealth the Kalang People accumulated is still easily recognizable by looking at about a dozen of their huge palace-like houses constructed during the earliest decades of this century. One of these houses, built in 1926 on the east bank of the Gajah Wong River, has two garages for eight sedans and a stable for twenty horses, besides an extremely extensive and gorgeous main building with many wings. A local tradition says that sometime around World War I, a Kalang family obtained such great wealth that they wanted to cover the floor of the open reception hall *(pendhapa)* of their house with thousands of rix-dollar coins. Hearing about this plan, the Dutch Resident of Yogyakarta was annoyed by the possibility that the face of Queen Wilhelmina on the coins would be repeatedly stepped on by the "natives". However, lacking any proper legal means with which to halt this attempt, he "suggested" that the coins be placed in an upright position rather

---

17. Perhaps this was related to the fact that money-lending for profit is prohibited by the orthodox Islamic teaching from which the Kalang People were remote.

than flat as originally intended. The family, immensely rich as they were, did not have enough coins to comply with the Resident's "suggestion" and were eventually forced to give up their plan.

The Kalang People thus lavishly displayed their fortunes. But, in one aspect, they were thrifty. It was their idea that no money should be spent for education (Western), religion (Islam), or culture (Javanese). So they did not send their children to school, did not pay any religious taxes or contributions *(zakat fitrah)*, and did not sponsor *wayang* puppet shows or *gamelan* music performances. They also avoided involvements in politics. They lived in an exclusive, pecuniary world of their own, surrounded by the envy, fear and hostility of the "native" Kotagedeans. Theirs was an extreme case of the *abangan* tradition in Kotagede.

THE IMPACT OF ADMINISTRATIVE REFORMS ON KOTAGEDE

The drastic change in Dutch colonial policy for the entire East Indies during the early decades of this century is known as the "Ethical Policy" in that ethical considerations for the welfare of the indigenous population were the primary justification for the policy change. It also brought various radical reforms in the fields of land system and administration in the Javanese principalities. To the new breed of Dutch colonial administrators who were inspired by the ideals of Ethical Policy, the Javanese principality authorities loomed as obstacles to such reforms and as impediments standing directly "in the path of a healthy development of the land and the people," who had been overburdened by various particularistic taxes and unpaid labour services with frequent instances of "utterly appalling abuses" of power by the indigenous authorities (van Mook 1958, p. 318f). As a result, in planning and implementing the reforms in the principalities along the lines of the Ethical Policy, the Dutch colonial government discarded its indirect approach and took "direct action" to introduce "drastic reforms" *(ibid.)*.

By 1909, guidelines for the reforms in the principalities were well delineated in S. de Graaf's *Hervormingsplan voor de Javaansche vorstenlanden* (Reform plan for the Javanese principalities), which included "the abolition of the appanage system and the bekel-ships, formation of 'native village community' *(Inlandsche dorpsgemeente)*, regulation and reinforcement of the land rights of the people, reformation of the system of taxation" (van Mook 1958, p. 321). By 1918, implementation of the reform plan in all of the principalities was well under way except for some places, including Kotagede, where the former territories of the principalities overlapped and laborious negotiations were necessary. Finally, by 1920, reforms in these places were completed. Since the process of the reforms in Kotagede is meticulously documented by van Mook (*ibid.*, pp. 324–31), I shall not dwell on it here at length. Only a few aspects of the reforms which had a bearing on the development of Muhammadiyah shall be discussed below.

Kalurahan

The abolition of the appanage system entailed the removal of ramified personal ties that had bound the townspeople to the *patuh*, appanage-holders. Formerly, the administration of the town was composed of a large number of particularistic dyadic clusters between the appanage-holders, the *bekel*, and the common people *(wong cilik)*. These clusters often ignored territorial groupings. Consequently, it frequently happened that a natural neighbourhood and its people were divided into two parts belonging one to the Surakarta and the other to the Yogyakarta principalities. No less frequent was the case in which neighbours belonged to different appanage-holders or *bekel* who imposed different kinds of obligations in the same Surakarta or Yogyakarta neighbourhood.

The new *kalurahan* was formed on the basis of a single, solid and continuous territorial unit disregarding the former allegiances of the people in the territory. This required the merging of former *bekel*-ships and also the exchange of fomer *bekel*-ships between the two principalities. In the end, six *kalurahan* (administrative village) were formed in 1920, four of them belonging to the Yogyakarta Sultanate and two belonging to the Surakarta Susuhunate. Each *kalurahan* consisted of two to ten neighbourhoods *(kampung)* with from 700 to 1,500 people apiece. The *kalurahan* became a legal personality, with communal resources such as its own cash funds, land, and buildings. It exercised regulatory power over the land transactions taking place in its territory. The *kalurahan* had a group of officials consisting of one *lurah* (chief), one *carik* (secretary), one *kamituwa* (vice-chief, also in charge of economic affairs), one *kebayan* (messenger), one *jagabaya* (constable), one *kaum* (religious official), and one *ulu-ulu* (irrigation supervisor). The *lurah* was eleced by the villagers from a list of candidates previously approved by the *wedana* (district chief) and formally appointed to the office by the grand vizier of the Surakarta or the Yogyakarta court. The rest of the village officials, also elected by the villagers, were confirmed by the regent *(bupati)* rather than by the grand vizier. No limits were set upon the terms of these offices and, once elected and appointed, an official could occupy the position for the rest of his life. Villagers who had the status of house-compound holders formed the village council in which important decisions concerning village life, such as the allocation of communal village resources, were made.

Most of the newly created *kalurahan* offices were occupied by former *bekel*. Those former *bekel* who failed in their bids for office were given compensations for the loss of their income in the pre-reform period as follows: (a) those who had previously had rice-fields under their jurisdiction obtained pension fields for the rest of their lives; and (b) those who had had a share of cash revenues received pensions in money from the treasuries of the courts. Of the pre-reform *bekel*, about half did not get into the new *kalurahan* administration and received compensation instead (van Mook 1958, p. 327).

The new *kalurahan* in Kotagede, especially those in urban residential areas without rice-fields, suffered several drawbacks from the outset. The *kalurahan* office did not have an aura of authority deriving from the sharing of royal power. The *lurah* was, after all, *primus inter pares* and was unable to go much further than the limit of consensus among his fellow villagers. The salary of the office (ranging from 30 guilders a month for *lurah* to 10 guilders a month for *jagabaya*) was not enough to attract talented Kotagedeans who were otherwise making good incomes from trade or craft. Former *bekel* who were assured of pensions greater than the *lurah's* salary found no reason to bother with the new office. Therefore, the *kalurahan* offices soon came to be occupied by second-rate former *bekel*. The majority of well-to-do people avoided the *kalurahan* administration. None of the former appanage-holders entered the *kalurahan* administration in spite of the fact that they had been residents of Kotagede for many generations. In their view, the *kalurahan* was the business of the "little people" *(wong cilik)* from whom they should stay aloof. Instead, the former appanage-holders preferred to seek higher positions in the corps of *pangreh praja* (civil services) of the principalities or to provide higher education for their children as professionals.

Having little authority or popular support, the *kalurahan* offices were precarious. It was the fear of van Mook that the rural *kalurahan* system imposed upon the urban sector of Kotagede might fail. As an alternative, he suggested that an urban community or municipality *(stadsgemeente)* with a municipal council *(gemeenteraad)*, which had already been established in many urban areas of Java, might be desirable for the administration of urban Kotagede. He expected that the emerging indigenous middle class in the town would assume the initiative in forming this urban community and taking up its leadership (van Mook 1958, pp. 312, 327–31). The expectation of van Mook, however, did no materialize, for the majority of the newly emerging middle class was not interested in serving the local administration. Instead, many of them devoted themselves to the formation of a new religious community in the form of the Muhammadiyah as shall be described later.

Royal Cemetery

The second significant consequence of the Dutch reforms was that which affected the institution of the Royal Cemetery. The key-keeper officials of the Royal Cemetery complex continued to exist but now they were completely severed from local administration. The officials lost appanage lands, taxes and labour services from the local inhabitants, receiving instead fixed salaries from the principality courts. The townspeople were no longer forced institutionally to contribute money or service to the maintenance of the Royal Cemetery. The Royal Cemetery, however, persisted as the locus of royal ancestral worship and a center of Javanese popular belief in mystical powers. Nevertheless, deprived of the political authority to rule the townspeople and of the administrative apparatus with which to tap local resources, the power, prestige and wealth of the key-keeper officials started to decline. *Kasekten* (mystical powers) were separated from *kakuwaosan* (political authority). Townspeople who continued to take part in traditional ceremonies and rituals centering around the Royal Cemetery were now doing so of their own choice.

In this new situation, the position of the Great Mosque of Mataram in the Royal Cemetery complex became extremely delicate. In the case of the Royal Cemetery itself and other historical remnants of the early Mataram court in the town, the principality courts could still place a full claim on the ownership and control of them. But the Great Mosque had been simultaneously a royal property for the performance of court rituals on the one hand and a holy place for the *adat* Islam of the ordinary townspeople in Kotagede on the other hand. As shall be examined later, the latter's religious orientation gradually shifted toward the orthodoxy. Formerly, one's allegience to the *raja* (the ruler) meant his obedience to Allah simultaneously: *raja* and Allah were co-terminous. However, this situation became no longer tenable: the two are separated now.

Reflecting this separation, a cleavage between the officals who were directly in charge of the Mosque (*penghulu, ketib*, and the like) and those who were exclusively in charge of the Royal Cemetery (*jurukunci*) developed and widened. The Mosque officials continued to receive salaries from the courts, but they were locals in origin and on the whole went along with the changing religious orientation of the townspeople and retained a place of respect in the religious leadership of the town, while the key-keeper officials were less and less respected. This process was accelerated by the fact that after the reforms anybody could become a key-keeper official if he so desired. An aspirant for the office had only to register himself on the waiting list for appointment and could start assuming apprenticeship *(magang)* at once without receiving an emolument. When the last generation of hereditary key-keepers died or retired, most of their sons did not take over their fathers' positions: they preferred to enter the ordinary civil service corps *(pangreh praja)*. In the course of time the majority of *jurukunci* were volunteers.

3

THE BEGINNING OF THE MUHAMMADIYAH
Court Religious Officials and the Urban Middle Class

> Let there be one group of you who call people to good, who urge them towards virtuous conduct and restrain them from evil deeds. Those are the ones who prosper. (Qur'an 3:104)

ABDI DALEM SANTRI IN KAUMAN, YOGYAKARTA

Serious cleavages were developing not only among the local religious officials in Kotagede but also in the court of the Yogyakarta Sultanate itself around the turn of the century. Some of the religious officials of the court, *abdi dalem santri*, became critical of the laxity of Islamic faith and practice among their fellow court officials. They urged the ruler and the *priyayi* to rectify their behaviour according to the standard of Islamic orthodoxy. Kyai Haji (K.H.) Ahmad Dahlan (1868–1923), the founder of Muhammadiyah, was one of these critical *santri* in the service of the Sultan of Yogyakarta.[1]

---

1. There are a number of well-known anecdotes transmitted among Muhammadiyah circles about Dahlan's early attempts at the restoration of orthodoxy in defiance of the established religious authorities of the Sultanate. For those and other

K.H. Ahmad Dahlan was one of the twelve *ketib* (*khotib*, Friday sermon giver) of the Great Mosque of Yogyakarta, receiving a meagre salary of seven guilders a month from the Sultan's treasury. He lived in the Kauman district of Yogyakarta, gave religious lessons in his own home and engaged in the batik trade, in addition to his official duties in the Sultan's Mosque. He travelled widely in Java for religious as well as commercial purposes. His education was solely religious, obtained from his own father Kyai Haji Abubakar, a *ketib* himself, and from various teachers *(kyai/ulama)* in several *pondok pesantren* in Java. He twice made the pilgrimage to Mecca for a total of several years.

K.H. Ahmad Dahlan was not a scholar or a writer. He has left no books or articles.[2] He was, however, obviously an excellent educator and organizer. According to an Indonesian biographer of Dahlan, he was a *"manusia amaliah* (man of action) rather than a *manusia ilmiah* (man of scholarship)" (Solichin 1962, p. 28). His religious lessons, given in his own house, attracted a number of Kauman youth. When the Budi Utomo, the organization of young *priyayi* of nationalist orientation, was established in 1908, he joined it with several of his pupils and associates.[3] He was soon elected to its leadership board as a commissioner and as a religious advisor. He also joined the Sarekat Islam, a mass political organization broadly based on Islam, from the time of its foundation in Surakarta in 1911: in 1914, he assumed the position of religious advisor to the organization as well.

---

stories on Dahlan's life, see Sosrosoegondo (1938), Solichin (1962, 1963b, 1965), Junus (1962), and Amir (1962). Unless indicated otherwise the description in this chapter relies primarily on a summary of the Indonesian sources by Alfian (1969). Some of the Dutch contemporary documents which have recently been published seem to shed new light on the relationships among Dahlan, the court authorities, and the Dutch who intervened the relationships between the two, suggesting that they were more intricate than hitherto have been understood: for example, Rinkes reported in 1913 that Dahlan, after a clash of views with the court religious authorities over the issue of *kiblat* (the direction of prayer to Mecca), was sent to Mecca to study the subject at the expense of the Sultan who wanted at the same time to put him in a peaceful exile until the situation cooled off (van der Wal 1967, p. 193).

2. Schrieke in 1922 mentioned a brochure written by Kyai Haji Dahlan and translated into Dutch by R. Kamil with the title, "Het bindmiddel der menschen" (The agglutinant of people), which apparently attracted some attention from Dutch circles. Unfortunately, however, the brochure seems to have been lost since then (Kwantes 1975, p. 448).

3. For a standard description of the early history of the Budi Utomo, see Nagazumi (1972).

The establishment of the Muhammadiyah took place in the midst of these events on 18 November 1912. There is no primary source of information referring to the reasons why Dahlan formed a new organization alongside the Budi Utomo and the Sarekat Islam, in both of which he had already occupied an influential position. Perhaps neither organization was fully satisfactory to meet the need of furthering Islamic propagation and education, which was of paramount importance to him. But, Dahlan's Muhammadiyah did not have any hostile or competitive relationship with either organization during his lifetime. Besides Dahlan himself, there were a number of individuals who had overlapping memberships in those three organizations.

The original Statute of the Muhammadiyah states the purposes of the Muhammadiyah as follows:

> Article 2: The purpose of this association is:
> a. to spread *(menyebarkan)* the teachings of the Religion of His Majesty Prophet Muhammad, 'May the Lord bless him and give him peace', among the indigenous inhabitants in the Residency of Yogyakarta.
> b. to promote the religious life of the members.[4]

One may notice the rather archaic and Javanese flavour of the original wording in the article (see note 4 below). The language used is unmistakably that of Yogyakarta *santri*: *Igama* for *agama*; the title of *Kanjeng*, a title for Javanese high nobility, for the Prophet Muhammad. However, one can also notice something innovative: that is the idea of what may be called a voluntary association for internal missionary work among the Javanese Muslims.

The new idea must have been a reflection of the atmosphere of an era in which numerous voluntary associations mushroomed (*perhimpunan, persarikatan, persatuan*, and the like). At the same time, it seems important to understand the foundation of Muhammadiyah in terms of its significances as a religious organization. The particular verse of the Qur'an which has already been quoted at the beginning of this chapter, is said to have inspired Dahlan to form the Muhammadiyah. The verse has become one of the mottoes of the Muhammadiyah: the Muhammadiyah is regarded as "one group of you" dedicated to calling people to good and restraining them from

---

4. The Indonesian original of the article runs as follows (changed to the new spelling): *Artikel 2. Maka perhimpunan itu maksudnya*:
   a. *menyebarkan pengajaran Igama Kanjeng Nabi Muhammad Sallalahu Alaihi Wasallam kepada penduduk bumiputra di dalam Residentie Yogyakarta.*
   b. *memajukan hal Igama kepada anggauta-anggautanya.*
   (Reprinted in the *Statuten ... Moehammadijah*, 1938, p. 10).

evil conduct. *Amar ma'ruf, nahi 'anil munkar* in the Arabic original, or its Indonesian rendering, *mengajak kepada kebajikan, mencegah perbuatan yang jahat* (meaning, "call to good and restrain from evil deeds"), has become a standard way of expressing what the Muhammadiyah is all about.

I have noticed an interesting feature about the Indonesian translation of this verse prepared by the Muhammadiyah:[5] the term *ummah* (*ummat* in Indonesian and Javanese) in the Arabic original is translated as "one group" (*segolongan*). In English, *ummah* is usually translated as "religious community" or "nation". Arberry's translation of this Qur'anic verse reads: "Let there be a nation of you, calling to good, and bidding to honour, and forbidding dishonour; those are the prosperers" (1955, vol. I, p. 87). A common understanding of the term *ummah* among Western scholars seems to be that it refers to an aggregate of Muslims of Arab and other countries and even of the entire world, a connotation much broader than that implied by the Muhammadiyah's translation, *segolongan* (one group). "One group" seems, however, not a mistranslation. When there is a group of individuals who obey the commands of Allah, then it constitutes an "ummah" regardless of its size (see *"umma"* in *Encyclopaedia of Islam*, 1934, vol. IV, p. 1015). The point is that the Muhammadiyah founders chose to select one meaning, the narrowest one, from a wide range of possible interpretations of the term: the interpretation best suited to define the character of the movement. The Muhammadiyah certainly started as a small group in contrast to the entire population of "indigenous inhabitants" *(penduduk bumiputra)*. But it was a group of those Javanese Muslims who were dedicated to the cause of spreading what they believed to be the true teachings of Islam.

In terms of the people constituting its leadership, the Muhammadiyah at its incipient stage seems to have been a movement of *abdi dalem santri*, or court religious officials. As mentioned above, Dahlan himself was *ketib* (sermon giver), a functionary of the Sultan's Mosque, a position he inherited from his father. His mother's father was the *penghulu* (chief of the religious bureaucracy) of the Sultanate. His wife's father was also the *penghulu* (Alfian 1969, pp. 228–30). The Kauman area of Yogyakarta in which he was born

---

5. The Indonesian version of this verse quoted in *Statuten ... Moehammadijah* (1938, p. 66) reads as follows (changed to the new spelling):
Hendaklah kamu mengadakan segolongan daripada kamu
yang mengajak kepada kebajikan
yang memerintahkan kepada perbuatan baik dan
mencegah perbuatan yang jahat
Orang-orang yang demikian itulah yang berbahagia.

The Beginning of the Muhammadiyah

FIGURE 3.1

Friday prayer in the inner hall of the Great Mosque (*minbar* dates back to Sultan Agung's time).

FIGURE 3.2

Religious lecture meeting *(pengajian)* on the front porch *(srambi)* of the Great Mosque.

and continued to reside is a neighbourhood located next to the Great Mosque of the Sultan, and the residents there were, like Dahlan, mostly religious functionaries of the Sultanate.

The nine members of the founding leadership of the Muhammadiyah submitted for the Dutch authorities' recognition in 1912 seem also to have been mostly *abdi dalem santri*: seven of them had the aristocratic title of *Mas* or *Raden*; three of them were religious officials (one *penghulu* and two *ketib*) and two, of general administration (one *carik* and one *kebayan*). All of them had the title of *haji*, a person who had made the pilgrimage to Mecca (ibid., pp. 241–42, and *Statuten ... Moehammadijah* 1938, p. 17).

Initially, Dahlan seems to have sought the audience for his propagation among the young *priyayi*, as indicated by the fact that he joined the Budi Utomo, and that he gave extra-curricular lectures on Islam to the students of the Government Kweekschool (Teachers' Training School) in Jetis, Yogyakarta, and of the OSVIA (Training School for Native Administrators) in Magelang. Some of these students, who had already been Budi Utomo members, reportedly became earnest disciples of Dahlan. An anecdote says that it was largely thanks to the prompting of these young disciples that Dahlan decided to establish the organization, the Muhammadiyah (Solichin 1963*b*, pp. 38–39).

It seems that those young followers of Dahlan, who held double membership in the Budi Utomo and the Muhammadiyah, contributed to a great degree to the subsequent growth of the Muhammadiyah through the late 1910s. The 1917 national congress of the Budi Utomo was hosted by Dahlan himself at his own house in Kauman, Yogyakarta. A religious lecture he gave at the congress made a deep impression upon the delegates. After the congress, he was asked by many of them to visit and give similar lectures in various parts of Java. The subsequent lecture trip Dahlan made marked the first step in the expansion of the Muhammadiyah beyond the Residency of Yogyakarta (Deliar 1973, pp. 75–76; Solichin 1963*b*, pp. 38–39).

From the above it may be observed that the Muhammadiyah started as a movement of *abdi dalem santri* (court religious officials) in the Sultanate of Yogyakarta. Dahlan first attempted to reform the religious life of court circles but was unsuccessful. He sought support among the young *priyayi* through the Budi Utomo. He also tried to inject his ideas into the Sarekat Islam. He had some success in both. Until the end of the 1910s, however, the activities of the Muhammadiyah were confined to Kauman, Yogyakarta, or to the Yogyakarta Residency at best. The expansion of the Muhammadiyah came with the support and participation in the movement of the "urban middle class", a process which developed rapidly in the next decade.

THE GROWTH OF THE MIDDLE CLASS IN KOTAGEDE

Already at the time of van Bevervoorde's observation (1903), the general prosperity of the town of Kotagede and a few instances of the enormous accumulation of wealth among some of the merchants there were well noted (see Chapter 2, pp. 43–44 above). Within the next two decades, these few instances seem to have grown into well-established social phenomena. The story of the economy of Kotagede between 1903 and 1922 seems to be that of continuous expansion and diversification as suggested by the result of a survey conducted in 1922 and reported by van Mook (1958). The survey (see Table 3.1) represents the occupational composition of a total of 1,073 house-compound holders in the four newly formed administrative villages (Prenggan, Basen, Sayangan [Alun-Alun], Mutihan).

TABLE 3.1
Occupations of House-Compound Holders in Kotagede, 1922

Description	N	%
I. Royal Servants and Government Officials	91	8.5
II. Wholesale Traders and Master Craftsmen	211	19.7
III. Craftsmen and Retail Traders	678	63.1
IV. Day-Labourers and Peasants	93	8.7
Total	1,073	100.0

Note: For a more detailed breakdown of the data by villages and occupations, see the original table of van Mook (1926a, p. 363) which is appended at the end of this book (Appendix I). Note that this survey did not include the neighbourhood of Tegalgendu where the rich Kalang people resided.
Source: van Mook (1958, p. 289).

The statistics of van Mook contain valuable information. First of all, it is observed that the number of house-compound holders in the second category of the "wholesale traders and master craftsmen" is significantly large: 211 individuals or 19.7 per cent of the total. Furthermore, according to the van Mook's original table (1958, p. 289; 1926a, p. 363), of these 211 individuals, 120 people or 11.2 per cent of the total, were in the wholesale trade of textile, batik and related goods, while the rest, 91 people or 8.5 per cent of the total, were master craftsmen *cum* entrepreneurs (*juragan* in local terms) in gold and silver smithing and jewelry. This entire group has been categorized as "wealthier inhabitants" by van Mook (ibid.).

A second point to be observed from van Mook's statistics is that, over the two decades, production and trade in batik and related goods continued to occupy a leading position in the Kotagede economy. Those house-compound holders who engaged in "batik-making, cloth-dyeing, and cloth-printing (*cap*, stamping)," subsumed in the third category of "craftsmen and retail traders" in Table 3.1, in fact, constitute the single largest occupational group of all, with 220 individuals or 20.5 per cent of the total house-compound holders (ibid.). As mentioned above, the number of wholesalers in batik and related goods was already considerable (120 individuals or 11.2 per cent). Taken together, almost one-third (31.7 per cent) of the total number of house-compound holders in 1922 was involved in trade or production of cloth, batik or related goods. The period certainly deserves its local name, *jaman batik*, or the "batik period". An elderly Kotagedean looked back on the period and stated:

> Everybody who had capital rushed into batikking or the sale of batik. Batik workshops mushroomed everywhere. Even those who did not have money were not left behind. They were easily able to find jobs as labourers. More often, those who did not have money but who were strong, diligent, and trustworthy got an advancement of batik cloth from wholesalers and peddled from market to market, from village to village. Some of them soon became rich enough to set up their own enterprise.

The trade networks in batik, textile, and a number of handicraft products centring around Kotagede extended far beyond the region of Central Java, reaching Batavia (Jakarta), Cirebon, and Purwokerto to the west, Pekalongan and Semarang to the north, and Surakarta, Madiun, Kediri, and Surabaya to the east (van Mook 1958, p. 288). In his famous *Batik Report*, de Kat Angelino noted the presence of Kotagedeans in the batik trade of Tulung Agung (a town on the Kediri plain) as follows: the "inlanders" who were operating twenty-five batik workshops out of the total of thirty-eight found in the town [of Tulung Agung] in 1930 were mostly "Wong Mataram" (Mataramese) originating from Kotagede and Yogyakarta city, and came to settle there about twenty-five years ago (1930, vol. III, pp. 56–57).

This was also the time when four or five of the richest merchants of Kotagede were given the nickname of *raja dagang* or *ratu dagang*, "merchant king" or "merchant queen" respectively, by the local people. A lady merchant who controlled a large portion of the supply of secondary crops from the Kediri plain to the Yogyakarta region was one such Merchant Queen. A textile wholesaler who was given the monopoly on the import of cambric, the material for batikking, in the Yogyakarta region was a Merchant King. Far more than a statistical category, those whom van Mook called "the wealthier

FIGURE 3.3

Main road (northern route) from Kotagede to Yogyakarta — Mt. Merapi in the background.

FIGURE 3.4

Front view of Kotagede market.

FIGURE 3.5

Inside scene of Kotagede market.

FIGURE 3.6

Main road (eastern route) from Kotagede to Plered.

merchants" formed a closely knit ingroup connected by kinship, marriage and business partnership.

Kotagede was now renowned for the existence of *raja dagang*, merchant kings, in addition to the *abdi dalem jurukunci*, royal key-keepers at the Royal Cemetery. In terms of wealth, *abdi dalem jurukunci* were no longer able to match those *raja dagang*. Accordingly, as van Mook has observed, in Kotagede in the early twenties "the administrative officials have much less influence there than elsewhere, especially when they are not well-to-do. It is often difficult, and financially disastrous, for them to keep up with the wealthier inhabitants of Kuta Gede" (van Mook 1958, p. 287). Some of the wealthier inhabitants of Kotagede even became the creditors of the courts of Yogyakarta and Surakarta or a " 'Rothschild' of Java" (ibid., p. 288).

The economic superiority of wealthy merchants in Kotagede went hand-in-hand with the elevation of their social status. Although they were not fully accepted into the rank of nobility, wealthier Kotagede merchants were nevertheless often included as equals in the social circles of the nobility and among the high-ranking officials of the principalities. There was at least one instance of a *raja dagang*, merchant king, being given a princess from the court of Yogyakarta as a wife for his son, as we shall see below (p. 84). Selosoemardjan has found that there were frequent contacts for the transaction of trade in gold, silver, and jewelry between wealthy Kotagede merchants and the wives of Yogyakarta court officials who otherwise rarely mingled with commoners (Selosoemardjan 1962, p. 119).

There were some among the wealthy merchants who endeavoured to convert their wealth into power and status in traditional terms by buying noble titles and honorary offices in the court government. It was an irony of history, however, that at the very time when wealth enabled a person of common origin to acquire a position in the traditional hierarchy of Yogyakarta society, the traditional structure was already hollowed out from within.

An elderly Kotagedean who became an activist in the Muhammadiyah and a teacher for its elementary school stated his experience as follows:

> I had an uncle who wanted to become a palace guard trooper. Formerly the position of royal troopers was hereditary and passed from father to son, but gradually it became possible to buy the position. You could pay money and become an *abdi dalem* (royal servant). That's how this uncle became an *abdi dalem*. I had another uncle, whose name was Bahuwinangun, father of Mr. Kasmat [a renowned Islamic politician in Yogyakarta]. Pak Bahuwinangun was an *abdi dalem* in the court of Yogyakarta and he was very happy to be respected by people for his closeness to the king. I could also have become an *abdi dalem* in the same way if I had wanted to, but I just didn't want to. I felt that it was only *gengsi kosong* (empty prestige).

The majority of the wealthy merchants remained rather indifferent to the prestige deriving from the court.

More positively, success in business and elevation in social status contributed to the development of a special kind of attitude among the wealthy merchants of Kotagede which van Mook has characterized in such terms as "self-reliance *(self-standigheid)*", "level-headed frankness *(bezadigde vrijmoedigheid)*", and "absence of obsequiousness *(onderdanigheid)*", an attitude which was rarely found among the rest of the population in the principalities (van Mook 1958, pp. 288, 313).

Self-confidence and indifference to the superfluous way of life inside the court seems to have created among the Kotagede middle class a general condition in which the propagation of Islamic reformism would find a sympathetic response.

THE BEGINNING OF THE MUHAMMADIYAH IN KOTAGEDE

Elderly Kotagedeans still recall the excitement and enthusiasm they experienced when they first encountered various so-called "national awakening" movements developed in the 1910s. The retired Muhammadiyah school teacher quoted above stated:

> *Rapat propaganda* (propaganda meetings) were often held in various places in Kotagede at that time. Large *pendhapa* (open reception hall) near the market were often used for gatherings of that sort. There came and spoke such *tokoh-tokoh* (leading figures) as H.O.S. Tjokroaminoto [president of the Sarekat Islam], Samanhoedi [founder of the same organization], K.H. Dahlan [founder of the Muhammadiyah], Ki Hadjar Dewantoro [leader of the Taman Siswa school system], and even Communist leaders, Semaun, Muso and Alimin. We listened to them attentively and then continued *debat* (debate) among ourselves.

By the middle of the 1920s it became obvious that two organizations were chosen by Kotagedeans from among a spectrum of "national awakening" movements: the Muhammadiyah and the PKI (the Communist Party of Indonesia). In the course of time, the two became mutually antagonistic and the tension between them was only removed as a result of the suppression of the latter by Dutch authorities in 1926–27. First, in this section, the organizational development of the Muhammadiyah in Kotagede during the 1910s and 1920s shall be traced. The next section shall examine its confrontation with the PKI in 1924–25.

It was apparently the Budi Utomo that first recognized the importance of the thriving middle class in Kotagede as a model for indigenous economic advancement and as a potential constituency for its organization. When the Budi Utomo's second congress was held in the Kweekschool of Yogyakarta in 1909, Raden Sastrowidjono, Public Prosecutor *(Jaksa)* of Sragen, made a speech on the desirable course of progress for the indigenous population of Java, which the Budi Utomo was to lead, and mentioned the significance of trading activities in Kotagede and elsewhere:

> A country cannot progess if she does not have a segment of her population engaged in trade, for those traders indeed form a middle class, *bangsa pertengahan* or *middenstand*. Are there not any Javanese who are engaged in trade? Yes, there certainly are. But they are few in comparison to the total number of the population on the island of Java. In fact, at present, there is not yet found among us Javanese what is called the *handelsgeest* (commercial spirit) in the Dutch language. [Nevertheless] it is true to say that wherever there is a grain of the commercial spirit, however small it may be, then there is prosperity. People [in such a place] seem content and calm *(ayem-ayem)* like those in Pasar Gede [of Yogyakarta], Lawiyan [of Surakarta], and Kauman of Kudus, and some other places (*Verslag Boedi Oetomo* 1910, p. 40).[6]

There is no evidence, however, that this *priyayi* organization obtained any significant support from among the townspeople of Kotagede.

Neither did the Sarekat Islam (S.I.) make any organizational headway in Kotagede. This may seem strange in view of the fact that the organization, especially in its formative years, put much emphasis on the protection and advancement of the economic interests of the indigenous trading class against those of the Dutch as well as the Chinese. It seems true that Kotagedeans were stirred by the Sarekat Islam's propaganda,[7] but they showed little enthusiasm in organizational affiliation with it.

I asked Haji Masjhudi, one of the founders of the Muhammadiyah in Kotagede (whose life history shall be described in detail in the next chapter), why the Sarekat Islam was not successful in Kotagede. The old Haji replied:

---

6. I am indebted to Professor Akira Nagazumi for the source of the information cited here.
7. For an episode in which a certain Hardjowirogo, a local official in charge of the sale of salt and opium, was so excited by the Central Sarekat Islam that he named his son "Central", see Rasjidi (1968, p. 10).

In the case of the Sarekat Islam, its ideology entered here first but its organization did not. We were already connected with *(berhubung dengan)* the Muhammadiyah through family ties *(hubungan keluarga)*. A few of us joined S.I. too, but as an organization it did not come alive *(hidup)* here. Moreover, S.I. was a political organization while the Muhammadiyah was a social one. In the case of the Muhammadiyah, it entered here through family relationships and frienships *(perantaraan persaudaraan)*.

Ideologically many Kotagedeans were receptive and even sympathetic to S.I.[8] But when it came to the matter of organizational affiliation, networks of family relationship and friendship were given priority. Another elderly member of the Muhammadiyah explained why it was so:

At that time a lot of organizations developed. These organizations first looked like one another. But we suspected that there must be some organizations which were set up by the government to deceive us. We did not like to be manipulated *(didalangi)*. In that kind of situation, we thought that we'd better rely on the relationships of family and friends. We already knew who was honest and could be trusted and who was not.

As shall be examined in the next chapter, the Muhammadiyah was the organization which had been well connected with some Kotagedeans through kinship, marriage, and friendship.

As briefly mentioned in the Introduction, the formation of a branch of the Muhammadiyah in Kotagede was preceded in the early 1910s by the establishment of a local organization, Syarekatul Mubtadi.[9] As indicated by

---

8. Contemporary Dutch information seems to support this local memory: Rinkes reports in 1912 that the Sarekat Islam of Surakarta approached similar associations ("clubs") in Yogyakarta and Pasargede but was unsuccessful to incorporate them (van der Wal 1967, p. 88). The "similar association" in Yogyakarta was Dahlan's Muhammadiyah (ibid., p. 89). The other one in Pasargede was very much likely to be Syarekatul Mubtadi. Unfortunately, he failed to mention its name (ibid., see also note 9 below).

9. No definite date of the foundation of the Syarekatul Mubtadi was given by its former members. As we shall see in the next chapter, one of its founders Haji Masjhudi came home from Mecca a few years prior to the outbreak of World War I (1914–18). The association mentioned by Rinkes in 1912 (see note 8 above) might well have been it. Rinkes has only the following to report: "I am not well informed of the above-mentioned association in Pasar Gede: apparently it consists of merchants who, following the fashion of the time and somewhat impulsively, founded the society for the purposes of pursuing together their business on a more modern basis and of developing the religious character of the members" (van der Wal 1967, p. 88).

the Arabic name of the organization (*syarekatul* means association or union; *mubtadi* means novice or beginners), it aimed at the advancement of basic religious education especially among adult men and women. The kind of religious education pursued by the new organization was markedly different in a number of ways from traditional Islamic education.

Traditional Islamic education was characterized by the teaching of Arabic script and the rote memorization of some verses of the Qur'an given by *kampung* teachers *(guru ngaji)* to young children, a more advanced teaching of various subjects to young men in *pesantren,* and the furthering of mystic learnings by adult men through *tarekat,* devotional orders.[10] The new organization was based on the conviction of its founders that traditional Islamic education was too incomplete, inadequate and out of touch to cope with the challenge of the modern world and the religious crisis which the community of Muslims faced. Those Kotagedeans who participated in the Syarekatul Mubtadi, when I asked them about the purpose of the new organization, invariably replied that it was organized to "deepen *(mendalami)*" the teachings of Islam, to "strengthen *(menguatkan)* the religious consciousness *(kesadaran agama),*" to pursue "progress *(kemajuan)*" and to "awaken *(membangunkan)*" the *ummat Islam* (the community of Muslims). Some also stated that the approach employed by the Syarekatul Mubtadi was quite different from that of the traditional Islamic learning in that the verses of the Qur'an and the Hadith were given direct explanations in the vernacular language: "Syarekatul Mubtadi promoted the learning of basics, the 'a, b, c,' of Islam. It made easy *(memudahkan)* the learning of the basics of Islam."

The new organization based upon this conviction was also markedly different in organizational forms from the traditional institutions of Islamic education represented by *pesantren* and *tarekat.* Unlike the *pesantren,* which

---

10. I realize now (in 1981) that the characterization of traditionalist Islam in general and of *pesantren* and *tarekat* in particular summarized in this study is somewhat biased in favour of their modernist critics: it should at least be admitted that traditionalists have made remarkable adaptations to modern conditions over the past half a century (Nakamura 1981). For an insightful description of the traditional *pesantren,* see Samudju Asjari (1967): Professor Benedict Anderson kindly showed his summary notes of this work to me, and I hereby acknowledge his help. For "standard descriptions" of *pesantren* and *tarekat* in English, see Geertz (1960, pp. 177–84, and *passim*) and Sartono (1966, pp. 157–65) respectively. For more recent works rectifying modernist prejudice in the study of traditionalism in Indonesian Islam, see Sudjoko et al. (1974), Dawam (1974), Abdurrahman (1979), and Zamakhsyari (1981).

had been almost exclusively operated for the education of young unmarried men, the Syarekatul Mubtadi was characterized by the education, or more precisely, re-education, of married men and women of middle age. Again, unlike the *pesantren,* in which the authority of *kyayi* or *guru* was absolute and the relationships among the *kyayi,* his trusted assistants, advanced students and novices were organized in a well-defined hierarchy, the new adult organization was characterized by the principle of equality among members and by emphasis on learning among themselves. In the Syarekatul Mubtadi there was no formal position of *guru*: those who were more learned in religious knowledge and more talented in teaching others naturally came forth as popular lecturers. A few people worked as *pengurus,* functionaries of the organization, but lecturers were widely sought from among the members as well as from outside. It was to these lecture meetings of the Syarekatul Mubtadi that many prominent leaders of Islamic and nationalistic movements of the day were invited to talk. Again unlike the traditional *pesantren* characterized by its geographic and social isolation, the lecture meetings of the Syarekatul Mubtadi were held in the midst of the town, easily accessible and always open to the public, and curious newcomers were welcomed to come and encouraged to participate in discussion (cf. Junus 1960).

Another feature of the new organization was that it placed equal emphasis on both sexes. The traditional *pesantren* was exclusively for young men, and masculinity was a dominant value in many aspects of its communal life. But the Syarekatul Mubtadi leaders explicitly encouraged its male members to bring their wives and daughters to public religious meetings. The women's section of the Syarekatul Mubtadi soon got under way with its own leadership.

The Syarekatul Mubtadi had another auxiliary organization — a foundation for fund-raising. The foundation was called Mardihartoko (lit., Supporter of Treasury). The foundation issued shares *(saham)* at five guilders each, and there were about 100 share holders *(andil).* The capital collected in this way was then invested to buy land in various neighbouring villages — about three hectares of rice fields and some dry land. The profits obtained from the land were divided in the following manner: 30 per cent for share holders; 40 per cent for reinvestment; and 30 per cent for the Syarekatul Mubtadi's treasury. The foundation continued its operation after the Kotagede branch of the Muhammadiyah was formed (Hardjono 1969, p. 30).

It has been well noticed by the historians of the early Muhammadiyah that it had put much emphasis on and was quite successful in the field of youth organization. It has also been suggested that this was largely due to the personal effort of K.H. Ahmad Dahlan himself who took inspiration from a Western style Boy Scouts organization in Surakarta, Javaansche Padvinders

Organisatie (Javanese Scouts Organization), or J.P.O., sponsored by the Mangkunegaran court and Dutch authorities: modelling on this example, Dahlan founded a Muhammadiyah counterpart, Hizbul Wathan (lit., "Defenders of Fatherland"), or H.W. (see Solichin 1963*b*, p. 50ff., Alfian 1960, p. 273, and Deliar 1973, p. 80).

Independent of and parallel to what was happening to the Kauman youth under the direct leadership of K.H. Ahmad Dahlan, numerous reformist Islamic youth organizations seem to have been developing simultaneously in various places. In Kotagede, the Syarekatul Mubtadi founded a local, independent youth organization, Krida Mataram, at almost the same time as its own founding. Haji Masjhudi was again one of the prime organizers of the Krida Mataram. He founded it with several of his friends. He stated:

> It [Krida Mataram] was an organization for "children" *(anak-anak)*. It was for them to learn the Qur'an together *(ngaji bersama)* and to go out and play together *(dolan-dolan)*. "Children" were invited to join in *(diajak ikut)* religious courses *(pengajian)*, sports *(olahraga)* like football *(sepak bola)*, parading *(pawai)* and the like. It was called *padvinders* ["Scouts" in Dutch] in the Dutch times. It is *pandu* [Indonesian word for Scouts] of today.

The retired Muhammadiyah school teacher already quoted above was also an "old boy" of the Krida Mataram and described how he had joined it as follows:

> I married in 1916. After it, I was [still] fond of playing with friends of mine *(suka dolan sama teman)*. One of them was Haji Masjhudi. I was then not observing religion yet *(belum menjalankan agama)*. H. Masjhudi invited me to come along to religious courses *(mengajak saya, mari datang pengajian)*... I was not observing religion yet but was willing to listen to religious courses. The longer the time passed, the happier did I become observing religion. So I went along [with H. Masjhudi] and was assigned a job in the organization. It was the beginning of my participation in the movement *(gerakan)* in Kotagede.

The Krida Mataram put equal emphasis on the learning of the Qur'an *(pengajian)* and playing *(dolan)*. In Kotagede, like elsewhere in Java, *langgar* (small neighbourhood prayer houses) and *rondha* (night watch) posts had been traditional centers around which neighbourhood boys gathered. Some even slept there rather than in their houses. The Krida Mataram seems to have been organized as a grand confederation and formal organization of such neighbourhood boys' peer groupings. The name itself is suggestive of this aspect. "Krida" in Javanese refers to doing something (together) for sport or fun-making activities such as *gamelan*-playing, dancing, and *pencak*-fighting (stylized self-defense art). "Mataram" is the colloquial generic term for the Kotagede area derived from the fact that it was the old capital of the kingdom of Mataram. So, put together, Krida Mataram means a "do-something" group for boys and young men in Mataram, which was quite an appropriate name for the nature and purpose of the group.

An interesting contemporary booklet reveals further information on the development of reformist Muslim youth organizations in the Yogyakarta region in the early 1920s including the Krida Mataram in Kotagede.[11] In the year 1921, when this booklet was written, there were three major youth groups in Yogyakarta: Hizbul Wathan (lit., Defender of the Fatherland) of the Kauman district with 250 members, Wira Tamtama (lit., Young Soldiers) of the Pakualaman district with 350 members, and Krida Mataram of Kotagede with 250 members. As the Syarekatul Mubtadi and similar independent local organizations were eventually amalgamated into the Muhammadiyah, headquartered in Kauman, Yogyakarta, so were these youth organizations incorporated into one single organization, Hizbul Wathan, in 1924 (Deliar 1972, p. 80). The booklet referred to here seems to reflect an earlier phase of this merging process in which the three youth organizations were forming a central coordinating body, Centraale Padvinders Vereniging (Central Association of Scouts) in August 1921. The document consists of a preamble and the statute of this central coordinating body.

Besides the information on the organizational aspect of this development, the document provides valuable information on the ideological aspect of these youth movements. For that reason an almost full translation of the preamble is presented below (the spelling has been changed to the new one):

> The land of the East Indies (Hindia Timur) is the land where we were born (*tanah tumpah darah kita*, lit., the land where our blood was shed). We, the people of the indies *(orang Hindia)*, are the native people *(bumiputra)* of this land, whose population is no less than 35 millions.
>
> We all know that our land is extremely rich and yields many kinds of products, whose usefulness is enormous for all peoples *(segala bangsa)*. Because of that, it is not strange that many thousands of foreigners *(orang bangsa asing)* have come here to acquire the riches of this land of ours. Up

---

11. This 18-page booklet is entitled *Statuten Centraale Padvinders Vereniging Di Djokjakarta: Dengan Beberapa Keterangan Jang Perloe Bagi Boemi Poetera Hindia Timoer* (The Statute of the Central Association of Scouts in Yogyakarta: with some explanation for the native people of the East Indies), 1921. I owe special thanks to the late S.K. Hardjono, a Muhammadiyah activist and a bibliophile in Kotagede, who showed me this booklet from his personal library.

until now most of them have settled here for many generations, while there are also many of them who have gone back to their respective countries. [In either case] they have all attained a noble *(mulia)* and comfortable *(senang)* life.

However, how about the lives of 35 million people, the indigenous inhabitants *(bumiputra)* of our land? We have all suffered *(sengsara)* and have become a people of extreme lowness *(rendah sekali)*, differing remarkably from those foreign peoples. It has become merely words that we have a land of richness: for the authorities *(peperintahan)* have been totally ignorant *(sama sekali tidak tahu)* and have only followed and fulfilled rules established in the past *(menurut dan menetapi aturan-aturan yang sudah jadi)*. The richness no longer exists but has been drained out. Our knowledge and skills *(ilmu kepandaian)* have remained small and extremely rudimentary. Our moral character *(perasaan budi)* has already been destroyed *(rusak)*.

Everywhere, on the streets or in the villages, we come across our people *(bangsa kita)* suffering because of poverty *(sengsara karena miskinnya)*. For instance, many people are sick or dying, for there is nobody who looks after them. It is indeed a matter of great pity *(kasihan)*. Who is the one that is responsible for helping them? We ourselves, aren't we? To help those suffering is our responsibility *(wajib kita)*, we, human beings, who live in this world.

Not only the poor suffer: an ordinary person may also find himself facing unavoidable suffering and in need of help: for instance, what if calamities like fire, flood, falling into a river, sudden illness, or death on the street, being struck by a vehicle, and the like, befall us?

If we let such a situation continue, or remain silent about it or just laugh at it, then it means that we have no human feelings *(tiada berhati kemanusiaan)*. It should be said that we have no love for our people with whom we live *(tidak cinta kepada sesama hidup)*. It should be said that such a person or a people is abject *(hina)* and their sensibilities *(perasaan)* are destroyed. A people whose sensibilities are destroyed is also certain to suffer the destruction of their language and land of birth, just like the situation we are in at present.

There are many among our people who certainly acknowledge love for our people and for our land of birth, but they just acknowledge it and never want to demonstrate *(membuktikan)* it. They are happier and more willing when they are asked a favor by a rich man *(orang kaya)* or a noble man *(orang luhur)* than when asked a favor by a poor man *(orang miskin)*. They get more excited *(gugup)* when visited by a noble man than when visited by a poor man. Help and respect to the rich or noble are more quickly and abundantly accorded than help to the poor man, and the like.

That way of thinking is wrong *(terbalik,* lit., the other way around): a person or a people, whose skills are high *(tinggi kepandaiannya)* or whose wealth is enormous *(banyak hartanya)* or whose position is superior *(luhur pangkatnya)* is preceived more exalted *(lebih mulia)* than a person of good and honest character *(baik dan lurus budi perasaannya)*. That is what is causing people at the present time to be always greedy for more education *(ilmu)*, higher position, or more wealth, but not at all eager to become aware of [the importance of] good and honest character and feelings.

Knowledge and skills *(ilmu kepandaian)*, knowledge of standards *(ilmu kederajatan)*, and knowledge for making wealth *(ilmu kekayaan)* all derive from school education, but school education at the present time is in fact less than satisfactory *(kurang baik)*; it does not yet satisfy our hearts *(tidak menyenangkan hati kita)*.

As long as school education remains as it is, our offspring will only continue to suffer *(terus sengsara sahaja)*. In order to exalt *(memuliakan)* our people and our land of birth, the feelings *(perasaan)* of our people must be exalted higher than other kinds of education.

Being aware of the enormous suffering befalling us, there have developed several groups of men and young men *(orang-orang atau kanak-kanak)* who are willing to help relieve this suffering as much as possible *(menolong sengsara itu sekuat-kuatnya)*, that is, the Padvinders (Scouts).

A number of observations may be made about the document quoted above. First, the anti-Dutch tone is unmistakable: the Dutch and other foreigners came to exploit the riches of Indonesia and the riches were drained out. Consequently the Indonesian people were suffering. Secondly, the criticism of the indigenous authorities is obvious. They had lost their vitality as leaders of the people and clung instead to the rules established in the past. Little could be expected from them for the the improvement of the condition of the populace. A third point in the preamble deals with the negative effect of the Western secular education which provided Indonesians with the practical knowledge and skills needed to acquire material wealth. However, it resulted in the decline of humane feelings and compassion and in the strengthening of the cult of the rich and the powerful among the Indonesians. Alongside the education of practical knowledge and skills, education, aimed at elevating the moral charcter of the people based upon Islam, must be promoted.

A fourth point that the preamble emphasizes is the necessity for immediate and concrete action. Lip-service to the idea of love for the nation and the people is useless. Action is required in order to help relieve "public suffering *(kesengsaraan umum)*". A clause in the statute further spelled out the action programmes which include: (a) hygiene and physical education to build and maintain healthy bodies; (b) skills of reading, writing and arithmetic, and first aid and natural disaster training; (c) "moral education *(ilmu perasaan,* lit., knowledge of feelings)" in order to cultivate "genuine humane feelings *(perasaan kemanusiaan sejati)*" like "love of body *(cinta badan)*, love of nation *(cinta bangsa)*, and love of motherland *(cinta tanah tumpah darahnya)*", and actions to express and carry out these loves; and (d) religious education, the understanding and performance of the teaching of Islam.

For the ear of a present-day political analyst, the ideology of the preamble may sound rather unsophisticated. However, it should be noted that the basic stance of social activism to alleviate public sufferings *(kesengsaraan umum)* is already remarkably clear. The Muhammadiyah youth organization was to continue this social activism.

CONFRONTATION WITH THE PKI (1924)

It was van Mook's observation that there was a growing antagonism between the Muhammadiyah and the PKI in Kotagede during the early 1920s. He described it primarily in terms of the conflict of economic interests, that is, the interest of the established merchants vis-à-vis that of the smaller craftsmen and traders, and the Islam of the Muhammadiyah and the Communism of the PKI representing ideologically each side of this conflict of interest. Referring to the occupational categorization among Kotagedeans (see Table 3.1), he further elaborated the corresponding ideological differentiation among them as follows:

> The craftsmen, together with the lesser tradesmen in foodstuffs and similar commodities, constitute the third group. There are a few prosperous persons among them, renowned artisans who fill costly orders from the kratons, but most of the group are highly dependent on their employers or their clientele. Despite the geniality usually dominating Javanese industrial relations, many of this group have been hard-hit by the pressure of the slump years, and it is no doubt partly as a result of that fact that "Communism" has gained some influence among them in recent years. (As might be expected, there has been a steady, fairly strong opposition to the "Communist" movement from the more prosperous members of the community. The Mohammadiyah association has found quite a large following among the better-off in this third group). (van Mook 1958, p. 288)[12]

Information collected locally for this study suggests, however, that the antagonism between the Muhammadiyah and the PKI in the local context

---

12. On the basis of van Mook's remarks, Wertheim argues that the case of Kotagede points up the inherently conservative nature of Islam as a bourgeois ideology (Wertheim 1959, p. 220). However, as shall be examined in the text, the reality seems to have been more complicated than his clear-cut characterization.

FIGURE 3.7

Open reception hall *(pendopo)* of Sopingin, Chief Key-Keeper *(Lurah Jurukunci)*.

FIGURE 3.8

Palace-like house of a Kalang family (used for R.K. head's election meeting).

of Kotagede during the early 1920s was not easily reducible to the conflict of class interests. According to the memories of local elders, there were about a score of core activists of the PKI in Kotagede at that time. They included one village *carik* (clerk, or secretary), one *prajurit kraton* (palace guard), one post office employee, two government elementary school teachers, one *tukang emas* (goldsmith), and a few other craftsmen *(tukang)*. None of them was a "poor artisan": the village secretary was from a family of the pre-reform *bekel* and was quite well-to-do; the palace guard was a relative of one of the "merchant kings"; the government employees were receiving lucrative salaries according to local standards; the goldsmith was quite rich — a master-craftsman and entrepreneur himself. The Communist leadership in pre-war Kotagede did not represent a poor segment of the townspeople.

The mass following for the PKI was organized in a local branch of the Sarekat Rakyat (S.R. or People's Union) with several core members. It is likely that the Sarekat Rakyat members were generally "worse-off" economically than the core Communist group. But it should be noted that neither the PKI nor the Sarekat Rakyat organized labour disputes in Kotagede during the 1920s. Indeed, labour disputes seldom occurred in the local industrial scene. No trade unions were organized.

The major issue of antagonism between the PKI and the Muhammadiyah was, then, purely "political" and "religious" as far as the Kotagede local scene was concerned. The PKI advocated direct action to overthrow the Dutch colonial regime. The Muhammadiyah, although no less anti-colonial, did not let the organization become involved in such an action. The Muhammadiyah took the religious enlightenment of individuals as its primary task and regarded its political involment rather detrimental to the performance of that task. Although individual members were accorded the freedom of political action as individuals, the Muhammadiyah took the stand that political action without religious conviction was groundless or even harmful to its task of religious enlightenment.[13]

This antagonism between religion and politics was dramatically expressed in an incident of a clash between the Muhammadiyah and the PKI in

---

13. Haji Misbach, a celebrated "red haji" of Surakarta, proposed to the 1923 Muhammadiyah congress the direct involvement of the Muhammadiyah in politics. The congress did not accept his proposal, but the report of the congress mentioned his name still in very cordial terms (*Verslag Moehammadijah* 1923, p. 10). For further information on Haji Misbach, see McVey (1965, p. 171ff). For more on the issue of Muhammadiyah's political non-invovement, see Alfian (1969, pp. 248, 333–35).

conjunction with a PKI congress held in Kotagede in 1924. This congress, in fact, marked a turning-point in the history of the PKI in colonial Indonesia. In the congress a decision was taken to start an all-out effort to make a revolution in the near future (McVey 1965, p. 273). This decision led the PKI to stage unsuccessful uprisings in the following years, 1926–1927. As a result of the subsequent repressions by the colonial government the party disappeared from the political scene entirely until 1945.

This historic 1924 congress of the PKI in Kotagede was not only nationally significant. The occasion also left a deep imprint on the experience of many Kotagedeans because the clash between the PKI and the Muhammadiyah had taken place at an open propaganda rally held as part of the PKI congress. At first, the PKI wanted to find a meeting place for the congress in Yogyakarta city itself. However, because of the strong anti-communist influence of the S.I. Putih (the anti-communist main stream of the Sarekat Islam) and the Muhammadiyah in the city, it was impossible for the PKI to secure a safe meeting place there. At an open propaganda meeting of the PKI held in Yogyakarta in August 1924, Communist speakers had been shouted down by the S.I. and Muhammadiyah members in the audience. So the PKI, determined to have its congress in a more secure place, chose Kotagede (see McVey 1965, p. 294). In the event, Kotagede turned out to be no more secure than Yogyakarta. The closed sessions of the congress were conducted without incident from 11 to 15 December in a *pendhapa* near the Kotagede market. But when the PKI attempted to hold an open propaganda rally in the same place on 14 December, a large number of the Muhammadiyah members showed up among the audience of 700 to 800 people.

The following is a description of the incident taken from a contemporary secret report sent by the Resident of Yogyakarta, Dingemans, to the Governor-General of the Netherlands Indies in Batavia (*Mailrapport* 18X/25). A free summary translation of the report reads as follows:

> Since it was already known to the Yogyakarta authorities that Muhammadiyah members, especially those who belonged to the organization, Ummat Islam, a political arm of the Muhammadiyah,[14] were planning to obstruct the PKI rally, a large number of police troops were mobilized and present in the meeting place, and put at the disposal of the Police Assistant Wedono (District Police Chief) who was personally present at the spot to maintain order.

---

14. The organization "Ummat Islam" appears to have been an ad hoc action group to counter anti-Islamic provocations.

Prior to the opening of the rally, the police authorities took a precautionary measure and removed two potentially disruptive Muhammadiyah members, Hani and Raden Reso, from the *pendhapa* in which the podium was located. Another Muhammadiyah leader, Haji Hajid, asked for an immediate debate without waiting for his turn while the Communist speakers were speaking, but was not allowed by the chairman. Haji Hajid was not satisfied with this and continued to say to the police, "Watch out, you policemen, otherwise there will be bloodshed." At this point, the police stopped him and led him outside the meeting place. Then Haji Hajid's supporters shouted, "Muslims should all get out of here!" To this some Communists shouted back, "*Moh* [No, we refuse it]".

Then Hani, who had not been on the podium that day, and his followers began to heckle the Communist leader Alimin's speech which they thought insulted Islam. His speech was interrupted, and Alimin got angry. He and his supporters all stood up and yelled, "Now those hecklers must get out!" Hani was then dragged away by the police, and his followers walked out of the place.

Things did not go as quickly as Alimin wanted, who complained, "The police are powerless." To this, District Police Chief Raden Danudinoto replied, "The police are not powerless, but we cannot distinguish between one and the other party members." (The party members were not wearing party symbols.) Then the Communist leader, Muso, said to his members sitting around him, "If the police can't do it, my own party will do it." Then Muso and his followers wanted to get up, but they were forbidden to stand up by the District Police Chief.

In the meantime, Hani and his followers, while leaving the meeting kept shouting, "True Muslims must also get out!", after which more people followed. For the remainder of the day, however, no other significant incidents occurred.

Resident Dingemans added to the report that "quiet but forceful" use of police forces was sufficiently effective to prevent a serious clash between the PKI and the Muhammadiyah members and the employment of regular military troops proved to be unnecessary. He admitted that the PKI earned a sort of minor success by having got rid of the Muhammadiyah obstructors, and for this consequence the "careless and tactless fanaticism" of some leaders of the Muhammadiyah and the Ummat Islam was to be blamed (ibid.).

Dingemans also observed that the antagonism between the PKI and the Muhammadiyah was a very recent development. He continued as follows: "The PKI are more against the present leaders of the Muhammadiyah than against Islam. The previous chairman, Haji Dahlan [who had died in the previous year, 1923] was known to be very tolerant. There were many points of agreement between the PKI and the Muhammadiyah, which is no longer the case with the latter's present leadership. Because of the tactless action of some of the leaders of the Muhammadiyah and the Ummat Islam, the PKI and the Sarekat Rakyat are now opposed to the Muhammadiyah. Government and Police should be alert lest there be a serious clash between them one of these days" (ibid.).

"Tactless" as it might have been from the viewpoint of the colonial administrator who was preoccupied with the maintenance of public order, the action taken by the Muhammadiyah at this PKI rally was regarded by the Muhammadiyah members themselves as a brave and sincere expression of their determination that Islam and Communism were incompatible and hence no true Muslims could adhere to the PKI. The action was based not so much on political calculation as on religous conviction. Leaders of this anti-Communist action, Hani, Raden Reso and Haji Hajid, came from Yogyakarta, but most of their "followers", who heckled the Communist speakers and who staged a walk-out of "true Muslims", were from the local Muhammadiyah in Kotagede. According to those local Muhammadiyah elders who had personally joined in this action, it was intended to make a forceful demonstration to the general Muslim audience that "true Muslims" should not support the PKI. In a Kotagede elder's words:

> It was not so much a direct challenge to the PKI, but rather a self-injection of the message to Muslims that they should never accept Communism, for it is opposed to Islam in principle. If a Muslim was weak-minded or inadequate in his religious consciousness, he might be attracted to Communism, but never a true Muslim.

Another elder put it more blatantly: "the PKI denigrated *(menjelekkan)* religion. We didn't like it. So we went to the PKI rally, and it became noisy *(ramai)*."

This strong anti-Communist position was, however, not predominant among politically-minded Muslims of the early twenties. Although the Sarekat Islam had already split into Islamic and Communist factions, many of its local branches had not yet been differentiated ideologically, and an "Islamic Communism" which asserted that the Communist programme for a proletarian revolution was justified in terms of the Qur'an had been earnestly believed and propagated by many "red ulama", such as Haji Misbach who had been extremely popular in Surakarta (see note 13 above). In general, the PKI emphasized the religious inclusiveness of its movement, sometimes directly playing on Islamic aspirations and trying not to arouse Islamic hostility. In this situation, the Muhammadiyah's demonstration of the incompatibility of Islam with Communism and the challenge of choice between the two before the Muslim masses, in the form of interruption and walk-out at the PKI rally in Kotagede, seems to have sent out significant shock waves to many parts of Java.

In spite of this anti-Communist position of the Muhammadiyah, the organization continued its criticism of colonial rule in its own terms. As McVey has stated, "Such opposition [to the PKI by the Muhammadiyah] may have inspired the official promotion of anti-Communist movements, but it was soon clear that the two counter movements had quite different sources" (McVey 1965, p. 294). In fact, when the attempted Communist uprisings in 1926–27 turned out to be a disastrous failure and thousands of the PKI leaders and activists, including a number of Kotagedeans, were arrested and sent to exile in Boven Digul in New Guinea, the Muhammadiyah showed a certain sympathy to them. The Muhammadiyah regarded most of the rebels as being motivated by Islamic aspirations but wrongly manipulated by a tiny group of Communist leaders.

4

THE DEVELOPMENT OF THE MUHAMMADIYAH
Religion and Social Action

> Less talk, more work!
> *(Sedikit bicara, banyak bekerja!)*
>   (A Muhammadiyah motto)

One of the ways of understanding the process of the Muhammadiyah development in Kotagede seems to be to take a look at the life histories of its founding leaders. For, in the life histories of those individuals, the transition to a new religious and social orientation is clearly embodied. The life histories of two such individuals, Kyai Haji Masjhudi and Kyai Haji Amir,[1] shall be presented below in detail. Both were the founders of the Kotagede Muhammadiyah. In addition, for the purpose of generalization and comparison, mention shall be made of some other individuals.

---

1. On formal occasions and in official publications, the names of the two individuals are usually referred to by Kotagedeans with the titles of *Kyai Haji*, or their abbreviation "K.H.". However, in ordinary conversations, K.H. Amir was more often referred to as "Kyai Amir" and K.H. Masjhudi as "Haji Masjhudi". This local practice is followed below.

MUHAMMADIYAH FOUNDERS IN KOTAGEDE

Haji Masjhudi was born in Kampung Boharen, Kotagede in 1888. His childhood name was Rusdi but he later changed it to Masjhudi upon his return from the Mecca pilgrimage. The exact date of his birth is not known. He told me: "My birth date is not certain, for there is no written document." When asked if he remembered his birthday according to the Javanese calendar, he answered: "I've already forgotten it. It's not important." It is likely that he did know it, but obviously he did not seem to think much of it. When he died on 28 February 1972, while I was still in the town, a biographical sketch was compiled by the Muhammadiyah leaders of Kotagede and read at his funeral:[2] according to this source, the *haji* was 84 years old at his death. The description of his life, which follows, is based upon this biographical sketch, other local publications, and the interviews I had with him, his family members and friends.

Haji Mukmin, Haji Masjhudi's father, was a wholesale trader in cotton goods and cloth for batik. He had a store in Danuredjan, one of the main business districts in the city of Yogyakarta. Mukmin's grandfather, Kyai Baghowi, came to settle in Kotagede from the Kauman district of Pijenan in Bantul prior to the Dipanegara War (1825–30). Haji Mukmin's father was called Kyai Sjafi'i. Haji Masjhudi was thus the fourth generation of a family migrated from the hinterland of Kotagede, but he, and others, thought himself to be Kotagede asli, "a native Kotagedean". Haji Mukmin, Masjhudi's father, married twice and from his first marriage he had five children (four sons and one daughter), of whom Masjhudi was the youngest. All four sons of Haji Mukmin grew up to become successful traders in their own ways and his only daughter also married a trader in Kotagede. She was soon widowed but remarried Haji Mudzakkir, a respected trader of Kotagede (father of Professor Abdul Kahar Mudzakkir). Haji Mukmin's second marriage was with a woman in Kampung Gedungkuning, a *kampung* located about two kilometres to the north of Kotagede itself, to which union three sons were born, all of whom also later engaged in trade. Haji Mukmin died in 1920. He was a pious man and spent a large amount of money on his children's religious education. He went on the pilgrimage and also sent all his sons and daughter on the pilgrimage to Mecca while they were rather young. All of his children later became involved in the Muhammadiyah movement in various ways. His descendants are now formally organized into a family organization, Bani

---

2. "Sedjarah Sugengipun Kjai Hadji Masjhudi Bin Mukmin. Ulama [Alim], Pemimpin Ing Kotagede." Muhammadijah Tjabang Kotagede, 1972. (Typescript).

Mukmin ("Descendants of Mukmin"), and they regard him as the initiator of strong religiosity among them.

The most religiously active among his children were the second son, Muchsin, and the youngest, Masjhudi, from his first marriage. Haji Muchsin later became one of the richest traders in pre-war Kotagede, a "merchant king", reportedly owing to the fact that he was given by the Dutch government the monopoly over the import of *kembrik* (cambric, fine cotton cloth for batik) from Japan for the entire region of Yogyakarta. Later, in the mid-thirties, Haji Muchsin represented textile importers in Java at a bi-national trade conference between Japan and the Netherlands East Indies. Haji Muchsin's third wife, born in Kauman Yogyakarta, was a niece of K.H. Ahmad Dahlan, the founder of the Muhammadiyah. This marriage took place in the late 1910s and this affinal connection seems to have been instrumental in drawing Haji Muchsin into the Muhammadiyah movement. His name starts appearing in the national leadership of the Muhammadiyah in the early twenties, as the one who was in charge of the management of religious foundations *(wakaf)* for the Muhammadiyah (see *Verslag Moehammadijah* 1923, p. 28). He himself is said to have been one of the largest financial supporters of the Muhammadiyah, contributing various amounts and at least 500 guilders annually to the national treasury of the Muhammadiyah.

Haji Muchsin married four times (including the one mentioned above); he died in 1948. His first wife was a sister of Atmosudigdo, another "merchant king" of Kotagede one of whose sons is Professor H.M. Rasjidi (see Chapter 1, note 6 above). She died in Mecca while the couple was there on pilgrimage. From his three subsequent wives (one, the above-mentioned niece of K.H. Ahmad Dahlan, another from Semarang, and the last from Kauman, Yogyakarta) a number of the second-generation leaders of the Muhammadiyah in Kotagede were born. He also financially sponsored his two nephews (sons of his sister) to study in Cairo in the twenties and thirties, one of whom is the late Professor Abdul Kahar Mudzakkir, another nationally famous leader of the Muhammadiyah.[3] He later married his daughter to Abdul Kahar upon the latter's return from Cairo. A daughter of Muchsin's sister married Kyai Amir.

Haji Mukmin's third son, Haji Masduki, himself a successful trader, married four times and had many children, most of whom were highly educated and later became, or married, well-established professionals, e.g., one

---

3. For a life history of this Muhammadiyah leader of national and international fame, see my essay (1977).

FIGURE 4.1

House of the "merchant king" Atmosudigdo.

FIGURE 4.2

Cemetery of the "merchant king" Bahuwinangun.

lawyer, two physicians, one professor and two teachers, including a daughter who became the wife of Professor H.A. Mukti Ali, the Minister of Religious Affairs, 1971–78, and professor of Comparative Religion, State Institute of Islamic Studies, Sunan Kalijaga, Yogyakarta.

I first met Haji Masjhudi at the festive prayer meeting for Hari Raya Idul Fitri in November 1970, shortly after the beginning of my fieldwork in Kotagede. Between then and the death of the *haji* in February 1972, I talked to him on several occasions. He had a large house on one of the main streets in Kotagede, the one leading north from the market. His house was markedly different from other old houses in Kotagede in that it did not conform to the traditional house plan. Instead of a *pendhapa*, there was a large living room *(kamar tamu)* furnished with many pieces of fine teak furniture from Jepara. The *kamar tamu* was located in the eastern front of the house. In the traditional house plan, the *pendhapa* is placed to the south of the main body of the house and accordingly the entire house is constructed to face the south. Local people say that houses must face the south so as to pay respect to Nyai Loro Kidul (Goddess of the Southern Ocean), the Guardian Goddess of Mataram. Haji Masjhudi's house was constructed in the late twenties when he became financially independent of his father. When I pointed out some "irregularities" of his house, he smiled pleasantly and explained that he himself had drawn up the house plan and ignored the tradition: the only consideration he had, according to him, was to accommodate most comfortably people visiting his house for religious gatherings at any time without being disturbed by bad weather or noises from outside. (*Pendhapa* are subject to these disturbances.) His house also originally had a large garage for automobiles which in recent years had been used by the Office of Religious Affairs (Kantor Urusan Agama or KUA) of the Kotagede Ward for a nominal rent. In this house he lived with his third wife, his daughter from his second marriage and her husband, the children of the couple, and a maid and a house boy.

Haji Masjhudi had a store immediately to the east of the Post Office of Kotagede on the road leading to Plered. The store, originally built at the same time as his house was constructed in the twenties, had been burned down by the scorched-earth tactics of the Indonesian Republican forces in 1948 and has since been rebuilt. Merchandise found in his store was a strange assortment of kitchen utensils, kerosene lamps and stoves, religious books and pamphlets, notebooks and stationery, various kinds of nails and wire, and even some agricultural tools. It was, in short, a very much abbreviated version of a general store. In Kotagede there were several general stores which were much superior to Haji Masjhudi's in their variety of merchandise, if less competitive in quality and price. But Haji Masjhudi seemed to have had a number of steady customers who enabled him to keep his store running. Every morning from eight to noon Haji Masjhudi himself, still in good health although he was more than eighty years old, worked in the store. From noon to four the store was closed for the afternoon nap, as were most of other stores in Kotagede, but reopened between four and six in the late afternoon. In the afternoons his daughter or his son-in-law, who returned home from his office, the Regional Office of the Department of Religious Affairs in Yogyakarta, worked in the store while the old *haji* received visitors at home.

While at work Haji Masjhudi wore a white shirt, *sarong*, and white round cap on his head. On formal occasions he dressed in a khaki suit and *sarong* with *surban*, an Arabic turban, on his head. From his simple attire and the rather modest appearance of his store, it was difficult to imagine that he was still one of the richest merchants in Kotagede. But, in fact, he was. An indication of his wealth was that about 2.7 per cent of all the residential land in R.K. Prenggan and R.K. Basen in Kotagede was registered in his name or those of his immediate family members, according to the land registration book of the Ward Office of Kotagede: two plots each for his house and store, a large plot for a *musholla* (special one for women), the rest consisting of several rent-out shops, houses and open spaces. He was a regular contributor to the treasury of the local Muhammadiyah until his death.

The biographical sketch prepared for his funeral described his life as that of "*ulama [alim]* (Islamic scholar), *guru* (teacher), *pemimpin* (leader), and *pejuang* (fighter) in the religious and national movement." He was also termed a "successful kyai *pedagang*" (religiously respected merchant) all through his life.

Haji Masjhudi's formal education started with his enrolment at the second-class elementary school *(sekolah rakyat angka loro)* in Keputran, Yogyakarta. The school was a special one catering to the children of Yogyanese *priyayi*. I failed to obtain an explanation as to how the young Rusdi, apparently a boy of common origin, had been able to enter this privileged school. Perhaps it was due to his father's enormous wealth and close business relationships with the court circles. This closeness of Mukmin's family to the Yogyakarta court is also suggested by the fact that Masjhudi's second wife was a princess of the Yogyakarta Sultan's family. What is interesting about the later phase of Haji Masjhudi's life history is that obviously he did not activate or effectively manipulate his connections with the Yogyakarta court. Rather, the course of his life was to play down these *priyayi* connections and to emphasize his commitments to the Muhammadiyah.

His own statement as to his education is as follows:

There were no schools in Kotagede when I was a young boy. So I went to the Keputran School in Alun-Alun, Yogyakarta. There was no railroad service extended to Kotagede yet, so I had to walk six kilometres to school everyday. My mind was not strong enough. So I could not continue going to school. I quit the school at the second grade. But I was still interested in religious learning *(mengaji)*. So my father sent me to *pesantren* in various places. At that time there were not as many *pesantren* as today.

He spent some time learning basic Qur'anic Arabic in Pondok Wonokromo and Pondok Kanggotan, both near Kotagede, and Pondok Punduh, Magelang. He wanted to pursue more advanced learning and decided to study with Kyai Zainuddin, a famous *alim* of the day, in Pondok Cepoko, Nganjuk, at the foot of Mt. Wilis in the Kediri plain, East Java. There he spent five years. After another few years in Pondok Mojodari and Pondok Termas, both in East Java, he went on the pilgrimage to Mecca around 1910, where he studied with Kyai Muhtaram and Kyai Mahfudz, the most revered teachers of the 'Jawah' (Malay-Indonesian) community in Mecca.[4] Through these studies at home and abroad, Haji Masjhudi became learned in *fiqh* (Islamic jurisprudence), *tafsir* (commentary to the Qur'an), *tasawwuf* (mysticism) and *ushuluddin* (theology). He returned to Java shortly before the outbreak of World War I. He settled in Kotagede and according to his words, "following the tradition of *kampung* here, got married and started to work with my father".

In 1914, the young Haji Masjhudi represented his family's batik business at the Colonial Fair held in Semarang with a group of representative traders and industrialists from Kotagede. The official publication of the Fair mentions that "Haji Masjhudi from Yogyakarta exhibited batik in the Yogyakarta Pavilion and was given a bronze medal for recognition" (*Koloniale Tentoonstelling Semarang* n.d., I. 205).

Haji Masjhudi married three times, serially, in his life. His first wife was a local and bore him a son who later became a medical doctor. After her death he married a woman from "*dalem beteng*", i.e., the court of Yogyakarta, as mentioned above. She was apparently a "princess", but I failed to obtain information on exactly how the princess was related to the current Sultan of Yogyakarta. The princess died before World War II leaving only one child

---

4. Kyai Mahfudz, or Shaikh Mahfudz al-Tarmisy as he was known in Mecca, originated from Pondok Termas, Pacitan, East Java and spent most of his life in the Holy City teaching students from "Jawah" until he died in 1918. For his position in the intellectual genealogy of *ulama* in Java, see Zamakhsyari (1981, Chapter 3, especially pp. 131–34).

with Masjhudi. After the War he married for the third time, a woman from Wonosobo. When I was in the town, he was living with this third wife who was rather old, but he jokingly said: "We have not got children yet. But you'll see."

As we have seen earlier, it was in the mid-1910s that Haji Masjhudi took the initiative of founding two reformist organizations locally: Syarekatul Mubtadi and Krida Mataram. At about the same time, Kyai Amir moved into Kotagede and became the closest colleague of Haji Masjhudi. For the next thirty years the two *haji* played vital roles in the development of the Muhammadiyah movement in Kotagede. Haji Masjhudi occupied the position of the *voorzitter* (president) of the Kotagede Muhammadiyah branch well into the post-war period, while Kyai Amir headed the Muhammadiyah school system in Kotagede over almost the same period.

The report of the 1923 national congress of the Muhammadiyah contains the information that the Kotagede branch had already established a second-class four-grade elementary school *(sekolah rakyat angka loro)* and that religious courses *(pengajian)* for adult men and women were held regularly there (*Verslag Moehammadijah* 1923, p. 52). At the 1932 national congress of the Muhammadiyah held in Makassar, Sulawesi, the Kotagede branch was represented by the two *haji*, Masjhudi and Amir (*Pringatan Congress Moehammadijah* 1932). In the late 1930s, as we shall see later, the two *haji* were prime organizers in the Muhammadiyah effort to establish a new mosque, Mesjid Perak (Silver Mosque), in Kotagede, and they also served as *khotib* (sermon givers) of the mosque.

When the Masjumi (Madjelis Sjuro Muslimin Indonesia, or Consultative Council of Indonesian Muslims) was established as the all-embracing federation of Muslim organizations during the Japanese occupation period, Haji Masjhudi headed its Kotagede branch. During the War of Revolution, 1945–49, Haji Masjhudi was the head of the Muslim para-military organization Sabililah (lit., Path of Allah) and also sat on the leadership board of the para-military youth organization Hizbullah (lit., Fighters for Allah). He then retired from an active role in the leadership of the Kotagede Muhammadiyah but remained as its *sesepuh* (elderly advisor). He also became a member of the local Tarjih (the Council of Scholars) of the Muhammadiyah which considered the interpretation and implementation of Islamic law *(Syariah)* in local contexts and served as an advisor to the townspeople on religous and ethical matters throughout the rest of his life.

Upon his death in February 1972, his funeral was attended by the national leadership of the Muhammadiyah, a delegate from the court of Yogyakarta, the officials of the two Great Mosques in Yogyakarta and Surakarta, the officials of the offices of the Department of Religious Affairs throughout Yogyakarta, a large number of Islamic leaders and scholars from many parts of Central Java, and virtually all adult residents of Kotagede.

While Haji Masjhudi represented the organizational side of the Kotagede Muhammadiyah, Kyai Amir, whose life history shall be given below, represented the educational side. Kyai Amir created and led the Muhammadiyah school system locally from the late 1910s until the coming of the Japanese in 1942. The following information is taken from an article in a brochure of the Kotagede Muhammadiyah published in 1969 and from interviews.[5]

Kyai Amir was not a native of Kotagede. He was born ca. 1892 in the village of Mlangsen, Kulon Progo, as the second son of Kyai Djalal Sajuthi, a renowned *alim*. Earlier Kyai Djalal stayed in Mecca as a teacher and scholar for about ten years; K.H. Ahmad Dahlan, the founder of the Muhammadiyah, was one of his students there.

Kyai Amir's childhood name was Samanhudi. While Samanhudi was still young, his family moved to the town of Purworejo, Kedu, Central Java. There he grew up and married a daughter of Kyai Amin, the *lurah* (chief) of the village of Bokongan, Purworejo. From this marriage, Samanhudi had a child, but both child and mother died soon afterwards. Many years later, around 1918, Samanhudi, who had changed his name to Amir upon his return from the Mecca pilgrimage with the title of Haji, married a granddaughter of Haji Mukmin, in Kotagede. Kyai Amir came to settle in the *kampung* of Selokraman, Kotagede, and pioneered the Muhammadiyah educational system in the town.

The young Samanhudi's education started with the study of Arabic and the basics of Islamic teachings with his own father, Kyai Djalal. By the time he reached his teens he had already displayed strong interest in *Shahihul Bukhari*, the Hadith compiled by Al-Bukhari (194–256H/810–870M). He continued his religious education in various *pondok pesantren* in Java, partly financed by his first father-in-law, Kyai Amin. He studied and obtained a certificate of mastery in the recitation of the Qur'an *(khufadz)* from K.H. Munawir of Pondok Krapyak, Yogyakarta, a *pesantren* famous for training students in the recitation of the Qur'an. He also studied some other religious books with Kyai Nawawi of Pasuruan, East Java. He learned *ilmu nahwu* (Arabic grammar) from Kyai Ibrahim in Nglirap, Karanganyar, Kebumen, Central Java.

---

5. The article is written by the then Chairman of the Kotagede Branch of the Muhammadiyah Youth, Pemuda Muhammadiyah, Muhammad Nizar Chirzin, "Biography K. H. Amir", *Brosur Lebaran*, No. 7, 1389H/1969M (Panitia Gerakan Ramadhan, Muhammadijah Tjabang Kotagede), pp. 14–19.

FIGURE 4.3

Portrait of Kyai Haji Amir (c.1892–1948).
Source: Courtesy of Drs. Achmad Charris Zubair.

It was in the famous *pondok* of Tebuireng, Jombang, East Java, that he experienced a turning point in his career as *santri*. There he became on of the *murid* (disciples) of Kyai Haji Hasjim Asj'ari, the most revered "traditional and conservative" *alim* of the day who later founded the Nahdlatul Ulama in 1926 (Deliar 1973, p. 229, and Zamakhsyari 1981 *passim*). Samanhudi spent fourteen months in this *pondok*, mostly learning Bukhari's work. Soon Kyai Haji Hasjim Asj'ari came to recognize the extraordinary brightness and earnestness of Samanhudi. K.H. Hasjim Asj'ari suggested that Samanhudi should go to Mecca and continue to study with Bukhari specialists in the Holy City. The young Samanhudi was so overjoyed by his master's recognition and encouragement that he immediately left Java for Singapore on the trip to Mecca without obtaining his family's approval. Now lacking any support from family, Samanhudi was short of funds to travel on to Mecca. So, like many other religiously zealous but poor youths of his day, he spent some time in Singapore to earn the money to finance his further trip to Mecca. In Singapore he worked for the publishing firm of Sayyid Shaykh, a Malacca-born Islamic scholar of Malay-Arabic descent and one of the promoters of the influential reformist journal, *Al-Iman*. Meanwhile, Samanhudi continued studying the work of Bukhari with this learned Islamic scholar.[6]

After ten months of work and study in Singapore, the young Samanhudi finally sailed for Mecca. Upon arriving in the Holy City, he made himself a disciple of Kyai Haji Mahfudz, the famous Javanese *alim* from Pondok Termas of Pacitan. In 1914, after six years of study, Samanhudi was awarded a certificate *(ijazah)* indicating that he had mastered the Hadith compiled by Bukhari. The certificate was originated by Bukhari himself more than one thousand years before and was handed down through twenty-three generations of *ulama* who had commanded the work of Bukhari — Kyai Haji Mahfudz being the latest in the line at that time.

As we have seen earlier, Haji Masjhudi was almost contemporary with Kyai Amir in his stay in Mecca. Moreover, both became students of the same teacher, Kyai Haji Mahfudz. Therefore it is very likely that the acquaintanceship between the two young Javanese Muslims, who were soon to become close colleagues in the same reformist movement and relatives through marriage, might well have started in the Holy City.

Like many *ulama* in his day, Kyai Amir engaged in trade as a means of livelihood and it is likely that he first came into contact with merchants in Kotagede through trade networks. Even prior to undertaking his pilgrimage, Samanhudi had often been sent on business trips by his father-in-law, Kyai Amin, to Cilacap, Yogyakarta, and other trade centres in Central Java. His second marriage, to the granddaughter of Haji Mukmin in Kotagede, brought him into the midst of Yogyakarta trading circles. He worked closely with his mother-in-law, Nyai Chotidjah, whose trade networks even extended to Mojokerto in East Java. Kyai Amir also worked in the shop of his grandfather-in-law, Haji Mukmin, in Danuredjan, Yogyakarta. Soon Kyai Amir became independent in retailing threads and yarns in Kotagede. He also participated with his mother-in-law in the trade of gold and jewelry. From the late 1920s,

---

6. According to William Roff (*The Origins of Malay Nationalism*, 1967), this renowned leader of the Malay-Muslim community in Singapore was born ca. 1862 in Malacca of a Malay mother and a Malay-Arab father of Hadrami descent. He was then adopted by the Heir-Apparent *(Raja Muda)* of the Riau Sultan. He many times accompanied the sons of the Sultan and Raja Muda to Mecca and became one of the most important linkages between the Holy City and the Malay-Muslim world. In 1901–09, he published the journal *Al-Iman* in Singapore as its editional staff and chief contributor. He was also a prominent jurist of *Syariah* (Islamic law), educator and merchant in Singapore in the early decades of this century (ibid., p. 59ff).

however, he was increasingly occupied with his activities in religious education and consequently the task of earning livelihood for his family gradually passed to the hands of his wife, Nyai Amir.

Kyai Amir's contributions to the advancement of the reformist Islamic cause were numerous. As we have seen above, he joined Haji Masjhudi to organize the Syarekatul Mubtadi for adult education in Kotagede in the late 1910s. At about the same time he started to teach children and young men and women in his own house in the *kampung* of Selokraman, Alun-Alun, Kotagede. The effort soon developed into the establishment of a second-class Muhammadiyah elementary school (for four years of general education with religious classes) and a *madrasah* (in which only religious lessons were taught, mainly to the pupils of the government second-class elementeray school). The former grew into an "HIS met de Qur'an" (Hollandsch Inlandsche School, or Native Dutch Elementary School with Islamic lessons) and, the latter into an Islamic teachers' training school, Ma'had Islamy. Kyai Amir was also one of the co-founders of the Mesjid Perak (Silver Mosque) in the late 1930s, as we shall see later.

Kyai Amir's activities were not confined to Kotagede but extended to the Yogyakarta region and Central Java. Prior to the formation of the Majelis Tarjih (Council of Scholars) of the Muhammadiyah in 1927, he hosted a conference of notable *ulama* held in Kotagede. The participants included K.H. Hajid (Kauman, Yogyakarta), K.H. Mawardi (Surakarta), K.H. Masjhud (Keprabon, Surakarta), K.H. Abdul Aziz (Wonokromo), K.H. Abdul Mukti (Jombang), K.H. Hamin (Ngadiwinatan), K.H. Iman (Kedungbanteng), K.H. Masjkur (Jejeran), K.H. Abu Amar (Jamsaren, Surakarta), K.H. Muhamad Haman (Purworejo), K.H. Fekih (Kauman, Yogyakarta), K.H. Siradj (Pakualaman), and many others including some *penghulu*. The purpose of the conference was to discuss urgent religious and legal issues of the day in terms of Islamic law and give advice *(fatwa)* to the Muslim community in Java. As a result of this conference, a journal entitled *Ummat Islam* was launched, with Kyai Amir as its chief editor. Soon the conference and the journal were absorbed by the Majelis Tarjih of the Muhammadiyah.

Just prior to the capitulation of the East Indies to Japan, the Dutch colonial government established in Surakarta, Mahkamah Islam Tinggi, or the Islamic Appeals Court, as the highest body of Islamic justice for Java and Madura, and Kyai Amir was appointed one of the judges *(hakim)* of the Court.[7] The

---

7. For a description of the scope and the function of this Islamic court, especially of its post-war development, see Lev (1972, pp. 117–22). See also Pijper (1977, p. 7).

Japanese, in addition, selected him to head the Office of Religious Affairs (Kantor Urusan Agama, or Shumuka) of the Yogyakarta Sultanate government. During this period, he developed a close relationship with Sultan Hamengku Buwono IX with whom he had constant consultations on the religious policy of the Yogyakarta Sultanate. It is reported that, upon Kyai Amir's advice, the Sultan initiated and implemented many reforms, among them a more strict adherence by the Sultan and his family to Muslim obligations and a drastic simplification and rationalization of court rituals and ceremonies.

During his lifetime Kyai Amir wrote and edited many books, most of which were commentaries to the Qur'an and Hadith. Many of them were used as textbooks for the Muhammadiyah school system. These included *Shahihul Bukhari, Al-Qur'an wal Mufadats, Al-Adzakaar, Fathul mannan fie tajwiedil Qur'an, Adabul walad ma'a walidhihi, 'Iqdul jauhar, Al-Ittiba', Fathul Malikis Shomad*, and *Kifayatul Muhtaj*. His *tafsir* (commentary) of the Qur'an, printed in *pegon* (Javanese in Arabic script), is said to have been very popular among Muhammadiyah circles.

Kyai Amir died at the age of 56 in 1948 ater a short illness and was buried in a cemetery in Kampung Boharen, Alun-Alun, Kotagede, next to the graves of his grandfather-in-law, Haji Mukmin, and his friend and uncle-in-law, Haji Muchsin.

Figure 4.4 may be of help to recapitulate kinship and marriage relationships among some of those individuals who have been mentioned in the preceding pages. It goes, however, without saying that the diagram is a gross abbreviation of actual relationships. It is intended just to illustrate several important linkages

FIGURE 4.4

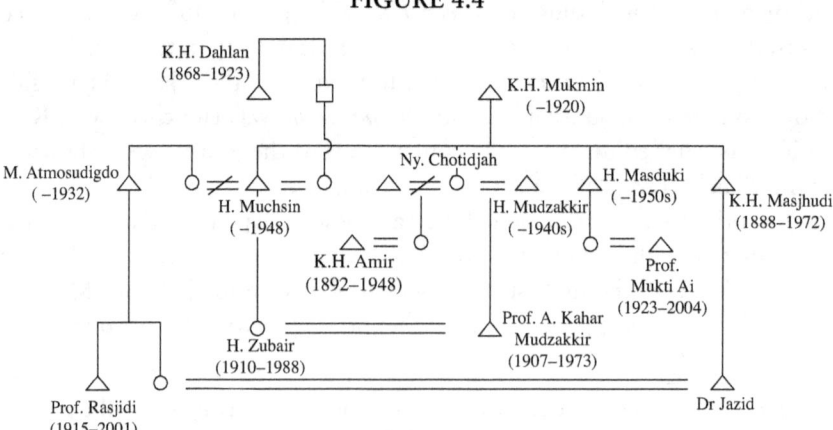

Kinship and marriage relationships among Muhammadiyah founders in Kotagede.

among the individuals who made up the core of the early Muhammadiyah in Kotagede.

The life histories of Haji Masjhudi and Kyai Amir represent the meeting of the thriving middle class and the increasing orthodoxy among Javanese *ulama* since around the turn of the century. Haji Mukmin and his son, Haji Muchsin, a merchant king of Kotagede, lavished their wealth for the religious education of their family members and relatives from among whom Haji Masjhudi emerged. Haji Muchsin also contributed further to the religious education of the townspeople: Muhammadiyah schools in Kotagede were established by donation from people like him.

The case of Mas Atmosudigdo, another merchant king of Kotagede in the early decades of this century, exemplifies the process of deepening religiosity among *abangan* traders of the town. His son, Professor M. Rasjidi (1915–2001), who has become one of the most prominent Islamic leaders in post-war Indonesia, recalls his family's *abangan* background as follows:

> My family was what was usually called an "*abangan* family" which meant that one professed Islam but did not perform daily prayers.
>
> In the month of Puasa, I was often sent by my parents to a *naib* [religious official] of the mosque to bring him a small sum of money every evening after *maghrib* [prayer at sunset] when fasting was over. But my family did not fast.
>
> My father, when he got old and felt weak, started to pray, and before he died he willed that part of his wealth was to be spent to send a person to Mecca to discharge the obligation of *haji* [pilgrimage] for him after his death (1968, p. 9).

The wealth of Atmosudigdo was also used to support his son Rasjidi's study in Cairo, Egypt. He later returned as one of the most active proponents of the Egyptian Islamic reformism of Muhammad 'Abduh and Rashid Rida in Indonesia. This was a far cry from his *abangan* family background a generation before.

Kyai Amir's career as a Muhammadiyah *alim* also attracts our attention in various ways. First of all, it should be noted that his education at home and abroad was thoroughly traditional: he studied at a number of *pondok pesantren* including the "bastion" of traditionalist *ulama*, Pesantren Tebuireng. There he obtained the recognition and blessing of K.H. Hasjim Asj'ari, who occupied the apex of the hierarchy of the traditional *ulama*. Kyai Amir specialized in the study of the *Hadith* compiled by Bukhari, which was a conventional subject in the curriculum of traditional religious education. Kyai Mahfudz, his teacher in Mecca, was one of the most orthodox scholars of the Shafi'ite

> **BOX 3**
> **Prayer for Snouck Hurgronje**
>
> I attended the Syawalan meeting of Bani Mukmin on 1 Syawal 1392H (23 November 1971). The late Prof Abdul Kahar Mudzakkir, a senior member of the Bani, dedicated a prayer to their ancestors. Among their names, I was surprised to find Christian Snouck Hurgronje, alias "Abdul Ghaffar". Later, I learned that those close to Snouck accepted him as a fellow Muslim. He had obtained trust from a number of prominent Indonesian *ulama* while in Mecca in the 1880s. He then came to Indonesia to work for the Bureau of Islamic and Native Affairs. He continued to mingle with *ulama* and married Hajjah Patmah, a daughter of Hasan Mustapa, Chief Penghulu of Ciamis, West Java. Snouck persuaded him to accept the position of Chief Penghulu of Kotaraja, Aceh. Hassan Mustapa's wife was an elder sister of the wife of Haji Muhammad Rusdi, Chief Penghulu of Tasikmalaya. Dutch Governor General, van Heutsz, appointed Haji Rusdi as Chief Penghulu of Kotaraja to succeed Hasan Mustapa, apparently upon the proposal of Snouck. A daughter of Haji Rusdi, Ainul Hayat, was married to Haji Zubair Muchsin of Kotagede, a central figure of Bani Mukmin. So, Snouck and Haji Zubair were related as in-laws. Snouck had several children from his marriage with Patmah. One of them was the father of Edi Yusuf, a Thomas Cup champion of badminton. Thus, Charris Zubair, a son of Haji Zubair and the current head of the Bani Mukmin, and Edi Yusuf are in uncle-nephew relationship via Snouck. The members of Bani Mukmin showed no particular feelings when the name of Snouck was mentioned in Prof Mudzakkir's prayer at the Syawalan of 1392H/1971M. He was obviously still treated as "one of them". This was contrary to the widely held view among the post-independence Indonesian public that he had been a scholar-politician of the Dutch colonialism who had tried to subjugate Indonesian Muslims, especially those of Aceh. (Personal communication with Drs. Charris Zubair, 27 November 2009. Cf. P. Sj. van Koningsveld, *Snouck Hurgronje dan Islam* (Jakarta: Girimukti Pusaka, 1989), also Ajip Rosidi, "Snouck Hurgronje dan H. Hasan Mustapa", *KOMPAS*, 22 October 2004.)

school at that time. Unlike the conventional image, the Muhammadiyah school system in Kotagede was initiated *not* by a Western-educated intelligentsia *but* by *ulama* with the background of traditional *pesantren* education like Kyai Amir and Haji Masjhudi. The fact that these individuals became the pioneers of the Muhammadiyah's modern education is somewhat puzzling. It is suggested that the phenomenon may be accounted for not so much in terms of their educational background but rather in terms of actual needs arising from their immediate social environment — an urban commercial situation in which the challenge of industrialization and monetarization of economy was directly felt. To this, a school-system with both secular and religious subjects was an answer.

SCHOOLS AND CLINICS: THE SOCIAL ACTIVISM OF THE MUHAMMADIYAH

In the Muhammadiyah's perception of true Islam, religious education was a must: it is a duty for a Muslim to keep learning God's message from childhood to death. Hence the promotion of one's own religious learning as well as that of other Muslims, especially one's immediate family members, formed an integral part of fulfilling one's religious obligations. Also the promotion of material and physical well-being of oneself and fellow Muslims was equally a God-given obligation, for natural resources are the trust of God to human beings who were to make best out of them. The Muhammadiyah emphasized the need for welfare activities to help fellow human beings in the form of hospitals, clinics, orphanages, etc., as a fulfillment of Muslim obligation. Religious taxes *(zakat fitrah)* were to be paid and to be redistributed directly to the poor and the needy. Further voluntary contributions to these educational and welfare institutions were highly recommended. Especially encouraged as a meritorious act of devotion to God was the donation of real property *(wakaf)* for religious and social institutions. (For the activities of 'Aisyiyah, see H. Nakamura 1981.)

Social activism of this kind was a conspicuous feature of the Muhammadiyah movement in Kotagede from the beginning. In the late 1910s when the Syarekatul Mubtadi was still an independent local organization, a Muhammadiyah "second-class native school" was founded in Kotagede using a *pendhapa* in a private home as its classroom.

Since the early 1910s there was a government second-class native school in Kotagede but it was not popular. Only a fraction of the townspeople were induced to send their children to this new school: only nine entered it in the first year. As a Muhammadiyah elder puts it:

> Kotagedeans did not think much of school education. They did not need "certificates" or "diplomas" because their livelihood came from being *bakul* (trader) or *tukang* (craftsman). Only government officials *(pegawai)* sent their children to this school but there were not so many *pegawai* in Kotagede.

In contrast, the Muhammadiyah school proved to be a great success. It soon acquired a permanent building by donation and enrolled a large number of boys and girls. In the late 1920s, an HIS (a seven-year primary school with the Dutch language) was added and also soon a girls' school specializing in housekeeping, sewing and childcare was started. It seems no exaggeration to state that the Muhammadiyah school system in Kotagede overshadowed the government counterpart throughout the pre-war period in that even some *priyayi* families sent their children to Muhammadiyah schools.

In the beginning, under the guidance of Kyai Amir, these Muhammadiyah schools were staffed by teachers educated at *pondok pesantren*. By the late 1920s, however, some of graduates of the Muhammadiyah primary schools continued their education in Mu'allimin or Mu'allimat (Muhammadiyah's teachers' training schools in Yogyakarta established in 1922) and started to come back to teach in Kotagede. By the middle of the 1930s, the Muhammadiyah educational system seems to have become a self-sustaining system. In addition, Kyai Amir's *madrasah* located in his own house moved to Tegalgendu, and became a full-fledged religious teachers' training school, Ma'had Islamy by the late 1930s, attracting mainly *santri* children from the rural hinterland of Kotagede.[8]

The attraction of Muhammadiyah schools seems to have lied in the fact that they provided alternative channels of education to the government school system, entrance to which was not quite open even to the children of wealthy merchants in Kotagede. Haji Zubair, son of Haji Muchsin, who studied at Muhammadiyah schools in the mid-twenties, states his experience as follows:

> I went to the Muhammadiyah's second-class elementary school in Kotagede and completed its four years. Then I went to a "normal school" of the Muhammadiyah in Yogyakarta [teachers' training school in general subjects]. In that school I met a young man whose Arabic was extraordinarily good. I asked him where he studied it, and learned that he had spent some years in an Arabic school in Surakarta. So I wanted to go to the same school in Surakarta and my father [Haji Muchsin] allowed me to do so. In the Arabic school I spent three years. Then I wanted to go on to a secondary school. But since I had no Dutch language training at all, the path to MULO (Dutch language middle school) was closed to me. I was already fifteen years old. There was no hope of getting secondary education in Java. My

---

8. A survey on religious situation in Java and Madura conducted by the Japanese military authorities in 1942 reports: "Mahad Islamij, Tegalgendoe, Giwangan, Bantoel-Ken, Djokja Kotji, Kepala Madrasah Kjai H. Amir, 33 moerid" (Osamu Shudan 1943, p. 282).

brother and cousins were already in Cairo and I thought I might try a way out in Cairo, too. My father agreed to give me financial assistance and in 1930 I arrived in Cairo.

Altogether, there seem to have been at least six young men sent to study in Cairo from Kotagede between 1925 and 1935: two sons of Haji Muchsin, two sons of Haji Mudzakkir, and two sons of Mas Atmosudigdo. The sending of these young men from Kotagede to Cairo was brought about by a juncture of several developments during the 1920s and the early 1930s: the rise of religiosity among certain prosperous families in Kotagede; the aspiration for more advanced education, religious as well as secular, among the younger generation of these families; the absence of opportunities for such education in Java; and the increasing attraction of Cairo as the place to meet these aspirations. These developments were taking place not only in Kotagede but also in many other Javanese urban centres; as a result, the 1925–35 period witnessed a peak of Javanese student pupulation in Cairo (see Roff 1970*a*). In the course of the 1930s, some of those who had studied in Cairo returned to Java and joined the central leadership of the Muhammadiyah and contributed a great deal to it in terms of intellectual and organizational sophistication and linked it directly with the Middle Eastern Islamic reformism.

Muhammadiyah schools spread to almost all cities and towns in Java (and almost all major urban centres in the Netherlands East Indies) by the end of the 1930s. The consequences of Muhammadiyah education were manifold. First, it enhanced an Indonesian national consciousness in Islamic terms. Second, through Muhammadiyah schools, the ideology of reformist Islam was widely disseminated. Third, it promoted the spread of practical knowledge of modern sciences.

A measure of religious nationalism of the Muhammadiyah was indicated by the adoption of Malay, or what later came to be known as Bahasa Indonesia (Indonesian), as its organizational language. Indonesian had long been the *lingua franca* of the Malay-Muslim world prior to the development of modern nationalism. As early as the 1890s, Snouck Hurgronje observed that in Mecca Malay was used as the medium of interethnic communication among the Jawah community consisting of "all people[s] of Malay race in the fullest meaning of the term; the geographic boundary is perhaps from Siam and Malacca to New Guinea" (Snouck Hurgronje 1931, pp. 215, 229ff.).

Many Indonesian *haji* who stayed long enough in Mecca or in other parts of the Malay-Muslim world often acquired a degree of fluency in Indonesian, which prepared a channel of political communication in the 1910s for the spread of the national awakening movement.

FIGURE 4.5

Indonesian students in Cairo, at the front gate of Al-Azhar University, 1928: (from left) Faried Ma'ruf (from Kauman, Yogyakarta), Zubair Muchsin (from Kotagede, Yogyakarta), Egyptian teacher, Abdul Kahar Mudzakkir and Rasjidi Atmosudigdo (both from Kotagede, Yogyakarta) and Hamid (from Cicalengka, West Java).
Source: Courtesy of Drs. Achmad Charris Zubair.

As it grew as a national organization, the Muhammadiyah adopted Indonesian (Bahasa Indonesia) as the official language of organizational activities. Kyai Dahlan was fluent in Indonesian. His successor, Kyai Ibrahim, was not, but Haji Fachruddin, the vice president, was an eloquent speaker in Indonesian and helped to cover Ibrahim's deficiency in this regard. The

Muhammadiyah's national meetings and publications were carried out in Indonesian. And most importantly, Indonesian was adopted as a subject in its school curriculum.⁹

The practice, well established over the period of two decades prior to the outbreak of World War II, created a large number of bilingual individuals fluent in Indonesian as well as in their native Javanese. (A considerable number of them also knew Arabic and Dutch as well.) This group of individuals made up the immediate audience for and often active participants in national politics when the independent republic was born in 1945.

In Kotagede a typical bilingual or multilingual speaker with Muhammadiyah education spoke Javanese in the family, neighbourhood, workshop or market, Indonesian in the Muhammadiyah organization, Arabic in religious studies and services, and Dutch in dealing with the government authorities. This was certainly a reflection of the existence of cleavages among these four cultural traditions, but at the same time it meant that the individual had acquired a capacity to bridge these cleavages.

The world of those who used Indonesian was no longer merely regional but had Indonesia as its point of reference. As an elderly Muhammadiyah member puts it:

> Children of my generation did not know what Indonesia was. What is Indonesia? There is no Indonesian people. What exists is "Javanese". In the [government] primary school the geography of Indonesia was not taught, only the geography of Java. The language taught there was also only Javanese. Teachers spoke Javanese in the classroom, too. Counting numbers was also in Javanese. The change of Dutch policy to what was named "Ethical Policy" brought higher education to Indonesian children. This was aimed

---

9. It has been customary in the post-independence literature (for example, Pringgodigdo 1950) to refer to the event of the Oath of Youth in 1928 as the origin of the official ascendancy of Bahasa Indonesia as the national language: the Oath of Youth which was participated in by the widest representation of the nationalist movement of the day declared the ideals of "One nation (Indonesia), one flag (red and white), one anthem (Indonesia Raya), and one language (Indonesian)". However, this view tends to underestimate the contribution of the Islamic community to the promotion of Indonesian as a common language prior to the nationalist development. Anderson's analysis of the political language in modern Indonesia (Anderson 1966), stimulating among others for the understanding of the Javanization of Islam in the pre-modern era in terms of obscurantism of Javanese-Arabic bilingualism, also seems to suffer from a neglect of the role of the *ummat Islam* for the advancement of Bahasa Indonesia.

not at raising education of Indonesian children, however, but at meeting the demand of Dutch offices. So MULO, HIS, AMS [senior high school], up to the higher education were established. But Indonesian children benefited from it, too, although indirectly. They got a ride *[membonceng]* of it and got well educated. The Muhammadiyah did not unfairly criticize the government or Christian missionary schools. The Muhammadiyah demanded fair competition with them and requested government subsidies and received them.

Another feature of the Muhammadiyah school education, a crucial step in the view of the reformists, was the separation of Arabic as an independent subject. In *pesantren*, Arabic was taught as part of the Qur'an recitation: after learning the Arabic alphabet and pronunciation, verses from the Qur'an were learned by rote, and exegeses of the particular verses were given in Javanese. The Muhammadiyah schools taught Arabic as an independent subject. (This had already been experimented with as an innovation in the Qur'an learning among the Jawah community in Mecca in the late 19th century when Snouck Hurgronje was staying there (cf. Snouck Hurgronje 1931, p. 267)). The new method employed by the Muhammadiyah school encouraged independent understanding of the Qur'an and Hadith by the students themselves. Questioning and discussion of the meaning of a particular word or verse were also encouraged in the classroom. "*Bocah-bocah, dimardekaaké pikiré!* (As for children, their thinking should be made independent!)", a statement quoted from a speaker in the 1925 Muhammadiyah congress, well depicts the mood of early Muhammadiyah schools *(Mailrapport 467X/25, p. 13).*[10]

---

10. The level of the Arabic fluency of Muhammadiyah activists in particular and of the Javanese Muslim community in general seems to have been often underrated by foreign observers. Since I am quite illiterate in the language, I have no standard to measure it. But, through my field observations, I have come to realize an interesting fact that the same Qur'anic verses are translated differently by the same *muballigh* (propagandist) on different occasions or by different *muballigh* on the same occasion. The propagandists usually quote the Qur'anic verses in Arabic and then add Javanese or Indonesian translations. In so doing, they do not use "standard translations" of the Qur'an. (See Chapter 6.) In fact, such a thing does not seem to exist. Translations are always *ad hoc* and adjusted to the situational context of the quotation. The fact that *muballigh are* capable of doing this smoothly seems to suggest that their knowledge of the Qur'anic Arabic is not based upon mechanical rote memorization but rather upon a deeper comprehension of Arabic grammar and vocabulary.

Muhammadiyah schools also emphasized the learning of Islamic history which was juxtaposed to the history of Indonesia. In teaching Islamic history, the glory and perfection of its early period were emphasized and contrasted to the regressions in the subsequent periods of Muslim world history, including that of Indonesia. The upshot of casting Islamic history in that perspective was to hold Muslims themselves responsible for the regression and degenerations, urging Muslims to realize their responsibilities and strive to restore the greatness of Islam in the modern world.

Another feature of the Muhammadiyah education to be remarked upon was the teaching of practical scientific knowledge. Mathematics as well as basic biology, chemistry and physics were taught as part of *ilmu kegunaan* (practical knowledge). Biology was connected to basic hygiene, and other natural sciences and mathematics were taught in connection with vocational training. Basic to all this was a religious notion that nature works regularly as a result of God's creation and that man, God's creature equipped with God-given rationality *(akal)*, was capable of understanding nature's regularity and was indeed obligated to make good use of it. This admonition to acquire scientific knowledge and apply it to everyday life seems to have been conducive to the introduction of various technological innovations by several Muhammadiyah members in the field of economic activities in Kotagede.

In summary, if we are to find "modern" education in Kotagede, it was not the unpopular government school, but the Muhammadiyah schools which were its prime embodiment. In Kotagede of the twenties and thirties the Muhammadiyah schools were practically synonymous with "modern" schools. Patrons of Muhammadiyah schools were not limited to Muhammadiyah members alone. Individuals from a much wider spectrum of religious orientations and status groups sent their children to Muhammadiyah schools.

Underneath a surface of quietism, the Muhammadiyah school system produced by the end of the 1930s a large number of young men and women who were literate, fundamentally nationalistic, religiously convinced, well adapted to modern economic conditions, and well trained in associational activities. This category of younger generation indeed formed an enormous reservoir for the outburst of radical nationalism in the following phase of Indonesian political history. At the end of the 1930s, Bousquet, a shrewd French observer of colonial Indonesia, noticed this "long-run danger" of Muhammadiyah for the Dutch colonial regime. He stated:

> In the political field the *Mohammadiyya* [Muhammadiyah] is neutral in the sense that it refuses to take sides officially. Its exclusive object is to spread

FIGURE 4.6

Kotagede youths in Holland, 1930: (from left) Zubair Muchsin, Kasmat Bahuwinangun and Djalal Muchsin. Back home, H. Zubair became a French teacher and Mr Kasmat a lawyer/politician while H. Djalal stayed on in Holland to become a medical doctor.
Source: Courtesy of Drs. Achmad Charris Zubair.

Moslem culture. For this very reason, in contradistinction to the nationalist groups, it is held in high favor by the [Dutch] authorities. It would be very wrong, however, to suppose from this its members entertain no political bias. Indeed, it would not be wholly incorrect to say that they are quite as anti-Dutch as other nationalists, Moslem or otherwise. I can vouch for this. Yet the government displays great solicitude toward this society, an attitude which I do not think shows much political intelligence. (Bousquet 1940, p. 5)

Subsequent developments in modern Indonesian history proved that Bousquet's observation was well grounded.

Besides schools, P.K.U. (Penolong Kesengsaraan Umum, or literally, Assistance for the Relief of Public Suffering) constituted another field in which Muhammadiyah's social activism was formally institutionalized. It was first begun in 1918 as an independent organization formed by several Muhammadiyah members in Yogyakarta in order to engage in emergency relief activities for the victims of the eruption of Mt. Kelud. In 1921, the organization was officially made a department of the Muhammadiyah (see Deliar 1973, p. 78ff.).

Mention was already made of the importance of the notion of "public suffering" in the reformist youth movement: what was meant was widespread general sufferings caused by foreign rule and the degeneration of Islamic morality. The relief of these sufferings through immediate action was regarded as a fulfillment of Muslim obligations and a path to the recovery of Islam's glory. Thus a number of poor-houses, orphanages, clinics, hospitals, and delivery houses were built and maintained by Muhammadiyah branches.

In Kotagede, a P.K.U. clinic was established in the late twenties through *wakaf* of land and building by Haji Bakar (Mas Atmosudigdo's son) and several other Muhammadiyah members. The clinic was staffed with a number of trained nurses and a midwife, and regularly visited by a physician from the Yogyakarta P.K.U. hospital. Until well after the independence of Indonesia, the Muhammadiyah P.K.U. clinic constituted the only modern medical facility locally available to Kotagedeans.

Muhammadiyah hospitals and clinics employing modern medicine posed a direct challenge to traditional Javanese healing practices. A patient who visited a Muhammadiyah clinic was explicitly discouraged from asking for simultaneous help from a *dhukun* (magical healer). Thus Muhammadiyah hospitals and clinics not only worked as pure medical agencies but also as agencies for the propagation of reformist Muslim ideas.

Beginning in the late twenties, reforms in the collection and distribution of *zakat fitrah* (religious taxes collected at the end of the fasting month) were made part of the programme of the Muhammadiyah. Prior to the reform, *zakat fitrah* in money and kind (rice) were collected by *kaum, modin, naib* and *penghulu* (religious officials of hamlet, village, subdistrict and district levels respectively) and distributed among themselves as reward for their religious

BOX 4
Kaum Rois: Baseline of Javanese Islam

Islamic religious functionaries at grassroots level in the Yogyakarta region — usually called "*kaum rois*" or "*kaum antek*" — seem to have existed for many centuries up to the present and have formed the baseline of traditional Islam. They have played a pivotal role in providing Islam-ness to a community. For a long time, *kaum rois* had formed small clusters of *santri* scattered among the sea of *abangan* in rural areas. Yet, the *abangan* people have needed the presence and service of them. They have taken care of prayers in Arabic at the *selametan*, i.e. ritual meals for individual life cycle — birth, circumcision, marriage, and death, and also community rituals like village cleansing. They had usually spent at least a couple of years at *pesantren* (Islamic boarding school) to acquire basic skills in reciting the Qur'an and saying prayers in Arabic. They have been elected to the post at hamlet meetings and served for life. Many of them have acquired the position hereditarily. So, most of them have been senior in age and well respected by hamlet people as their "*sesepuh*" (eldermen). With the development of contemporary religious bureaucracy under the Department of Religious Affairs (Departemen Agama) after Independence, the status of *kaum rois* has been lowered to a great degree since they have not been included in the national bureaucracy; that means that they were not salaried. Yet, their services have been widely called for the rituals held by the hamlet, neighbourhood or individual families. Often, they still play an indispensable role in the case of death since they can direct the ritual cleansing of the body and the proper manner of burial with appropriate prayers. For those services, they are given rewards in kind or in cash by their clients. Thus, they are village *santri* whose services are needed even among a mostly *abangan* community. A research done in Plered in the 1970s, a neighbouring sub-district south of Kotagede, has found an interesting positive correlation between the activeness of *kaum rois* and the religious orientation of a community: i.e., the stronger its *abangan*-ness is in a community, the more prominent the role of *kaum rois* is (see Hazim 1977). *Abangan* and *santri* are thus mutually dependent and complementary in traditional Javanese Islam. Many of *kaum rois* have formed a grass-roots constituency for Nahdlatul Ulama. However, recently, Muhammadiyah has made an in-road into their circles. In Kotagede, there still exist a total of twenty-five *kaum rois* at present. Now the most senior *kaum rois* among them in Kotagede is Mbah Sis ("Grandpa Sis", or Siswo Harjono, b. 1929), who is an active member of Muhammadiyah. He heads the association of *kaum rois* in Kotagede and is also a member of its Yogyakarta city leadership (see *Brosur Lebaran*, No. 43, 1425H/2004M, pp. 68–71).

services.[11] But the Muhammadiyah claimed that the practice was wrong in the light of the Qur'anic teaching and the matter should be entrusted to a group of representatives of *ummat:* furthermore, the amount of the tax should be as prescribed by the Qur'an, and it should be distributed for the relief of the poor and needy *(fakir miskin)*. Muhammadiyah reforms in *zakat fitrah* presented a direct challenge to the authority and the material foundation of traditional religious officials. Naturally many of them vehemently resisted the reforms and the Muhammadiyah gained varying degrees of success according to local conditions. In the most successful cases these religious officials were won over to the Muhammadiyah and *zakat fitrah* started to be collected and distributed as the Muhammadiyah claimed.

"SILVER PERIOD" AND "SILVER MOSQUE"

Muhammadiyah schools and clinics, despite their conspicuousness, constituted not so much a complete alteration of the traditional social and spiritual order as an introduction of new institutions alongside the old ones. It was a matter of personal choice for individuals to select between the new and the old. However, the Muhammadiyah's reform effort did not stop at that. It raised the issue of control over the Great Mosque in Kotagede, which posed a direct infringement on the established religious authority of the principality courts and the interests of local officials who derived their status and income from them. The Great Mosque had been an all-embracing institution through which the local population and the court authorities were bound together. The Muhammadiyah's challenge presented a grave threat to this *status quo ante*. It was towards the latter half of the 1930s that the antagonism reached its zenith and resulted in the establishment of a new mosque, Silver Mosque (Mesjid Perak), by the Muhammadiyah. This section shall attempt to reconstruct this antagonism on the basis of contemporary documents and local information.

The period roughly between the late 1920s and the late 1930s is remembered by elder Kotagedeans as the "silver period", or *jaman perak*. The reason for this designation is that the silverwork industry of the town

---

11. A former *penghulu* in Kotagede told me that in older days the amount of rice presented to him at the end of the fasting month was enough to support his household for half a year. See also Chapter 2, p. 34 above, for *kaum*.

FIGURE 4.7

Tukang perak (silver craftsmen) pounding out silver trays.

had experienced a boom in this period. Causes of the boom were multiple but perhaps the most important was the simultaneous presence of capital, entrepreneurial skills, technical innovations, and a new market. The former two were obviously the result of the preceding boom period in the batik industry of which mention was made in Chapter 3. There now emerged a category of people called *juragan*, or entrepreneurs. They had money and skills to invest in a wide variety of business enterprises. To the development of technical innovations and marketing, the intervention by the Dutch and Yogyakarta principality authorities seems to have given a great stimulus. They helped organize an association of craftsmen from traditional industries in Yogyakarta, Pakarjan Ngajokjakarta, in which silverwork occupied a leading position. They gave a subsidy of 1,500 guilders annually, held training courses, provided a showroom, and induced craftsmen and entrepreneurs to participate in domestic and international trade fairs. In spite of the generally dismal state of the economy in the 1930s as a result of the great depression, certain areas in traditional industries, especially the silverwork industry, experienced a considerable growth and increasing employment in the same period. A 1934 Dutch report states:

FIGURE 4.8

Engraving motifs on silver trays.

FIGURE 4.9

Smoothening and polishing silverware.

FIGURE 4.10

Extending and thinning silver threads.

FIGURE 4.11

Pak Dullah Siddiq, an entrepreneur with craftsmen at his tortoise-shell workshop *(kerajinan penyu)*.

FIGURE 4.12

Buruh jahit (sewers) at *konfeksi* (ready-made clothes) workshop.

FIGURE 4.13

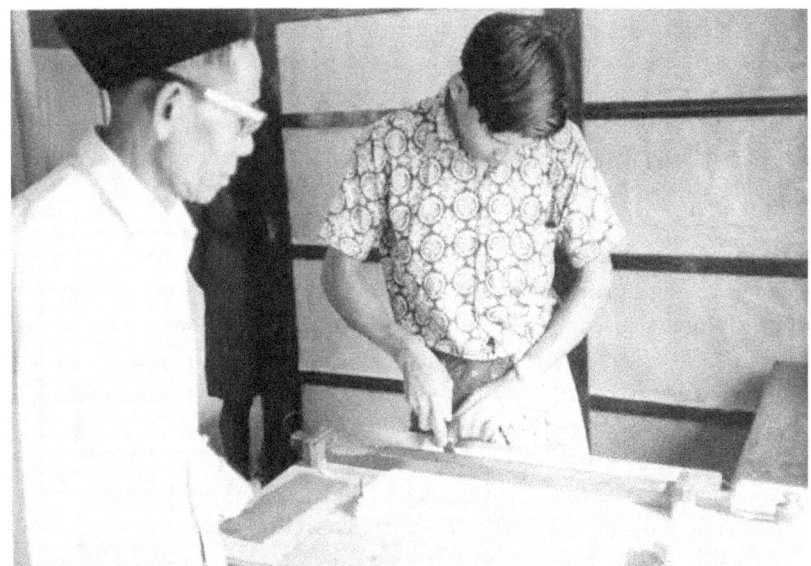

H. Humam Siradj with a cutter at *konfeksi* workshop.

FIGURE 4.14

Workers at *imitasi* (imitation accessories) workshop.

> The number of workshops for silverwork, turtle, horn and bonework, leatherwork and woodcarving has increased a great deal which means that more people can be employed ... The silverwork industry of Kotagede is steadily progressing and the output of the showroom of the Pakarjan Ngajokjakarta has increased considerably with a annual turnover of 40,000 guilders. (*Mailrapport*, Geh. 1320/1934)

The peak of the silver period seems to have been reached between the years 1935 and 1938. During this period 25,000 kilograms of silver was processed within a year by seventy silver enterprises employing about 1,400 workers (*Republik Indonesia* n.d., XII, p. 721). When the Indonesian journalist, Parada Harahap, visited Kotagede in 1939, he met a number of "*raja-raja wang*", or the kings of money, there. He reports:

> ... so numerous buildings and such beautiful houses in Yogyakarta now are mostly the property of Kotagedeans. Here, like in Kudus, we can enumerate actually by fingers and say that it is Indonesians who are holding number one position. (Harahap 1952, p. 139)

Not only entrepreneurs but also workers in the industry were assured of comfortable incomes: an unskilled worker received 0.35 guilders a day and a skilled craftsman 1.50 guilders a day when the price of rice was only 0.05 guilders per kilogram (Tedjo 1971, p. 31). The construction of the Silver Mosque got under way against this economic background.

The Great Mosque of Mataram in Kotagede had been used for court rituals as well as for communal and personal rituals of local Muslims. It was not only a royal property but also *the* mosque for the local *ummat* Islam, community of Muslims. Traditionally, the local population accepted the leadership of court-appointed Mosque officials in community rituals. In addition, a number of specialists of *adat* Islam centring around the Complex were patronized by the kraton authorities. The status of these semi-official specialists was derived from and was rooted in the legendary past, and it had been sustained by the personal favor of successive rulers.

The earliest clash between the Muhammadiyah and *adat* Islam over the Pasaréyan Mosque complex was instigated by the former's attack on the role of a particular woman *dhukun* (magical healer), who had been living in the kampung located in the front court of the complex (see Chapter 2, p. 37 above). Lesser Mosque functionaries whose ancestors were said to have been brought to settle there by the founder of Later Mataram, Panembahan Senapati, lived in this kampung. The woman was believed to have a special mystical ability to communicate with the spirit of Senapati and her mediation was often sought by visitors who came to the Pasaréyan to request Senapati's help.

As a part of its campaign against superstition, the Kotagede Muhammadiyah declared that what she had been doing was nothing but *tahyul* (superstitions) and indeed a negation of *tauhid* (the unity of God), and demanded that local authorities forbid her to perform her *dhukun* role in the Pasaréyan. Hizbul Wathan (Muhammadiyah Boy Scout) youths picketed the Pasaréyan, and minor skirmishes occurred between these youths and the woman's family members and neighbours. Police were called in to separate the quarrelling parties (see Rasjidi 1967, p. 12). The woman was eventually allowed to continue her magical performances while the Muhammadiyah remained openly hostile, seriously injuring her reputation.

In the late 1920s the Muhammadiyah also requested that the practice of distribution of small sums of money on the occasion of *maleman* (all night prayers) in the Great Mosque in the month of Puasa should be forbidden (see Chapter 2, p. 32 above). The Muhammadiyah argued that the practice was attracting people to the religious meeting by luring them with monetary rewards and, further, it disturbed the quiet and orderly atmosphere which was necessary for the performance of prayers. This request was granted by the authorities, and thereafter the practice disappeared from the grounds of the Great Mosque.

Another, more serious conflict occurred in the mid-1930s when the Muhammadiyah attempted to reform the ways in which Friday prayers and sermons were traditionally given. The issue led to the establishment of a new mosque, the Silver Mosque. The following description of the processes leading to the formation of the Silver Mosque has been taken mainly from a locally published booklet entitled *Riwajat Mesdjid Perak Kotagede* (*History of the Silver Mosque in Kotagede*, Nawawi 1957).

The booklet was written by a member of the Tabligh (Religious Propagation) Section of Kotagede Muhammadiyah in 1957. The purpose of the booklet was, according to its preface, to dispel misunderstandings concerning the Silver Mosque which was still found in a certain segment of the local population even after twenty years of its existence in Kotagede. Since the booklet was addressed to a non-Muhammadiyah local audience, it was written in Javanese and took the typical Javanese tack of approaching the issue in a round about way. The booklet is, therefore, not only a good documentation of the foundation of the Silver Mosque viewed from within, but also a good example of the way in which Muhammadiyah's messages were put before the wider audience.

The preface states that the book attempts to give adequate answers to four questions which are raised by some people in Kotagede: (a) the reasons for the construction of a new mosque in addition to the old one; (b) the question whether the new mosque was exclusive to Muhammadiyah members; (c) the meaning of the name, Mesjid Perak; and (d) the relationship of the new mosque to the court authorities. The author phrases the questions as follows:

> Why should there be a new mosque in the community of Islam in Kotagede in which there already had been a large and beautiful mosque which was the royal property *(kagungan dalem)* of the Surakarta and Yogyakarta courts? Why was it necessary for the able *(pinisaged)* and the wealthy *(parasugih)* to conceive and construct a new mosque? Is it true that the new mosque was the contribution of the Muhammadiyah and therefore it is only to fill the need of the Muhammadiyah and was visited exclusively by its members and sympathizers? Is it true that the new mosque the Silver Mosque, was so named because of the fact silverware entrepreneurs *(juragan perak)* exclusively contributed to its construction? Is the view correct that there was discord *(pasulayan)* between the royal servants *(abdi dalem)* who were entitled to control over the royal mosque *(kaparingan panguwaos-panguwaos masjid kagungan dalem)* and the religious leaders

(panuntuning agami) as well as the Muhammadiyah leaders? As a result of these doubts some people are led to believe that the Silver Mosque is less holy and less valid because its construction was not based upon (the devotion) "To God, the Almighty alone" *(Lillahi Ta'ala)* but rather derived from the outlet of lowly desire *(hawa napsu)*. Some people are inclined to believe that the Silver Mosque is disharmonious with the proper qualities *(mboten cocog kawontenan saleresipun)* [which a mosque should possess]. (Nawawi 1957, pp. 1–3)

The author of the booklet observes that these views are all inappropriate *(panggalihan ingkang boten-boten)*. These misguided views derived from an inadequate understanding of the circumstances *(lingkungan)* for the construction of the Silver Mosque. The author asserts that there are no bases in keeping the general public of Muslims *(saderek Islam umumipun)* in Kotagede from making use of the Silver Mosque, which indeed is a "property of God, the Lord *(kagunganipun Gusti Allah)*" (ibid., p. 3).

Then the author gives a general picture of the religious situation in Kotagede between 1925 and 1940 leading to the foundation of the Silver Mosque:

The years around 1925 were a golden age *(wekdal kemasan)* for Muslims in Kotagede. Especially the Muhammadiyah was active in holding religious courses *(pangaosan)* in every hamlet *(dusun)* for the old as well as for children so that Kotagede came to be recognized as "*kampung Islam*". The Muhammadiyah also establihed schools and a clinic ... There were many *langgar* (prayer houses) constructed in numerous places and a number of religious courses were given there as well as in ordinary houses. Among those meetings, the one that attracted the largest number of pupils was Kyai Amir's in Kampung Selokraman. Although Kyai Amir's house was a large one, it soon overflowed with pupils who came to receive lessons from him. Older boys among his pupils then went out to hold religious courses in the neighbouring villages ... Everywhere religious courses progressed, becoming larger and larger, the religion of Islam spread wider and wider, followers of the religion increasing (ibid., pp. 4–8).

The author then returns to the position of the Great Mosque in this general upheaval of religiosity, whose immediate consequence was the absolute increase in the number of people who came there to pray daily and especially on Fridays:

The porch *(srambi)*, which was large, was not large enough. Especially for Friday prayers in the fasting month, people had to sit on the ground in the yard of the Mosque (ibid., p. 8).

As a result, *khutbah* (sermons) given in the inner hall of the Mosque were heard only with difficulty by those who sat on the edges of the porch, not to mention the people sitting on the ground in the yard. Seeing this situation, the Muhammadiyah proposed that the *minbar* (pulpit for sermon) be moved from the inside of the inner hall to the porch. So as not to invite the government's rejection on the basis of tradition (the existing *minbar* had a particular legendary past dating back to Sultan Agung's reign), the Muhammadiyah proposed that a new *minbar* be made and placed on the porch so that it should become easier for the audience to listen to the sermon. The proposal was eventually accepted by the authorities. This was around the year of 1926 or 1927 (ibid., pp. 9–12).

Another consequence of the increased religious intensity in Kotagede, according to the author, was the fact that when a religious meeting or lecture addressed to the general public was held, there was no one place large enough to accommodate a large attendance. Kyai Amir held the view that the Great Mosque was the most appropriate place for such an occasion. The reason was that it was not only physically large but that a mosque should be the place for acquiring religious knowledge *(ilmu)* and engaging in religious discussions in addition to performing prayers *(sembahyang)*. However, the Great Mosque, as the property of Surakarta and Yogyakarta royalty, was already in frequent use for the courts' ceremonies, especially on Islamic holidays.

In order to have public religious meetings in the Great Mosque, a written request for permission had to be submitted to both the Surakarta and Yogyakarta courts. It usually took weeks and sometimes even months to obtain permission. Permission for the use of the Great Mosque for a public meeting was usually granted unless it conflicted with a court ceremony, but it happened time and again that requests were denied. If permission was denied by one government, it was the same as being denied by both. Especially from 1937 the government's regulations on public meetings, even including religious ones, were tightened, and it became more difficult and cumbersome to obtain permission (ibid., pp. 12–16).

Facing this situation around the year of 1937, Kyai Amir and his colleagues thought of the idea of constructing a new mosque for Kotagede Muslims themselves "a mosque which was not bound by regulations and which was free from any hindrances" (ibid., pp. 16–17). This idea was also accepted by the Muhammadiyah leadership, which appealed for wider cooperation from the general Muslim community in Kotagede. Organization of the construction of the new mosque got under way without the formation of a formal committee *(panitya)* or functionaries *(pengurus)*. The effort was voluntary and spontaneous:

With sincerity *(ikhlas)*, everybody participated according to one's own capability. Indeed Muhammadiyah leaders, the able *(pinisaged)*, the wealthy *(parasugih)* and others, all formed a committee without writing down their names, only reciting *Bismillahir Rahmanir Rahim* ("In the name of God, the Merciful, the Compassionate") and saying "I make a mosque *Lillahi Ta'ala* (For God, the Almighty alone)" (ibid., pp. 20–21).

Every Sunday, the informal *panitya*, which was always attended by more than one hundred people, met in Kyai Amir's house. The rich contributed money: the poor, skills and labour. Haji Muchsin and Haji Mudzakkir each contributed 300 rupiahs. Haji Mudzakkir also contributed another 700 rupiahs to buy the land for the mosque. In collecting money, women folks contributions were very significant, for in Kotagede the position of women in economic matters was extremely essential. Youths also contributed their labour and ideas. Thus with the accumulation of about 3,000 rupiahs in money and an abundant supply of skills and labour, the new mosque was completed in 1939 and officially inaugurated on the Islamic New Year's Day in 1940 or 1359 A.H. (ibid., pp. 21–31).

Toward the end of the booklet, the author explains that the name Silver Mosque (Mesjid Perak) derived not only from the fact that silverware enterpreneurs *(juragan perak)*, like Haji Mudzakkir, were among the primary promoters but also from the fact that the white colour of silver meant purity and holiness and was appropriate to symbolize the unselfish religious devotion *(ikhlas)* expressed in the construction of the Mosque (ibid., pp. 31–32). Later a committee of functionaries for the management of the Mosque was organized and headed by Kyai Amir. The committee included two *penghulu* from the Great Mosque in its members. After the death of Kyai Amur in 1948, Haji Masjhudi succeeded him as head of the committee (ibid., p. 38).

The booklet ends here. Obviously, the conflict with the principality authorities is deliberately de-emphasized. This may be partly because of the Javanese value of avoiding disharmony in public and partly because of the Muhammadiyah's concern not to injure the name of the new Sultan of Yogyakarta whose reputation was high among Muslims. However, the conflict with the court authorities was undoubtedly a major factor in the construction of the Silver Mosque. When I asked Haji Masjhudi about the beginning of the Silver Mosque, he answered frankly:

> The Great Mosque was under the control of *abdi dalem* and we [Muhammadiyah] were not so free to do this and that according to our needs *(semaunya kami)*. We were not satisfied *(kurang puas)* and decided to build a new mosque which we can use freely *(secara bebas)*.

FIGURE 4.15

Haji Masjhudi, founder of Kotagede Muhammadiyah, in front of his general store.

FIGURE 4.16

Haji Masjhudi and Professor Mukti Ali at Bani Mukmin's annual Syawalan meeting.

FIGURE 4.17

Syawalan meeting of Bani Mukmin — descendants of Haji Muchsin and spouses.

FIGURE 4.18

Syawalan meeting of Bani Mukmin — descendants of Haji Masduki and spouses.

FIGURE 4.19

Haji Masjhudi in prayer *(do'a)*.

FIGURE 4.20

People paying last tribute to Haji Masjhudi's body.

FIGURE 4.21

Haji Masjhudi's body carried to cemetery in Alun-Alun for burial.

FIGURE 4.22

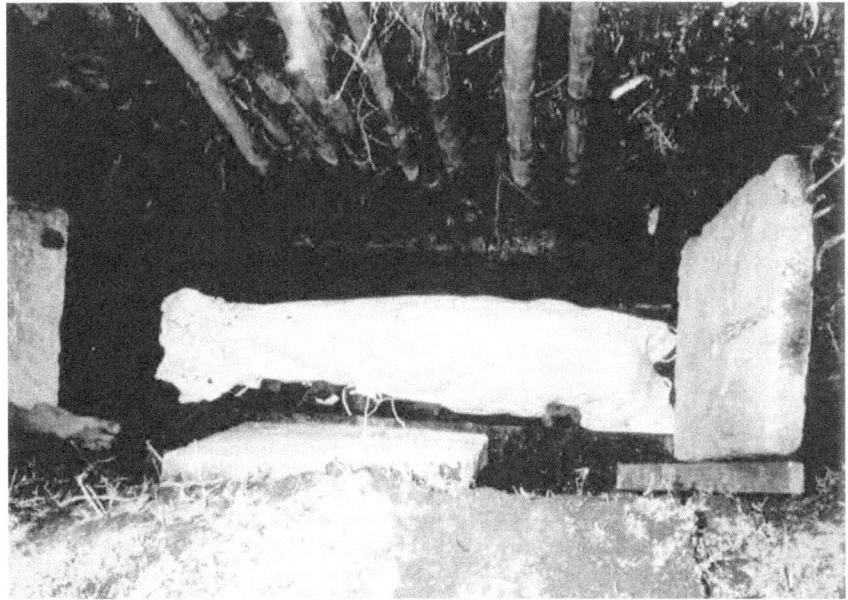

Haji Masjhudi's body placed in his grave facing west.

Another elderly Muhammadiyah member also told me:

> In the 1930s, there was a Surakarta *abdi dalem* who was particularly stubborn, sticking to traditional regulations in order to check Muhammadiyah activities. We just could not stand him.

The Silver Mosque symbolized the independence and separation of reformist Muslims from the court's religious authority and *adat* Islam. By constructing the new mosque, reformist Muslims acquired independence and self-control. They stood out, distinct from the traditional spiritual order. A second generation Muhammadiyah leader who was once Kyai Amir's student stated to me:

> In fact there is another meaning for Silver Mosque. The meaning cannot be understood if one is not good at Arabic. In Arabic, *firaq* (*pirah* in Javanese pronunciation) means "being separated and independent", *terpisah* in Indonesian. Thus Mesjid Perak in fact means *mesjid firaq*, "a mosque of separation", an independent mosque. [It symbolized the] separation of *ummat* from *kekotoran* (dirts) and *kebekuan* (stagnation) of the past. Only *santri* people were able to understand this hidden meaning.[12]

It should be remarked at the same time that the Silver Mosque not only embodied a separation but a continuity as well. The fact that two *penghulu* were included in the committee for the new mosque points up the line of continuity the Muhammadiyah endeavoured to maintain. The two *penghulu* commanded respect from *abangan* as well as *santri* for their unselfish personalities, strict orthodoxy in their religious behavior, and genuine devoutness. Later mainly through the efforts of these two *penghulu*, the Great Mosque was made available for the Muhammadiyah's full participation in its management.

With the establishment of the Silver Mosque the pre-war Muhammadiyah in Kotagede was equipped with a full set of organizational apparatus to promote its activities. However, the outbreak of World War II changed the situation drastically. In the next chapter we shall follow the subsequent development.

---

12. This statement seems to be a good example of how a *santri*, presumably deeply Arabized and therefore most alien to Javanese cultural traditions, enjoys a typically Javanese linguistic art of *kerata-basa*, i.e. "a kind of folk etymology" (Moertono 1968, p. 21, note 14). Similar cases were numerous in the field and have induced me to suspect the validity of the conventional *abangan-santri-priyayi* categorization.

5

THE SOCIOLOGY OF UMMAT ISLAM
Structure and Anti-structure

> Nowadays anybody can become any kind of person *(siapa-siapa bisa menjadi apa-apa saja)*. The main point is how one behaves; like *priyayi (berpriyayi)*, like *santri (bersantri)*, or like *abangan (berabangan)*. It is *ber, ber, ber* ("doings") that makes the difference. (Interview with Kyai Haji Masjhudi, 2 November 1971).

The Muhammadiyah movement was characterized by its non-political stance from the outset as we have seen above (Chapter 3, p. 73). Besides the factor of circumspect avoidance of government repressions of "Muslim fanatics", the position was a manifestation of the high value placed by the movement on an individual Muslim's personal faith which could uphold self-reliant and independent Muslim life under any political condition. The achievement of religious devotion was regarded as a matter lying within the range of an individual's personal control in whatever situation. A religious community composed of such individuals could transcend any particular forms of secular polity. Throughout the Dutch period, the Muhammadiyah's stance towards the colonial government was rather passive and defensive; if the government interfered with Islamic matters, it certainly reacted to defend its interests with full strength, but otherwise it took no political initiatives of its own. Formation of or affiliation with political organizations was completely left to individual choice.¹ Towards the latter half of the 1930s, an Islamic political party, Partai Islam Indonesia (PII), closely connected with the Muhammadiyah, was formed. However, the party's role was a "diplomatic" representation, i.e., negotiations with the colonial government and other secular political parties for the defence of Islamic interests.² The basic non-political position of the Muhammadiyah helped to maintain a stable condition favourable for the steady growth of its membership and the establishment of educational and social welfare institutions.

THE POST-WAR POLITICAL DEVELOPMENT

Conventionally, the history of Indonesian politics in the next two decades (1940s–1950s) has been viewed as a history of the failure of Muslims' political attempt at making independent Indonesia an Islamic state. Under the Japanese occupation authorities, Muslim political forces acquired organizational strength and a stature in national politics comparable to that of civil servants and secular nationalists. In post-Independence politics, Muslim political parties were strong enough to keep playing a dominant role in successive coalition governments, but not strong enough to realize their goal of an Islamic state through parliamentary means. The insufficient strength of the Muslim political parties for their claim to power was typically shown by the results of the first general elections held in 1955 in which they failed to obtain a majority in spite of the fact that approximately 90 per cent of Indonesians professed to be Muslims. No other political parties did secure a majority either, and the Constitutional Assembly came to a stalemate over the issue of the foundation of the state. The Muslim frustrations found an outlet in a number of local armed revolts culminating into large-scale rebellions in cooperation with regionalist military officers in the major outer islands. With the defeat of these rebellions and the suspension of parliamentary democracy, however, Muslim political parties were largely incapacitated, and forced into cooperation with Sukarno's Guided Democracy or simply banned. The Java-based traditionalist Muslim party, the Nahdlatul Ulama (NU), took the first course, and the outer islands-based reformists, the Masyumi Party, the latter. The Muhammadiyah, by appealing to the personal favour of President Sukarno (who once taught at a Muhammadiyah school while he was in exile in Bengkulu, Sumatra, in the late 1930s), barely escaped the government repression.

---

1. For an interesting discussion on the relationship between religion and politics by a Muhammadiyah leader in the early 1930s, see Mahfoeld (1933).
2. For more on this short-lived Islamic party, see Deliar (1973, pp. 158–61).

As a political analysis, the foregoing conventional view seems to present no problem. However, in a wider perspective of the relationship between religion and politics, the view poses more questions than answers. A central question to be asked is whether it is appropriate to regard Muslim political forces as having contended for power in competition with secular political forces in the same terms as suggested by Harry Benda (1958, p. 203; 1965, p. 131). When I entered Kotagede and first met some of the former local leaders of the Masyumi Party there, who were supposed to have been "failed" and "defeated", I was impressed by the fact that they showed no bitterness or lament over their past. This impression led me to question the conventional view on the place of Islam in modern Indonesian politics.

During the Japanese occupation Muslim organizations including the Muhammadiyah and the Nahdlatul Ulama were allowed to continue their religious activities while all other pre-war nationalist political parties and organizations were forbidden. The Muslim leaders were given positions of national prominence alongside secular nationalists and *priyayi* representatives. The position of Islamic bureaucracy (office of religious affairs) was enhanced and given semi-autonomy from the secular bureaucracy. The Muslim local leaders were encouraged to sit in leadership positions of various mass organizations, and even exclusively Muslim military and para-military organizations were allowed to be formed. All this was intended to mobilize Indonesian popular support, especially that of politically active Muslims, for the Japanese war effort. Hence the view is that the Muslim ascendancy during the occupation is the result of the Japanese political manipulation.

However, from the Muslim side, their relationship vis-à-vis the Japanese military government was quite differently conceived. They felt that the Japanese rulers were from the outset forced to acknowledge the importance of Islam among the Indonesian population in obtaining their genuine cooperation with the government. What the Japanese authorities did for Muslims and Islam in Indonesia was a long overdue rectification of numerous wrongdoings committed by the Dutch colonial rulers. Even so, the Japanese Islamic policy was far from satisfactory, and Muslim support for the Japanese was conditional: as long as the Japanese helped to promote the Islamic cause, Muslims would support and cooperate with Japan in resisting the return of the Dutch rule; otherwise, they might withdraw to the position of non-cooperation or even turn against Japan. There was a manipulation of the situation as much on the part of the Muslims as the Japanese.

With the defeat of Japan and the Declaration of Independence, Muslims participated in revolutionary politics on a massive scale. In their conception, the defence of Islam was equated with the defence of national independence. Islamic symbols inspired the struggle for independence and against the re-establishment of the old colonial social order. Muslim mass organizations, especially of the youth, spearheaded a number of spontaneous "social revolutions" in various parts of the archipelago and formed one of the important elements in popular revolutionary forces.

The mode of Muslim participation in the Revolution at the mass level attracts special attention. In this revolutionary situation it was felt that an extraordinary time in history had arrived. It was as if Islamic ideals were momentarily realized on earth — unselfish devotion and sacrifice for the defence of Islam and the community of Muslims, comradely unity and egalitarianism among the independence fighters and the population at large, and the endurance of material hardships for the higher cause. The struggle for independene and social justice was not merely a political action in the narrow sense of the word but rather the expression of religious devotion and fulfillment of religious obligation.

Another important aspect of the mode of Muslim participation in the Revolution was that it came mainly through numerous "struggle organizations" rather than through religious organizations already in existence. Neither the central leadership of the Muhammadiyah nor the Nahdlatul Ulama was able to coordinate its own local branches, for the communication system was very bad and the situation extremely fluid. Instead, numerous units of Hizbullah, Sabillilah, Lasykar Rakyat and many other "struggle organizations" were formed, and they became the organizational framework through which the revolutionary energy of the masses were channelled. Muslim elements in these organizations as well as in the regular republican troops were quite significant from the beginning of the Revolution.

The Revolution was thus the time when religious consciousness was much heightened. The vision of a new social order was often congruent with the Islamic vision of a true *ummat*, the community of the faithful, and daily experience in the Revolution confirmed it. The Indonesian Revolution ended as a national revolution, not as a social one. With the return of "normalcy", religion and politics once merged in the revolutionary period were again separated out. The religious community became distinct from the existing social order again. Instead of local, spontaneous "struggle organizations", the Muhammadiyah and many other Islamic organizations reestablished themselves and resumed their religious activities. Many Muslim activists of the Revolutionary period had not regarded their political or military roles as the ultimate goal of their life but rather as a temporary suspension of their normal life and self-sacrifice enforced by circumstances. They soon returned to normal life and engaged in religious activities *per se*.

The experience of the Muhammadiyah in Kotagede during the Japanese occupation and the Revolution followed the general pattern described above. A number of Kotagedeans were appointed to key positions by the Japanese authorities as we have already seen above: Haji Masjhudi became the chairman of the local Masyumi, and Kyai Amir, the head of the regional office of Religious Affairs. Perhaps the most remarkable is the emergence of Abdul Kahar Mudzakkir, first as an employee of the local Japanese government in Yogyakarta, then as deputy-head of the central office of Religious Affairs in Jakarta, culminating in his participation in the highest circles of national politics during the late Japanese occupation period and the earliest stages of the post-war politics. Abdul Kahar could have stayed in politics, but he did not. He devoted himself to the foundation and the growth of an Islamic university (Nakamura 1977). Similar but less conspicuous cases were numerous in Kotagede. (For example, see the case of Pak Ja'far in Chapter 6, pp. 169–74 below).

Political developments in Kotagede during the 1950s and the early 1960s followed the general national trend, i.e., the decline of the Masyumi Party and the ascendancy of the PKI. On the occasion of the 1955 general elections, the Masyumi Party and the PKI showed almost equal strength, with 40 per cent each of the local votes. The Masyumi Party was narrow first with about 2,000 votes and the PKI a close second also with about 2,000 votes. The PNI remained as a poor third with some 500 votes, and votes for other parties were less than 500 in total. In the 1957 regional elections, however, the order of the Masyumi Party and the PKI was reversed with a slight margin again. The PNI made headway mainly at the expense of smaller parties but remained the third.

From the late 1950s on, the PKI's ascendancy was remarkable in the general Yogyakarta region including Kotagede. With the banning of the Masyumi Party in 1960, its members were purged from governmental bodies (legislative and executive bodies at the village, regency and residency levels) as well as from semi-governmental or public bodies such as neighbourhood associations and cooperatives. Some former Masyumi members changed their affiliations to the NU and survived the purge. Vacancies created by the purge were filled mostly by PKI, PNI and NU members. In Kotagede, two Masyumi village chief *(lurah)* switched their party affiliation to the NU, and two Masyumi-affiliated chairmen of neighbourhood association *(rukun kampung)* were replaced by PNI men. In the case of the silverwork production cooperative, the leadership changed from that of consisting of PKI/Masyumi members to a PKI/PNI coalition. In retrospect, the Guided Democracy period is remembered by many Kotagedeans as "jaman PKI" or the "PKI period".

A curious local phenomenon during this period is the PKI's failure in the field of trade union movement. Nationally the rapid growth of the PKI was closely associated with the increase of the membership of SOBSI (Central Labor Organization of All Indonesia). Locally in Kotagede, too, the SOBSI was the largest union in terms of registered membership. However, in the actual scene of management-labour relations, the SOBSI was rarely active to organize labour demands. This was especially so in the field of the silver industry, the major private industry in Kotagede.

Local people explained this phenomenon in terms of a peculiar situation in Kotagede. The management and the labour sides of the silver industry were represented by two PKI members who were brothers. The elder brother, a former goldsmith and the owner-manager of one of the largest silverwork enterprises in post-war Kotagede, was a returnee from Dutch political exile in Boven Digul. He was instrumental in organizing the Production Cooperative of Silverwork Enterprises of Yogyakarta (KP3J, Koperasi Pengusaha Produksi Perak Jogjakarta) in the early 1950s and since then continuously occupied the chairmanship of the Cooperative until 1965. He also played the role of *sesepuh* ("eldery advisor") in the Communist movement in post-war Kotagede. His younger brother, a silversmith less politically sophisticated than himself, started the unionization of silver industry workers under his close guidance and established a SOBSI affiliate, occupying its General Secretary position himself. In the mid-1950s, there were some silver entrepreneurs who suffered a strike by SOBSI workers demanding the application of a uniform wage scale and working conditions agreed upon by the SOBSI and KP3J representatives. However, other than this, management-labour disputes rarely flared up in the silver industry of Kotagede. Before anything serious developed, the two brothers personally mediated the disputants.

The SOBSI attracted little enthusiasm from the workers in Kotagede. A silversmith said, "SOBSI was just the matter of a membership card." The membership card was a necessity because, in theory, a worker must produce a union membership card when obtaining employment with an enterprise affiliated with the KP3J. Otherwise the SOBSI was used only as a tool for the mobilization of masses for political rallies and paradings. The insignificance of the SOBSI in popular eyes was furthered by an incident in the early 1960s when the General Secretary was found to have made private use of the union funds but was allowed to retain his position upon "self-criticism". The SOBSI became all the more ineffective thereafter.

The increase of PKI influence in Kotagede was achieved rather in the field of other mass organizations, youth (Pemuda Rakyat, or People's Youth); women (Gerwani, or Indonesian Women's Movement); and cultural activities (Lekra, or League of People's Culture). Especially active was the last organization, using such traditional cultural media as *wayang kulit* (puppet shadow play) and *kethoprak* (folk drama) for PKI propaganda purposes. The intensity of the Lekra activities during the period of PKI dominance was such that the period is remembered by many locals as "*jaman kethoprak*" or the "*kethoprak* period".

The banning of the Masyumi Party in 1960 did not entail the weakening of the Muhammadiyah movement. As we shall see later, Muhammadiyah started a new membership drive in the early years of the 1960s and, as a result, its membership made a remarkable increase nationally as well as locally. This reconsolidation process of the Muhammadiyah continued during the period of the general deterioration of the economy with sky-rocketing inflation, blackmarketing and the widespread corruption of civil servants. Arbitrary repressions of Muslim leaders did not deter the process of Muhammadiyah growth, and incidents of clashes between the Muhammadiyah activists, especially *muballigh* (religious propaganists) and the PKI members, increased towards 1965. The air was getting "hot" (*panas*), and many Muhammadiyah activists were anticipating an impending showdown with the PKI on the eve of the abortive coup of 1 October 1965.

THE POST-WAR ECONOMIC IMPOVERISHMENT

A most important change in the post-war Kotagede economy compared to its pre-war counterpart seems to be the general impoverishment of the people in the town. The enormous wealth witnessed by van Bevervoorde around the turn of the century is today (1972) only discernable in decaying old palatial houses. In place of van Mook's thriving entrepreneurial class of the mid-twenties, one finds numerous small traders and daily workers striving hard just to survive for another day. Kotagede is no longer a prosperous town but an economically depressed one. Consequently, the economic environment in which the Muhammadiyah movement is operating has also vastly changed.

Table 5.1 illustrates various aspects of this general economic impoverishment. The table compares the change in the occupational composition of the townspeople between 1922 and 1971. The 1971 figures are based on the government census, supplemented by my own survey. For the purpose of securing the equivalent units of comparison, only three administrative villages *(kalurahan)* out of the four in the van Mook's original table are selected. These three *kalurahan* became three neighbourhood associations *(rukun kampung)* after Independence, but the boundaries of the former were retained intact and are the same as the latter's.

TABLE 5.1
Comparison of Occupational Composition of House-Compound Holders in 1922 and Household Heads in 1971[a]

Category	A 1922		B 1971		B–A
	N	%	N	%	
I. Officials and professionals	76	8.4	170	10.3	+94
II. Entrepreneurs	207	23.1	135	8.2	−72
III. Craftsmen, small traders and workers	600	66.8	1,139	69.3	+539
IV. Others	15	1.7	201	12.2	+186
Total	898	100.0	1,645	100.0	+747

Note: (a) In the three *kalurahan/rukun kampung* of Prenggan, Sajangan (Alun-Alun) and Basen.
Sources: A. van Mook (1926a, p. 363; also 1958, p. 289).
B. 1971 Census plus supplementary survey of my own.

From the data in Table 5.1 we can make several important observations. First of all, the absolute decrease in the number of entrepreneurs (Category II) is most remarkable. This is all the more significant in view of the fact that the population of the town has almost doubled over the fifty years' period. Consequently, the proportion of entrepreneurs in the total has decreased drastically from 23.1 per cent to 8.2 per cent. In contrast, the absolute number of individuals in the third category increased considerably in the fifty years, but it has only made an increase of 2.5 per cent from 66.8 per cent to 69.3 per cent in terms of proportion. As to those in the fourth category, there were only fifteen individuals in van Mook's original data, and most of them were day-labourers. In 1971, the bulk of those belong the fourth category, "others", are unemployed and non-employed: the rest are students, who were totally absent in 1922. Finally, more-than-doubled number of individuals in the first category over the past fifty years is largely made up of government official (civil and military), teachers and other white collar workers. This fact itself is quite consistent with the general expansion of modern bureaucracy. What should be kept in mind is, as we shall see later, that in terms of actual standards of living, a government official of 1971 is much more impoverished than a *priyayi* of 1922. As a general observation, it can be stated that the number of rich entrepreneurs has decreased significantly from the Kotagede economic scene, and small traders, daily workers and the jobless have vastly increased. The bulk of the population has been pushed downward on the economic scale.

BOX 5
One Morning in 1970

On Tuesday, 17 November 1970, I woke up early at around 4.00 a.m. and went out to the balcony of the house, which I had just rented from an Orang Kalang family. The house was built facing the main street, Jalan Tegalgendu, near the western edge of the bridge over the Gajah Wong River. I was on a strategic spot to observe the movement of people across the river to and from the directions between Yogyakarta and Kotagede. The day was an ordinary weekday in Gregorian, Hijrah and Javanese calendars. People started to move at about 4.30 a.m., but the peak period of their movement was between 5.30 to 6.30 a.m. I watched and recorded their movement for one hour at those times. The results of my observation were as follows:

(1) From Kotagede to the direction of Yogyakarta

Table 1: People to Yogyakarta by Means of Transportation

Means	Male		Female		Total	
	N	%	N	%	N	%
Bicycle	66	63.5	57	52.3	123	57.8
On foot	17	16.3	25	22.9	42	19.7
Andong	3	2.9	22	20.2	25	11.7
Motorbike	9	8.7	3	2.8	12	5.6
Becak	8	7.7	2	1.8	10	4.7
Automobile	1	0.9	0	0	1	0.5
Total	104	100	109	100	213	100

In total, 213 people moved from Kotagede to the direction of Yogyakarta across the Gajah Wong River during the observation period. Of them, 104 (48.8 per cent) were male, 109 (51.2 per cent) female. For both, the most popular means of transportation was bicycle. Sixty-six men (63.5 per cent) were on bicycle, while 17 (16.3 per cent) on foot, 9 (8.7 per cent) on motorbike, 8 (7.7 per cent) on *becak*, 3 (2.9 per cent) on *andong* (horse-carriage), and 1 (0.9 per cent) driving a car (jeep). Additional information on men is as follows: Out of 104 men, 29 (28 per cent) carried goods. Apparent age categories among men were: 59 (56.7 per cent) middle-aged, 38 (36.6 per cent) young, 5 (4.8 per cent) senior, and 2 (1.9 per cent) boys.

Of the 109 female, a majority (57 or 52.3 per cent) were riding bicycle, 25 (22.9 per cent) on foot, 22 (20.2 per cent) riding *andong*, 3 (2.7 per cent) on the backseat of motorbike, and 2 (1.8 per cent) on *becak*. Thirty-one (29.8 per cent) of female carried goods, almost all of those on *andong* and some on foot and on bicycle did so. Apparent age categories were: 72 (66.0 per cent) middle-aged, 30 (27.5 per cent) young, 5 (4.6 per cent) senior, and 3 (2.75 per cent) children.

continued on next page

> **BOX 5** — *continued*
>
> *(2) To the direction of Kotagede*
>
> Table 2: People to Kotagede by Means of Transportation
>
> | Means | Male | | Female | | Total | |
> |---|---|---|---|---|---|---|
> | | N | % | N | % | N | % |
> | Bicycle | 64 | 64.6 | 35 | 43.2 | 99 | 55.0 |
> | On foot | 25 | 25.3 | 43 | 53.1 | 68 | 37.8 |
> | Motorbike | 9 | 9.1 | 0 | 0 | 9 | 5 |
> | *Becak* | 1 | 1 | 3 | 3.7 | 4 | 2.2 |
> | *Andong* | 0 | 0 | 0 | 0 | 0 | 0 |
> | Automobile | 0 | 0 | 0 | 0 | 0 | 0 |
> | Total | 99 | 100 | 81 | 100 | 180 | 100 |
>
> In total, 180 people moved towards the central part of Kotagede: 99 (55 per cent) of them were male and 81 (45 per cent) female. Sixty-four males (65 per cent) were on bicycle, 25 (25 per cent) on foot, 9 (9 per cent) on motorbike and 1 in a *becak*. Those who were carrying goods numbered 20 (20 per cent) among the total male. Fifty-five (56 per cent) of them were middle-aged, 34 (34 per cent) young, and 10 (10 per cent) children. Distinctively, there were 11 men taking 20 cattles. There were also several men going down to the river apparently to ease themselves. I also saw some boys carrying fishing poles going down to the river, too. Of the 81 female, a majority (43, or 53 per cent) were on foot, 35 (43 per cent) on bicycle, and 3 (4 per cent) riding *becak*. Sixty (74 per cent) of the total female were carrying goods. It was obvious that those women were headed for *pasar*, the market. Sixty-five (80 per cent) of them were middle-aged whereas 12 (14 per cent) were young, and 2 (2 per cent) children.

The war in the Pacific deprived the silverwork industry of the supply of raw materials as well as the market forcing it to a complete halt during the Japanese occupation. After the war the industry started to operate again, but until 1950 it was hampered by the scarcity of materials and the unstable market conditions. Between 1950 and 1960 the industry experienced a degree of recovery but did not reach the pre-war peak level. Organized into the Production Cooperative of Silverwork Enterprises of Jogjakarta (KP3J), the industry then gained new vigour. But during the Guided Economy period of 1960–65, the Cooperative was placed under government control, and the supply of materials and even the sale of products were determined by the whim of government agencies and the Cooperative leadership dominated by the PKI.

Since 1966 the government control of the Cooperative has gone, and the silverwork enterprises have been completely left to "free" competition among themselves. The Cooperative is now almost defunct, and with the increasing influx of foreign tourists, the larger (actually only two giant ones) enterprises are getting larger while the rest are losing their ability to compete as independent enterprises. These changes are reflected to some extent in Table 5.2.

TABLE 5.2
Silverwork Industry in Kotagede, 1935–71

Year	Number of enterprises	Number of employees	Annual production
1935–38	70	1,400	25,000 kg.
1945	50	250	4,500 kg.
1946	70	350	6,500 kg.
1947	80	400	14,500 kg.
1948	90	500	16,000 kg.
1949	30	150	2,700 kg.
1950	50	300	4,500 kg.
1951	100	1,000	18,000 kg.
1952	80	700	12,000 kg.
1955	164[a]	—	—
1956	165	—	—
1957	194	—	—
1958	199	—	—
1959	197	—	—
1960	202	—	—
1961	202	—	—
1962	179	—	—
1963	178	—	—
1964	161	—	—
1965	147	—	—
1966	147	—	—
1967	123	—	—
1968	137[b]	—	—
1971	117	400[c]	6,000 kg.[c]

Notes:
(a) All the enterprises in 1955–71 were the KP3J members.
(b) KP3J sources say that in recent years only about 10 per cent of the enterprises were in operation.
(c) Estimate by KP3J sources.
Sources: 1935–52 *Republik Indonesia* XII, p. 721.
　　　　　1955–71 Tedjo (1970: Appendix II), and annual reports of the Production Cooperative of Silverwork Enterprises of Jogjakarta (KP3J).

With the silverwork industry in a slump, where are the numerous day wage workers finding employment in recent years? In fact, no single replacement has been found. The trades in prevalence recently are *konfeksi* (garments, simple ready-made clothing) and *imitasi* (accessories of gold imitation). In both trades not much skill or experience is required. Among *buruh* (daily workers), *buruh jahit* or sewers are the greatest in number.

The impoverishment of the Kotagede economy is also reflected in a marked decrease in real income and a consequent lowering in standards of living. According to local elders, the highest daily wage for a skilled *tukang perak* (silversmith) during the 1930s was 1.50 guilders while a *buruh* was paid at least 0.35 guilders a day (see Tedjo 1970, p. 30). In the 1930s, rice was bought at 0.05 guilders per kilogram. So, the daily earning of a highest paid silversmith was an equivalent of 30 kilograms of rice and that of an unskilled worker 7 kilograms. To measure the standard of living, a common local practice is to assess if one is eating enough rice, and in this measurement a half kilogram of rice for an adult (and 1/3 to 1/4 kilograms for a child) is held to be a minimal necessity. The average number of members in a household in Java has been and is about 4.5. So, an average household needs at least two kilograms of rice every day to feel it is eating properly. The greater the positive difference between income and the amount of money spent for purchasing rice, the more well-off a household is considered to be. This index may seem rudimentary but nonetheless it is very practical and essential in providing a concrete measurement of living standards for ordinary Javanese. When this system of measurment is applied to the above-mentioned wages, we can visualize the fact that a skilled craftsman in the pre-war time never felt hungry and was in fact able to enjoy a fairly comfortable life. Silversmithing was an ideal career for Kotagedean boys, and girls were eager to marry such men (Tedjo 1970, p. 31). It was also easy for a skilled silversmith to save from his earnings and accumulate capital to start his own workshop with hired labour (ibid.). Even an unskilled worker's daily earnings, equivalent to 7 kilograms of rice, was more than enough to feed him and his family. A former Muhammadiyah high school teacher (who says that he received the same salary as a government school teacher) recalls that his starting monthly salary in 1929 was 12.50 guilders (or the rice equivalent of 8 kilograms a day). He remembers that "with that salary, life was easy enough for me. I ate enough every day, wore a pair of trousers and a pair of shoes, and still had a surplus. I was even able to go see movies every night if I wanted to."

In 1970–72, the price of rice was fairly stable at 32 to 35 rupiahs per kilogram. For a *buruh* whose cash income is only 50 to 100 rupiahs, his real income is only the rice equivalent of 1.5 to 3 kilograms. This means that a *buruh*'s real income today has been pushed down to less than half of the pre-war level. Even the highest-paid silversmith now receives 400 rupiahs a day, or the rice equivalent of 12 kilograms. The majority of silversmith wages now range from 150 to 200 rupiahs a day, which is the rice equivalent of 5 to 6 kilograms. Here again the real income of silversmiths has been reduced to 1/3 or 1/4 of the pre-war level. A high school teacher at present is paid from 2,000 to 5,000 rupiahs a month, which is approximately equivalent to 2 to 5 kilograms of rice a day. Besides rice, he must wear a pair of trousers (about 500 rupiahs) and a pair of shoes (about 700 rupiahs), too. His salary is barely enough to feed him and his family. Thus we can see that many of those individuals who are included in the category of "Officials and professionals" in 1971 in Table 5.1 are in fact much worse off than their counterpart in 1922.

Besides the general stagnation and even retrogession of the national economy of post-war Indonesia, which were ultimately responsible for the impoverished state of the Kotagede economy, there were several factors of more direct local relevance. First of all, mention should be made of the deterioration in the infrastructure of the local economy over the past thirty years of war, revolution and economic instability: war and revolution brought direct destruction in transport and communication systems, electricity, irrigation and drainage systems, public buildings and the like. Not many were reconstructed, and maintenance was not catching up with the speed of wear and tear. Even the short-distance transport by road between Yogyakarta and Kotagede becomes unreliable during rainy months. The supply of electricity is limited to only about 15 per cent of the total number of buildings in Kotagede, and the supply is irregular and not to be relied on. Blackouts occur quite often and the voltage is almost always far below the official 100 volts. This generally very poor state of infrastructure has hampered local economy greatly.

Secondly, there was an exodus of a significant number of active entrepreneurs from the town. With their departure many jobs were lost to the local work force. The most conspicuous was the almost complete desertion of the Kalang People from Tegalgendu leaving their huge houses to slow decay. In Kotagede itself several families from the top layer of the wealthy entrepreneurial group moved out from the town mainly to the central business area of Yogyakarta. For example, the largest and the most representative batik retail shop located in the prime spot of the city of Yogyakarta is owned by a former Kotagede family (one of Haji Mukmin's descendants). Several other batik retail shops in the same district also originated from Kotagede. A few large-scale silver workshops have also moved out from Kotagede to the city.

Many of the wealthy families of the pre-war time were simply pushed out of business through the turmoils of war and revolution. This is clearly observed with the descendants of the pre-war "merchant kings". Among the descendants of Haji Mukmin, there are still many entrepreneurs, but there is no one who has been able to compare to the level of prosperity achieved by Haji Mukmin himself. Bahuwinangun's descendants still own many houses and shops to let, but they are only living off their ancestor's wealth. The house and factory complex of Atmosudigdo with a spacious underground construction is now falling into ruins, for the maintenance and repair costs are beyond the capability of his descendants. An interesting phenomenon to be observed with the descendants of these "merchant kings" is that quite a large portion of their family wealth has been spent for the education of children who have become professionals rather than entrepreneurs. Among the second generation offspring of Haji Mukmin, almost one half have become professionals (see Table 5.8 below). A similar process of professionalization can be observed with the descendants of Atmosudigdo and Bahuwinangun.

Despite constant sloganizing, the economic policies of succesive governments of independent Indonesia were not much help to the recovery of entrepreneurial activities in Kotagede. Because of tremendous inflation, the freezing of banks accounts, currency devaluation, corruption, the bank and credit system was discredited in public eyes. The production cooperatives were often only a disguise for blackmarketing, for the matirial supplied through the cooperatives was better sold on the blackmarket than worked on. Arbitrary policy changes ruined many entrepreneurs overnight. The history of the post-war Kotagede economy is full of stories of sudden ups and downs of individual entrepreneurs, and there were indeed more downs than ups. Ups were mostly attributed to speculations or windfall gains. For example, several nouveaux riches allegedly acquired their sudden gain in wealth by looting the Kalang People's treasures. But more often heard are failure stories. A batik workshop owner went bankrupt and became a taxi driver. A *kuningan* (brasswork) entrepreneur failed in business and now is peddling batik. A once-prosperous garment factory owner manager was reduced to tailoring all by himself because of the debts incurred in business. All in all, the entrepreneurial group in post-war Kotagede has been weakened considerably, diminished in the size and scale of operation, and has become less innovative and enterprising compared to its pre-war counterpart. With the discouraged entrepreneurs, the post-war economy of Kotagede has never had a chance to "take off".

Now a brief mention should be made of changes which occurred in the non-economic fields of post-war Kotagede. The most important change seems to be that of the status system directly caused by the political and administrative changes in the Yogyakarta Sultanate. Shortly after the Declarations of Independence, the entire Yogyakarta Sultanate with the Pakualaman principality became an integral part of the new Republic (see Selosoemardjan 1962, especially Chapters 4 and 5). The former "royal servants" *(abdi dalem)* were changed into "civil servants" *(pegawai negeri)* of the Republic and received salaries from the Republican government. However, a small number of the *abdi dalem* remained in the service of the Sultan's palace and several other institutions including the Royal Cemetery Complexes in Imogiri and Kotagede. Now the new civil servants, although many of them were still from traditional *priyayi* (aristocrats) families, represented not so much the Sultan, who remained in the position of the Head of the Special Region of Yogyakarta, but rather the Republican government.

Prior to the administrative reform of 1920, the *abdi dalem jurukunci* (royal key-keepers) occupied the top layer of the Kotagede society in terms of power and prestige (see Chapter 2). They functioned to supvervise the unkeep of the Royal Cemetery Complex and governed the territory and the people of Kotagede. There were four positions of *lurah jurukunci* (chief key-keepers), which had been hereditarily occupied by four families. The 1920 reform separated the religious and territorial aspects of the functions of the *jurukunci*, and the latter, the function of territorial administration, was now taken over by the newly formed *kalurahan* (village) officials. Despite the loss of the territorial power, however, the pre-war *jurukunci* had maintained their prestige and spiritual authority for some time on the basis of their function of the upkeep of the Royal Cemetery.

By the post-war reform, however, both the territorial *kalurahan* officials and the functional officials *(jurukunci)* suffered a heavy loss of their power and prestige. First of all, the urban *kalurahan* in Kotagede were incorporated into the City of Yogyakarta, and the *kalurahan* system itself was changed into that of *rukun kampung* (neighbourhood association). The *rukun kampung* officials received no salaries or lands to go with their office *(lungguh).* They were neither *priyayi* nor *pegawai* in terms of their source of power, but merely elected community leaders. Their status was not comparable, either. Above the neighbourhood associations, the office of *kemantren* (ward) was placed to link them with the city government. The *kemantren* office was manned by the officials of the old *priyayi* turned new civil servants, but their power was much restricted and more dependent on the city government and the cooperation of the neighbourhood association leadership. The decline in the prestige of both the *jurukunci* and the *kalurahan*/neighbourhood association leadership in the post-war times was such that no one except one person, among the descendants of the four pre-war *jurukunci* families ever occupied either of the positions. When I first moved from Yogyakarta to Kotagede I was impressed by the inconspicuousness of the *priyayi* group in the Kotagede's social scene, which made a clear contrast to the city of Yogyakarta in which old-*priyayi*-cum-new-*pegawai* still formed a distinct upper class.

In the pre-war Kotagede society, the entrepreneurial group stood outside the status system deriving from the Sultan. They were generally richer than the local *priyayi* and enjoyed certain social prestige, but they scrupulously avoided involvement in government affairs. Now in post-war Kotagede the entire entrepreneurial group was pushed down on the socio-economic scale. Yet many entrepreneurs are still wealthier than most of the *pegawai negeri*. Relative positions in prestige between the two groups are difficult to generalize. They seem to hold ambivalent attitudes mutually; the entrepreneurs fear, envy, and despise the *pegawai negeri*, and vice versa.

Craftsmen, skilled workers, unskilled workers and peddlers increased absolutely in number and relatively in proportion. Their positions in the status system were often exalted by political leaders as the real masters of society. They were also able to assert their numerical strength in votes and voices through various mass organizations during the 1950s and the Guided Democracy period. But in reality, their condition in society was not improved at all and now with the banning of those mass organizations, their collective bargaining powers vis-à-vis other segments of the local society have been significantly weakened. They were and still are the "little people" *(wong cilik)* in contrast to the "big men" *(penggedhe)*.

To sum up: in contrast to Kotagede of the 1920s and 1930s which was undoubtedly a lively, prosperous town of indigenous *dagang* (merchants), *tukang* (craftsmen) and *juragan* (entrepreneurs), Kotagede of the 1950s and 1960s became an impoverished town of numerous *buruh* (daily labourers) and *bakul* (peddlers). The change in status system blurred the boundaries between traditional status groups, and social mobility was enhanced by education. The economic stagnation to some extent levelled off the differences between various groups in terms of material well-being, but more serious was the process of general impoverishment as a result of which the vast majority of the local population must strive to survive day to day.

WHO ARE THE MUHAMMADIYAH MEMBERS?

In this section, I shall examine a number of statistical features of the Muhammadiyah membership in Kotagede. I was very fortunate to have been allowed by the Muhammadiyah branch leadership to study its official membership registration book, *Buku Daftar Anggota Muhammadiyah Cabang Kotagede Yogyakarta*. The book includes for each member such items as name, address, birth date or age, date of registration, date of withdrawal or death, level of *rukun Islam* achievement, and membership fee. In addition to the information covered by these items, I also acquired from the Muhammadiyah branch leaders additional information on the occupation and education of each member. These sources have certainly rendered extremely valuable information on the Muhammadiyah membership in Kotagede. However, for the sake of completeness, I still needed to obtain similar information on the memberships of all the "sister" and "child" organizations of what they call "Keluarga Besar Muhammadiyah" (The Grand Family of the Muhammadiyah), i.e., 'Aisyiyah (women), Nasyiatul 'Aisyiyah (young women), Pemuda Muhammadiyah (young men), Ikatan Pelajar Muhammadiyah (high school students) and Ikatan Mahasiswa Muhammadiyah (students of higher education). I was in fact unable to do so. Therefore, the following information has a marked bias in sex and age: what is represented below covers mostly adult males in the Grand Family of the Muhammadiyah while young men, adult women and young women are, to a considerable degree, under-represented.

GEOGRAPHIC DISTRIBUTION

As of February 1972, the Muhammadiyah membership book lists a total of 980 members in Kotagede. Of these, 630 members are in Kotagede *kota* (urban Kotagede) and 350 members are in Kotagede *desa* (rural Kotagede). (For this division, see Figure 2.1.) In July 1971 when the general election was held, the total number of adults in Kotagede *kota* was about 5,600. Taking the number of 630 as the most conservative representation, it is estimated that at least 11.2 per cent of the entire Kotagede *kota* adults are Muhammadiyah members. For Kotagede *desa* the percentage drops to 2.3 per cent. The contrast between urban and rural Kotagede in terms of the Muhammadiyah membership is clear. The Muhammadiyah in Kotagede is certainly a predominantly urban religious organization as elsewhere.

Within urban Kotagede, however, Muhammadiyah members are not distributed evenly throughout the area. Table 5.3 shows this unevenness. The strongest Muhammadiyah R.K. is Alun-Alun and the weakest Basen. With the exception of Kampung Joyopranan which will be mentioned below, the rank order of the relative strength of Muhammadiyah membership in these territorial units roughly correlates with such social geographic aspects as geographic centrality, population density and land use pattern. The closer a territorial unit is to the geographic centre of the town — the market, the stronger the

TABLE 5.3
Distribution of Muhammadiyah Members in Kotagede Kota

Rukun Kampung/Kalurahan	A Muhammadiyah members	B Total adults	A/B
Alun-Alun	231	1,191	19.4%
Jagalan	185	1,300(a)	14.2%
Prenggan	105	1,565	6.7%
Basen	57	923	6.2%
Purbayan	30	415	7.2%
Joyopranan	22	250(a)	8.8%
Total	630	5,644	11.2%

Note: (a) These figures are estimates from the 1971 monthly population reports.
Sources: A. Muhammadiyah Membership Registration Book.
B. 1968 Regional Census *(Rekan Susunan Kelamin Dengan Umur Dalam Kemantren Kotagede)*.

Muhammadiyah membership is. The denser the population is, the more frequently one is to find Muhammadiyah members. The more open spaces of *pekarangan* (yards with fruit trees) there are, the less the Muhammadiyah is represented. Translated into economic terms, it can be generalized that the more thoroughly the life in a *kampung* is dependent upon cash income through trading, handicraft or wage labour, the more likely it is to have more Muhammadiyah members. Politically, prior to 1965 the PKI was the strongest in R.K. Basen and the weakest in R.K. Alun-Alun. In other words, the exact reversal of the rank order of the Muhammadiyah's relative strength was that of PKI. The result of the 1971 general elections showed that the fomer PKI strongholds switched to that of Golkar, the govenment party. Joyopranan is an old, thoroughly "urban" *kampung* and strongly Islamic. But the NU's influence is reducing the Muhammadiyah's strength there.

AGE AND SEX

Information on Muhammadiyah members' age is incomplete: information on age has been obtained from less than half of the total of 630 individuals. The classification by the interval of twenty years of age as of 1971 is shown in Table 5.4.

It is clear that the Muhammadiyah is an organization of *orang tua* (parents). Members are mostly middle to old-aged, married and stable residents in Kotagede.

As to sex distribution, the data at hand show that 462 are male and 168 are female. But as mentioned above, this excludes the separate 'Aisyiyah

TABLE 5.4
Age Distribution of Muhammadiyah Members

Age	N	%
–19	3	1.0%
20–39	117	40.5%
40–59	137	47.4%
60 +	32	11.1%
Total	289	100.0%

Source: Muhammadiyah Membership Registration Book.

membership. My estimate is that there are at least another 300 female members to be added. It has been my observation that, when a public meeting of the Muhammadiyah is held, the female participants usually outnumber the males by a ratio of approximately three to two. (The male vs. female ratio of the entire Kotagede population is about 100:106.)

EDUCATION

Table 5.5 compares the terminal education of Muhammadiyah members and the entire Kotagede population. In both, dropouts are included. Even so, the percentage of 38.7 per cent — i.e., two out of five among those ten years old and over have never been to school — is the reality of public education

TABLE 5.5
Terminal Education of Muhammadiyah Members and Kotagede Adults

Level of Education	A Muhammadiyah members		B Kotagede adults[a]	
	N	%	N	%
No School	51	10.7	3,081	38.7
Elementary[b]	284	59.4	3,722	46.7
Secondary	106	22.2	1,095	13.7
Tertiary	37	7.7	75	0.9
Total	478	100.0	7,973	100.0

Notes: (a) Ten R.K. in the entire Kemantren Kotagede, 10 years old and over.
   (b) Includes religious education *(pesantren)* only.
Sources: A. Muhammadiyah Membership Registration Book.
   B. 1968 Regional Census *(Rekap Susunan Kelamin Dengan Pendidikan Dalam Kemantren Kotagede)*.

in Kotagede. In this regard, the high levels of Muhammadiyah members' education are quite remarkable. Almost 90 per cent of the members have at least an elementary education. In fact, forty-six of the fifty-one non-schooled Muhammadiyah members are women, and all men are educated at schools except those five, who make up only 1 per cent of the male membership. The Muhammadiyah scores high in terms of secondary and tertiary education,

FIGURE 5.1

Exhibition by the Publications Division of the Muhammadiyah at the Sekaten Festival of Yogyakarta, 1932.

too. Especially remarkable is the fact that it supplies almost half of the total tertiary-educated individuals in Kotagede. (Most of the other half are government officials who are not natives of Kotagede but who are living there because of government housing.)

YEAR OF MUHAMMADIYAH AFFILIATION

The years of affiliation with the Muhammadiyah are as shown in Table 5.6. The number in the pre-1945 cohort confirms interviewed information that there were about two hundred members before the War. The membership drive after the War seemed to have begun around the year 1955. It should be noted that, if broken down further, the increase in the years 1956–65 actually accrued after 1960, that is, after the ban of the Masyumi Party. It seems that the curtailment of the political activities of the reformist Muslim party did not result in their weakening socially but rather stimulated their vigour in the religious sphere. The relatively slow rate of increase after 1966, that is, after the ban of the PKI, should also be noted. A few Muhammadiyah leaders stated to me that they had been extremely careful about preventing opportunistic anti-Communists from joining the organization after 1965. The statistics seem to confirm this statement.

TABLE 5.6
Years of Affiliation with Muhammadiyah

Year	N	%	Cumulative %
Pre-1945	113	17.9	17.9
1946–1955	1	0.2	18.1
1956–1965	316	50.2	68.3
1966–(1972)	181	28.7	97.0
No information	19	3.0	100.0
Total	630	100.0	

Source: Muhammadiyah Membership Registration Book.

OCCUPATIONAL COMPOSITION

The occupational composition of Muhammadiyah members is enumerated into four large categories of (I) officials and professionals, (II) entrepreneurs, (III) craftsmen, small traders and workers, and (IV) others, and is compared with the corresponding data from the entire Kotagede population (household heads).

TABLE 5.7
Occupational Composition of Muhammadiyah Members and Household Heads in Kotagede, 1971

Category	A Muhammadiyah members		B Household heads[a]		A/B%
	N	%	N	%	
I. Officials and professionals	81	12.8	236	9.5	34.3
II. Entrepreneurs	148	23.5	184	7.4	80.4
III. Craftsmen, small traders and workers	284	45.1	1,777	71.7	16.0
IV. Others	117	18.6	281	11.4	41.6
Total	630	100.0	2,478	100.0	

Note: (a) Kotagede Kota excluding Joyopranan.
Sources: A. Muhammadiyah Membership Registration Book.
B. 1971 Census plus supplementary survey of my own.

Explanation seems appropriate for the occupational categorization employed here (and in Table 5.1). The four categories are my own secondary classification of those primary ones which are actually used in the 1971 Census as well as by Muhammadiyah leaders in reporting the occupation of its members. My secondary classification has been made in such a manner to correspond to that of van Mook for the purpose of comparison (see Table 3.1). The first category of "officials and professionals" includes *pegawai negeri* (government officials), and *pegawai swasta* (white collars in private offices). Retired officials on pension are also included here. In addition, free professionals in the Western sense, i.e., medical doctors, lawyers, university teachers are subsumed in this category. Further, school teachers, "key-keepers" of the Royal Cemetery, artists, and entertainers are covered by this category.

The second category of "entrepreneurs" consists of those individuals who are called *pengusaha* (lit., entrepreneur in Indonesian) or *juragan* (lit., masters in Javanese) and *pedagang* (lit., merchants in Indonesian) or *sudagar* (in Javanese). *Pengusaha* or *juragan* have capital and hire labour to produce commodities. *Pedagang* are wholesalers with or without shops, large shopkeepers (retailers), or well-established merchants in the central market of Yogyakarta. The itinerant trader or small shopkeepers is sometimes called *pedagang,* too, but I have placed them with the *bakul* who is included in the third category.

The third category is composed of *buruh* (workers), *bakul* (small traders, peddlers) and *tukang* (craftsmen). *Buruh* is an extremely generic term which covers various kinds of semi-skilled, non-skilled, and manual labourers. They may have fixed employers or they may not. Invariably they are paid daily wages even though the wages may be compounded weekly. In an enterprise in which the specialization of the production process is fairly well developed like a silver workshop, *buruh* are employed for simple work such as looking after the furnace, pounding silver bars, or preparing silver threads. When a *buruh* works to produce a complete commodity by himself like a *buruh jahit* (lit., sewing worker) who machine-sews children's shirts, the *buruh* may be paid by the piece.

Tukang is also a very broad term covering various kinds of specialists. To be a *tukang*, one needs a learned skill and some reputation. A *tukang's* dependency on an employer varies according to his trade, skill, need and relative wealth. He may contract with a *pengusaha* to finish a certain number of commodities at his own house on a piece-work basis. He may be hired by a *pengusaha* to do fixed wage labour in the *pengusaha's* workshop with meals. Or a *tukang* can be completely independent and self-employed as are bicycle repairmen, tailors and watchmakers.

Bakul is also a very broad category: itinerant market vendors, snack sellers on the street, flower sellers in front of the Pasaréyan, firewood sellers, etc. Their capital is extremely small and the quantity of their commodities is limited by what they can carry by themselves. In this third category I have also included extremely small shopkeepers, for example, those selling cigarettes and sweets only, and *warung* (prepared food stalls) operators.

The fourth category, "others", covers the unemployed, the "not-working" and the college students. The sick, invalid and old-aged are also included in this category.

Table 5.7 shows that Muhammadiyah members are found among (a) one out of about three household heads in the category of "officials and professionals" (KUA officials and teachers form the majority), (b) four out of five entrepreneurial household heads, and (c) one out of six *buruh, bakul*, or *tukang* household heads. It is obvious that the Muhammadiyah is still most strongly represented in the category of "entrepreneurs". However, it should also be noted that in absolute numbers the Muhammadiyah draws its largest membership from the third category.

In the leadership of the Kotagede branch of the Muhammadiyah, the individuals belonging to the first and second categories are well represented. The presiding nine-member leadership board consists of four from the category of "officials and professionals" (two Islamic college teachers, one high school teacher and one cooperative office clerk), three entrepreneurs (one garment factory owner-manager, one goldsmith workshop owner and one Yogyakarta market trader) and two from the third category (one itinerant market trader and one radio repairman). In the *kampung* sub-branch leadership, the third category has a larger proportion of leaders than at the branch leadership level. One conclusion that may be drawn from the above is that, in terms of the overall membership, the Muhammadiyah is supported by various segments of the population and is not confined to the entrepreneurial class. The Muhammadiyah seems to have lost to a great extent the domination of commercial elite which characterized its pre-war memberships. As mentioned earlier in this chapter, the change in economic environment has had a profound bearing upon the constituency of the Muhammadiyah. The Muhammadiyah is no longer an elite organization of the economically better-off. It has become an organization of the economically poverty-threatened, if not poverty-strucken, people who constitute the bulk of the town's population.

The other side of the coin of this "de-entrepreneurization" of the Muhammadiyah is the process of professionalization. In absolute number as well as in relative proportion, professionals with academic degrees in the Muhammadiyah have increased vastly over the past thirty years. Two general social factors seem to have contributed to this process. First, the elevation of the value of an academic degree in post-colonial Indonesia. Second, post-war educational reforms have made tertiary education more accessible to wider segments of the population. In this general situation, reformist Islam's emphasis on the continuous education of oneself and one's children as a religious obligation works congruently. Many Muhammadiyah parents, not only wealthy ones but also modest merchants or craftsmen, spend a disproportionately large amount of money for their children's education up to the tertiary level. By thrifty and simple living, a large proportion of business profits are saved up for their children's education. (See the story of Pak Darwin in the next section.)

The generational change from entrepreneurs to professionals is most clearly observed with the case of Bani Mukmin, "Descendants of Haji Mukmin". On the basis of the genealogical record of the Bani, *Silsilah Bani Mukmin*, the total of forty-nine children and grandchildren of Haji Mukmin have been classified into three categories of entrepreneurs, professionals and others as shown in Table 5.8.

All of the eight children of Haji Mukmin were entrepreneurs. His forty-one grandchildren are almost equally divided into entrepreneurs and professionals with nineteen individuals each: the remaining three individuals of "Others" consist of two college students and one farmer. Thus Haji Mukmin's descendants show a remarkable degree of professionalization.

TABLE 5.8
Descendants of Haji Mukmin by Occupation

Generation from Haji Mukmin	Entrepreneurs	Professionals	Others	Total
Children	8	—	—	8
Grandchildren	19	19	3	41

Source: *Silsilah Bani Mukmin* (Genealogy of Mukmin's Descendants) plus supplementary information by interview.

HARD WORK, SIMPLE LIFE, AND CHILDREN'S EDUCATION

The Muhammadiyah's emphasis on the education of the children can be well illustrated by the life history of Pak Muhammad Darwin,[3] a silversmith and a small-scale entrepreneur, as follows:

Pak Darwin was born in a southern *kampung* of Kotagede kota in 1922. His father was a regular attendant at Kyai Haji Amir's religious lectures. Young Darwin entered the Muhammadiyah primary school in Kotagede, and in 1937 when he reached the fifth grade he started to work part-time every afternoon after school as an apprentice at Haji Mudzakkir's silver workshop, earning 5 *sen* or rice equivalent of 1 *kati*, 0.6 kilograms a day. After leaving school at the sixth grade, he worked full-time as a *buruh perak* (silver worker) at the same enterprise with the starting daily wage of 1 *ketip* (1 dime) or rice equivalent of 1.5 kilograms. He continued this, acquiring skills and experience as a *tukang perak* (silver craftsman), until 1942 when the Japanese came.

In 1944, he volunteered to the Heiho, Auxiliary Forces, of the Japanese Occupation Army and after the war, joined the new Republican Army fighting a number of battles until 1948. In 1949, he returned to Kotagede, got married and started a modest silver enterprise of his own with two workers. In 1953, he joined the KP3J, the Production Cooperative of Silverwork Enterprises of Jogjakarta. The silverwork industry then was recovering significantly, and the quota from the Cooperative as well as orders from retail shops in Yogyakarta were constantly coming in. The period between 1950 and 1955 was a period of gradual expansion of Pak Darwin's enterprise which was employing seven workers in 1955. However, from around 1960 on, the situation reversed.

---

3. "Pak" is a short for "Bapak" (lit., Father), an honorific term for a married man.

FIGURE 5.2

K.H. Pringgo Hastono (b. 1884), retired *penghulu* (chief religious official) of Kotagede Surakarta.

FIGURE 5.3

Muhammadiyah leaders in Kotagede (from left: Pak M. Jamhari, Pak Boshori Anwar and Pak M. Chirzin).

FIGURE 5.4

Pak Mudjono, Parmusi (Indonesian Muslim Party) politician in Kotagede.

FIGURE 5.5

Nizar Chirzin, Muhammadiyah youth leader.

The quota from the Cooperative became irregular and unreliable, the general market situation deteriorated with the tremendous inflation. Pak Darwin's enterprise was reduced in size employing only three workers on the average since then. The present situation (1972) is still depressed. Pak Darwin can hire only two workers now, one regular semi-skilled worker *(buruh)* for general work receiving Rp150 daily and the other, a skilled engraver *(tukang natah)*, earning by the piece at an average of Rp200 a day.

Pak Darwin gets orders from three sources: first, from the retail shops in Yogyakarta with which he has long business relations; second, from the Cooperative (nowadays it becomes active only when a large quantity of orders come from the Presidential Palace for souvenirs of state visits); third, from one of the two largest silver enterprises in Kotagede, which often needs the cooperation of smaller enterprises like Pak Darwin's to process a bulk order in a limited time. For routine business profits, Pak Darwin relies mostly on the first type of orders, but the latter two can also yield considerable amounts of extraordinary business gains. In all cases Pak Darwin does not have to purchase the material, i.e., silver bars, for the customers provide them. Pak Darwin gets paid for the workmanship alone when the complete products are delivered to the customers. He also manufactures ready-made products using the silver alloy of lower quality which does not require a large amount of capital.

The net monthly profit of Pak Darwin rarely exceeds Rp10,000 when the wages and other necessary expenses for production are paid. The profit from this small silver enterprise of Pak Darwin all goes to the maintenance of his household. His wife, Bu Darwin,[4] also makes her own contribution to the household economy from her peddling of batik in the market of Bantul, Kabupaten capital, about 20 kilometres southwest of Kotagede. She goes there by bicycle almost everyday and always on the market day which comes in five-day cycles. The joint income of Pak and Bu Darwin amounts to somewhere between Rp15,000 and Rp20,000, a month. They have five children — the eldest is 22 years old and the youngest, 10 years old.

Pak Darwin's is a typical ordinary Muhammadiyah family. He himself says, "I am an ordinary member *(anggota biasa),*" and he has never been in a leadership position even in his *kampung*. He and his family strictly observe daily prayers, Friday prayers, and fasting. Pak and Bu Darwin also contribute *zakat fitrah* as well as *korban* annually. Bu Darwin is also a graduate of the

---

4. "Bu" is a short for "Ibu" (lit., Mother), an honorific term for a married woman.

Muhammadiyah primary school in Kotagede, and is a member of the 'Aisyiyah. Pak Darwin's education policy was to send boys to government schools for professional training up to the tertiary level while girls to the Muhammadiyah and other Islamic schools for religious education. So, his two sons were sent to government schools from elementary level to higher education. The eldest son entered the Medical School of Gadjah Mada University and the younger one to the Faculty of Social and Political Sciences of the same university. His daughters started off with a neighbourhood elementary school run by government but then switched to the Muhammadiyah and other Islamic schools for further education.[5]

The Darwin family are living in a modest house of their own constructed in the mid-1950s. They are living simply, clothed neatly, and look healthy. What struck me as a great puzzle was the question of how Pak and Bu Darwin could afford to send all their children to school with that limited amount of income. The official tuition and fees of the University cost annually Rp15,000 for the Faculty of Social and Political Sciences and more than Rp30,000 for the Medical School. The school expenses for their three daughters may not be so large. But Pak and Bu Darwin must save up at least Rp50,000 a year for their children's education. When this is compared to a possible income of Rp240,000 a year for the couple, it is clear that they are spending an extremely large portion, more than one fifth, of their income for the education of their children. Pak and Bu Darwin are prepared to send all the rest of their children up to university level. The older children sometimes bring

---

5. His eldest son became a medical doctor and the younger one, after obtaining an overseas PhD, a professor at his alma mater. The eldest of his three daughters became a qualified nurse, after going through government and Muhammadiyah elementary schools, Ma'had Islamy and PIRI (Ahmadiyah school) for secondary, and then a nurse training school run by Hospital Bethesda. His second daughter also started off with a neighbourhood government elementary school but switched to the Muhammadiyah one in Bodon. She then entered Ma'had Islamy and went to Teachers Training College (IKIP) Muhammadiyah, Yogyakarta. She further pursued postgraduate studies (S1 and S2) at Gadjah Mada University's Faculty of Philosophy and became a lecturer at the same faculty. The third daughter went to a neighbourhood government school and Muhammadiyah elementary school at Bodon, and the Muhammadiyah Junior High in Kotagede and then to PIRI's senior high but stopped there. All in all, four out of five children of Pak and Bu Darwin became professionals through education. (Interview with Prof. Dr Muhadjir Darwin on 2 June 2011 and additional information via personal communication with him.)

home irregular incomes of their own. But still, it is obvious that the burden of the education of their children is mostly carried by Pak and Bu Darwin, and they are proudly doing so.

Pak and Bu Darwin are not exceptional. There are a number of similar hardworking fathers and mothers in Kotagede who are sending their children to schools and universities out of their modest incomes. There are altogether about one hundred university and academy students in Kotagede *kota* now. This is quite a disproportionately large number for a small town like Kotagede. The majority of their parents are Muhammadiyah members, and most of the students themselves are active in Pemuda Muhammadiyah (young men), Nasyiatul 'Aisyiyah (young women), or an independent Islamic youth organization like Pelajar Islam Indonesia (PII, or Indonesian Islamic Students), or Himpunan Mahasiswa Islam (HMI, Islamic Students Association).

Muhammadiyah parents' dedication to the education of children is difficult to be explained solely in terms of rational calculation of present frugality and investment for future gains when the children finish university. For it has been generally hard for university graduates to find appropriate jobs. There are many cases of unemployed and underemployed university graduates in Kotagede. "B.A." as *belum apa-apa*, meaning "not yet anything", and "M.A." for *masih ada di rumah*, meaning "still staying home" are standard jokes referring to the plight of many unemployed degree-holders. Muhammadiyah parents' behaviour should be understood in religious terms as well. The Muhammadiyah teaching exhorts the continuous pursuit of knowledge as a God-given obligation of the faithful. The very action of saving up from the daily income in order to provide education for the children is viewed as a fulfillment of this obligation. What matters for the faithful is not so much the possible future gain resulting from the present action but the religious significance of their present action itself.

This seemingly "secular" action of spending a large amount of money for the education of children is, therefore, an integral part of the religiosity of the faithful. Other sociological factors, such as the democratization of the Indonesian educational system and the heightened prestige of degree-holders, certainly have facilitated and induced their religiosity to be materialized in the field of education. But what seems more essential than these circumstantial factors is the religious factor.

I was very much impressed by the significance of the religious factor, not so much as a marker of social grouping like the Geertzian *abangan-santri-priyayi* trichotomy, but rather as a matter of self-identification and self-evaluation and as the ultimate point of reference for the individual's action. When I had a conversation with Haji Masjhudi a few months prior to his death, I outlined for him the Western (American) understanding of the Javanese religious situation *à la* Geertz and asked for his comments. The following is his answer:

> Yes, the understanding is all right *(pengertian itu baik)* but it is already a past *(sudah dulu-dulunya)*. Formerly there were the separate groups *(golongan)* of *abangan, santri* and *priyayi*. Their ways of life *(cara hidup)* were different from each other. *Priyayi*, called *amat dalem* here, were ordered by the kraton to guard *(jaga)* the Pasaréyan, received salary land *(tanah gaji)* and the people, and governed *(menguasai)* this place *(daerah ini)*. *Santri* prayed in the Mosque, officiated marriages, registered divorces, and when people died, called in for funeral. *Abangan* was the rest of people, the "little people" *(wong cilik)*. They were under *priyayi*. When ordered to pray *(sembahyang)*, they just prayed. When ordered to contribute labour *(kasih tenaga)*, they just offered it. In return, they were given meals and prize money *(wang hadiyah)*. The three groups were separate *(terpisah)* and differences were obvious. But recently, after the salary land of *amat dalem* was abolished, the differences started to disappear. *Priyayi* no longer behaved like *priyayi (mriyayi)*. If a *priyayi* has no salary land, or no people under him, what is the use of behaving like *priyayi*? It is more so when he has no official status *(pangkat)* or wealth. The same is true with *santri*. Nowadays many people pray like *santri*. Marriage and death are taken care of by KUA (Religious Affairs Office). So there is no longer a particular group of *santri*. The same with the little people, *abangan*. If well educated, even an *abangan* can get an official position *(pangkat)*. He can even have much more religious knowledge *(ilmu agama)* than an old-fashioned *santri (santri kolot)*. So the former differences have disappeared. Nowadays anybody can become any kind of person *(siapa-siapa bisa menjadi apa-apa saja)*. The main point is how one behaves; like *priyayi (berpriyayi)*, like *santri (bersantri)* or like *abangan (berabangan)*. It is *ber, ber, ber* ("doings") that makes the difference. The important difference today is if one is a bit progressed *(sedikit maju)* or still left behind *(masih ketinggalan)*, especially in the field of religious consciousness *(kesadaran agama)*. It is true that there are those who are a little wealthier than others and those who are a little poorer than others: or a little higher or lower in position *(pangkat)*. But the differences are not so large as the past. The essential thing *(pokoknya)* is if one is already deep *(dalam)* in one's faith *(keimanan)* and performs religious obligations *(beribadat)*.

The statement by Haji Masjhudi points up the fact that it is getting increasingly difficult to locate the Muhammadiyah members in society in socio-economic terms. It is less meaningful now to regard the Muhammadiyah movement as an expression of socio-economic interests of a certain group or a segment of the population.

If we are to look at the Muhammadiyah, it seems more meaningful to do so in the context of the general economic impoverishment already mentioned above. And in coping with daily subsistence amidst poverty, there seem to operate two distinctive ways in which religious factors come in to distinguish them. These two alternative strategies for subsistence and survival are also contrasting in their mutually distinctive social ethics and patterns of interpersonal relationships. They are both available and accessible as simultaneously existing choices of action for the people in Kotagede.

One strategy is to find a powerful and wealthy patron and obtain his total protection as a loyal client. This is basically an *abangan* alternative and still a dominant pattern in Kotagede. The other alternative is to strive to maintain one's economic independence as much as possible by avoiding deeper involvement with others and by keeping one's economic activity within the range of one's immediate control. The second alternative is a *santri* minority pattern, yet followed by a significantly large number of people in Kotagede.

The *abangan* pattern is characterized by the mutual asymmetrical dependence of individuals. When the Communist Party was alive, this pattern seems to have had much egalitarian emphasis in the form of cooperatives or trade unions: the economically less privileged organized themselves, and exerted group pressures on the relatively wealthy in order to secure a favourable distribution of economic benefits. With the disappearance of the PK1 and its mass organizations, the poor have apparently lost such bargaining powers. They have now to secure patronage of the wealthy on an individual and personal basis. Expressing personal loyalty in the form of diffused services, a poor individual attaches himself to a relatively wealthy patron for protection and assurance of continuous income to survive. A most extreme case of this clientship is found in the form of the household servant, who is completely servile to the patron and is given food, clothing and shelter at the level of minimal necessity. In such a case, monetary reward for the services of a servant is almost negligible and in fact is given not as a wage but as an allowance.

A more generally asymmetrical patron-client pattern underlies relationships between the local government officials and their apprentice-assistants *(magang)*, between the workshop owner-managers and their hired daily labourers, between the entrepreneurs and dependent craftsmen or between the wholesalers and their clientele, i.e., small peddlers. The relationships are coated with the emotion of pity *(kasihan)* and the sense of the moral duty to help the poor on the part of the relatively wealthy job-givers and the feeling of appreciation for the patron's personal favour and the personal loyalty on the part of the job-receivers. The practices of advancement of wages for daily labourers, advancement of credits in the form of commodities for the small peddlers, and advanced payment with orders for craftsmen are concomitant with thsse patron-client relationships. The patron is expected to show care and extend his favour for such personal matters of the client and his family members as birth, circumcision, weddings, funerals, schooling, and sickness. In return the client and his family members' services are always made available to the patron.

The *abangan* ethic is congruent with this patron-client pattern, for the aspect of superordination and subordination is often coated with and embedded in ritual interactions of gift exchanges, communal feasts, paternalistic care of the patron for the client and obedience of the latter to the former. Especially interesting to note is the fact that many of these *abangan* patrons are practitioners of mystical cults. These patrons engage in various traditional mystical practices: meditation in the *kramat* places, occasional fasting, and intaking of special herbs — supposedly accumulating mystical powers in their persons. Wealth, number of clients, personal appearance and virility in the number of wives are regarded to be the measure of a patron's potency in mystical powers. The *abangan* client tries to attach himself to a patron of high potency who is supposedly able to protect him effectively and secure him livelihood.

REZEKI: "LUCK" OR "LIVELIHOOD"?

The Muhammadiyah ethic concerning the way of making livelihood and forming interpersonal relationships is contrasting to the *abangan* counterpart. Basic to the Muhammadiyah's ethic concerning livelihood is the notion of *rezeki*. Like many other value terms in Javanese as we shall see more in the next chapter, this one has ambiguity. *Rezeki* on the one hand means "luck" or "gains by chance" — gains which were not expected nor earned through one's labour. In Indonesian the term is often used in this sense, and its meaning is almost the same as another Indonesian word *untung* ("luck", "fortune". See Echols and Shaddily 1963, p. 423). On the other hand, *rezeki* in Javanese means "livelihood" and more specifically "daily necessities" (rice and food in general). This meaning seems more "original" than the above-mentioned one etymologically (see Pigeaud 1938, p. 490). In the latter sense, *rezeki* is almost synonymous with *nafkah* in Indonesian ("subsistence" in Echols and Shaddily 1963, p. 253).

The Muhammadiyah seems to de-emphasize the first meaning of *rezeki*, "luck" or "fortune", and expound the connotation of the second, "daily necessities". It propagates that if a Muslim is really sincere in belief in God, performs ritual obligations properly, regulates social conduct according to the command of God (Syariah), then he or she is assured of *rezeki* (livelihood) by Him. The All-Mighty, All-Merciful, and All-Compassionate will unfailingly give *rezeki* to all His faithful followers. So the faithful need not and must not worry about securing *rezeki*. It will surely come.

The significance of the Muhammadiyah concept of *rezeki* is manifold, but here I mention three impotant aspects, most often observed in the usage of the term. First is that by taking the matter of everyday life as that of God's grace, the mundane matter of "bread-earning" has come to be regarded as a matter of religious faith. In other words, to work to earn money and to spend it to live is a matter in which the same religious devotion is required as in the performance of "purely" religious obligations. The Muhammadiyah preaches an extremely "totalistic" doctrine and I take it not as exceptional but logically consistent with other aspects of the reformist tenet.

The second aspect is that when the Muhammadiyah's notion of *rezeki* is applied to actual economic conduct, it works from the outset to reject what seems to be excessive gains: it is not that to gain profits by whatever means and then to donate the surpluses to religious causes, but that to limit from the beginning the target of gains to the amount appropriate for modest spendings. In other words, the goal of economic activities is to maintain one's subsistence. The simple subsistence level of life is taken to be the proper level of life for the truly faithful.

A third aspect of *rezeki* in Muhammadiyah teaching is that it entails a sort of individualism in economic activities. Each individual is taken as the agent of faith and devotion and the object of God's judgement. The individual's ultimate salvation is solely dependent upon one's own deeds. And one's deeds include economic conduct. One cannot and must not share responsibilities with others in economic activities, and one cannot and must not alienate from others the result of one's economic conduct. Hence an extreme kind of individualsm in economic conduct quite opposite to any degree of corporateness.[6]

Muhammadiyah members' economic conduct is affected by a conviction that this-worldly matters such as wealth, prestige and status are only

---

6. James Siegel has made critical comments on Geertz's assumption that reformist Islam may work for the development of corporate type of economic organizations from atomistic market traders (Siegel 1969, p. 200n). Siegel attributes the lack of corporateness in Acehnese economic activities to the Islamic notion of *akal* (see ibid., pp. 242–50, especially 245).

temporary and essentially irrelevant to the ultimate salvation of individuals in the afterlife. To maintain a decent life in this world, only a minimum of daily necessities is required and the ultimate salvation is conditional upon the deeds of individuals in this world. One's deeds must follow the Muslim obligatory prescriptions, and, furthermore, one is advised to meet various ethical admonitions recommended in the Holy Scriptures. The agent of faith and devotional action is the individual for he is the object of divine salvation.

On the basis of these notions Muhammadiyah members try to avoid economic or any other kind of dependency on others. In economic interactions this is explicitly evidenced. A Muhammadiyah wage-labourer is likely to request his employer that rights and obligations, wages and fringe benefits, and other conditions be spelled out in specific terms, for he is rendering his labour to the employer under certain terms but not his person. Muhammadiyah traders prefer short-term cash transactions to prolonged debtor-creditor relationships. Muhammadiyah entrepreneurs rarely expand their business enterprise indefinitely but often attempt to split it up into smaller independent units and keep the size of the unit manageable under personal control. In forming business partnerships or employer-employee relationships, the most valued criterion is one's religiosity which is regarded as the surest measurement of the trustworthiness of the other party.

With the emphasis on *rezeki* as a key notion for its economic ethics the Muhammadiyah encourages independence and self-sufficiency and provides a moral principle not to surrender to the socio-economic pressures threatening to engulf Muslims. Here seems to lie an answer to the question of why more people are getting religiously pious in spite of the increasing general impoverishment. Also it is to be sought here an answer to the question: why Muhammadiyah Muslims are not desperate but rather self-confident in the face of poor material conditions of their lives.

The *abangan* life style is relaxed, nonchalant, and unpredictable, for one's fate is trusted to the patron. The *santri* life style is regulated by self-discipline and long-term plans. Yet the *abangan* and *santri* differentiation does not necessarily create mutually exclusive social groupings. Both are patterns of behaviour found side by side in the same residential unit, workshop, office, market, informal and formal social and economic associations (e.g., credit associations, cooperatives, neighbourhood associations). Even within a single individual, the two orientations may exist side by side and alternate from time to time. The two orientations are alternative ways of action always at hand. The fact that the Muhammadiyah is growing steadily means that increasingly a large number of individuals are more frequently abandoning the *abangan* pattern of interpersonal relationships and ethic and choosing the alternative pattern propagated by the Muhammadiyah.

UMMAT ISLAM

The action-aspect of the Muhammadiyah discussed in the previous section leads us to the re-examination of the concept of *ummat Islam*.

First of all, if we take the term to mean the totality of individuals who are professed to the religion of Islam, 99 per cent of the Kotagede population may be covered by the term. However, as a sociological entity, this totality of individuals does not have much significance. It does not have a marked boundary other than the one vaguely territorial. It lacks internal cohesion. There are no organizational devices to create and maintain even a measure of cohesion and solidarity. In fact, it is not social organizational reality at all. In this case, the notion of ummat Islam is a postulate rather than a reality.

If we take the criterion of self-consciousness and self-identification, then *ummat Islam* shall be reduced to the size almost identical with the Muhammadiyah membership and its followers. Here again we come to confront peculiarities of the Muhammadiyah which do not conform to the notion of a "religious community", or even that of a "sect" in the Western sense. It is not an equivalent of the Church or a congregation, either. It does not receive any particular ontological justification for itself from Islamic theology other than that it is an organization of the pious. There are no differentiations of roles between the ecclesiastical order and that of laymen in Islam. The leadership of the Muhammadiyah is literally a group of functionaries (*pengurus*, "those who manage", *urus* = to manage), and it does not claim any religious superiority of authority vis-à-vis the rest of the membership. Neither are there any institutional devices for internal discipline other than the self-discipline of individual members.

As to the relationship between the Muhammadiyah and the larger population of "99 per cent Muslims", again there are no institutional devices that enable the former to claim to be representative or the leadership of the latter even in the purely religious sphere. Nor can the Muhammadiyah impose its version of Islam onto others through institutionalized sanctions. After having destroyed the institutionalized Islam of traditional Javanese version, the Muhammadiyah has created nothing whatsoever to replace it other than the "movement", directly appealing to personal conviction and conduct. The Muhammadiyah is thus in every aspect a voluntary association *par excellence*.

The Sociology of Ummat Islam

Ummat Islam is not a sociological entity in the ordinary social structural sense. It is created and experienced momentarily here and now through the ritual action of the faithful. It may be understood as an "anti-structure" in Victor Turner's sense, and the mode of ritual action and the relationship of individuals in the ritual context are characterized by 'liminality' and "communitas" (Turner 1969 and 1972).

One of the fundamental ritual actions for the Muslims is *sholat*, ritual prayer. Muslims must perform *sholat* five times a day, individually or in group, of which the Friday noon prayer must be performed in group in a mosque. In addition, on the mornings of the two Muslims annual festivals of Hari Raya Idul Fitri and Hari Raya Idul Adha, a festive prayer, *sholat ied* is performed in an open field. The performance of festive prayer in the open field has been a distinctive reformist ritual innovation. (Of course, from the reformist viewpoint it is not an "innovation" but a restoration of an Islamic tradition.) The festive prayer forms an essential part of the Muhammadiyah rituals. A brief description of a festive prayer I observed in Kotagede on the morning of Hari Raya Idul Fitri, the First of Syawal, 1391 AH (19 November 1971 AD), is as follows:

FIGURE 5.6

Takbiran on the last night of Ramadhan.

FIGURE 5.7

Girls gathered for *takbiran*.

FIGURE 5.8

Collection of *zakat fitrah* (religious tax) in rice on the eve of Idul Fitri.

FIGURE 5.9

Distribution of *zakat fitrah* on the eve of Idul Fitri.

FIGURE 5.10

Procession to *sholat ied* (festive prayer) on Idul Adha.

FIGURE 5.11

Men and boys in *sholat ied* (festive prayer) on Idul Adha.

FIGURE 5.12

Women and girls at *sholat ied* (festive prayer) on Idul Adha.

FIGURE 5.13

Khutbah (sermon) at *sholat ied* (festive prayer) on Idul Adha (Drs. Nur Bari as *khotib*, Pak M. Chirzin as *imam*).

FIGURE 5.14

Korban (sacrificial animals) led to the slaughter on Idul Adha.

FIGURE 5.15

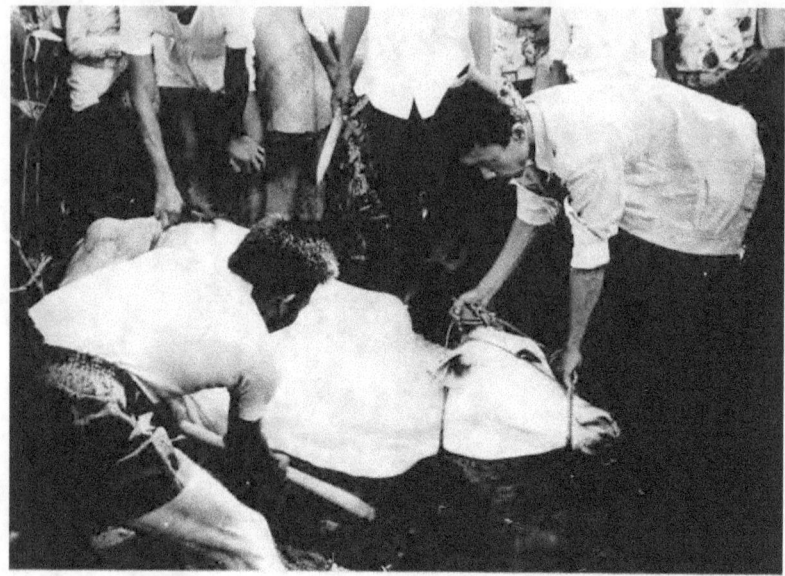

Cow being sacrificed.

FIGURE 5.16

Goat being sacrificed.

FIGURE 5.17

Slaughtered animals taken for distribution of meat.

Prior to participating in the festive prayer, each participant performs the ablution in a prescribed manner at home and thereby cleanses all the dirt of mundane world from his or her body. Clad in washed-clean or new clothing, the participants gather at a crossroad or the yard of a *langgar* (prayer house) of their own *kampung* reciting "Allahu Akbar" ("God is the Greatest") in low voice. Men and women form separate groups in a row and start a procession to the open field where the festive prayer is going to be held. Small streams of the participants from narrow *kampung* alleys meet and join on the main road and eventually form a single column of a mile-long procession. An extensive vegetable field *(tegalan)* located about two kilometres northwest of the centre of the town has been used for the festive prayers. Now the vegetables are all removed and weeds cleared, the place is simply an open flat field without any hindrances. Rope lines are laid at a regular interval to indicate the rows to sit facing in the exact direction of Mecca. No decorations are provided except for the two flags, one, the red and white flag of the Republic of Indonesia, and the other, the green flag of the Muhammadiyah, both on bamboo posts.

A podium, *minbar*, is located in front but it is not used for the performance of the festive prayer but for the sermon, *khutbah*, to be given after the prayer. An amplifier system is provided, and a microphone is placed in front of the seat of the *imam*, the leader of prayer.

To this open field, now the participants approach in a long procession with the Muhammadiyah Youth's drum band at the head. The participants are chanting "Allahu Akbar" loudly in melody, repeatedly in unison, with solemn expressions. Upon entering the open field, men and boys sit in the order of arrival in the front half of the field, and women and girls, their entire bodies covered by white clothes except their faces, in the back half of the field still chanting "Allahu Akbar".

The prayer itself begins with the *imam's* (prayer leader) reciting "Allahu Akbar" seven times in a rapid pitch without melodization. Then the entire participants start the morning ritual prayer with the recitation of the first chapter of the Qur'an, Surat Al-Fatihah, with the accompanying prescribed body movements (the basic sequence of the ritual prayer, *raka'at*, on this occasion was not different from the one finely described by James Siegel (1969, pp. 110–13)). The *imam* sets the pace of the prayer through the loudspeaker and the participants more or less follow it. The ritual prayer is fundamentally an individual action, and everybody has to perform it as accurately as possible. So some go slower than the rest, and others, faster. Especially those who are late to arrive in the field go through the entire prayer sequence at their own pace even when the rest are far ahead. The ritual prayer itself is brief and it does not take more than five minutes to complete, and it ends with the Muslim greeting, *Assalamu'alaikum warahmatullahi wabarakatuh* (May God give you peace, His mercy and His blessing), given to one's neighbours on the right and the left. Now the participants are visibly relaxed, and the women and girls take off their white covers, suddenly revealing their colourful and festive dresses worn underneath. Then the sermon is given in Javanese for about twenty minutes by a sermon giver *(khotib)* different from the *imam*. After the sermon, an announcement is made by a Muhammadiyah functionary on the results of the *zakat fitrah* and the like. The festive prayer meeting is now over, and the participants return to their *kampung* again in procession but this time with the drum band at the end. The participants chant repeatedly "Allahu Akbar" as before, but this time in an openly cheerful mood. The procession gradually dissolves itself when its units come to their own *kampung* entrances on the main road. In this particular festive prayer meeting, it seemed that about 6,000 people participated. (There were several other smaller festive prayer meetings held for the outlying *kampungs* of Kotagede.)

The entire ritual sequence may be recapitulated as follows: first, the act of ablution sets the motion of the ritual and physical separation of the participants from the mundane world. The prayer meeting was held in an outside place where no decorations were found and utter simplicity prevailed. In this liminal state, the relationships between the participants were least structured. All social differences in terms of status and positons were ignored. The participants were seated without reflecting social hierarchies at all, which was quite a contrast to other ceremonial occasions where the seating pattern was rigidly hierarchical. The internal differentiation of the ritual roles was minimal — the *imam* being the leader of the prayer and the rest undifferentiated. The distinction of the sexes was made, but sexuality, especially that of the females, was ritually negated by the white covers. The recitation of the formula "Allahu Akbar" induced the state of *ikhlas*, sincere devotion. Other emotions than that of devotion to God were minimized, and the participants prepared themselves for encounter with God. It was an encounter of the individuals with God in the purest and simplest manner. The utmost formality of the prayer erased all individual peculiarities from social contingencies. The participants meet God as His creatures without other attributes, and they meet each other in the ritual context as fellow creatures by Him. The ritual reality thus created was that of *haram*, or inviolability.[7] The procession back to the *kampung* is the process of re-aggregation to society, to which they return with heightened religiousity and festivity.

Sholat ied, the festive prayer, is the largest ritual ocassion in which a majority of Kotagede Muslim population participates, but on a smaller scale many of them perform essentially similar prayers daily. The daily ritual prayers also create the state of inviolability at intervals within a day. The ritual state

---

7. "In *salat [sholat]* ... he [the Muslim] is transformed into a state of inviolability or *haram*. He has left behind him the temporal world with its uncertainties, ambiguities, doubts and vexations. He is before Allah in a formal manner and his presence is sanctified ..." (Majul 1974, p. 16). The common understanding of the concept of *haram* by outsiders is that of Muslim taboos such as the prohibition of eating pork. However, besides this negative aspect, *haram* has a positive meaning, the state of divine consecration. I somehow became aware of the difference of understanding of the concept between Muslim-believers and non-Muslim observers through my field experience, but it was Dr C. A. Majul, a renowned Muslim and Islamologist of the Philippines, who personally enlightened me on this matter. Hereby I acknowledge his help.

reminds the faithful of an ideal state which they must endeavour to attain in the mundane environment. *Ummat Islam*, "community of Muslims", is thus temporarily but directly created and experienced through the ritual action by the faithful every day. As a different order of reality, or as an "anti-structure" in Victor Turner's sense, it presents itself as the ultimate point of reference for the faithful. *Ummat Islam* may also be regarded as a "reference group", whose point of reference is God, rather than as an actual social grouping.

6

THE IDEOLOGY OF THE MUHAMMADIYAH
Tradition and Transformation

> So, to get along well with your neighbour, the way must be proper. When the neighbour just drops in to chat with you *(omong-omongan)*, just welcome him and chat. If he doesn't pray yet, that's all right. You should not make a fool of him *(aja ngolok-olok)*. You should not tease him irritatingly *(aja ngece-ece)*. If he falls sick, then just go and see *(tuwéni)*; if in need, go and help; if down with a cold, go and give a coin-massage *(keroki)*. Well, it is up to you how you actually do your help. But that is what is called *sasrawungan ingkang saé* (harmonious way of social intercourse). 'Aisyiyah people, Muhammadiyah people, must be able to do this. (Speech by Bapak A.R. Fakhruddin, President of Muhammadiyah, 28 November 1971, Kotagede).

RELIGIOUS COMMUNICATIONS AMONG JAVANESE MUSLIMS

In the preceding chapters I have attempted to make two major points. The first, a historical point, has been that the Muhammadiyah movement must be regarded as a development from within Javanese society rather than as a ready-made import from without. The second, a more contemporary and sociological point, has been that the social basis of the Muhammadiyah movement has become greatly widened and it is no longer confined to a small segment of society like the urban bourgeoisie. In this chapter I shall examine critically another aspect of the conventional view that reformist Islam, including the Muhammadiyah, is fundamentally alien to Javanese or non-Javanese, in cultural terms (e.g., Benda 1965, p. 133; Geertz 1968, p. 16). I shall argue that reformist Islam is not antithetical to Javanese culture but an integral part of it, and what reformists have been endeavouring is, so to speak, to distil a pure essence of Islam from Javanese cultural traditions. The final product of distillation does retain a Javanese flavour, just as any highly pure liquors cannot lose their local flavours. But the universalistic essence of Islam is more fundamental, and it should be appreciated as it is first and foremost.

When I first arrived in Kotagede, I had, as mentioned earlier in the Preface, a very low regard of the significance of Islam for the Javanese lives. My pre-field readings of Western literature on Indonesia had made me think that the Islamic phase of modern Indonesian history had long gone, perhaps for good, with the decline of the Sarekat Islam as a mass organization in the early 1920s. I had accepted Wertheim's idea that the Islamic mass upheavals of the 1910s and 1920s were basically the expression of a "pre-nationalism" and, with the increasing socio-economic differentiation of the population and the development of more explicitly nationalistic and revolutionary political movements, Islam rather took on a conservative character:

> It [modern Islam] gradually lost its lively optimism and was forced on to the defensive. A certain rigidity was the outcome. A mature bourgeois Islam arrived too late on the scene to be what Protestantism had been for centuries: the bearer of new ideas and a fructifying influence on civilization. No sooner had a bourgeois Islam come into existence than the conditions permitting it to exert a regenerating influence on society disappeared. It soon lost its élan and became conservative (Wertheim 1959, pp. 217–18).

So when I first experienced the prevailing Islamic religiosity in the Kotagede society, I was rather shocked by the strength of "historical residues" and the "backwardness" of the town in that regard. I also suspected that the political climate of the New Order must have something to do with the situation in which so many "religious reactionaries" were kept active there.

As to the modern history of Islam in general, my pre-field knowledge had been extremely limited, and I had been quite happy to go along with Clifford Geertz in regarding modern Islam as a misfired reformation:

> Stepping backward in order better to leap is an established principle in cultural change; our own Reformation was made that way. But in the Islamic

case the stepping backward seems often to have been taken for the leap itself, and what began as a rediscovery of the scriptures ended as a kind of deification of them... Islam, in this way, becomes a justification for modernity, without itself actually becoming modern (Geertz 1968, p. 69).

Therefore when I first saw Muhammadiyah schools and clinics and heard what its *muballigh* (propagandists) were preaching, I just found in them a whole lot of pseudo-modernity, second-rate imitations of Western culture, and unimaginative Arab-Javanized replications of already familiar themes in Protestantism. To me, the contemporary religiosity in Kotagede seemed nothing but an inertia of a historical religion or its transitional phase on the way to a more complete secularization. The contents of local religious communications sounded like they were stuffed with repeated quotations of stereotyped apologistic expressions in bluffing solemnities and formalities.

Nevertheless, in the course of time, I came to feel that there was something meaningful in these communications than cliches and formalities. My increasing language ability to comprehend them helped (although I could not achieve any more than passive fluency in Javanese after all). It was, however, not that I was of able to grasp the "logic" of what was being talked about. Nor was it that I developed a comprehensive theoretical framework to analyse and explain the forms and contents of these religious communications. It was simply that what was being talked about began to make sense in the context of my daily experiences there. My everyday observations were rendered meaningful when interpreted in religious terms employed by the local people.

In fact, during the first half of my stay in Kotagede I did not do any systematic data collection on religious communications. They just naturally flowed into my fieldwork as part of my general encounter with the local people. Most of the contents of these religious communications were addressed directly to various existential problems the townpeople were facing. It was only in the later period of my stay that I started to attend religious meetings more regularly, interviewed Muhammadiyah leaders, and solicited their life histories. Toward the end of my fieldwork, I finally came to realize how rich, vivid and to the point these religious communications were and how immensely fascinating and interesting cultural idioms and religious expressions used in them were.

Benedict Anderson has once made a contrast between the spontaneous, direct, informal, spoken or "Ngoko" type of speech and the organized, formal, often printed, indirect or "Krama" type of speech in Indonesian political communications, and has emphasized the necessity of studying the former to get a deeper understanding of Indonesian political life (Anderson 1966, pp. 89–116). In my view a similar case can be made with the study of religious communications. What I shall attempt in the following is an ethnography of the "Ngoko" mode of religious communications among Javanese Muslims.

The following part consists of several sections in each of which a pair of contrasting vernacular terms are presented and discussed. These pairs are: (a) *gadho-gadho* vs. "true Muslim", (b) *lahir* vs. *batin*, (c) *kasar* vs. *alus*, (d) *hawa nafsu* vs. *ikhlas*. One side of each of these pairs represents the "traditional" aspect of Javanese Islam while the other, the reformist aspect expounded by the Muhammadiyah. The point that the reformist Islam is a transformation of traditional Islam shall be made by discussing the relationship between the two sides of these pairs. I shall also discuss the significance of the Javanese language as the medium of religious communication.

GADHO-GADHO VS. TRUE MUSLIM

The consciousness which Muhammadiyah *muballigh* (propagandists) are trying to instil among their local audience is that traditional Islam is confused and imperfect. One of the most frequently used metaphors to illustrate this perception is *gadho-gadho*, Javanese vegetable salad. Let me quote from the text of a sermon *(khutbah)* which a Muhammadiyah leader acting as sermon giver *(khotib)* gave to a Friday prayer meeting held in the Great Mosque of Kotagede. (This particular *khutbah* was given in Indonesian.)

> Honorable Participants of the Friday Meeting! The Great Prophet Muhammad passed away from this world more than 1,300 years ago. His teachings in the form of the Qur'an and the Hadith are as old [as that many years]. In these hundreds of years, the call and echo of his teachings have left deep impressions and have been felt in many personalities and many good deeds since then. However, it is also true that sometimes they have been only dimly felt and often remained only in name so that deeds of the [Muslim] community have come to take the appearance of *gadho-gadho* [Javanese vegetable salad]. [Like *gadho-gadho*] there are some ingredients that are well-cooked *(masak)*, but some are only half-cooked *(setengah masak)*, and the rest are still raw *(mentah)*. Ingredients like *kerupuk* (fried shrimp chips) and eggs are well-cooked; but cabbages and tomatoes are still raw.
>
> This picture of *gadho-gadho* salad is apt to illustrate the present situation of the community of Muhammad. Those who are well-cooked pray five times a day, fast in the month of Puasa, and perform obligatory religious duties; they faithfully follow the example shown by the Prophet Muhammad. Those who are half-cooked may or may not contribute *zakat* (religious taxes); but they ask for the help of magical healers *(dhukun)* and diviners *(juru ramal)*; they seek blessings at the sacred graves of saints

(kuburan wali-wali keramat). Sometimes some of them may even retreat into the world of *wirid* [repetitive chanting of Qur'anic formula], perform asceticism *(zuhud)*, and become learned mystics *(wiragi)* who completely abandon this-wordly matters despite the fact that the body is still in this world. Those who are still uncooked are stingy *(bakhil)*, close-fisted *(kikir)*, greedy *(serakah)*, covetous *(tamak)*, and cannot be trusted by others for they take advantage of others mercilessly. [Consequently], as long as our Islam continues to have the quality of *gadho-gadho*, we must never be a *tukang amin-amin* [= he who repeats amen only] sitting behind the crowd: Islam must always be placed in the front line *(di depan barisan)*. If we remain *tukang amin-amin* in the back, then we are to blame for leaving Islam in the *gadho-gadho* situation. If we regard the Great Prophet Muhammad as the truest and most absolute example, then we must also follow him in an absolute way ...

The sermon giver goes on to emphasize the importance of courage *(keberanian)* in carrying on the fight against *gadho-gadho* and the necessity of the unity *(kesatuan)* of the Muslim community for the task, stressing that final success is guaranteed by God as He said in the Qur'an:

> O Prophet, urge on the believers to fight. If there be twenty of you, patient men [in Indonesian, *orang yang berhati teguh*, lit., people who are firm-minded] they will overcome two hundred [enemies]; if there be a hundred of you, they will overcome a thousand unbelievers *(kafir)* for they are a people who understand not [in Indonesian, *kaum yang tidak mengerti*] (The Qur'an 8:65, English translation from Arberry 1955, vol. I, p. 204).

The categorization of the *ummat* by the degree of understanding is characteristic of the reformist perception of the entire population. The tone of self-confidence in "he who understands" sounds almost arrogant and contemptuous of "those who do not understand yet". However, in order better to appreciate the conviction of a Muhammadiyah activist like this sermon giver *(khotib)*, it is necessary to see how he has reached this degree of conviction. Most Muhammadiyah activists including this person were themselves born *abangan* but later chose to be *santri*. The life history of this *khotib* shall illustrate the point.

I shall call him Pak "Ja'far", a *santri* name.[1] Pak Ja'far was born in 1922 in one of the oldest *kampungs* of Kotagede as a son of a government school teacher. His grandfather was a *bekel*. Before he entered elementary school he

---

1. His real name was Djumairy Martodikoro (1922–92), a combination of *santri* and Javanese names.

was attracted to religious courses for small boys given by Kyai Amir in the neighbouring *kampung*. In spite of the fact that his father was a teacher of the Javanese language at the government elementary school in Kotagede, he went to the Muhammadiyah's second class elementary school and then to its HIS. He was an active member of Hizbul Wathan, the Muhammadiyah's Boy Scout movement. He continued his secondary education in the Muhammadiyah's Mu'allimin (high school for religious teacher training) in Yogyakarta. Then he learned English at the Muhammadiyah's language course and still has a fairly good command of it. After graduation, he started to teach at the Muhammadiyah's HIS in Kotagede. With the coming of the Japanese, he was apointed to head the Seinendan (Youth Corps, one of the Japanese-created para-military organizations) in the Surakarta part of Kotagede. Shortly after Independence he became the commander of the Badan Keamanan Rakyat, or People's Security Organization (the forerunner of the Republican regular army) in the same territory. In this capacity he participated in the battle of Semarang-Ambarawa in October–November 1945 in which the young Republican forces repulsed for the first time the attempted advancement of the allied (British) forces into south Central Java. After this battle experience, Pak Ja'far decided to quit the military to get back to education. He then taught at various Muhammadiyah schools in Kotagede and later in the city of Yogyakarta, which led him finally to the position of the inspector of private schools in the Yogyakarta region in the Department of Education and Culture just prior to the outbreak of the G30S affair in 1965. In addition to this government position, he was the secretary of the Masyumi Party in Kotagede until the Party was banned in 1960 and a member of the local leadership board of the Muhammadiyah for many years. From 1964 to 1966 he was one of the sermon givers *(khotib)* of the Great Mosque in Kotagede and his sermon quoted above was given during this period.[2]

Unlike other sermon givers, Pak Ja'far always gave his sermon in Indonesian rather than in Javanese. Perhaps partly because of this and partly because of his uncompromising personality, he was not so popular among elderly Muslims, who regarded him with mixed feelings of fear and respect. But he was immensely popular among younger Muslims, many of whom were his former pupils. A few months prior to the outbreak of the G30S incident, he organized a semi-secret Muslim Youth Organization, Pasukan Pemuda

---

2. Pak Ja'far kept typewritten texts of all the sermons he gave during this period, and he gave me permission to read and quote from the texts. I would like to thank him for this.

Senapati (Youth Troops of Senapati) which recruited devout Muslim young men locally. The organization was formed for the self-defence of the Muslim community in anticipation of the impending final showdown with the PKI, who reportedly set up a military training centre in a Communist-dominated *kampung* in Kotagede in August of the same year. The Senapati youths were given para-military training including *pencak*, the traditional Javanese self-defence art, which was Pak Ja'far's favourite sport. Eventually the Pasukan Pemuda Senapati grew to a force of four platoons of about forty troopers each, or about two hundred in total, including the staff and commanders. In August 1965, Pak Ja'far also began to establish contacts with Muslim veterans of the Revolutionary War secretly to organize a network of Muslim para-military forces in Central Java. But before this effort materialized, the G-30-S affair broke out. From November 1965 to January 1966, the Pasukan Pemuda Senapati under Pak Ja'far's command, now surfaced above the ground, was instrumental in arresting local PKI leaders and cadres and handing them over to the Yogyakarta military authorities who were sometimes not so eager in detaining PKI members. In May 1966, the Pasukan Pemuda Senapati was again active in showing support for the anti-Sukarno campaign in Jakarta. During this period, Pak Ja'far was arrested in a skirmish with the PNI members supporting Sukarno. He represented the Muslim political element in the New Order forces in Kotagede and personally embodied a linkage between the so-called '45 Generation (the youths of the '45 Revolution) and the '66 Generation (the youths of the '66 Anti-Sukarno Movement). However, after this arrest, he was deprived of his government post and the right to engage in political activities in 1969 for the reason of his former leadership position in a trade union of government employees. He then withdrew from the public scene and has since taught statistics and English at a private academy in Yogyakarta for his livelihood.

I first met Pak Ja'far in the fall of 1970 right after I settled in Kotagede. He was living with his son in an old house which he had inherited from his father in the Surakarta part of Kotagede. When I visited his house, I found autographed pictures of former Masyumi leaders, M. Natsir and Burhanuddin Harahap, hung on the living room wall. He noticed my surprise at such an open defiance of the official unfavourable attitude of Soeharto's government toward these and other former Masyumi leaders. He said smilingly, "They were called 'extreme-right' before. They are still called so now. I do not know if the labelling is appropriate. But I do know that they have been democrats consistently and conscientiously." Despite the fact that Pak Ja'far was in a very difficult personal situation he showed no signs of frustration but maintained good spirits and physical fitness. Since 1966 he has been a faithful reader and subscriber of the weekly paper *Mahasiswa Indonesia* (Bandung edition) — an organ of KAMI (Indonesian Students Action Front) — one of the few newspapers outspokenly critical of the performance of the New Order regime. He defined himself as "genuine, original Muhammadiyah *(Muhammadiyah yang asli dan orijinil)*." He foresaw difficult times for the Muhammadiyah movement in the coming years. They must, he said, adhere to the ideal shown by K.H.A. Dahlan, "To live the life of a true Muslim in fullest compliance with the Islamic teachings *(hidup sebagai orang Islam yang se-benar-benarnya sepanjang ajaran agama Islam)*." The most dangerous thing for the Muhammadiyah now is, according to him, to be lured by government positions and compromise one's own principles. He looked up at the pictures of the former Masyumi leaders on the wall and said, "They were men of principle. They never thought of positions *(pangkat)* or personal security *(keselametan pribadi)*."

Now let us examine the sermon he gave in the light of his personal background. As mentioned earlier, the categorization of the entire population in terms of degree of religious orthodoxy and devoutness is typical of the reformist perception of Indonesian society. One might find a parallel between this reformist Islamic categorization of "those who understand" vs. "those who do not understand yet" and a more general social categorization of the aware *(insyaf, sadar)* vs. the unaware *(masa bodoh)* (see Geertz 1965, p. 129ff.). However, one critical point of difference between the two seems that reformist Muslims make it their task to convert "the unaware" to "the aware" while, for leaders of some other ideological persuasions, *masa bodoh* (the indifferent masses) only calls for paternalistic care *(momong,* lit., to nurse, to babysit). Those in power position especially play on the "stupidity" of the *masa bodoh* and no serious effort is made to close the gap between the aware and the unaware. Perhaps they fear that the increasing "awareness" of the unaware may undermine their privileged position. For reformist Muslims the existence of the unaware is a constant reminder that their Muslim duties have not yet been fulfilled. They feel they are burdened with historical inertia. Traditional Islam which they have inherited from the preceding generations can be valued as an asset only if it constitutes a point of departure for the effort to attain a purer Islam. Once "aware", one cannot be content with the *status quo* but instead must work to alter the *gadho-gadho* situation. Pak Ja'far's life history presents a good example of how a Javanese Muslim has striven to develop himself out of *gadho-gadho* in order to become a "true Muslim".

As mentioned earlier, prior to the Dutch reform of administration in 1920, Pak Ja'far's grandfather was a *bekel* (assistant) for a *jurukunci* in the Surakarta territory of Kotagede. As a *bekel,* he had control over a considerable amount of rice fields, kept a number of personal followers, and was economically better off. He held the title of Raden, a title for the lesser nobility. He was pensioned after the reform, but one of his sons, Ja'far's uncle, became a village official in the newly-created *kalurahan* (administrative village). Another of his sons, Ja'far's father, became a *guru bahasa Jawa*, Javanese language teacher, at a government elementary school. He was an *abdi dalem* (royal servant) of the Surakarta Susuhunate and was given an appropriate name for his position and function as a teacher. He was also allowed to use the title of Raden. Pak Ja'far was thus born and raised in this lower *priyayi* milieu. Since his childhood Pak Ja'far learned from his father what is called by the generic term "*tata-cara*" (lit., "order" and "way" in Javanese), the proper ways of Javanese life, including traditional Javanese literature, etiquette and ethics, and aesthetic and physical training. He still has a good knowledge of what is proper *tata-cara*, and is rather sensitive about it.

For example, when I distributed ritual food among neighbours and acquaintances in Kotagede in a *besek* (small bamboo slat box) on the first birthday of my son who had been born in Yogyakarta, Pak Ja'far immediately sent me a thank-you letter in which he meticulously enumerated what he found wrong with my way of performing *slametan* for a birthday. His criticism was twofold. First, he pointed out that the ingredients of the ritual food and the way they were cooked did not follow the ways people do in Kotagede. (I had entrusted the preparation of the ritual food to an elderly maid who was not a Kotagedean but a Yogyanese). Another, more important point of his criticism was that I was not advised to indulge in this custom of *musyrik* (polytheism) at all because every ingredient had magical meaning which constituted the negation of *tauhid*, the unity of God. (Later he told me, "As a Protestant, you don't want to compromise in the principle of monotheism, do you? I don't either, as a Muslim.")

In his letter he stated that there were in Kotagede three categories of people: those who adhere to the Islamic teaching only, those who practise *tata-cara* Jawa only, and those in between who say Islam was all right but *tata-cara* was also all right. He himself belongs to the first category and asked my forgiveness as he would not be able to reciprocate my gift according to the *tata-cara* way in the future, since it would constitute a violation of the principle of the unity of God.

Another example shall also indicate his familiarity with the traditional Javanese way. In 1971, I contributed a short essay on the history of Kotagede to a local Muhammadiyah publication (Nakamura 1971). Pak Ja'far again sent me a letter pointing out several factual mistakes contained in my essay by quoting seemingly off-hand from various *babad* (Javanese court chronicles)

Obviously he has memorized all the major *babad* stories. Even by Javanese traditional standards, then, he could be regarded as a well-learned man of *sastra*, literati. But he rejects this. Already in the day of the Revolution he had ceased to use the title of Raden to which he was entitled. Now he rarely uses his full name (which must include his father's name) which unmistakably reveals his *priyayi* origin. Instead he prefers to use his Islamic given name only. His life history exemplifies a constant and conscious effort to discard from his deeds and thoughts what he conceives of as non-Islamic and anti-Islamic elements and to replace these by what he considers to be "truly Islamic". When he talks about the *gadho-gadho* situation he is indeed talking about his own past.

Apparent arrogance in Pak Ja'far or in other reformist Muslim activists is actually a reflection of their conviction that they "understand better" than the rest of the population. This must be related to the fact there is no notion of "God's chosen ones" in reformist ideology. Ascribed qualities such as royal descent or genealogical relationship with famous *kyai* have no significance. What is valued is the individual's deed accomplished by self-discipline. If one realizes that one is still *gadho-gadho*, he himself is responsible for and capable of cleansing *(membersihkan)* himself.

Pak Ja'far projects this notion to the history of Islam in Indonesia. In these same sermon quoted above, he says:

> It is true that *ummat Islam* has never been defeated from the outside but only from within. There is no Aladdin's lamp to help us except ourselves. We must realize that "half the truth is not the truth" and strive for the realization of Islamic teaching as perfectly as possible.

And quotes from the Qur'an, "God changes not what is in a people, until they change what is in themselves" (13:11, English translation from Arberry 1955, vol. I, p. 268).

How to change onself then? According to the Muhammadiyah teaching the way is already revealed in the Qur'an and exemplified by the deeds and sayings of the Prophet Muhammad: To believe in the truth revealed in the Qur'an and to live in compliance with God's prescriptions. Leaving behind the *gadho-gadho* half-truth, one has to become a true Muslim in full compliance with God's commands. The idea of the "true Muslim" is then what is contrasted to the *gadho-gadho* situation.

In speeches and writings, Muhammadiyah propagandists *(muballigh)* exhort that one must become a "true Muslim". In Javanese this is expressed as *dados tiyang Islam ingkang sa-èstu-èstu-nipun*, which literally means "to become (*dados*) a Muslim (*tiyang Islam*) who is the most real (*sa-èstu-èstu-nipun*)".

> **BOX 6**
> **Protest of *Orang Halus* (Ghosts)**
>
> On one night in 1971, I was talking with a middle-aged Muhammadiyah activist on the porch of his house. He looked at an empty space in front of his house and said: "That space used to be an old graveyard for my hamlet. But, it became crowded and the government decided to turn it to a space to build an elementary school. The neighbourhood association agreed after several meetings of discussion. But, those who were buried there seemed to have disagreed. While sitting here on the night before the land was cleared, I saw a number of corpses bound in white clothes rise up from beneath the ground, stood upright, and started to dance swaying their bodies silently back and forth, left and right, as if they had been protesting the plan to build a school on their graveyard. As I supported the plan to build a school there, I tried to pacify those *orang halus* (ghosts) by reciting the Qur'an. I recited it earnestly and emphatically until they returned to the underground. They never appeared again." He told the story in a serious manner.

*Sa-èstu-èstu-nipu*n is derivative of *èstu* which means "real, true, certain, honest, sincere, and earnest". Sometimes *sa-èstu-èstu-nipun*, is replaced by or affixed with *sampurna* which means "perfect, complete, ideal". In Indonesian the phrase is expressed as *menjadi orang Islam yang se-benar-benar-nya*. *Se-benar-benar-nya* means "the truest, the most real". Sometimes this too is replaced by or affixed with *se-sungguh-sungguh-nya* ("the most earnest, sincere") or *sempurna* ("perfect, complete, ideal"). The current Constitution *(Anggaran Dasar)* of the Muhammadiyah states:

> The purpose and intention of the Association *(Persyarikatan)* is to raise *(menegakkan)* and hold high *(menjunjung tinggi)* the religion of Islam so that there shall be formed *(terwujud)* an Islamic society *(masyarakat Islam)* which is the most real *(yang se-benar-benar-nya)*. (Anggaran Dasar Muhammadiyah 1967, p. 8)

To see how this theme of "true Islam" is presented to the local audience, I shall quote from a speech given by another Muhammadiyah propagandist, whom I shall call Pak Asy'ari.[3] The speech was given at a Parmusi (Partai Muslimin Indonesia, or Indonesian Muslim Party) campaign meeting held in a Kotagede *kampung* during the 1971 general elections. The meeting was held in the hall of the *musholla* (mosque for women[4]) from 8.00 to 11.00

---

3. His real name is M. Asrofie, father of Yusron Asrofie.
4. For this "mistake", see Chapter 9, note 4.

in the evening. The audience was mostly the middle- and old-aged, about ninety in total, one-third of them were male and the rest female. According to my observation, roughly twenty people were Muhammadiyah members and the rest were non-members.

As in the case of Pak Ja'far, a brief biographic sketch of the speaker, Pak Asy'ari, shall provide a background to the speech. Pak Asy'ari was born in 1927 in a rural *kampung* in the southern part of Kotagede as a son of a well-to-do farmer. He was first educated at the Muhammadiyah elementary school in Kotagede and then entered the HIK Muhammadiyah (Hoogere Inlandsche Kweekschool or high school for teacher training in Dutch in general subjects) in Yogyakarta. He did not finish the high school but instead went to the *pesantren* of Termas, Pacitan, and spent two years there. Then the Japanese came and he was made a Seinendan (Youth Corps) leader in his native *kampung*. During the revolutionary years he was a member of Hizbullah, Muslim para-military organization. He married a trader's daughter in Kotagede *kota* in 1948 and, with the assistance of his father-in-law, started to make a livelihood in the retail and wholesale trade in *emping*[5] in the central market in Yogyakarta, Bringhardjo. In 1952 he became independent of his father-in-law and has since specialized in the sale of ready-made clothes (for which Kotagede has also been famous since the end of the war) in the market of Piyungan, a town about ten kilometres east of Kotagede. Today he visits the market every day on his bicycle. He has also been the organizer of a Muhammadiyah branch in Piyungan and still gives regular religious courses *(pengajian)* there. Since 1966 he has been one of the Muhammadiyah board members in Kotagede in charge of the *tabligh* (religious propagation) section. Almost every day, after returning home from Piyungan, he has an engagement to give a religious lecture somewhere in Kotagede or in its vicinity. In addition, since 1968 he has been elected the vice-chairman of the Rukun Kampung (Neighbourhood Association) of the urban neighbourhood in which he and his wife have been living since their marriage.

His wife is a graduate of the Muhammadiyah's Mu'allimat (religious teachers' training school for girls) in Yogyakarta and is an active leader of the 'Aisyiyah (the women's association of Muhammadiyah) branch in Kotagede. Two of their three children ware born in the delivery house of the

---

5. Crackers made from the endosperm of *gnetum gnemon* tree for which production Kotagede was and still is famous.

Muhammadiyah PKU polyclinic in Kotagede and all have been educated in the local Muhammadiyah school system. The eldest, a daughter, is a graduate of the Mu'allimat in Yogyakarta; the second, a son, is now a student of the State Institute of Islamic Studies in Yogyakarta; and the youngest, another daughter, is still in the Muhammadiyah's elementary school in Kotagede. His wife is also engaged in the trade of ready-made clothes and twice a week travels by bus to a market in Wates, the *kabupaten* (regency) capital of Kulon Progo, about 40 kilometres southwest of Kotagede.

Although it was not a *pengajian* (religious lecture) meeting but a political meeting, the format of this meeting exactly followed that of a *pengajian*: opening with the recitation of the Qur'an by a young Mu'allimin student from the *kampung*, speeches by two speakers interrupted by a recess for tea and snacks, and closing with a question and answer period. Pak Asy'ari was the first speaker and the second was the secretary of the Kotagede branch of the Parmusi (also a clerk of the KP3J, the silver industry cooperative and a board member of the Muhammadiyah). Pak Asy'ari talked for about forty minutes on what might be entitled "The true Muslim's task in the general elections". The content of his speech was mostly religious, and explicitly political arguments were relegated to the second speaker. Compared with religious lectures or with sermons at Friday prayer meetings which usually focus on some specific topic, the speech Pak Asy'ari gave to this meeting was an excellent general statement of the Muhammadiyah's tenets. Therefore I shall quote rather extensively from it.

He opened his speech with the customary greeting of Muslims, *Assalamu'alaikum warahmatullahi wabarakatuh* ("May God give you peace, His mercy and His blessing!"), and the audience returned the greeting, *Wa'alaikum assalam warahmatullahi wabarakatuh* ("May God also give you peace, His mercy and His blessing!"). Then he recited the opening chapter of the Qur'an, Surah Al-Fatihah, first in Arabic, followed by its line-by-line translation into Javanese:

> In the Name of God, the Merciful, the Compassionate. Praise belongs to God, the Lord of all Being, the All-Merciful, the All-Compassionate, the Master of the Day of Doom. Thee only we serve, to Thee alone we pray for succour. Guide us in the straight path, the path of those whom Thou has blessed, not of those against whom Thou art wrathful, Nor of those who are astray (The Qur'an 1:1–7, English translation from Arberry 1955, vol. I, p. 29).

Pak Asy'ari sang out, rather than recited the last few lines of the above verses in Arabic. The chairman of the meeting, a graduate of Mu'allimin, later mentioned to me that it was a traditional *pesantren* style of reciting the Qur'an.

Next Pak Asy'ari read the Confession of Faith in Arabic followed by its almost word-by-word translation into Javanese whose English equivalent is as follows:

> I truly believe that there is no god to which I am responsible for praying except God who is the most Glorious, the Only One, the Greatest. And I am convinced and I believe that our master the Great Prophet Muhammad is the servant and the messenger of God.

When the name of Muhammad was mentioned, the audience recited with Pak Asy'ari the formula, *Salla llahu 'alaihi wasallam* ("May God bless him and give him peace").

With these preliminaries, the atmosphere of the meeting was perfectly set for a *pengajian*. Then Pak Asy'ari went on to touch upon the subject of this particular meeting:

> *Bapak-Bapak* (Gentlemen, lit., Fathers) and *Ibu-Ibu* (Ladies, lit., Mothers), all those who are present here, you and I have all been Muslims since our childhood, since the time of your parents and mine, since the time of your ancestors and mine. Therefore, let us face the problem before us tonight, the problem of the general election, which is going to be held on Sabtu Pahing (Saturday, Pahing [of Javanese five-day week]) the 3rd of July, 1971, as Muslims who follow the teaching of God revealed in nothing other than the Holy Book of the Qur'an.

Pak Asy'ari then asked a question of the audience: "What is the purpose of our life in this world?" He continued to answer it by himself: "Let us look for the answer in the words of God in the Qur'an." He cited a verse of the Qur'an, first in Arabic, then in Javanese: "I *[Ingsun]* have not created jinn and mankind except to serve *[ngibadah]* Me" (The Qur'an 51:56, Arberry 1956, vol. II, p. 239). Pak Asy'ari went on to explain this verse as follows:

> Honourable audience, God created us, all of us, as followers *(ummat)* of God, as servants *(kawula)* of God. What is essential for you and me, for all of us, is that we are commanded by God to serve *(ngabdi)* God, the Lord *(Gusti Allah)*. What is essential for us is to be ever His faithful servants *(kawula)*. God commands us to disregard this-worldly things *(kadonyaan)* and to choose *akhérat* (the world of the after-life), to perform good deeds *(tumindak sing apik)* in this world only in the hope of receiving reward *(ganjaran)* in the world of the after-life: these are the ones who shall be favoured by God, blessed by God.

Then Pak Asy'ari dwelt on the relationship between this world *(donya)* and the world of the after-life *(akhérat)*:

> You and I, all of us, who are living in this world are certainly going to die; all living people are certain to die. There is nothing living that will not die. Everybody must die. Then what is important is not that we think of "what is it like to die?". That we do not need to think about. What we must think about is "what are we going to take along with us as *sangu* (provision) to the world of the after-life when we die". We must seek *sangu* for death, for the world of the after-life. That *sangu* is in fact the fear *(takwa)* of God and many good deeds *(amal)*. Life in this world should be regarded only as a road *(margi)* or a market *(peken)* leading to the world of the after-life on which we purchase necessities for the life to come. We must direct ourselves solely towards the *akhérat*: to live in this world is only to seek God's reward in the world of after-life. This world is like *sabin* (rice field) or *pasiten* (house garden) into which we plant *(menanem)* [paddy or fruit tree], and then tomorrow *(mbenjing,* tomorrow or at a certain time in the near future) we shall collect the harvest in the world of the after-life.
>
> What are good deeds *(amal)* and what are not?: what is evil *(awon)*? That which is commanded by God is good, and that which is prohibited by Him is evil. Let us all endeavour to complete *(sampuranaaken)* our conduct as Muslims who are the most sincere *(sa-èstu-èstu-nipun)*. To become true Muslims, we must fulfill our religious duties *(ngibadah)* in all aspects of life. When we work *(nyambut gawé)*, the way must be as true Muslims. When we are married as husband and wife *(bebojoan)*, the way must be as true Muslims. When we send our children to school, the way must be as true Muslims.
>
> In contrast, there are people who say they are Muslims but whose way of life is still that of unbelievers *(kafir)*. For example, they often like to reduce the contents [of merchandise], reduce the weight of a scale, knowingly buy and sell defective things. They say they are Muslims but the way they behave is not different from that of unbelievers. Tomorrow in the *akhérat,* when we face God, our mouths will be locked; we cannot mouth excuses; only our hands and legs will talk and tell what we have done in this world.
>
> We know that our life here in this world is only to serve *(ngibadah)* God, to become loyal servants *(kumawula)* of God, the Lord *(Gusti Allah)*. What is meant by *ngibadah* then? There are three ways to *ngibadah* (to serve God). The first is what is called *rukun iman* (Pillars of Faith) and *rukun Islam* (Pillars of Islam). These are found in two fields *(bidang)*. One is in the field of *batin* (internal self); the other is the field of *lahir* (external self). In the field of *batin,* deep inside our heart *(ati)*, we believe in *(pitados)* the existence of God, in the existence of His angels *(malaikat)*, we believe in the Book of God, in the prophets of God, the world of the afterlife *(akhérat)*

and in the predestination *(takdir)* by God. This we firmly believe in our hearts. In the external field of *lahir* we behave *(mlampah)* as servants of God, the Lord *(Gusti Allah)*; we recite *(maos)* the Confession of Faith *(shahadat)*, pray *(sholat)* five times a day, perform fasting, contribute *zakat* (religious taxes), and go on pilgrimage *(hajj)* if we can afford it.

The second way to *ngibadah* is to control *(ngempet)* our *napsu* (= *nafsu*, "passions, lowly desires"). *Napsu* induces us to do something evil *(awon)*, likes to divert human beings for wrongdoing. We must control *napsu* all the time, and that is our *ngibadah*. The third way to *ngibadah* is to live harmoniously *(rukun)* with our fellow creatures *(makhluk sesami)* in this world. We are not alone here in this world. Let us use our good character *(akhlak)*, behave well *(tumindak ingkang sae)*, and follow good manners of social intercourse *(tata krama ingkang sae)*.

The point is that *(pokokipun)*, the one who is called perfect *(sampurna)* in his services *(pangibadahipun)* is he who understands the fundamental responsibilities *(kawajiban ingkang baku)* towards God, the Lord, he who controls his passion, and he who develops good character *(akhlak)* and makes it a practice to perform good deeds *(amal)*. It is not yet sufficient *(kirang cekap)* if you pray five times a day and go to a religious lecture *(pengajian)*, but at the same time still remain arrogant *(kemaki)* toward others, do not respect *(ora ngajene)* your parents, do not keep promises, continue to be obstinate and irritate others *(ngeyel lan mangkelke)*, do not mingle with neighbours *(ora tepung)*, do not go to help them *(ora réwang)* on social occasions *(ewuh)*, do not visit others when someone in the family has died, do not go to help when someone is sick. If someone behaves like that, then even though he prays *(sholat)* he is not yet a Muslim who is true *(tiyang Islam ingkang saèstu)*; he cannot be called a perfect Muslim *(tiyang Islam ingkang sampurna)*. Let us not be like that.

After presenting this summary statement of the Muhammadiyah on the ways to be a true Muslim, he went on to mention the political responsibility of a true Muslim: since a true Muslim strives to perfect his behaviour in all aspects of life, politics is no exception; in the coming general election he must support the fighters of God, the party of God, the Lord *(golongan Gusti Allah)*. (For more on his speech, see p. 201 below.)

JAVANESE SPEECH LEVELS

Two general points can be observed from the speech of Pak Asy'ari as an example of Muhammadiyah ideology. The first is to do with the language of his speech. The second concerns the effort of the Muhammadiyah in the transformation of traditional Islam in Java.

Earlier I stated that Indonesian has long been used as the official intra-organizational language of the Muhammadiyah. In contrast, religious communications between Muhammadiyah speakers and their local audience are almost invariably carried out in Javanese. (Pak Ja'far's Indonesian sermons to Friday prayer meetings were an innovation which has not been followed by other Muhammadiyah leaders. See p. 168 above.) Indonesian is used publicly (i.e., outside Muhammadiyah membership meetings) as the official medium of communication only in public lectures and cultural entertainments held by Muhammadiyah youth organizations. Even on these occasions, it is essential to insert proper Javanese expressions from time to time to enliven the atmosphere. Javanese is thus the essential medium of communication used in public meetings held by the Muhammadiyah.

Javanese is a language of extreme subtlety, with multiple speech levels.[6] A Javanese speaker cannot make any utterance without linguistically differentiating in terms of politeness and formality the relationship between the speaker and the addressee, and the speaker's relationship to the third person referred to in his utterance. Religious communications in Javanese are no exception.

In fact, Javanese speech levels are apt to facilitate the differentiation and the understanding of such concepts as God as the Absolute and Supreme Being and human beings as His servants, and the latter's relationship with the former. It also helps to qualify the topic and context of speech. For example, Pak Asy'ari's speech is basically spoken in *Krama*, indicating the formal and polite relationship between him and the audience and the respectful quality of the subject. However, when he refers to God and describes His deeds and words, he switches to *Krama Inggil* showing the highest degree of respect. When God speaks to human beings, His utterances are naturally on the *Ngoko* level. And when Pak Asy'ari presents his own ideas, internal monologues, supposed

---

6. For the linguistic aspect of Javanese speech levels, see Soepomo (1968). For its socio-cultural implications, see Geertz (1960, pp. 248–60). According to Soepomo (ibid.), there are four types of vocabulary levels; (1) *Ngoko* (non-polite and informal), (2) *Madya* (semi-polite and semi-formal), (3) *Krama* (polite and formal) and (4) *Krama Inggil* ("high *Krama*") and *Krama Andhap* ("humble *Krama*"). "Respect vocabulary" and two types of affixes differentiating *Ngoko* and *Krama* levels are combined to form three basic speech levels, *Ngoko Madya*, and *Krama* with three sub-levels for each of the three (Soepomo 1968, pp. 56–61). A good Javanese speaker must be familiar with the proper use of these speech levels, which form an integral part of Javanese *tata-cara* (proper manners and etiquette).

conversations with his friends, or describes mundane human activities, the expressions are made in *Ngoko* or *Madya*. He never addresses the audience directly in *Ngoko* or *Madya*.

Here are some notable examples: Pak Asy'ari, quoting from the Qur'an, states that "God says, 'I *(Ingsun)* have not created jinn and mankind except to serve Me'" (see p. 178 above). The Javanese word for "says" here is *ngendika*, a *Krama Inggil* word which refers to the act of "talking" of a highly respected person — God in this case. Similarly, *Ingsun* for "I", first-person pronoun, is a *Krama Inggil* word only appropriate for a king or God to use (see the use of *Ingsun* in the royal letter of appointment, Chapter 2, p. 27 above). The same is true with another *Krama Inggil* word, *dhawuh*, which is frequently used in religious terminology. This word means "to tell someone to do something", and its connotation is always a person of a higher status giving a command to a person of a lower status to do something. When God commands mankind to do something, the word most fitted is, therefore, *dhawuh*. The use of the particular respectful vocabulary is thus well-suited to express the lord-servant relationship between God and man.

Even reformist Islamic ideas, then, once expressed in Javanese cannot escape from being moulded by the Javanese language structure. A fact to be observed is that these linguistic features of Javanese do not necessarily constitute strictures upon religious communications of the Muhammadiyah. The relationships among God, the Absolute Authority, mankind as His servant, and the Prophets as His messengers are rather finely conceptualized and expressed not only by individual words but also by the structure of Javanese speech levels themselves.

What distinguishes the reformist ideas off from traditional Javanese ideas concerning the cosmos and society is the fact that the Muhammadiyah has made a number of shifts in emphasis and alterations of meaning in the use of traditional religious terms. To illustrate this point the pair of words *kawula* and *gusti* merit special consideration. This is said to be one of the core concepts derived from traditional Javanese *ngelmu* (esoteric knowledge) rather than from orthodox Islam. Moertono has produced an elegant explication of this concept (Moertono 1968, Chapter II). According to him, in traditional Javanese terms, the concept denotes the fundamental order in the cosmos and society. *Kawula-gusti* (servant and master) is simultaneously the basis of the social order (the ruled and the ruler) and of the cosmic order (man and God). To quote Moertono:

> In Javanese mysticism the words *djumbuhing kawulo-gusti* (the merging of servant and master) describe the highest goal of man's life, namely the achievement of ultimate "oneness" *(manunggal)* with God. This is the more

dramatic since the words *kawulo* and *gusti* denote the very lowest and the very highest status of man in society. However, and this is important to our argument, unity of servant and master is possible only because there are certain ties between and properties common to "man and God". (Moertono 1968, p. 15).

Traditional and reformist ideas agree in that *gusti* refers to the Highest Being and *kawula* to the humblest. However, whereas in traditional ideas the social and cosmic orders are juxtaposed implying that they are in essence one and the same, in reformist ideas the terms *gusti* and *kawula* are exclusively used for God and man respectively. The result of this narrowing-down of meaning in the reformist terminology is that God becomes absolute, and there is nothing else comparable to Him in authority and power while mankind is His most humble servant. At the same time, "certain properties common to man and God" are subtly denied. Likewise, in place of the interdependency and reciprocity between God and man implied in the traditional ideas, reformists, using the same terminology, emphasize an asymmetrical relationship between God and man, a relationship of total dependency of man on God: man is created by God only to serve Him. Then the service *(ngabdi)* a servant *(kawula)* does for Lord *(Gusti)* is nothing other than the fulfillment of his religious duties *(ngibadah)*. (A Muhammadiyah *muballigh* explained to me that the Javanese words *ngabdi*, *ngibadah* and *ibadat* are actually derived from the same Arabic root-word, *'abd*, and all mean the same thing — "to serve".) Instead of the traditional teaching of the mystical unity of God and man *(manunggal)* in this world through *semedi* (meditation), reformists inform us that man should expect reward *(ganjaran)* from God in the world of the after-life through service *('ibadat)* and good deeds *(amal)* performed in this world.

LAHIR VS. *BATIN*

A similar example of the reformist use and reworking of Javanese traditional ideas is indicated by the pair of concepts, *lahir* (outer self) and *batin (batos* in *Krama*, inner self). Pak Asy'ari has explained that *Rukun iman* and *Rukun Islam* (principal religious beliefs and rituals) are expressed in two ways, *lahir* and *batin*. In the internal self, one believes in God and His attributes and actions. In the outer self, one performs rites which are prescribed by God and exemplified by Muhammad. As we know from Geertz's work, the pair concept, *lahir* and *batin*, is a fundamental and all-prevasive idiom for Javanese conceptualization of one's self (Geertz 1960, pp. 238–41 and *passim*). Indeed, we hear the expression *lahir* and *batin* used on numerous occasions in numerous ways. For example, when the month of Puasa (Fasting) is over and Lebaran comes, the Javanese greet their parents, relatives, neighbours, colleagues, teachers, office supervisors and bosses with the formalized expression, *Nyuwun pangapunten sedaya kalepatan kula lahir lan batos.* ("I ask your forgiveness for my wrong-doings externally as well as internally, i.e., most earnestly"). School children are taught to love their fatherland wholeheartedly, *lahir* and *batin.* This is a most prevalent notion shared by all Javanese regardless of their differences in religious orientation and commitment. Therefore when Pak Asy'ari preaches that true Muslims have to serve God *lahir* and *batin,* the point of his ideas is well expressed in a familiar Javanese idiom and is perhaps well understood by his audience.

However, it is interesting to point out that the same notion, *lahir* and *batin,* can be used in different ways by individuals of different religious-political orientations. Let me cite an example I recorded in the field:

> I went to see Pak Mantri Anom [Vice Chief] of the Kemantren (Ward) office of Kotagede. [This was a few months prior to the general election of July 1971]. I talked with him and Pak Sastro [another *kemantren* official] about the election. I asked if the branch of Golkar (the Government's "Functional Group") had already been formed here and, if so, who were its leaders.
>
> Pak Mantri Anom answered that he and several other *kemantren* officials had become its leaders. Then he went on to say, "People say that we, *pamong praja* [local administration officials] are *bunglon.*" Pak Sastro interrupted and asked me a question, "*Tuan tahu bunglon itu apa?* (Do you know what *bunglon* is, Sir?)." I said, "No, I don't." Pak Sastro continued, "It's a small animal like a *toké* (house lizard) whose skin colour changes according to circumstances." "Ah *itu, namanya chameleon kalau bahasa Inggris* (Oh, that's it. Its name is chameleon in English)," I said. *"Ya, itulah, chameleon* (Yes, that's it, chameleon)," Pak Sastro repeated. Pak Mantri Anom returned to his subject. "People say we are chameleons and change the colors of our skin according to circumstances. Formerly, in the period of Dutch colonial rule we went along with *(ikut)* the Dutch. Then the Japanese military came, and we went along with *Dainippon* ("the Great Japan"). Then in the independence period, we went along with R.I. (Republic of Indonesia), and most recently when Pak Harto (President Soeharto) replaced Bung Karno (Presiden Sukarno), we went along with Pak Harto. Therefore they say we change the colours of our skin. That is true. The main point is that we go along with whoever gets power in Jakarta. We can be and we have been skilful in adjusting ourselves *(menyesuaikan diri)* to current situations and conditions *(situasi dan kondisi sekarang).* Because of this, people say we are chameleons, inconsistent *(kurang konsekwèn)* and don't have principles. But in fact we are not like that. We are not *opporcunis* (opportunists). We do have principles. Our principles are to defend the interests of people *(membela*

kepentingan rakyat) in whatever situation. If we don't do so, who else can protect the people, lead the people? *Batinnya* (in inner self) we have been continuously consistent. We have been loyal to our role: that is, to *momong rakyat* (to look after, to babysit the people). *Lahirnya* (outwardly) we have changed colours; formerly PNI, now Golkar, for example. But our principles have remained the same. Not inconsistent, is it?

The same situation is, however, viewed differently by a *santri* in the same terminology of *lahir* and *batin*. Talking about the various tactics used by the Golkar in the election campaign, Pak Ja'far told me:

> The most sinful thing is to force people by means of social pressures. If one is *yakin* (convinced) to be a Communist, it is all right. If one is *yakin* to be a Marhaenist (PNI's ideology), it is all right, too. But "social economic pressures" *(tekanan sosial ekonomis)* like *monoloyo* [the principle of monoloyality which Golkar has imposed on all government officials] is wrong. It makes people believe one way in *batin* (internally) but behave the other way in *lahir* (outwardly). Discrepancy *(kurang setujunya)* between *lahir* and *batin* leads to the destruction of morality *(akhlak)*. Monoloyo abets widespread hypocrisy. That I cannot accept *(tidak bisa menerima)*.

For a "true Muslim" discrepancy between one's *lahir* and *batin* is the most horrible thing. Outer self *(lahir)* must reflect the inner self *(batin)* and the two must always agree with each other. Whereas for an *abangan*, especially for an *abangan* of *priyayi* status, the manipulation of *lahir* is viewed as a measure of self-control and if circumstances force him to adopt a different *lahir*, as in the case for the *pamong praja* cited above, such a smooth compromise is justified in terms of perseverance of their *batin*.

In contrast to the *abangan priyayi's* emphasis on *batin*, internal self and its perseverance, reformist Muslims seen to consider *lahir*, external self, or more precisely, the externalization of one's true internal self, much more important. For example, the role of an organization for religious enlightenment like the Muhammadiyah is viewed as an aid in getting rid of "'dirt and dust" in the overlayer of one's self which in itself has God-given ability and natural tendency to comprehend and obey His commands. The organizational activities of the Muhammadiyah, especially those providing facilities and opportunities for prayers, education, *zakat*, etc., are viewed as making it much easier for Muslims to fulfil religious obligations without outside hindrances. The existence of a prayer house *(langgar)* near one's home is likely to induce a less devout Muslim to start praying more often and more regularly. A Muhammadiyah school in the neighbourhood may attract more children of *abangan* families for the systematic learning of Islamic teachings.

A retired Muhammadiyah teacher stated to me that the most important contribution of the Muhammadiyah in the field of education was that it made much easier *(memudahkan)*, more accessible and more comprehensible *(lebih mudah untuk difahami)* the learning of Islamic teachings for average Muslim children so that their inborn faith in God in *batin* can acquire a definite, refined shape in *lahir*. The reformist view is that all Javanese are Muslims in *batin* but are only prevented from expressing and realizing their faith outwardly. This view covers former PKI members and followers as well. In a self-confident tone a Muhammadiyah leader stated to me as follows:

> Almost one half of the total population in Kotagede went along with the PKI before 1965. But in fact they were all Muslims and white *(putih*, [the colour for Muslims, especially pious Muslims]) in *batin*. They were red only in *lahir*. Therefore once the outside conditions are improved, and above all once Muhammadiyah further invigorates its educational activities, it is not impossible to hope that most former PKI supporters will become "true Muslims".

This conviction seems to underline the Muhammadiyah's attitude towards the former PKI members and supporters. The categorization of self into *lahir* and *batin* is also employed by the Muhammadiyah to induce the performance of good deeds *(amal)* in *lahir* in this world to secure reward *(ganjaran)* in the world of the after-life. The performance of concrete and visible virtuous deeds in this world constitutes the surest guarantee *(jaminan)* of receiving God's reward in the world of the after-life.

KASAR VS. *ALUS*

The ideology of the Muhammadiyah is expressed in the Javanese language through its linguistic structure and cultural idioms. But, as we have seen, there are a number of subtle alterations in meaning and shifts in emphases to adapt to reformist ideas. This transformation can further be observed in the Muhammadiyah's frequent use of another pair of Javanese value terms, *kasar* and *alus*. Geertz has given a lucid explanation of this pair concept: "*Alus* means pure, refined, polished, polite, exquisite, ethereal, subtle, civilized, smooth ... *Kasar* is merely the opposite: impolite, rough, uncivilized..." (1960, p. 232). I would like to add another point to this. In the reformist view, *alus*-ness is a God-given quality in human beings, and this must be brought forth when human beings interact with each other. Hence, the notion of *sasrawungan ingkang saé*, "the harmonious way of social intercourse" as the God-commanded way of interpersonal relationships in this world, comes to occupy a central position in the Muhammadiyah ideology.

The Ideology of the Muhammadiyah   187

The campaign speech of Pak Asy'ari cited above has already touched upon this theme, but as a supplement and support, I would like to quote from another speech which I recorded in Kotagede. The speech was given by the present national president of the Muhammadiyah, Bapak Haji A.R. Fakhruddin on the occasion of Syawalan of the Kotagede branch of the organization in November 1971 (1391 AH). A Syawalan meeting (derived from the name of the month, Syawal — the month following the Fasting Month, Ramadhan) or Halal-bihalal (meeting asking for mutual forgiveness) is held every year for the entire Muhammadiyah membership in the beginning of the month of Syawal. The meeting was held in the building, still under construction, of a new Muhammadiyah junior high school *(wakaf,* donation of Professor H.M. Rasjidi) and was attended by about 800 people. Approximately 60 per cent of the audience were women who occupied the front half of the hall, and the rest, men, occupied the back half of the hall; both groups sat on mats spread on the earthen ground.

Pak A.R., as Muhammadiyah members affectionately call him, the ninth and present top leader of the Muhammadiyah, is originally from an *alim* family in Kulon Progo, Yogyakarta. Like his many other colleagues in the

FIGURE 6.1

Syawalan meeting of R.K. Prenggan (speaker is the sub-district military commander, Pak Rasjidin).

FIGURE 6.2

Syawalan meeting of Kotagede Muhammadiyah (speaker is Pak A.R. Fakhruddin, national chairman of Muhammadiyah).

national leadership of the Muhammadiyah, he is another example of a reformist *alim* with a traditional background. His big round face and rather fat body remind one of Semar, the comic figure in the Javanese *wayang* shadowplay. In keeping with his appearance he has a real talent for *dhagelan*, comedies spattered by improvised jokes played out by *panakawan* (clown) figures. (For *panakawan*, see Anderson 1965, pp. 2–22.) A *dhagelan* player must possess above all an immense skill in manipulating the complexity of the Javanese language, jumping from high to low speech levels, mimicking every type of Javanese speaker, deliberately twisting and misusing proper speech etiquette, invoking an uproar of laughter from the audience while maintaining a sober face with the utmost self-control. Pak A.R. is equipped with that ability.

Just as Pak Asy'ari emphasized *tata krama ingkang saé* (good etiquette of social intercourse), so did Pak A.R. dwell at length on the importance of *sasrawungan ingkang saé* (harmonious social interaction) stressing the point that fulfilment of *rukun Islam* is not enough: what is important is to improve one's character (*akhlak* in Arabic, *budi pekerti* in Javanese) so that one can become a more perfect Muslim. According to him, Muhammadiyah members must know how to behave well in social intercourse with others who are all fellow creatures by God, the Lord. The passage from Pak A.R.'s speech which

The Ideology of the Muhammadiyah

follows is of interest both for the content of his ideas on the subject and for the manner in which they are expressed. After quoting in Arabic a Hadith exhorting the cultivation of a good character *(akhlak)* and interpreting it in Javanese, he went on as follows:

> There are many ways which a good character [of a person] takes form, if not in speeches, then in the ways a person gets along with others. If a person's character is good, then the way he gets along with others must be good, too.
>
> For example, when we see each other, we certainly greet each other. You and I are all Muhammadiyah people, and thus we already know the way Muslims greet as exemplified by the Prophet, *Assalamu'alaikum* (May God give you peace). But when you greet a friend *(sedulur)* who is not Islamic yet *(durung Islam)*, then you of course do not need to greet him with *Assalamu'alaikum*. You just greet him in the Javanese way only *(cara Jawi mawon)*. [Imitating a woman's voice in *Krama*, High Javanese.]
> "Where are you going, Madam?" *(Badhé tindak pundi, Bu?* [A common polite greeting])
> This is already a greeting.
> "Well, just to the market." And then later, when you see her returning, you greet again,
> "Going home, Madam?"
> "Yes, going home now."
> You see, this is already a good greeting. This is a substitute greeting for those who do not yet understand *(dereng mangertos)*. Don't say to yourself, [in *Ngoko*] "Alas, this one doesn't understand yet, not yet a *santri!* Can't even say *Assalamu'alaikum!*" (Laughter)
> This is not *akhlak*. (Light laughter) [Imitating a tone of utmost disgust.] "Yeh, she must be a G30S (Communist rebel)!" (Explosion of laughter) Having been greeted, just to keep silent and to think that way, that is wrong; it's not a proper way. *Inggih* (Yes)? *Inggih* (a chorus of of "y-e-s" from the audience).
> So you and I, we all must be able to get along well with others *(srawungan sing apik)*: when you meet a person, you just smile; just question *(takon)*. You must know the question is just etiquette *(tata krama)* and you don't actually need to know something [expect an answer]; [in a woman's voice in *Krama*]
> "Where are you going, Madam?"
> "Just to the market."
> "What are you going to buy?"
> "Well, buying some rice."
> "What kind of rice, Madam?" (Laughter)
> "Well, hulled rice."
> "What price of rice, Madam?" (Louder laughter)

Just to keep on asking like this is not a greeting. If you do so, the one who is being questioned will be annoyed in the heart *(mangkelati)*. If [you] meet [a person] and question like what Pak A.R. [I] has done right now, then [the person] will try to avoid seeing you again so as not to be questioned about this and that. That is not the way to get along well with others but just to annoy others; it means you do not know the proper way yet.

So, to get along well with your neighbor, the way must be proper. When the neighbour just drops in to chat with you *(omong-omongan)*, just welcome him and chat. If he doesn't pray yet, that's all right. You should not make a fool of him *(aja ngolok-olok)*. You should not tease him irrtatingly *(aja ngece-ece)*. If he falls sick, then just go and see *(tuwéni)*; if in need, go and help; if down with a cold, go and give a coin-massage *(keroki)*. Well it is up to you how you actually do your help. But that is what is called *sasrawungan ingkang saé* (harmonious way of social intercourse). 'Aisyiyah people, Muhammadiyah people must be able to do this.

Please do not say, "... but my neighbour just doesn't pray yet." And when asked about your neigbour, you say, "Ah, that neighbour of mine? Don't worry about him. He doesn't pray yet." And if you hear he is sick, "Let's not worry about him." "Dead? All right, let's not worry." (Laughter). This means that you just cannot get along well with others *(ora isa srawung)*. All Muhammadiyah people, ladies and gentlemen, must be able to behave properly with others, talk with others in a refined manner *(alus)*. For if a person speaks in a way to annoy others, then the other side also talks back in a harsh manner; [in *Krama* but in a fast and blunt tone of *Ngoko*]

"*Where are you going, Sister* (Mbakyu)?"

"*We* (My God)! How come you keep asking that way *(kok takén-takén)?*" (Uproar of laughter)

O my dear! Just to ask (greet) in such a way! This is what is called hurting each other's hearts. So Muhammadiyah people, 'Aisyiyah people, let us avoid being like that as much as possible, *inggih?*

Inggih ("Yes", the audience responded loudly).

It is obvious from the above quotation that the Muhammadiyah shares basic Javanese ethical value on harmonious social intercourse with the rest of the population. In fact, several lines of Pak A.R.'s speech make even perfect parallels with statements which Geertz has regarded as representing typical *priyayi* ethics (1960, Chapter 17). Sometimes Pak A.R., a representative *santri*, and Geertz's teacher of *priyayi* mysticism even employ exactly the same expressions and metaphors (for example, see ibid., p. 242). However, the two differ radically when it comes to the source of "truth" for these ethical teachings. For Geertz's teacher of mysticism, the harmonious state itself has an intrinsic value. For Pak A.R., human beings must live together harmoniously because God commands so. What Pak A.R. is endeavouring to do in his speech is to give new interpretations to traditional Javanese ethical themes which are already familiar to most of the people. He is trying to make his Javanese audience realize that these already familiar themes in fact have much deeper religious significances than commonsensical wisdom. Ethics are God's commands for mankind. Harmonious social intercourse has a value for it is God's command to do so, and to obey His command is to serve Him.

HAWA NAFSU VS. *IKHLAS*

Javanese Muslims regard human nature as consisting of mutually antagonistic elements, *hawa nafsu* and *nafsu mutma'innah*. Both are God-given. The concept of *hawa nafsu* seems to have been incorporated into traditional Javanese ideas for a long time, probably since the time of the early Islamization of Java. As a result, *hawa nafsu* has acquired an extremely broad spectrum of meanings. *Nafsu*, an Arabic word in origin, means in contemporary Javanese "passion", "lust", "desire", and "anger". *Nafsu* is also often pronounced *napsu* or *nepsu* since the sound of "f" is not an indigenous Javanese phoneme. (See, for example, p. 180 above.) Moreover, it has even been "corrupted" into *nesu*, whose primary meaning is "anger". A similar-sounding word, *nafas (napas)* probably of Malay origin, has come to be used as a synonym of *nafsu*, adding the meanings of "breath", "breathing", and "soul" into the spectrum of the meaning of *nafsu-nafas*.[7] Perhaps here again the working of Javanese folk etymology, *kerata-basa*, has been responsible for the blending of these words and meanings. (For *kerata-basa*, see Chapter 4, note 12 above.)

Geertz has observed that in some mystical sects breath and the technique to regulate breathing occupy a place of central importance (Geertz 1960, pp. 317–19). Breath is regarded as the essence of life, and its conscious regulation by mediation constitutes an elementary step toward mystical attainment. In fact, the equation of life and breath is commonly held by Javanese, and it is not restricted to any mystical sect. The more Javanese aspect seems to come in when the physiological mode of breathing is linked with particular psychological states like anger and passionate desire. Then the control of disturbed feeling or emotion is achieved through the control of breathing.

As with the cases of the pair concepts of *lahir/batin* and *alus/kasar* mentioned above, *nafsu* taken into the reformist terminology emphasizes

---

7. For dictionary definitions of *hawa, nafsu, nafas*, etc. see Pigeaud (1938) and Echols and Hasan (1961). Further etymological explanations have been obtained from the speech of Pak A.R. Fakhruddin and Kotagede informants.

exclusively one element in one of the many meanings of the term, i.e., "desire". *Hawa* in Arabic and *hawa* in Javanese are perhaps accidentally homologous. In Arabic *hawa* means "to descend" and "to be low in morality". In Javanese, *hawa* means "air", "climate", and "weather". When *hawa* and *nafsu are* combined as an idiom, it comes to mean "desire to do something low in morality". Pak A.R. states in the same speech quoted above as follows:

> The month of Puasa is over. But we must keep trying energetically to add up our devotion to God *(takwa)*. We must, with increased earnestness, continue to work for the fulfillment of God's commands and try to keep ourselves away from His prohibitions. We must not be completely dominated by *hawa nafsu* which is always the nest of Satan. Ladies and gentlemen, we are all given *hawa nafsu* by God. We are given *nafsu* (desire) which can *hawa* (descend). *Hawa* in Arabic means "to descend, to go down" *(mandhap, anjlok* in Javanese). [*Hawa nafsu* is] the desire which can [make us] behave rudely *(tumindak ingkang saged asor)*, look sourly *(nylekuthis)*, beggarly *(dermis)* or in other ways that are intractable *(mbeler)*.

Pak A.R. mentions, as examples of *hawa nafsu*, telling lies and being dishonest, especially in trade, buying lottery tickets, and being covetous of one's neighbour's better food and clothing. He summates that all these are caused by the work of *hawa nafsu*. Pak A.R. goes on to say:

> We must all be able to control *(ngencengi*, lit., "tighten, not to let loose") our *hawa nafsu*. Fortunately we are also equipped with another God-given element, *nafsu mutma'innah*, a *nafsu* which can [make us] do good deeds. This is *taufik* (God's help). For example, when you are invited to attend a religious lecture *(ngaji)* and when you feel you'd like to go along willingly, that is [the work of] *nafsu mutma'innah*, the desire for good deeds. Then while listening to a religious lecture, you keep listening willingly, keep concentrating your attention on the lecture without falling asleep (laughter), then that is [the work] of *nafsu mutma'innah*.

Hawa nafsu, if unrestrained, will lead man astray from the way prescribed by God. However, *hawa nafsu* is a God-given element in human nature, and man is incapable of eradicating it completely. It is the desire for this-worldly satisfaction; the desire for tasty food, sexual gratification, pretty clothing, money, status, prestige, power and the like. There is nobody who is totally lacking in *hawa nafsu*. However, the critical point of difference between being "true Muslims" and being less so is that the former know how to control *hawa nafsu* and do not go to excess in satisfying those desires: a minimal amount of food to maintain a healthy body, lawful marriage to satisfy sexual desire and to procreate, a decent income to be clothed properly and to have a safe shelter — that is enough. Excesses are sinful and the work of unrestrained *hawa nafsu*.

FIGURE 6.3

Pak A.R. and his audience

FIGURE 6.4

Visit of General Nasution to Silver Mosque in Kotagede.

FIGURE 6.5

(From left) Prof. Abdul Kahar Muzakkir, Pak Wardi, Pak Jamhari, Pak S.K. Hardjono, and the author in Alun-Alun, Kotagede.
Source: Courtesy of an anonymous photographer.

In order to illustrate further the Muhammadiyah's ideas about *hawa nafsu*, it may be helpful to make a brief digression into *kethoprak*, folk drama, which is regarded by the Muhammadiyah as the expression of unrestrained *hawa nafsu*. *Kethoprak* is a south Central Javanese counterpart of *ludruk*, the "proletarian drama" of East Java studied by James Peacock (1968). In south Central Java *kethoprak* is extremely popular among the lower class masses in the regional and local urban centres and also to some extent in the rural areas. *Wayang kulit*, the puppet shadow play, and *kethoprak* contrast sharply, each representing an extreme end of the Javanese ethical and aesthetic value scale of *alus* (refined) and *kasar* (crude). The world of the *wayang*, stories of which are Javanese adaptations of Indic epics, is characterized by stylized politeness, elegance and refinement, with the emphasis on order, harmony, mystical oneness and the interdependence of all beings in the universe and their predestined roles. The *dhalang*, who narrates the story moves all the puppets and directs the *gamelan* orchestra through the entire overnight show, displays the utmost power of self-control and perseverance. *Wayang* is essentially an *alus* art-entertainment encompassing both *priyayi* (aristocrats) and *wong cilik* (commoner). In contrast, *kethoprak* is an art-entertainment of, for and by *wong cilik*. It has never reached the *kraton*, or court circles.

The world of *kethoprak* is that of wildness and disorder, the world of *édan-édanan* (fool and madness) to use the common Javanese expression. The basic tone is seriocomic, and clown figures play much more dominant roles than in the case of *wayang*. Most *kethoprak* stories are taken from folk versions of historical events. (Out of the seven shows I saw in Kotagede, two stories were taken from the Majapahit period, three from Later Mataram, one from Imperial China and one apparently from Mughal India.) The stories are mostly about bitter struggles over such this-worldly desiderata as women, kingships or other power positions, territories, treasures, and magical objects. The ways through which those spoils are acquired are also this-worldly: rapes, abductions, conspiracies, betrayals, assassinations, sorceries, massacres, etc. The language used includes most *kasar* expressions in *Ngoko desa*, village *Ngoko*; filthy words and swear words are used freely. The players (consisting of both sexes playing "natural" roles — transvestites are rare) also act out scenes of wildness in extremely exaggerated ways which are not allowed in the context of everyday public life. For example, physical contact between males and females, direct expression of bliss, lust, anxiety, fear, disgust, anger, hatred, or sorrow is freely and exaggeratedly shown. The audience also responds directly and wildly to what is transpiring on the stage. Even the seating pattern of the audience in a *kethoprak* theatre is a "deviation" from Javanese norms and everyday practice. Young men and women of the late teens and twenties constitute the core of the audience, along with their younger brothers and sisters; older people are rare. The audience seat mixedly disregarding sex and age categorizations which in the rest of life are decisively important. The audience jeers, boos, yells, shouts, laughs, weeps, or applauds unrestrainedly. Prostitutes are seen in and out of the theatre. Around the theatre snack *warung* (stalls) and small food vendors are clustered. Various types of gambling — roulette being most popular — are also going on around the theatre. Backstage, it is said that *kethoprak* troupe members often engage in promiscuous relations, both heterosexual and homosexual, taking indigenous narcotics and alcohol.

Despite the fact that most *kethoprak* plays end happily (the good hero-prince finally gets the kingship after destroying its usurpers, the honest lovers finally get married and live happily ever after, etc.), the kind of emotional experience the audience undergoes seems quite different from its *wayang* counterpart. At the end of the overnight performance of a *wayang* show, accompanied as it is with the dim lights of the morning sun and cool fresh air, the audience feels catharsis: the self cleansed through an *alus* experience. At the end of a *kethoprak* show (which ends around midnight usually), however, after hours of emotional ups and downs, shouting at top voice and hilarious laughing, one feels physical exhaustion and an as yet unsettled sense of excitement. A Muhammadiyah elder, noticing that I had been to *kethoprak* shows, once asked me how I felt when the show was over. Without awaiting my answer he said:

> You must have been exhausted *(payah)* and lazy *(malas)* but not so much satisfied yet *(kurang pitas)*. Your body felt hot *(panas)* and trembling *(gemetar)*, and you felt thirsty *(haus)* for anything [implying, as I understood it, "thirst" for food, drink and sex]. That's the way *kethoprak* is.

I confessed that it was exactly the way I felt when the show was over. The elder man continued:

> You see that's the work of *hawa nafsu*. The determination *(tekanan,* lit., "pressure") to work hard is impaired *(dilemahkan)* and *hawa nafsu* is set free *(dilepaskan)*. You want to do whatever you like *(semaunya saja)* without thinking what is good and what is bad. That is the reason why *kethoprak* is so dangerous *(bahaya)* for the personality of young people *(jiwa muda mudi)*.

The recent revival of *kethoprak* (after its demise with the banning of the PKI and the Lekra, PKI's cultural organization) with the coming of the 1971 general election at the encouragement of government authorities has been received by Muhammadiyah activists with dismay. This has contributed in part to the development of their rather sober view of the New Order regime.

The above quoted Muhammadiyah elder and some other members pointed out to me that, during a recently-held four-week marathon show of *kethoprak* with the ostensible purpose of raising funds for a "young farmers association", petty thefts occurred frequently in the neighbourhood around the *kethoprak* theatre. (This was confirmed by the "social relations" police officer). During this period there were an unprecedented twenty-two reported cases of thefts including one in which 20,000 rupiahs in cash for the monthly salaries of the local religious affairs office (KUA) were stolen from the office's safe. Although it was of course difficult to verify the Muhammadiyah allegation that the *kethoprak* show was chiefly responsible for the actual ocurrence of these crimes, it was observed that from the time of the general election semi-professional criminals, who were generally known as *penjahat*, came under the patronage of the local authorities. Some of them were given positions in Hansip, the local security corps, and some others were officially enlisted in the committee which ran the notorious four-week *kethoprak* show. A horse racing meeting (where official and unofficial gambling was allowed) was also held by a similar committee a few months before the above-mentioned *kethoprak* show in order to raise funds for "the repair of the police office building".

In the light of what has been described above, it is interesting to note that the Muhammadiyah's hostility toward the PKI was explained by its members not so much in terms of the latter's political and economic programmes (e.g., land reforms) nor its philosophical standpoint (historical materialism or atheism) but rather on moral grounds that the PKI encouraged the release of *hawa nafsu*.

I asked Pak Marto (an old-guard Muhammadiyah who experienced the historic "clash" with the PKI in 1924) why the PKI was able to build up such a large following in Kotagede after World War II. His explanation was:

> PKI people were clever in deceiving people *(pintar menipu)*. They promised this and that, although the promises were empty *(janji kosong)*. In essence, the PKI promised that if it gets power people can get anything they want *(semaunya saja)*. The PKI did not attack religion [Islam] directly. They only said, "when stomachs are empty, what is the use of prayer *(kalau perutnya kosong, apa gunanya sholat)*? If the PKI gets power, just ask for anything *(minta apa-apa saja)*. Every demand will be met (food, clothes, house, land, etc)." It was a lie. Nothing is achieved only by asking. We have to work hard to get something. Empty promises only make people lazy and let *hawa nafsu* free *(membiarkan hawa nafsu)*.

Being part of human nature, man cannot get rid of *hawa nafsu*. But man must and can control it by conscious effort. The unrestrained expressions of *hawa nafsu* advocated by the PKI will lead to anarchy, tyranny and sinful acts which go astray from God's command: the Muhammadiyah reasons this way and takes the stand of moral opposition to the PKI as well as to any other group which it regards as encouraging the release of *hawa nafsu*.

IKHLAS VS. *PAMRIH*

Let me focus now on the notion of *ikhlas* in Muhammadiyah ideology. The notion of *ikhlas* is in fact not a monopoly of the Muhammadiyah, either. It is again an extremely pervasive value notion among the Javanese. The Muhammadiyah has taken up this notion and reworked it. The result is the addition of a very powerful conceptual weapon in the hands ot the Muhammadiyah for linking traditional and reformist ideas. Clifford Geertz has attempted at a definition of *ikhlas* as the "state of willed affectlessness" (Geertz 1960, p. 73). He goes on to explain that *ikhlas* means:

> ... detachment from contingencies of the external world so as not to be disturbed when things go awry in it or if something unexpected occurs. It is "not caring" on the premise that if one does not care about worldly things they cannot hurt or upset one (ibid., pp. 240–41).

This explanation seems to be too psycho-philosophical whereas the notion of *ikhlas* is, as I see it, primarily religio-ethical. Perhaps this psycho-philosophical bias is related to the omission in the work of Geertz of the fact that a short chapter in the Qur'an is entitled "*Ikhlas*" (Surah Al-Ikhlas, The Qur'an 112:1–4). This is one of the few chapters that even an extremely unsophisticated *abangan* Javanese is surely to have heard on many occasions or even learned by heart to recite by himself after learning the Confession of Faith from a village Qur'anic teacher.[8]

In order to elaborate this point I shall quote again from statements of Muhammadiyah activists who are already familiar to us: Pak Ja'far, Pak Asy'ari and Pak A.R. Fakhruddin. The core of the Muhammadiyah notion of *ikhlas* seems to take its model from the deed of Prophet Ibrahim (Abraham) whom God ordered to sacrifice his beloved son Ismail. It emphasizes sacrifice as a deed of complete faithfulness to God and as a means to glorify Him. (In the Qur'anic tradition not Isaac but his older brother Ismail was ordered to be sacrificed.)

---

8. In spite of the fact that Geertz has more recently come to emphasize the "scripturalist" aspect of modern Indonesian Islam (1968), there was little indication in his initial monograph on the Javanese religious life (1960) that he had given his attention to the literary sources of Islamic tradition in Java including the Scriptures. Drewes has remarked (I suspect with no little indignation about the fact that the Dutch pre-war scholarship on Javanese religion was totally ignored by Geertz in his earlier writings) that "the Javanese emerge from his [Geertz'] description as an almost illiterate people" (Drewes 1968, p. 211, n. 2). I cannot disagree with Drewes.

The theme of sacrifice is most explicitly expressed on the occasion of Hari Raya Idul Adha (Hari Korban) or the Day of Sacrifice. *Sholat ied* or festive prayer is held, after which cattle (buffaloes, cows and goats) are slaughtered and their meat is distributed to the poor and needy *(fakir miskin)*. I quote from Pak Ja'far's *khutbah* (sermon) to a Friday prayer meeting which was held a few days prior to the Day of Sacrifice in April 1965 (Dulkijah 1384 AH):

> On the Day of Sacrifice (Hari Korban) the entire Muslim community *(ummat Islam)* over the world will be getting together in festive prayer meetings *(sholat ied)* to praise the name of God and with the intention of slaughtering *korban* (sacrificial animals) to fulfill and to carry out the command of God. *Korban* in the form of slaughtering cattle is to commemorate the sacrifice of the Prophet Ibrahim [Abraham] who with sincere devotion *(ikhlas)* sacrificed the feeling of affection *(rasa cinta kasih)* as father to son, sacrificing human feelings *(rasa perikemanusiaan)*. The required sacrifice was quite unusual to comply with for any human being of noble character *(budi luhur)* like him. Hari Korban is also to commemorate the devotion *(keikhlasan)* held in the heart of Ismail, his son, who was ready to sacrifice his life, to die entirely filled with the conviction in the truth that his father Ibrahim had received the divine revelation from God. The Prophet Ismail, who was still so young to face this trial of God's *(ujian Tuhan)*, stood death, unmovedly *(ikhlas)*, to be cut apart by his father's knife whose edge was very sharp.

Pak Ja'far goes on to say that since the days of Ibrahim and Ismail the believers of God followed the model exemplified by them in order to glorify the religion of God. He cites heroes and heroic deeds which contributed to the victory of Islam in early Islamic history. Then he views modern Indonesian history from the same viewpoint and states that in the history of Indonesia, both before and after Independence, Muslims sacrifice themselves for the victory of Islam and the Indonesian nation:

> Their sacrifices *(pengorbanan)* took various forms — thinkings and ideas *(fikiran)*, energy *(tenaga)*, wealth and property *(harta benda)*, and even blood *(darah)*, soul *(jiwa)* and body *(raga)*. Burned with the fighting spirit of Islam *(semangat api Islam)* the Indonesian Muslims made wholehearted self-sacrifices *(pengorbanan ikhlas)* for the nation and revolution. The victory of Islam [in its early Golden Age] was not possible through mere meditation *(tafakur)* or the repetition of rosary counting *(menghitung-hitung tasbih)*. It was achieved only through concrete deeds of self-sacrifice. So was the independence of Indonesia.

Then he quotes from the Qur'an and urges the audience to examine themselves to see if their deeds are up to the standard set by God:

> The believers are those who believe in God and his Messenger, then have not doubted, and have struggled with their possessions and their selves in the way of God: those — they are the truthful ones (The Qur'an 49:15, English translation from Arberry 1955, vol. II, p. 232).

Pak Ja'far asks the audience: "Have we really believed in God without doubts, straightforwardly *(tidak plintat-plintut)*, without inconsistency? Have we really struggled *(jihad,* lit., 'extraneous effort', 'Holy War') for the interest of Islam?" In more specific terms, he continues:

> Have you already counted and made note of what percent of your total wealth and income should be used for donations *(amal)* to Muhammadiyah schools, hospitals, libraries, etc.? Have you even come to the point that you feel so devoted to the defense of Islam that you forget about your own personal interest and your family's?

Here it can be observed how *ikhlas* has come to provide a basis for the social activism of the Muhammadiyah movement (see Chapter 3 above, for the Muhammadiyah's activism). Far from being a resignation from this world or a psychological defence to avoid unexpected emotional disturbances, *ikhlas* in Muhammadiyah ideology has been generalized to mean the positive, willing abandonment of this-worldly concerns in the form of concrete deeds. In order to express the belief that this-worldly possessions do not have significance of their own but are only significant as a creation of God's and as a means to glorify God, the Muhammadiyah urges that actual deeds of negating this-worldly concerns must be done in tangible and positive ways: surrendering properties and human energy for the interest of Islam. The often-heard "shorthand" characterization of the Muhammadiyah as a "religious, social and educational organization" will become less appropriate in the light of the foregoing understanding of the notion of *ikhlas*. Instead of arranging the *religious, social* and *educational* on the same plane, we must see that the first, the *religious,* is the *sine qua non* of the Muhammadiyah movement, and the latter two are the outward expressions and realizations of the religious consciousness of the movement and are properly understood only when explained in terms of it.

Ikhlas might have been the watchword for self-resignation and non-involvement in traditional Javanese ideas as Geertz has suggested. With the Muhammadiyah, however, the notion has been transformed into a battle-cry for its active social concern and involvement. The word, *ikhlas*, is indeed shouted out. For example, Pak A.R. in the same address cited above appealed to the audience: "I heard earlier that this building [for a Muhammadiyah junior high school] needs some 800,000 rupiahs more to bring it to completion. *Ikhlas!* Ladies and gentlemen, I urge your contributions for its completion."

In the Muhammadiyah terminology *ikhlas* is also applied to political activities. Pak Asy'ari, in the campaign speech quoted above, uses the term in the political context:

> The coming general election is a trial *(ujian)* for us. We are going to be tested to see whether or not we are true Muslims *(tiyang Islam ingkang saéstu)*. Today you say that you are a Muslim but tomorrow you may say that you are forced *(dipekso-pekso)* by someone [to vote for a non-Islamic party]. But it cannot be a good excuse. Even if forced, it is only before you enter the voting booth *(bilik)*, isn't it? Once you are in the booth, there will be nobody else watching over you except God, the Lord. So whether or not you vote for a party of God, the Lord *(golongan Gusti Allah)* is entirely up to you. It is your own and my own responsibility … In the booth you do not have to be *bingung* ("confused, lost"). For if you and I, all of us, keep firmly in mind the command of God, the Lord, we will not be confused. Once there is established in our hearts a deep wish *(hasrat)* that we support the party of God, the Lord, nothing can confuse us any more and we will be safe *(slamat)* … Once we are in the booth, we face God, the Lord, alone. Then we must forget all this-worldly concerns *(kadonyaan)*. Forget the intimidations *(intimidasi)* you have suffered before, and *ikhlas!* Reciting *bismillah* ("in the name of Allah"), vote for the party of God, the Lord. *Ikhlas!* Because we do so not because of our selfish desire *(pamrih)* but because of our genuine willingness to fulfill the command of God, the Lord. That will become your good deed *(amal)* which later you can take along as provision *(sangu)* to the world of the after-life *(akhérat)*…

It should be obvious from the foregoing presentation in this chapter that Muhammadiyah ideology is essentially an ethical teaching, a doctrine for individual conduct based on Islam. It focuses on the individual and urges him to conform to its admonitions. Being an ethical theory for individuals, Muhammadiyah ideology lacks specific programme for social reform or political strategies to achieve them. The image of an ideal society for the Muhammadiyah is a society in which every man becomes a true Muslim and behaves as such. And the means to attain this society is that every man endeavours to become a true Muslim. In the sociology of Muhammadiyah (or perhaps more correctly, in the absence of sociological thinking in the Muhammadiyah in the sense of the Western tradition of social thought), society is no more and no less than the aggregate of individuals. The totality of individuals does not acquire a quality which surpasses the sum total of

FIGURE 6.6

Pak M. Asrofie speaking at a *pengajian* (religious lecture meeting) in Purbayan.

FIGURE 6.7

Professional *dhagelan* troupe performing at Independence Day celebration.

FIGURE 6.8

Amateur *kethoprak* group performing in Purbayan.

FIGURE 6.9

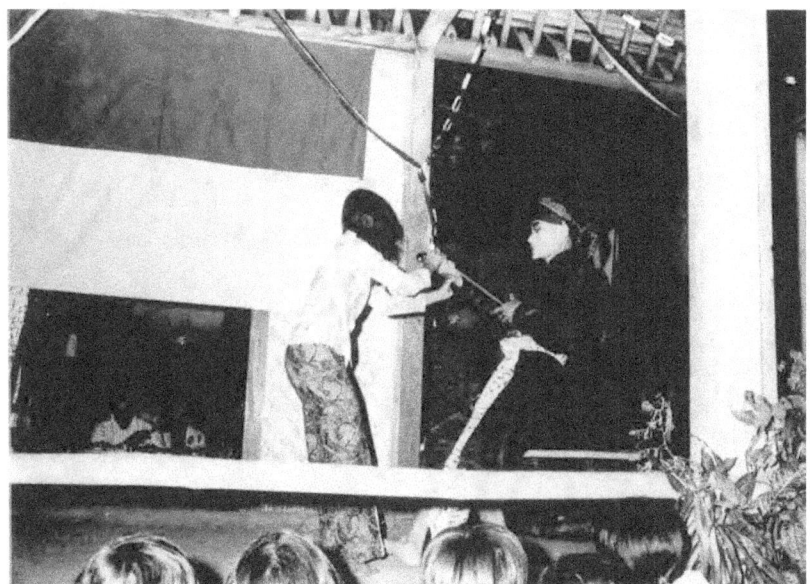

Commercial *kethoprak* troupe performing in Gedongan.

FIGURE 6.10

Gambling near *kethoprak* show.

FIGURE 6.11

1971 general election posters in front of Kotagede market.

FIGURE 6.12

Parmusi (Indonesian Muslim Party) campaign posters.

individuals. The reason for why we find repeated emphasis on *akhlak* (good character, personality which behaves properly) in Muhammadiyah literature and verbal communications can be explained in the light of the above discussion (cf. Kessler 1972).

To conclude this chapter, it seems appropriate to sum up the Muhammadiyah ideology in terms of its ideal personality type. The Muhammadiyah's ideal person is a true believer in God who never ceases to learn directly from the Holy Scriptures; who faithfully performs *rukun Islam*; who is independent and willing to assume responsibility for his own deeds; who lives a simple material life and avoids luxuries; who is anti-traditional and egalitarian in outlook but yet likes to humble himself; who can and prefers to speak polite language and behave harmoniously with others; who is honest and willing to help others; who values and is capable of controlling his selfish desire and avoiding instinctual behaviour; and who is ready to sacrifice himself for the interest of Islam and the community of the faithful (cf. Faded Ma'ruf 1961/62 and "Achlaq" in *Almanak Muhammadijah* 1960/61, pp. 114–23).

As a nomenclature of virtues, the above list may not be much different from any other religio-ethical teachings. A critical point is then how the reality approximates to the norms — the degree of religious intensity and the extent of religious commitment of an individual. And in that regard, Muhammadiyah members seem to score very highly. Many of the Muhammadiyah members I came to be acquainted with in the field indeed conformed to the ideal personality types. Of course, this is an extremely subjective judgment, and it is difficult to verify my statement by any "objective" means. I can only state that this assessment is based on my own personal experience among Japanese Christian circles and my limited exposure to the religious life in the United States. At least I can say this much: for the first time in my life, I felt that I was able to see in Kotagede what a religious man looked like and what religiosity meant.

Personal confessions aside, another interesting observation to be made on Muhammadiyah personality is that it coincides in many respects with the Javanese traditional ideal of *satrya*, or knighthood. For example, Pak Marto stated to me that he respects the Sultan of Yogyakarta, Hamengkubuwono IX, the former Vice President of the Republic, not because he is a hereditary sultan but because he is a good Muslim and a genuine *satrya*. *Satrya* is a Hindu-Javanese notion. Pak Marto's statement contains a peculiar contradiction that an ideal Muslim is an ideal Javanese. However, this contradiction holds only for those who think Islam and Javanese-ness are mutually exclusive and antagonistic. For Muhammadiyah members in Kotagede, who are born in the Javanese world and are striving to approach what they conceive of as the purer Islamic essence in their tradition, being a good Javanese and being a good Muslim mean one and the same thing (cf. Nakamura 1977, pp. 14–15).

Interestingly enough, from the viewpoint of *abangan*, too, a Muhammadiyah-type *santri* is regarded as peculiarly Javanese. To an *abangan*, a devout and socially active *santri* who is actually fulfilling the Islamic obligations, which the *abangan* knows to be required in theory but which he feels himself not up to, seems to possess extraordinary spiritual power *(kasektèn)*. As a result, the *abangan* tends to develop a complex of fear, admiration, envy, guilt, and inferiority vis-à-vis the *santri*. For example, many *abangan* people in Kotagede described our Pak Ja'far, a military commander in both the 1945 and 1966 crises, as a man of invincibility, superhuman cleverness, courage, and unlimited physical energy which enables him to fight a hand-to-hand combat for days and nights without eating, drinking, or resting, yet showing no signs of exhaustion: Pak Ja'far is a superman in *abangan* eyes. The often-heard appellation, "fanatic", given by *abangan* people to a Muhammadiyah-type activist, then seems not so much a derogatory term but reflecting a secret admission of inferiority on the part of the *abangan*. The *abangan* attitude towards *santri* is ambivalent in essence. An *abangan* may turn to a *santri* as his positive reference point. The relationship between the two is fluid and dynamic. In fact, a large part in the steady increase of Muhammadiyah membership in recent years seems to have occurred in this way.

The social categorization of Javanese society in terns of *santri* and *abangan* (and in a qualified sense, *priyayi*), presented and refined by Clifford Geertz and adopted by many other students of Javanese culture and society, has been a useful tool of analysis in order to make sense out of rather chaotic Javanese social groupings. However, once it is fixed as a bundle of cultural traits and employed to classify actual individuals into mutually exclusive categories, its analytical usefulness seems to start diminishing. The result has been a kind of tautology that an *abangan* behaves like an *abangan* because he belongs to the *abangan* group, and so with a *santri*. It is hoped that the foregoing discussion in this chapter will be of use for the review of this somewhat absurdly mechanical picture of Javanese religious behaviour which has been an unfortunate consequence of the Geertzian formulation.

BOX 7
The Beatles in Kotagede

One night in 1971 when I was coming home from an interview to my newly rented house in Basen, I heard a familiar melody drifting from a shophouse. The house was facing Jalan Karanglo, one of the main streets in Kotagede, stretching eastward from the post office. The music was *Ticket to Ride* by the Beatles. I came closer to the house and peeped through a gap at the front door. There I saw three young men dancing to the music under the dim light of an unmoving colour ball. They were almost in a trance. The street was dark, already deserted by people. The voices of the Beatles were mixed with the sound of frogs coming from the sewage ditch in front of the house. I felt somehow relieved and went home.

7

CONCLUSION
Re-Islamization of Java

> The struggle *(perjuangan)* to achieve a truly Islamic society *(masyarakat Islam yang sebenar-benar-nya)* is a struggle which has no breaks *(tak putus-putus).* It is like a relay race *(permainan estafet)*; generation by generation *(generasi demi generasi)* taking turns to carry forward the relay baton [of the struggle] on the track of history. *(Bulletin Lustrum Ke-I, S.M.P. Muhammadiyah VII, Kotagede,* 1970, p. 21).

The thesis that has been developed in the foregoing chapters is that orthodox Islam in the form of a reformist movement, Muhammadiyah, has arisen from within the traditional Javanese Islam as its internal transformation rather than as an outright import of a new ideology made complete elsewhere. The reformist version of orthodox Islam has been a vigorously proselytizing religious ideology and has brought, is bringing, and will bring about profound changes in social, cultural, economic and political aspects of Javanese life. To support this thesis, attempts have been made to document, describe and analyse major aspects of this ongoing process of re-Islamization as it occurred in a local town, Kotagede in south Central Java, over the past seventy years or so.

If the thesis can be regarded as having been substantiated sufficiently, at least for one local case, then the view expressed here may appear to come into direct conflict with an assumption widely held among students of contemporary Indonesia that Islam, especially its reformist version, is losing political strength. For example, George Kahin has recently expressed such a view in his preface to Ken Ward's *The Foundation of the Partai Muslimin Indonesia* (1970). Kahin states:

> Today [1970] Islamic political power in Indonesia has become considerably weaker [than in the early 1950s], and the influential Modernist Islamic elements who previously led the Masjumi are without political focus and organization (ibid., p. iii).

Another foreign observer of Indonesian politics, studying the results of the 1971 general election, noted a "surprisingly poor showing" of the electoral support the Parmusi obtained (Nishihara 1971, p. 50): the Parmusi votes of 5.36 per cent of the total votes in 1971 are compared to the Masyumi votes of 20.9 per cent of the total in the 1955 general election, and the figures have been regarded as firm evidence for the drastically weakening political strength of reformist Muslims (ibid., *passim*).

Nowadays it has become common among the circles of Indonesian observers to hear expressions of surprise, "Muslims are *still* strong!", or "They are *still* holding out!", when there has happened a show of Muslim political strength. Foreign observers were certainly surprised by the NU's persistence in the rural areas of Central and East Java in the 1971 election or by a more recent event of the passage of the Marriage Law with numerous amendments to appease Muslim critics despite Muslim political parties' numerical weakness in the post-election parliament. Obviously, the assumption underlying this kind of surprise is that the weakening of Muslim political strength is a natural process to expect, and the opposite is rather exceptional. So much so that academic interest now (mid-1970s) seems to be shifting to studying how long and how far Muslim political forces can survive and resist this process in terms of their relationships vis-à-vis the overwhelming power of the military dominated government.

In this general climate of opinion, the thesis of this study seems to belong to a tiny minority view which holds that Islam has been getting stronger. Drewes, the great Dutch scholar of Indonesian Islam, observed in the early 1950s that "the Islamization of Indonesia is still in progress, not only in the sense that Islam is still spreading among pagan tribes, but also in that peoples [sic] who went over to Islam centuries ago are living up more to the standard of Muslim orthodoxy" (Drewes 1955, p. 286).

Hoesein Djajadiningrat, the Indonesian Islamologist of international reputation, assessed the situation in the mid-1950s that "the number of 'white people', or those who have knowledge of Islam and are living up to Islamic principles, is increasing" (1958, p. 384). Daniel Lev, the American political scientist studying the social basis of Islamic legal institutions, obtained a strong impression in Jakarta in 1971 that many people are now undertaking Islamic obligations such as fasting in the month of Ramadan more seriously than before, "almost enthusiastically" (1972, p. 263). These observations seem to apply perfectly well to Central Java as well.

To be exact, however, the majority and the minority are *not* differing in opinion on the assessment of the same phenomenon. The majority is focusing on the weakening of the *political* strength of Muslims. The minority is, however, concerned about the growth of the number of serious believers in *socio-religious* terms. Their opinions may not be mutually exclusive and both can be right. Yet, there remains a problem of how to account for the relationships between the waning of Muslim political strength and the waxing of Muslim social force.

I think that this is a real problem arising from the current situation (1970s) in Indonesia and challenges our understanding of it. I feel that it is a kind of problem which can educate us in terms of substantive knowledge as well as theoretical sophistication when we attempt to seek a proper intellectual solution. I have tried to address myself to this problem in various parts of this study with particular reference to Kotagede society, even though my solution may not have been persuasive enough.

In addressing this problem, I have stood by an obvious but often forgotten truism that Islam is a religion, a faith for the believers and not a marker for political grouping. Politics in fact forms only a peripheral concern for most Muslims' daily lives. Instead of merely looking at Islam as a symbol of political solidarity, I have tried to understand the intellectual content, ethical relevance and significance of ritual actions of Islam as they are practiced in the real-life context of Kotagede. As I have stated in the Preface of this book, my field work in Kotagede was an experience of revelation to me. While I was living amidst Javanese Muslims I gradually started to feel and realize that there is nothing peculiar for a Javanese to be a pious Muslim. If this study conveys something of that feeling, I think I have done my job.

The Muhammadiyah may look doctrinaire at a distance. Yet at a closer examination, we realize that there is little theological systematization. What is there is rather an array of moral admonitions taken direct from the Qur'an and Hadith. It may appear exclusive when viewed from outside, but in fact it is extremely open when you are within. It may look organizationally imposing, but, actually, it is an aggregate of individuals who value personal devotion highly. It may appear as an organization of high discipline, but in fact there is no effective disciplinary device other than the individual's conscience. It looks aggressive and fanatic, but in fact its ways of propagation are gradual and tolerant. And finally but perhaps most important, it may appear anti-Javanese, but actually it embodies Javanese virtues in many ways. Perhaps we can say that here is a case of a universal religion, like Islam, having become a living religious tradition in the Javanese environment.

POSTSCRIPT TO PART I

> The reality of Islam is a personal, living faith, new every morning in the heart of individual Muslims.
>
> (Wilfred C. Smith 1957, pp. 17–18)

1. My stay at Harvard University, September 1981 to June 1982, as a visiting scholar of the Department of Anthropology and the Center for the Study of World Religions, has caused delay in the publication of this book for more than a year. I must apologize for this to the publisher and whomever else concerned.
2. At Harvard I was initiated into Qur'anic Arabic. I was also exposed to introductory courses in Islamic studies and comparative religion. My newly acquired knowledge, although still meagre, has enabled me to see my previous experience with the Muhammadiyah in Kotagede in a new perspective. I now realize a number of errors and shortcomings contained in this book. Most of them are of such nature that I took matters of universal significance in Islam and the Muslim world as something peculiar to the Muhammadiyah in Kotagede or Islam in Java. At the same time, I now feel assured of the basic soundness of my approach — to take Islam seriously as a religion.
3. I am encouraged by favourable comment on my original dissertation coming from a leading Indonesianist (McVey 1981). I am also heartened to observe growing interest among young Indonesian scholars in the empirical study of religious developments in Indonesia. Their contribution includes two recent *sarjana* theses by Kotagede students (Hazim 1977 and Charris 1979). Perhaps the "intellectual stagnation" I mentioned in the Preface applies only to Western or more precisely American scholarship which seems still enchanted by Geertzian paradigms.
4. I would also like to mention a brief but important contribution by H. Zaini Ahmad Noeh, a senior official of the Department of Religion. In his introduction to the Indonesian translation of Daniel Lev's *Islamic Courts in Indonesia* (*Peradilan Agama di Indonesia*, Jakarta: Intermasa, 1980), he emphasizes, among other things, the duality of *penghulu* officials in the indigenous Javanese polity as "*kyai* in the circle of *priyayi*, and also conversely *priyayi* in the circle of *kyai*" (ibid., p. 7). (Cf. *abdi*

dalem santri, p. 15 in this book.) He further points out the significance of this religious officialdom as a basis of the Islamic legitimization of the Kingdom of Later Mataram and successive Javanese authorities (even under the Dutch rule), and as a source of leadership for modern Islamic movements (both Muhammadiyah and NU), and the forerunner of the Department of Religion in the Republic of Indonesia. I hope his call for full scholarly investigation on the *penghulu* will be heeded.

5. The role of the Muhammadiyah in the field of women and marital life — a topic briefly touched upon in my original dissertation — has been dropped almost entirely from this book for various reasons. Those who want to know something about this subject are advised to consult the M.A. thesis of my wife, Hisako (H. Nakamura 1981). The thesis will be published by the Gadjah Mada University Press before long.

6. I would like to repeat my invitation of criticism and correction on this book from readers. I would especially welcome comments from Muhammadiyah people. (Please correspond through the publisher.) For I believe that the anthropologist is academically and morally obligated to keep striving for the improvement of his or her ethnography with the help of the people he or she studies. For the time being, let me only say: *nyuwun pangapunten sedaya kalepatan kula lahir lan batos* ("I beg your pardon for all my mistake most sincerely").

Mitsuo Nakamura
Tokyo
12 July 1983M/1 Syawal 1403H

PART II

Kotagede Revisited,
1972–2010

Coming Home

By Nur Atika

Smiles…
My old town
My small town

Warmth…
At every corner
An old friend of mine

Stories…
Of alleys separated by walls, and
Laughters from childhood days

Echoes…
Of *santri*s chanting the Qur'an
Rising and lowering

Faces…
Of my old town
Always the same

From: "Pulang", *Brosur Lebaran*, AMM Kotagede, No. 39, 1421H/2000M, p. 77.
English translation by Mitsuo Nakamura

MAP 2
Kotagede Region

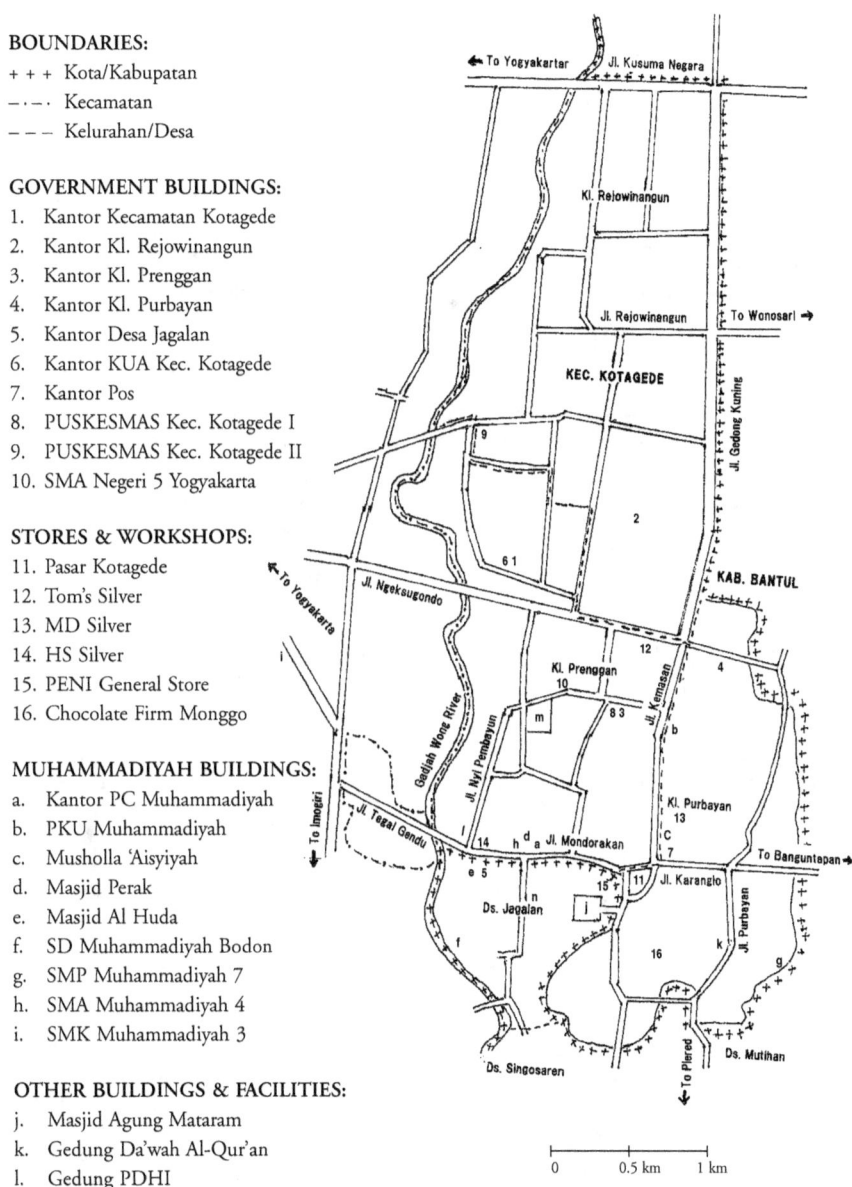

BOUNDARIES:
- + + + Kota/Kabupaten
- –·–·– Kecamatan
- – – – Kelurahan/Desa

GOVERNMENT BUILDINGS:
1. Kantor Kecamatan Kotagede
2. Kantor Kl. Rejowinangun
3. Kantor Kl. Prenggan
4. Kantor Kl. Purbayan
5. Kantor Desa Jagalan
6. Kantor KUA Kec. Kotagede
7. Kantor Pos
8. PUSKESMAS Kec. Kotagede I
9. PUSKESMAS Kec. Kotagede II
10. SMA Negeri 5 Yogyakarta

STORES & WORKSHOPS:
11. Pasar Kotagede
12. Tom's Silver
13. MD Silver
14. HS Silver
15. PENI General Store
16. Chocolate Firm Monggo

MUHAMMADIYAH BUILDINGS:
a. Kantor PC Muhammadiyah
b. PKU Muhammadiyah
c. Musholla 'Aisyiyah
d. Masjid Perak
e. Masjid Al Huda
f. SD Muhammadiyah Bodon
g. SMP Muhammadiyah 7
h. SMA Muhammadiyah 4
i. SMK Muhammadiyah 3

OTHER BUILDINGS & FACILITIES:
j. Masjid Agung Mataram
k. Gedung Da'wah Al-Qur'an
l. Gedung PDHI
m. Karang Sports Field
n. Rumah Pesik

MAP 3
Yogyakarta City and Kotagede Region

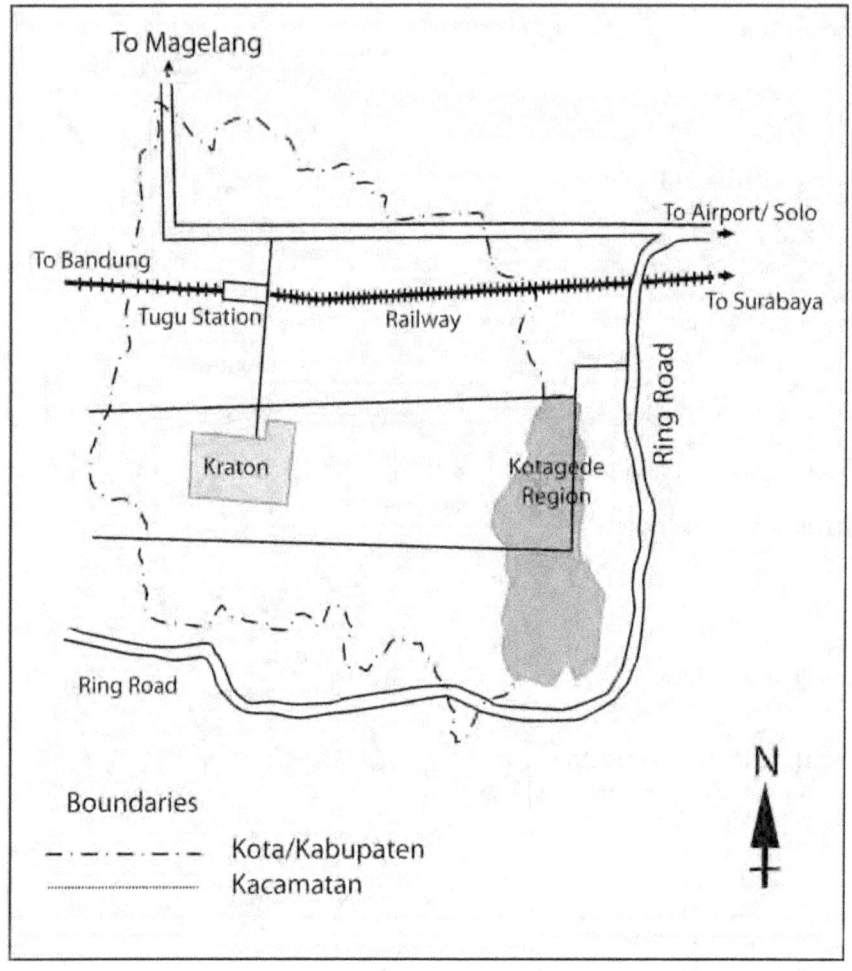

INTRODUCTION TO PART II

Part II of this book covers the history of the Muhammadiyah movement in Kotagede for the period of approximately forty years since my first fieldwork, i.e., from 1972 to 2010. During the period 1972–98, General Soeharto ruled Indonesia with his strategy of *pembangunan*, i.e., economic development under military control with the aid of Western powers. During the period 1998–2010, Indonesia experienced years of turbulent political change, in which the dictatorship of General Soeharto fell before the widespread protests and the era of Reformasi (Reformation) was launched. In Part II, attention is focussed on the local scene of Kotagede against the background of developments at the national level.

Chapter 8 reviews social changes occurring over the forty year period in the town of Kotagede in terms of urbanization, diversification, and globalization. Then, in Chapter 9, the achievements of the Muhammadiyah during the same period are described and discussed. In the following Chapter 10, the internal dynamics of the Muhammadiyah, especially of the conflicts between generations, and the process of change in its leadership are examined. In Chapter 11, a number of challenges currently faced by the Muhammadiyah movement in the post-Reformasi situation are taken up. In Chapter 12, an interesting and important recent development in the town, i.e., the Festival Kotagede, is discussed in relation with the Muhammadiyah. Chapter 13 deals with the impact of the 2006 earthquake and the efforts for rescue, recovery and reconstruction undertaken by the Muhammadiyah and others.

An exact chronological approach is not taken in historical narratives because of the paucity of appropriate data. Instead, I have presented for description and discussion a series of snapshots of major events and developments concerning the Muhammadiyah movement with some statistical data.

After the Concluding Remarks in Chapter 14, which summarizes major points of findings through the "revisit" study and discusses the future direction of the Muhammadiyah movement, Part II is followed by a Post-Postscript including acknowledgements. There, I have offered my personal reminiscences and appreciation of the help of others given to me during the forty years of my observation on the Muhammadiyah movement in Kotagede.

8

SOCIAL CHANGES IN KOTAGEDE, 1972–2010

ADMINISTRATIVE RE-DESIGNATION

It must be mentioned in advance when dealing with social changes in Kotagede that the town has undergone administrative re-designation since the original study for this book was conducted in 1970–72. The "Kemantren (Ward) of Kotagede, Jka (Jogjakarta)", has changed its name to "Kecamatan (Sub-district) Kotagede" and is one of the fourteen sub-districts constituting the City (Kota) of Yogyakarta. The geographic boundary of Kecamatan Kotagede, however, remains the same as that of former Kemantren Kotagede. The ten Rukun Kampungs (RK or neighbourhood association) which constituted the Kemantren of Kotagede before (see Figure 2.1) are now rearranged into three groups, forming three Kelurahans (Kl. or urban community) as follows: (1) Kl. Rejowinangun consisting of four ex-RKs, i.e., Rejowinangun, Gedongkuning, Pinalan and Tinalan; (2) Kl. Prenggan, of two ex-RKs, i.e. Prenggan and Tegalgendu; and (3) Kl. Purbayan, of four ex-RKs, i.e. Gedongan, Basen, Alun-Alun, and Purbayan. Each Kelurahan is further divided into Rukun Warga (RW or residents association), and the RW further into Rukun Tetangga (RT or neighbours association). There are all together 40 RWs and 164 RTs in the Kecamatan Kotagede. The area of Kecamatan Kotagede is sometimes called "Kotagede Administratip (= administrative Kotagede)".

Meanwhile, those areas, which were formerly designated as "Kotagede Ska (Surakarta)" belonging to the Kabupaten (Regency) of Bantul, no longer bear the name Kotagede, not to speak of Ska, at all at present. Former Kalurahan Jagalan Kotagede Ska, Kalurahan Singosaren Kotagede Ska and Kalurahan Mutihan Kotagede Ska are now simply called Desa Jagalan and Desa Singosaren, both belonging to Kelurahan Banguntapan, and Desa Mutihan belonging to Kelurahan Wirokerten — all forming part of Kabupaten Bantul. Desa Jagalan, which occupies the core part of the old town of Kotagede, has five RWs divided into fourteen Kampungs (abbreviated as Kp.).

In spite of all these new administrative designations, the former core areas of Kotagede (see Figure 2.2) are still regarded by most of the residents as a single socio-cultural entity in terms of geographic proximity, network of family and marriage, closeness in social interaction, cooperation in economic activities, commonness in customs, and a shared local history with a number of prominent remnants from the past. Perhaps for these reasons, those areas of Kotagede are still semi-officially called "Kawasan Kotagede" (= Kotagede Region)[1] especially for the promotion of tourism.

FIGURE 8.1

Front view of the village office of Jagalan.

---

1. This designation seems, however, not necessarily being shared by some people among local residents. For example, a PDIP member of Kabupaten Bantul Council (DPRD) living in Desa Singosaren declined my request for an interview on the ground that he had nothing to do with Kotagede.

FIGURE 8.2

Village office of Jagalan with multi-purpose hall constructed after the 2006 earthquake.

FIGURE 8.3

Sign of "Kawasan Kotagede" at the western end of the bridge over Gajah Wong River.

In addition, on the basis of its commonness in the history of development, the Muhammadiyah branch of Kotagede employs the term "Kotagede Kultur" (Cultural Kotagede), for its area of operation which consists of the areas of "Kawasan Kotagede" plus the rest of the Kotagede administrative. Organizationally, thus, the Kotagede branch *(cabang)* of the Muhammadiyah, whose office is located on the main street of Kotagede, Jalan Mondorakan, in the Kecamatan of Kotagede, City of Yogyakarta, incorporates within its fold not only all of those branches in the Kecamatan Kotagede but also those sub-branches *(rantings)* in Desa Jagalan, Kp. Mutihan of Desa Mutihan, and Kp. Joyopranan and Kp. Semoyan of Desa Singosaren — all in Kabupaten Bantul. In the following part of this book, when the term Kotagede is employed, it most often refers to the Kotagede region in the widest sense, i.e., the above Bantul part inclusive.

URBANIZATION

In spite of the disappearance of the name "Kotagede" from a substantial segment of the Kotagede region and of its enhanced "rural" character by new designation, i.e., Desa Jagalan, etc., in fact, urbanization has engulfed the entire region in social reality over the past four decades.[2] The distinction between "*kota*" (urban) and "*desa*" (rural) made at the time of the original study (see Figure 2.2) no longer holds. Almost all parts of the Kotagede Region have become urban. Rural scenery of continuous rice and sugar cane fields with a view of Mt Merapi at a distance — a familiar landscape just outside the "Kotagede kota" in the 1970s (see Figure 3.3) is lost for good.[3]

Growth of Population

The population of the entire Kotagede areas (Kemantrean Kotagede in the City of Yogyakarta plus Kelurahan Singosaren in Kabupaten Bantul) has doubled since 1970, as shown in Table 8.1.

---

2. For a short but useful survey of Kotagede in 1979 from the viewpoint of social ecology, see Pranoto Hadi, "Spintas tentang ekologi sosial di Kotagede" [Briefing on social ecology of Kotagede], *Brosur Lebaran*, No. 17, 1399H/1979M, pp. 34–35, 50. Also for a depiction of urbanization ten years later through the eyes of a resident, see Agus Suryantoro, "Kilas balik Kotagede 1992" [A flashback on Kotagede 1992], *Brosur Lebaran*, No. 30, 1412H/1992, pp. 28–32. *Brosur Lebaran* has been a brochure published by AMM Kotagede (Angkatan Muda Muhammadiyah Kotagede or Young Generation of Muhammadiyah, Kotagede) annually on Idul Fitri.
3. See Figure 8.4 below. The reader is also advised to see an aerial view of the Kotagede region via the website of Google Earth, Indonesia/Yogyakarta/Kotagede.

FIGURE 8.4

Mt. Merapi seen from Ring Road.

TABLE 8.1
Population Growth in Kotagede by Kelurahan/Desa, 1970–2007

No.	Kelurahan/Desa	A	B	B/A	C	D	D/C
1	Rejowinangun	3,971	12,233	3.08	894	2,612	2.92
2	Prenggan	5,146	11,484	2.23	1,269	2,701	2.13
3	Purbayan	6,485	9,704	1.50	1,554	2,063	1.33
4	Jagalan	1,300	1,750	1.35	637	867	1.36
5	Total	16,902	35,171	2.08	4,354	8,243	1.89

Notes: A = 1970 Population, B = 2007 Population, C = 1970 Households, D = 2007 Households.
Source: 1970 data from Offices of Kemantren Kotagede and Kelurahan Singosaren. 2007 data from various *Monografi Kelurahan and Desa 2007*.

The most remarkable increase has occurred in the Kelurahan of Rejowinangun. The area was rural in character at the time of my initial fieldwork in 1970–72. Its population has since tripled. Also, the population of the Kelurahan of Prenggan, used to be half rural and half urban, has since more than doubled. These two *kelurahan* are located to the northwest of the core part of Kotagede, bordering to the city of Yogyakarta proper. An influx of migrants to those areas has changed their character from rural to urban almost completely. Land-owning farmers there have sold their lands to developers for the construction of extensive housing complexes, governmental as well as private, and for other purposes. They have also built new buildings for themselves or enlarged their houses to provide living spaces to rent for newcomers who commute to Yogyakarta for work or study. Roadside lands are now occupied by continuous rows of government and business offices, banks, hospitals, schools, hotels, factories, stores, restaurants and some private houses.[4]

FIGURE 8.5

Remains of *pendhapa* Sopingin. The wooden structure was sold to an outsider in 1994.

---

4. For an interesting field study on the marginalized "urban farmers" in Kl. Rejowinagun, see a *sarjana* thesis by I. Setyobudi, "Dunya yang paradoks: Pandangan petani tentang posisi diri dalam tata ruang kota (Kasus Pilahan Lor di Kotagede, Yogyakarta)" [A paradoxical world: Farmers view on themselves in an urban space (The case on North Pilahan, Kotagede, Yogyakarta)], Faculty of Cultural Studies, Gadjah Mada University, 1997.

Meanwhile, the slow rate of population increase in Kl. Purbayan and Desa Jagalan are contrasting. Those areas are inhabited by a number of families who trace their ancestry for generations. Some are descendants of court officials and well-established merchants. Except for the stores facing the main streets, buildings here are almost all residential or combined with stores or workshops. Some of the families have moved out, leaving their old houses unattended. The 2006 earthquake has accelerated this trend. Yet, a majority has stayed on and, as a result, those areas are still keeping the essence of the "Old Kotagede". Narrow alleys, extensive compounds surrounded by high walls, in which typical *pendhapa* (open reception halls) are located with symmetrical structure of other spaces, reflecting the traditional Javanese architectural concept. Most of the compounds still keep *pekarangan* (inner yards) as their integral part, in which fruit trees such as banana, papaya, coconuts, and rambutan grow.[5]

Buildings

Not only have the patterns of land use changed but also the buildings constructed on the lands. According to official data,[6] both in the newly developed as well as old established areas, houses are now mostly of "permanent construction" in administrative designation with bricks and cement. For example, in 2007, out of the total number of 5,932 houses in Kecamatan Kotagede, 5,608 or 94.53 per cent are "permanent". Only 286 or 4.82 per cent are "semi-permanent" (partially bricks and cement) and the rest amounting to 38 or 0.64 per cent are "temporary" (shacks, made of bamboo and wood). My memory of 1970 is that about half of the houses in Kotagede were "temporary" shacks with earthen floors then. That was especially so with the houses in the fringe areas of Kotagede *kota* and in most areas of Kotagede *desa*. In addition, a significant change to be observed in the urban scenery of Kotagede over the past forty years is that the appearance of two-storeyed buildings (see Figure 8.6). A significant number of two-storeyed offices, shops and even private houses have been constructed, especially on the main roadsides. This is a clear defiance of the traditional taboo observed in Kotagede as a former capital of the Mataram Kingdom (see Chapter 2, p. 39).

---

5. See the website of Green Map, Kotagede. The reader can also take a virtual tour of "Heritage Trail" through the Old Kotagede region via this site.
6. *Monografi Kecamatan Kotagede 2000.*

FIGURE 8.6

Two-storeyed bildings on Jl. Kemasan.

Public Infrastructure

In public areas, modern infrastructure and facilities are well provided now. Roads are widened or constructed anew, and all are asphalted or cemented even in the inner neighbourhoods with proper drainage. Heavy rains during the rainy season rarely cause flooding of roads now. Frequent flooding used to hinder traffic in the past. Electricity supply to the buildings — offices, shops, workshops and private houses — is almost 100 per cent. The main streets are well lit with neo-classical lamp posts, and even small alleys are sufficiently lit up by neon lamps. Many houses have electric pumps and tanks to utilize underground water. Only a minority still relies on manual power to get water from wells. The sewage system is well developed where residential areas are concerned. The City of Yogyakarta collects garbage regularly although illegal disposal of garbage is still detected sporadically especially at the river banks of Gajah Wong River.

Communication

Improvements in telecommunication are also remarkable. The number of households with fixed telephone lines increased gradually. In Kecamatan Kotagede, there were 1,908 fixed lines for the total households of 7,376 in 2007.[7] However, lately, fixed lines have been overtaken by a more rapid increase in mobile phones. There are no statistics on the latter, but the number might have exceeded the total adult population as there are many people who possess more than one mobile phone. At any rate, the widespread use of mobile phones has been affecting people's way of life to a significant degree. (See Box 8.)

BOX 8
Mobile Phones Spared Tsunami Panic

Mobile phones have been widely used since early 2000s even in Kotagede, and it showed an amazing effectiveness at the time of the earthquake in 2006. The village head of Jagalan, whose hobby was fishing, was planning to join his friends for fishing on the beach of Parang Tritis facing the Indian Ocean on that fateful day. However, he had to stay on in his office because of an urgent matter. When the earthquake struck, the earth trembled and many houses collapsed causing a number of casualties. After the initial tremors, with the memory of the disaster in Aceh two years before still fresh in their minds, people started to worry about a tsunami, even though the village was located 50 kilometres away from the seashore and at a height of 100 metres above the sea level. The village head called his friends on the shore through his mobile phone. They told him that there were no signs of an impending tsunami such as the sudden withdrawal of seawater. The village head transmitted the information to the villagers who gathered in front of his office. He assured them that there was no likelihood of a tsunami. Even if there is a tsunami, Kotagede is too far from the sea. The news was immediately spread to the other residents. As a result, there was no tsunami panic at all in the village, and the villagers turned their attention to rescue work. In neighbouring areas, many people panicked and ran to higher places, including a huge flyover bridge of Ring Road over Solo Highway. It was soon packed with a huge number of people. After several hours and with no tsunami in sight, they eventually went home.

---

7. Ibid.

Statistics on mass media for the whole of Kotagede are incomplete. However, it is obvious that a large number of townspeople subscribe to national as well as local newspapers. Television sets are now owned by a majority of the townspeople. For example, in the case of Desa Jagalan in 2007, there were 564 TV sets and 1,956 radio sets among 864 households in total.[8] Perhaps, these figures represent the general situation in the entire Kotagede. A few scores of parabola antennas are visible on the roofs of houses in the town today. There are several Wartel (*warung telephone* or telephone and fax service stations) and Warnet (*warung Internet*, or Internet service stations) in and around the town. In addition, a significant number of people possess personal computers by now. The recent popularity of Facebook and Twitter is further stimulating the use of mobile phones and personal computers among the young people. Networking through these media is so extensive that the term "*trah/bani fesbuk*" (extended kinship through Facebook) has been heard recently.[9]

Transportation

A "revolution" has taken place in transportation. The number of motorbikes has exceeded that of households. For example, 7,376 households in Kecamatan Kotagede possessed 8,554 motorbikes as of 2007. In other words, on average each household had more than one motorbike. I counted more than one thousand motorbikes parked on the streets in the vicinity of the market of Kotagede on the morning of a Sunday Legi (market day) in January 2009. (See Figures 8.7 and 8.8.) In 2007, private cars numbered at 626 in the Kecamatan of Kotagede, meaning a little less than one car per ten households. There are also 30 buses and 21 trucks owned and operated by the townspeople. Of course, bicycles were still popular at 7,228, but significantly the number is less than the total number of motorbikes. This compares with the day when bicycles were one of the most important means of transportation. (See Box 5.)

Main roads going through Kotagede connecting its rural hinterlands with the centre of the City of Yogyakarta are filled with roaring sounds of motorbikes day and night. Especially since the construction of Ring Roads neighbouring to the east and south sides of Kotagede Region, the volume of traffic through the town has increased significantly (see Figure 8.9). If a traffic

---

8. *Monograf Desa Jagalan 2007*.
9. Kang Iping, "Trah Bani Fesbuk" [Facebook Kinship], *Brosur Lebaran*, No. 48, 1430H/2009M, pp. 47–48.

FIGURE 8.7

Front entrance of Kotagede market on Legi day.

FIGURE 8.8

Traffic jam in front of Kotagede market on Legi day.

FIGURE 8.9

Traffic on Jl. Karanglo looking to the east.

survey is conducted on the same spot where I had done one in 1970 (see Box 5 in Chapter 5), traffic volume of probably ten times more than that of 1970 might be observed, with the majority being motorbikes. Traffic accidents happen very frequently now, and air pollution caused from automobiles and motorbikes is reportedly reaching a dangerous level.[10]

Education and Health Care

Public services in the areas of education and health care have developed enormously. Government as well as private — mostly the Muhammadiyah's — schools of various levels are dotting almost every corner of neighbourhoods in the town. Especially after the 2006 earthquake, several schools were repaired, renovated and upgraded thanks to domestic as well as international aids (see Figure 8.10). In recent years, a number of private schools, from playgroups and kindergartens to secondary schools and tertiary institutions

---

10. Cf. M. Fathurahman, "Smurawtnya lalulintas di Kotagede" [Traffic congestions in Kotagede], *Brosur Lebaran*, No. 43, 1425H/2004M, p. 3.

FIGURE 8.10

Muhammadiyah elementary school at Bodon — reconstructed after the 2006 earthquake.

including vocational and professional training centres outside the fold of the Muhammadiyah have been established. Gone are the days when the Muhammadiyah schools pioneered modern public education. As we shall see later (see p. 370), a competition for excellence and accessibility is developing among the various schools, which affects the course of action taken by the Muhammadiyah.

Improvements in public health service are also quite noticeable. At present (2009), Kecamatan Kotagede has two full-scale government health clinics, PUSKESMAS (community health care centre), with facilities for hospitalization (see Figure 8.11). These government facilities provide relatively cheaper medical and health care (including family planning) services and see a large number of visitors. The Muhammadiyah PKU, now specializing in maternity and childcare, is still popular. It should, however, be noted that the Muhammadiyah PKU is no longer the only provider of modern medicine and health care for the townspeople. Implications of this fact for the Muhammadiyah movement shall be discussed later (see p. 277).

FIGURE 8.11

PUSKESMAS, community health care centre, Kotagede II.

Lifestyle

All in all, rapid urbanization has brought drastic change in the lifestyle of townspeople in Kotagede. They can now enjoy (and suffer from) urban ways of life not so different from those in major cities like Jakarta and Surabaya, let alone those of Yogyakarta. Almost all contemporary urban amenities are available. Yet, the uniqueness of living in Kotagede is that native residents (also newcomers) can still choose to enjoy a traditional way of life inherited from their ancestors, providing them with a specific identity and an emotional attachment to the old town. The physical, social and cultural environments of Kotagede make this possible.[11]

GROWING DIVERSITY IN ETHNICITY AND RELIGION

The influx of migrants from outside Kotagede has naturally brought an increasing diversity among the population in terms of ethnicity, religion and political orientation.

Yet, pure "foreigners" in Kotagede are still very small in number. Kecamatan Kotagede has only three foreign nationals in 2007: two Indians and one Japanese. There are also fourteen individuals of so-called "WNI

---

11. This aspect of life in Kotagede has been beautifully captured in a book entitled *Kotagede: Life Between Walls* (Text: Revianto Budi Santosa and Photography: Bambang Tri Atmojo) (Jakarta: PT Gramedia Pustaka Utama, 2007).

Keturunan" (Indonesian nationals of foreign descent, mostly referring to those of Chinese ancestry). The presence of those WNI individuals is a new development since Kotagede has never had overseas Chinese residents (see p. 42 above).

I have met one of the WNI individuals living in the outskirts of town. He was a gentleman in his seventies whose parents originated from Fukien Province of China and came to East Indies in the pre-war time. He had worked for a long time in a small but famous department store in the City of Yogyakarta. He had retired but was still working in the store occasionally, doing accounting. He said he was a Buddhist and showed me a poster of Mengtse's sayings, which he put up on the wall of his house and was visible from outside. Pointing to the poster, he said he felt quite comfortable and safe living among Muslim neighbours in Kotagede. (See Figure 8.12.)

FIGURE 8.12

A man of Chinese descent living on the outskirts of Kotagede.

Ethnicity

Other than WNI Keturunan, statistics on the ethnic composition of Indonesian nationals in the town are difficult to obtain. I was only able to find figures from Kl. Prenggan, the northern part of which has received a large number of migrants. Out of the total population of 11,484, 11,200 or 97.52 per cent are reportedly Javanese, 135 or 1.18 per cent are Sundanese, 84 or 0.73 per cent are Sumatrans, 34 or 0.30 per cent are from Kalimantan and the rest, 31 or 0.27 per cent were from various other regions of Indonesia.[12]

So, Kotagede is still predominantly Javanese in ethnicity. Data on demographic movement of the Kecamatan Kotagede also supports this point. During the first half of 2007, 344 individuals moved out of Kecamatan while 469 individuals moved in, resulting in the net social increase of 125. Of the 469 individuals who moved in, 283 or 60 per cent originated from within the Special Region of Yogyakarta. In addition, there were 269 newborns and 141 deaths, resulting in the net natural increase of 128 individuals during the same period. Altogether there was a population increase of 253 individuals who were supposed to be predominantly Javanese.[13]

Religion

When it comes to religious affiliation, the picture becomes more diversified than that of ethnicity. We have statistics from the KUA (Office of Religious Affairs) of Kecamatan Kotagede for the year 2007 and those from Desa Jagalan for the year 2006, both of which combined produce an overview of the religious situation in Kotagede Region as shown in Table 8.2.

Kotagede is still predominantly Islamic as Table 8.2 indicates. Yet, the increase in the number of Christians, both Protestants and Catholics — whose existence was almost negligible in 1970 — is quite significant. The above data as well as those in the previous section suggest that many of the Christians are Javanese in terms of ethnicity. There are two Protestant churches in the bordering areas of the town. Catholics, however, seem to go to the cathedral in the City of Yogyakarta.

An interesting development, which is not detected in Table 8.2, is the diversification among Muslims. First, the resurgence, or perhaps more aptly, "resurfacing" of the NU elements in the town is quite visible. The regional

---

12. *Monografi Kelurahan Prenggan 2007.*
13. *Data Monografi Kecamatan Kotagede 2007.*

TABLE 8.2
Religious Affiliation in Kotagede, 2006–07

	Kecamatan Kotagede 2007		Desa Jagalan 2006		Kotagede Total	
	N	%	N	%	N	%
Islam	30,149	91.78	3,410	98.2	33,559	92.39
Protestant	1,362	4.15	32	0.9	1,394	3.84
Catholic	1,255	3.82	33	0.9	1,288	3.54
Hindu	44	0.13	0	0	44	0.12
Buddhist	36	0.11	0	0	36	0.1
Others	2	0.01	0	0	2	0.01
Total	32,848	100	3,475	100	36,323	100

Source: Data Monografi Kecamatan Kotagede 2007; Profil Monografi Desa Jagalan 2006.

office of NU is located on Jalan Gedongkuning, the main street connecting Yogyakarta and Kotagede. Two *pesantrens* in the tradition of NU, one for girls and the other for boys, and a *madrasah* have been established by two local *kyais* in Prenggan since the 1980s. One of the two *kyais*, Kyai Haji Abdul Muhaimin (b.1953) of Pesantren Nurul Ummahat is very active in interfaith dialog, and is well known both nationally as well as internationally.

In addition to the NU, the PKS (Partai Keadilan Sejahtera, or Prosperous Justice Party) branch is also active in the town and has established a number of kindergartens named TA (Taman Asuhan) IT. IT is an abbreviation for Islam Terpadu, meaning "intensively Islam". The intensity refers to the curriculum and length of classes. Classes are conducted until two o'clock in the afternoon instead of until noon like other TKs. There are also a few primary schools and a secondary school designated as "Islam Terpadu" under the management of PKS activists located just outside the limits of Kecamatan Kotagede.

DIVERSITY IN POLITICAL CHOICE

During the era of the New Order, there were only three choices available in politics: the huge vote-getting machine Golkar, in which the powers of bureaucracy and the military were combined; the political forces of Islam eventually united in Partai Persatuan Pembangunan (PPP), or United Development Party; and a small but diehard group of secular nationalists, PDI, carrying the tradition of PNI through the symbolic presence of Sukarno's family. The political scene of Kotagede was characterized by the persistent strength of the Islamic political party, PPP. It had captured a good one-third of the votes at every general election throughout the New Order period. The town was regarded as a bastion of political Islam supported by a constituency mainly comprised of the Muhammadiyah members and its sympathizers.

Void Created by the Removal of the PKI

It should be remembered that the Muhammadiyah's dominance in the town was ushered in by the crush of its arch-enemy — the PKI — in the late 1965 on the national scale. According to my observation, the details surrounding the G30S/PKI Affairs[14] still remains to be a big "black hole" in the local history of Kotagede. The townspeople know that the crush on the PKI is a publicly sealed page of their history. However, an actor of this history had entrusted me a document directly related to the incident. The late Pak Djumairy had recorded the details of the members and sympathizers of the PKI who were captured by their fellow citizens during the months of November 1965 through January 1966. For a glimpse into the PKI's strength before October 1965, refer to Box 9 (pp. 239–41) on Ex-Tapol. I would also suggest that via this data he/she may realize that in the recent political development in Kotagede, the PKI had since been totally removed as a player. Obviously, the Muhammadiyah, which had been the strongest counter-force of the PKI, took advantage of the void created by the suppression of the PKI.[15]

---

14. G30S/PKI refers to the failed coup of 30 September 1965. After the incident, a large number of PKI members and their sympathizers, estimated at tens of thousands to half a million, were killed nationwide. Many more were arrested and jailed by the military under the leadership of General Soeharto in cooperation with anti-Communist Muslim forces, including the Muhammadiyah and the Nahdlatul Ulama.
15. I was unable to gather information on the G30S/PKI Affairs during my first field work in Kotagede in 1970–72 as it was strictly forbidden for foreign researchers to touch on the subject. Furthermore, all topics concerning SARA (*suku* = ethnicity; *agama* = religion; *ras* = race; and *antar-golongan* = inter-group relations) were not allowed to be approached by foreign as well as local researchers until the last days of the Soeharto's reign. In fact, when I submitted my application for research permit to Indonesian authorities in 1969, I did not mention the Muhammadiyah at all. I just stated that I was interested in studying the social history of a traditional Javanese town. That was my true intention then.

BOX 9
Ex-Tapol (Political Prisoners)

In Kotagede, the PKI and its front organizations were very strong before the G30S/PKI incident of 30 September 1965. Tense situations developed before and after the incident. Before the incident, PKI, Gerwani (its women's wing) and Pemuda Rakyat (People's Youth) had set up a paramilitary training centre in Basen, and the use of firearms was reportedly instructed there. On 2 October, a large demonstration was held in Yogyakarta to support Colonel Untung's Revolutionary Council, and a large number of PKI members and its sympathizers from Kotagede joined it. On 20 October, a large number of people participated in the last and biggest pro-PKI rally in Yogyakarta.

A few months before the outbreak of the conflict, Islamic forces in Kotagede, i.e., ex-Masyumi activists and Muhammadiyah members who had anticipated a show-down with PKI, formed a counter-PKI organization, Pasukan Pemuda Senopati (Young Troops of Senopati). In early October (when the situation was not settled yet), Muhammadiyah leaders and young activists were said to have changed their sleeping places every night for fear of possible PKI attack. When the failure of the attempted coup in Jakarta became clear, anti-PKI forces took an initiative to "secure" PKI members and its sympathizers before the advent of the anti-PKI military forces. Thus, altogether more than 100 people were captured through this form of civil arrest and handed over to the military. The Commander of the Pasukan Pemuda Senopati, the late Pak Djumairy, made a detailed record of those arrested. He provided the record to me. The following is the information based on Pak Djumairy's document and supplemented by current official data.

Out of 147 people arrested by the Pasukan, the largest number, 54 (51 males and 3 females), came from RK Basen — now known as RW Basen under Kelurahan Purbayan. The next largest group came from RK Alun-Alun with 27 people (25 males and 2 females) — the area under Kelurahan Purbayan now. RK Purbayan, now forming the southern half of Kelurahan Purbayan, had 22 arrested people (all males).

The ages of the arrestees were as follows: the oldest was 60 years and the youngest 16. The 46–55 years old cohort had 6 people; 36–45 years old, 33; 26–35 years old, 38; the youngest cohort of 16–25 years old, 66, i.e. 70.75 per cent of the all arrested were below 36 years. Therefore, those who belonged to the youngest and the largest age cohort then (1965) are between 60 to 69 years old in 2009 if they are still alive.

In terms of occupation, the largest group was just simply "workers" (*buruh*) with 48 people. The next largest was the group of artisans (*tukang*) which numbered at 41, including silversmiths and turtle-shell carvers (*tukang penyu*). There were 19 individuals belonging to the category of *pegawai* or office workers, of whom 8 were civil servants, 7 private office workers, and 4 teachers. There were also 6 businesspeople (*pengusaha*), 6 shop owners, 7 students, 3 farmers, and 2 peddlers.

In terms of organizational affiliation, the largest 61 people belonged to PR (Pemuda Rakyat) — PKI's Youth Front, and 41 PKI itself. Lekra, the cultural and artistic groups of the PKI front, had 12 persons. There were 9 members of Gerwani, PKI's female

continued on next page

front, and others belonging to the PKI-led organizations like SOBSI (trade union) and BTI (farmers union). No information on educational background was included in the record except that one had a Bachelor of Science degree and another was a lecturer at the Universitas Rakyat (People's University). Neither was there specific information on religion, except for two persons recorded as Catholic: others were all presumably Muslims.

Documented reasons for their arrest, in addition to their membership and leadership positions in the PKI and its front organizations, included the followings: the establishment of a paramilitary training centre in Basen and their participation in it, participation in the demonstrations on 2 October and/or on 20 October; and protection of the outside PKI cadres trying to escape from the pursuit of the military at their houses.

There was apparently no serious resistance against those arrests. I did not hear any stories of blood shedding in the town around this period. The reasons were explained in the following terms: both captors and the caught were mostly families, friends and neighbours — and the latter had even submitted themselves to the former peacefully. In the terminology of the captors, those arrested were "secured" (*diamankan*) in the sense of being protected in a safe place. This was perhaps true because those arrested by civil arrest in Kotagede were spared of immediate ill treatment by the military (who often resorted to tortures and summary execution). They tended to be extremely cruel to the PKI members and its sympathizers in revenge against the murdered generals. There was also no evidence of open class conflict in Kotagede leading to blood shedding like the ones between NU's *kyais*/landlords and the PKI peasants in East Java.

Many of those arrested in Kotagede were imprisoned in the City of Yogyakarta and elsewhere. Several of them (categorized as B-Group) were sent to the Island of Buru and held captive until 1979. Most of those captured in Kotagede were released and returned to their families by 1970. But they were kept under the tight control by the local military and police forces with the help of civil administration who registered those released and their family members. Also, the local office of the KUA (Kantor Urusan Agama), the lowest level of the Department of Religious Affairs, was made responsible for religious education of those ex-PKI members and sympathizers in a project called P2A (Proyek Pembinaan Agama) to "guide them back to true path". They were gathered for a roll-call held every 35 days, given instructions by military and civil authorities, and made to listen to lectures by religious leaders including Muhammadiyah speakers.

All those who were "registered" as "ex-TAPOL/G30S-PKI" as well as their family members had been stripped of basic civil rights including rights for political participation (voting rights), geographic mobility, and the access to jobs and educational opportunities. They were unable to obtain certificates of "clean environment" (*bersih linkungan*) from the authorities. They stayed in their neighbourhoods and made their living in informal sectors. The stigmatization of ex-PKI members and sympathizers started to lessen significantly during the period of "opening-up" (*keterbukaan*) of the late 1980s. More recently, their political rights have been re-established with the advent of Reformasi in 1998 although the lifting of the ban on the PKI and the propagation of Commmunism, Marx-Leninism were still rejected by the People's Consultative Assembly (TAP MPR No. 1/2003). In the current official registration of local population (*Monografi Kelurahan/Desa*), the category of "ex-TAPOL/G30S-PKI" is still existent. The 2007 Kelurahan statistics show that more than 600 of those people who are labelled as such are still living in Kotagede.

Ex-TAPOL/G30S-PKI by Kelurahan/Desa, Kotagede, 2007

No.	Kelurahan/Desa	N in 2007		Cf. N of Civil Arrest in 1965
1	Jagalan	Golongan B	6	3
		Golongan C	32	
2	Purbayan	Golongan B	34	83
		Golongan C	307	
3	Prenggan	Golongan B	11	46
		Golongan C	200	
4	Rejowinangun	Golongan B	9	6
		Golongan C	47	
5	Kotagede Total	Golongan B	60	
		Golongan C	599	
		Total B+C	659	147

Notes: Golongan (Group) A = those involved in G30S. B = members of PKI and its front. C = PKI sympathizers.
Source: *Monografi Kelurahan/Desa 2007*, Record of Pasukan Pemuda Senopati, 1965.

It is puzzling that such listing is still officially continued even now at the village level after ten years of democratization and the official rehabilitation of their political rights.

As shall be described in Chapter 9, the advancement of the Muhammadiyah movement since 1965 happened against a backdrop whereby its antagonists were totally incapacitated.

Post-Reformasi Situation

Reformasi — the political reformation since the fall of Soeharto's regime — has brought many significant changes. Early enthusiasm for the Reformasi subsided soon after the 1999 general elections. People were becoming more discerning after several years of experience with parliamentary democracy. They had voted a number of times at various levels of legislature by then. A general tendency in the voting pattern is the increasing diversity in the choice of political parties as Tables 8.3 and 8.4 suggest.

In 2004, Partai Amanat Nasional (PAN) still maintained the dominance that it had held since the beginning of the Reformasi period, thanks to the support of Muhammadiyah members. Also, the combined votes for Islamic parties reached more than half (55.73 per cent) of the entire votes cast. However, the growing force developed among Islamic parties, reflecting a new diversity of the population. In addition to the obvious contrast based upon

TABLE 8.3
The Results of 2004 Election for Yogyakarta City Council in Kecamatan Kotagede

No.	Political Party	N of Total Votes	% of Total Votes
1	PAN	5,645	33.39
2	PDIP	3,112	18.4
3	Golkar	1,973	11.67
4	PKS	1,757	10.39
5	PPP	1,159	6.85
6	Demokrat	1,139	6.73
7	PKB	863	5.1
8	17 Others	1,264	7.47
9	Total	16,912	100

Source: KPU (General Election Commission), DIY.

TABLE 8.4
Results of 2009 Election for City Council of Yogyakarta in Kecamatan Kotagede by Kelurahan

No.	Political Party	Rejowinangun	Prenggan	Purbayan	N of Total Votes	% of Total Votes
1	PAN	704	1,176	1,151	3,031	19.05
2	Demokrat	1,487	810	505	2,802	17.62
3	PPP	431	628	1,240	2,299	14.45
4	PDIP	866	831	565	2,262	14.22
5	PKS	759	459	699	1,917	12.05
6	Golkar	356	803	439	1,598	10.05
7	Hanura	171	314	222	707	4.45
8	Gerindra	184	165	124	473	2.97
9	36 Others	331	323	164	818	5.14
10	Total	5,289	5,509	5,109	15,907	100

Source: KPU DIY.

the traditionalist NU versus the modernist Muhammadiyah, i.e. between the PAN/PPP and Partai Kebangkatan Bangsa (PKB), a new element of the Islamist Partai Keadilan Sejahtera (PKS) has emerged.

Over time, a more diversified picture has emerged as the results of the 2009 election for Yogyakarta City Council indicate (see Table 8.4).

The three major Islamic parties (PAN, PPP and PKS) managed to garner less than half of the entire votes cast, i.e. 7,247 votes or 45.55 per cent. Meanwhile, the three major nationalist parties (Golkar, PDIP and Demokrat) obtained 6,662 votes or 41.88 per cent. If these are added by the votes for the two parties recently formed by ex-generals, i.e. Hanura and Gerindra, the total nationalist votes become 7,842 votes or 49.29 per cent. These results show that the dominance of Islamic political parties, which has been maintained in Kotagede since the beginning of the Reformasi period, is now threatened.

Change in Political Choice

Changes in the political orientation of voters can be analysed further by breaking down the votes cast by *kelurahan* shown in Table 8.4. In Kl. Rejowinangun, which is the newly "urbanized area", the nationalist parties are apparently dominant. Golkar, PDIP and Demokrat obtained 2,709 out of 5,289, or 51.22 per cent there. The Islamic parties (PKS, PAN, PPP) obtained only 1,984 votes, or 35.81 per cent. Significantly, among the Islamic parties, the PKS's 759 votes exceeded the PAN's 704 votes. Meanwhile, Demokrat made a remarkable gain among the nationalist parties with 1,487 votes or 28.12 per cent.

Even in Kl. Prenggan, an area made up of new and old Kotagede, the nationalist parties (Golkar, PDIP, and Demokrat) are becoming stronger than before, obtaining 2,444 votes or 44.36 per cent of the votes cast. The Islamic parties (PAN, PPP and PKS) are rather strong enough with 2,263 votes or 41.08 per cent, with the PAN capturing about half of the total with 1,176 votes or 21.34 per cent. The PKS remains relatively small there with 459 votes or 8.33 per cent, and the PPP is relatively strong with 628 votes or 11.40 per cent.

In Kl. Purbayan, where the most established neighbourhoods of old Kotagede are found, the nationalist parties (Golkar, PDIP and Demokrat) are least strong among the three *kelurahans* with 1,509 votes or 29.53 per cent. The Islamic parties (PAN, PPP and PKS) occupy a majority position with 3,090 votes or 60.48 per cent. Here the "old" Islamic party PPP with 1,240 votes or 24.27 per cent slightly supersedes the PAN's 1,151 votes or 22.53 per cent. The PPP's strength here reportedly derives from the existence of a prominent local politician who has represented the PPP in the City Council for a long time since Soeharto's era. In contrast, the PKS is relatively small here with 699 votes or 13.68 per cent.

From the observations presented above, it can be generalized that Reformasi with a series of legislatures for democratization and decentralization in national and local politics has brought in a wider freedom of political choice for voters. As a result, voting behaviour is getting less "primordial" or less ideologically motivated. Especially at the city council level factors such as the personality of the candidate and consideration for practical interest of voters have become significant. Even for the PKS, seemingly the most ideological of all political parties, its election campaign was reportedly explicitly "interest-oriented", for example, an emphasis on less expensive and more accessible health care, child care and education appealing to newcomers to the area. Many of them are young families who have moved and settled in newly urbanized areas of Kotagede recently.

Nationalism vs. Islam

Another point to be mentioned here is the fact that the nationalist parties campaigns were not exclusively "nationalistic" or secular. On the contrary, all of them, especially Demokrat — President SBY's party — have emphasized the image that their candidates are pious Muslims. So, the nationalist parties are not exclusively "nationalistic" at the expense of Islam, the majority religion. Conversely, the Islamic parties, especially those who have adopted Pancasila as their political foundation, are no longer exclusively Islamic at the exclusion of nationalism.

Non-Parliamentary Extremism

It should also be mentioned here as a sign of widening political choice, creeping extremist influences are felt outside party politics. In fact, the infamous MMI (Majelis Mujahidin Indonesia or Indonesian Council of Holy War Fighters) — a federation of radical Muslim organizations — is headquartered just outside the city limits of Kotagede. Also, Hizbut Tahrir, a transnational political group advocating the re-establishment of a caliphate as the goal of worldwide Muslim struggles is actively spreading pamphlets and posters in Kotagede.

Consequences of Political Diversification

Diversification in politics has brought a direct bearing on the Muhammadiyah. A Muhammadiyah activist in Jagalan has written as follows:

> From 1970 to 1999 was a period for the prosperity of the Muhammadiyah in Kotagede. All the townspeople, even down to the lower social class, knew the progress of the Muhammadiyah as a mass organization with a drum band, scout, martial art, and *pengajian* held everywhere .... However, after Reformasi political parties have become many more than three, PPP, Golkar and PDIP, so that the Muhammadiyah started to be left behind. Its leaders were absorbed into PAN, PPP, PKS and others. Compactness of the Muhammadiyah leadership was broken and everybody became busy in one's own effort to make each one's party bigger. As a result, there

developed conflicts among leaders, and now nobody is looking after the Muhammadiyah's social activities.[16]

Although the situation is not as bad as depicted above, it seems undeniable that the energy of the Muhammadiyah cadres is now consumed for party politics to a great extent, in addition to a substantial loss of young members to the PKS. It will need a considerable amount of time and energy for the Muhammadiyah to repair the damage done to the organization and re-establish its constituency solidly.

Further implications of growing political diversity shall be discussed later in the section dealing with the challenges that the Muhammadiyah is facing (Chapter 11).

GLOBALIZATION

Globalization has been keenly felt in the economy. The forces of world market most drastically affected local economy during the time of the 1997–99 multidimensional crises. As elsewhere in Indonesia, the townspeople of Kotagede suffered from the hike of prices of the "*sembako*" (nine essential commodities for daily life). The most complained about was the hike of the prices of rice, cooking oil and fuels. Many also struggled with the skyrocketing prices of imported medicine.

Globalization of Economy

In the area of economic activities, local industries producing souvenirs for foreign tourists, the most representative being silverware and also other various handicraft products, were hard hit because of the significant decrease in foreign tourists since 1998. In addition, before recovering from this slump, terrorist attacks in Bali and Jakarta in 2002–03 worsened the situation. Then, the 2006 earthquake in Central Java hit the local economy of Kotagede for the third time. Competition from foreign imports especially from China are getting fiercer by the day. Results of all these disasters over the past ten years are devastating to the town's economy to say the least.

In reaction, many small-scale silverware workshops have stopped producing high-priced products for foreign tourists and switched to producing cheaper accessories for domestic customers. Big firms are surviving by developing direct contacts with overseas traders or with leading domestic travel agents.

---

16. H. Bambang Sumantri, "Orsos Muhammadiyah" [The Muhammadiyah as Social Organization], *Brosur Lebaran*, No. 46, 1428H/2007M, pp. 29–30.

A new import tax on the silver alloy made the Indonesian products less competitive vis-à-vis foreign products. Thus, many silverware craftsmen and workers have lost their jobs. After the 2006 earthquake, they found temporary employment in the removal of debris and reconstruction work but that did not last long.[17] All these economic downturns have increased the number of daily workers, small traders, and peddlers besides widespread unemployed and underemployed, especially among young school leavers. We shall discuss the details of this situation and its implications for the Muhammadiyah later (cf. section on "Overcoming the 'Culture of Poverty'" in Chapter 11).

Positive Side of Globalization

As have been heard from several townspeople, globalization has brought not only negative aspects to the town. International aids for recovery and reconstruction after the 2006 earthquake have made a number of significant contributions. As a result, a programme assisted by overseas aid agencies started preserving historic buildings. A World Bank scheme for the reconstruction of the damaged houses of the local residents operated extensively (see Figure 8.13). Some residents obtained better houses than before through the scheme.

FIGURE 8.13

A standard house built with aid from the World Bank after the 2006 earthquake.

---

17. *Laporan Tahunan 2006 KP3Y* [Koperasi Produksi Pengusaha Perak Yogyakarta] (2006 Annual Report of KP3Y [Production Cooperative of Silverwork Enterprises]): Kotagede, Yogaykarta.

With international aid, a number of primary and secondary schools have been reconstructed and upgraded. A Red Cross Emergency Aid Centre has been built and equipped with advanced facilities. Many of these international aid are not one-off in nature but are likely to continue in the future via close ties and personal contacts developed between local NGO activists and international aid workers.

There is another positive aspect of globalization involving Kotagede. Some of the townspeople are becoming senders of messages, technology and goods, instead of mere receivers of those. The most obvious early case of this trend was the invention and the export of the methodology of Iqra' (an innovative way of learning the recitation of the Qur'an) with its textbooks and cassette tapes to the Malay-speaking world. The attempt was most successfully received in Malaysia and Brunei. (This shall be discussed in more detail in Chapter 11.)

Rumah Pesik and "Monggo"

Outside the Muhammadiyah circles, the recent appearance of Rumah Pesik and a Belgian-Javanese chocolate firm Monggo may also be regarded as the positive aspect of globalization originating from within Kotagede. Rumah Pesik (House of Pesik) was the house of a former merchant king in Desa Jagalan. It is now owned by a Manadonese businessman, Rudy Pesik. He has rebuilt the house into a small museum and guesthouse (see Figures 8.14 and 8.15).

FIGURE 8.14

Outer wall of Rumah Pesik.

FIGURE 8.15

Rumah Pesik seen from a narrow alley.

In the village of Jagalan, there used to be several *istana raja dagang* (palaces of merchant kings) including the one that belonged to the family of Bahuwinangun. In 1970 when I first visited the area, the palace of Bahuwinangun was empty, decaying gradually, but still showing the grandeur of the past. However, when I returned to the place in 2008, it was undergoing renovation, and by early 2009 when I was back there again, the complex was completely redone with a nameplate attached on the front door saying "Rumah Pesik". I had a couple of chances to interview the new owner of the house. Ir. Rudy Pesik is a graduate of Bandung Institute of Technology (ITB).

He is the CEO of DHL Indonesia, and owns a number of international firms. The following is his story:

He had a friend named Gordon Bishop, a Jewish American, who came to Indonesia as a journalist in 1969. He fell in love with a Javanese lady named Nanies Siti Ahadiah Suryodiprodjoa — member of the Bahuwinangun family, and they got married. They had a daughter, Naomi, and were living happily in their "palace" in Kotagede until a tragedy struck. The family of three was involved in a car accident in 1993. His wife, Nanies, was killed instantly. Bishop himself was badly injured, only Naomi escaped unhurt. Bishop went home to America to undergo a series of surgeries including the amputation of his left leg. In 1996 Bishop started Joyo News Service — a free online news service gathering and sending rather critical news and analyses of Soeharto's dictatorship from his hospital bed in New York. That was only possible from outside Indonesia. His news service was instrumental in reporting the rise of the Reformasi movement to the outside world in 1998. Unfortunately, Bishop was then discovered to be suffering from breast cancer. The treatment required a huge amount of money. Pesik, being a close friend of Bishop, extended financial help, and the house changed owners. Bishop passed away in 2007. Pesik, as the new owner, completely redesigned the house, adding features somewhat like Thai or Burmese structures, and also made it into a small museum to house artefacts he had collected from all over Southeast Asia. The house has a number of guest rooms, too. He intends to contribute to the post-earthquake restoration of the town physically as well as socially and to promote its tourism and folk industry. He is on friendly terms with the local leaders including those from Muhammadiyah.[18]

In the Dalem area of Kotagede — *dalem* literally means "inside", referring to the place where the court complex was once located — there is a modern and Western-style building with a sign "Monggo" ("Please" in Javanese). This is the location of a chocolate firm which opened in 2007. Its owner and manager is a Belgian, Thierry Detournay (b. 1966). He came to Gadjah Mada University as a lecturer in French literature in 2001. He had once joined a chocolate cooking course back home and has become a chocolate connoisseur himself. When in Indonesia, he was disappointed to find the chocolates to be of very low quality, with no uniqueness. They were just sweet. He ventured to produce tasty chocolates himself. He got the idea of fusing European and Javanese recipes using top quality ingredients. After all, Indonesia is the

---

18. Interviews with Pak Rudy Pesik on 20 January 2008 in Kotagede and 5 February 2010 in Jakarta.

third largest producer of cacao in the world. He combined the typical bitter sweetness of dark chocolate with ginger and other local flavours.

At present, about thirty employees at the modern Monggo factory in Dalem produce a variety of chocolates. They are attracting not only foreign tourists but also becoming popular among young Indonesians. Monggo products are sold in a number of hotels, department stores and supermarkets in major Indonesian cities. Recently, the products have started to be exported to Singapore, Australia, and other overseas destinations. People around the chocolate firm are generally welcoming the presence of this Javanese-European amalgam in the midst of the old town. They appreciate the fact that it is creating job opportunities for the locals. Besides, the fusion of Javanese and European tastes was not new for the townspeople. Silverwork, which made the town very famous in the past, was also a combination of Javanese and European tastes in designing, worked by Javanese skills and widely marketed in Europe.[19] (See Figures 8.16 to 8.18.) The case of the Monggo chocolate firm illustrates one of the ways of globalization occurring in this old town of Kotagede.

FIGURE 8.16

Front view of the Monggo chocolate firm.

---

19. *Jakarta Post*, 14 February 2009. Also personal communication with Andhi Kurniawan in Kotagede, January 2010.

FIGURE 8.17

Inside view of the Monggo chocolate firm.

FIGURE 8.18

Factory floor of the Monggo chocolate firm.

Kotagede as a World Capital

A young Muhammadiyah member has contributed an interesting essay entitled "The Capital of the World moves to Kotagede in 2012" to a recent issue of

Brosur Lebaran.[20] He emphasizes the possibility of Kotagede becoming the sender of positive message of friendly and progressive Islam to the rest of the world, thereby attracting domestic as well as overseas visitors to appreciate its historical heritage and unique cultural creativities. This, in my view, might not be a dream at all since there has been a steady increase of young men and women from Kotagede going overseas for postgraduate studies, government and private business trips or even extended overseas stays. They are bringing back home higher academic degrees and a wider knowledge and human contact in the world today. An accumulation of these young people's intellectual power might soon reach a critical mass from where an explosion of cultural vitality, like the one that occurred during the 1920s and 1930s, might take place again for the revitalization of the town's life. They might contribute to making the name of Kotagede known worldwide indeed.

---

20. Fakhruddin Hadi, ST, "Tahun 2012 Ibukota Dunia Pindah ke Kotagede" [By 2012, World Capital will move to Kotagede]", *Brosur Lebaran*, No. 44, 1426H/2005M, pp. 112–15. The essay was originally a more serious thesis submitted to the Department of Architecture, Faculty of Engineering, Gadjah Mada University, 2004 with the title, "Pusat Pengembangan Budaya Kotagede (Centre for the Cultural Development of Kotagede)."

9

THE ACHIEVEMENTS OF THE MUHAMMADIYAH

BACKGROUND: A BLACK HOLE IN HISTORY

Before reviewing the achievements of the Muhammadiyah in Kotagede, it seems necessary to make a sober reminder for ourselves about one of the starting points of the period which we are looking at. I have already mentioned the point in the section on political diversification in Chapter 8. I am referring to "a black hole" in the history of Kotagede (see Box 9, pp. 239–41) as the background for the subsequent growth of the Muhammadiyah. Communists were undoubtedly the ideological and social force that was the most antagonistic to the Muhammadiyah movement in the town of Kotagede since the pre-war time. They were, however, incapacitated almost overnight in late 1965 by the arrest of a large number of PKI members and its front organizations, and the permanent outlawing of their activities thereafter.

The Muhammadiyah developed its strength since then in a very favourable condition in which there was a void created by the disappearance of the PKI from the public scene. The national government took a policy of staunch anti-Communism. For that, the government launched its propaganda via the P2A (Proyek Pembinaan Agama or Religious Guidance Project) at the local level. The project involved local religious leaders, mostly from the Muhammadiyah in the case of Kotagede, as speakers at a series of *pengajian* (religious lectures) held in a thirty-five-day cycle. Those *pengajian* were aimed at gathering the

"G30S/Ex-PKI people" for regular roll calls and debriefing of their ideology. As stated by one of its leaders, the immediate task of the Muhammadiyah movement after 1965 was to "'regain' the ex-PKI people to its fold".[1]

It was difficult to gather information on how effective these "brainwashing sessions" were since any topic related to the PKI was to be avoided during my first field stay. But, I became aware that many of the familiar faces at the ex-PKI *pengajian*, which I was allowed to join in, were also active in such communal Islamic rituals as the collection and distribution of *zakat fitrah* during Idul Fitri and the slaughtering of sacrificial animals and distribution of their meats during Idul Adha. It seemed that a number of those ex-PKI people were being socially rehabilitated via religious paths.[2]

Having this historical background in mind, let us take a look at the achievements of the Muhammadiyah movement in the town over the past some forty years. As a socio-religious movement, the Muhammadiyah endeavours to attain its goal of a "truly Islamic society" (*masyarakat Islam sebenar-benarnya*) via (1) religious propagation (*dakwah*), (2) school education (*pendidikan*), and (3) promotion of social welfare.[3] So, my assessment shall be focused on those three areas.

RELIGIOUS PROPAGATION (*DAKWAH*)

It is difficult to measure the success or failure of religious propagation in exact terms since the result is ultimately a matter of individual conscience. One way, however, to approach the matter is to look at the external behaviour of people and institutions created by people. For that, the growth of mosques in

---

1. "Diskontinuitas dan stagnasi: Cermin kemacetan kita dewasa ini [Discontinuity and stagnation: Reflection of our stoppage at present time]", *Brosur Lebaran*, No. 29, 1411H/1991M, p. 15.
2. There are some literary writings on the violent removal of the PKI and its sympathizers from the public life of Kotagede and its aftermaths as follows: A short story by Erwito Wibowo, "Pasar Kotagede 1960–1965", *Brosur Lebaran*, No. 33, 1415H/1995M, pp. 122–30; an essay and short stories in Darwis Khudori, *Orang-Orang Kotagede* (Yogyakarta: Yayasan Bentang Budaya, 2000), and a short story entitled "Interogasi" in *Bayi-Bayi Bersayap*, by Mustofa W. Hasyim (Jakarta: Progres, 2003). A comprehensive academic research on the subject is yet to be done before long since those who have been involved are passing away one by one.
3. Raker PCM Kotagede 2008 [Material for Working Conference of Kotagede Branch of the Muhammadiyah, 2008].

the town may be one good indicator. So, I shall trace the growth of mosques first, and, then, the activities held there.

Mosques

In 1972 when I left Kotagede upon the completion of my first fieldwork period, there were only two mosques in the town, the old Great Mosque of Mataram and the new Silver Mosque.[4]

In 1978, a survey done by a Muhammadiyah activist listed eight mosques and eighteen *langgar* existing in the area of Kemantren Kotagede (see Table 9.1). To the list, two more mosques in the Bantul part of Kotagede, i.e. the oldest Masjid Mataram and a newly built Masjid Al-Huda in Bodon (Figure 9.1) should be included in order to cover the entire Kotagede region for 1978. Also, this list did not include the newly built mosque, Baiturrahman

TABLE 9.1
Mosques and *Langgggar* in Kemantren Kotagede, 1978

No	Rukun Kampung	Masjid	Langgar	Daily Prayers	Friday Prayers
1	Tegalgendu	0	0		
2	Prenggan	1	6	265	300
3	Alun-Alun	1	7	260	
4	Purbayan	0	1	8	
5	Basen	2	2	110	240
6	Gedongan	0	1		
7	Tinalan	1	0	10	200
8	Pilahan	1	1	25	40
9	Rejowinangun	1	0	10	50
10	Gedong Kuning	1	0	20	200
	Total	8	18	708	1,030

Note: blank cells mean no information.
Source: Darwinto, "Sudah saatnya dibangun Islamic Centre di Kotagede" [It's time for Islamic Centre to be constructed in Kotagede], *Brosur Lebaran*, No. 16, 1398H/1978M, pp. 1–4.

---

4. At that time, I made a mistake of regarding the *musholla* of 'Aisyiyah in Basen as "a mosque for women" since it was used by 'Aisyiyah women very frequently. Obviously, however, it was not a mosque but a prayer house since it was not used for Friday congregational prayers. See p. 7, p. 83 and p. 175 of this book for the same "mistakes".

FIGURE 9.1

Al-Huda Mosque in Bodon for the central *pengajian* of Kotagede Muhammadiyah.

in Selokraman, Alun-Alun, in that year (Figure 9.2). In all, there seems to have been eleven mosques existing in Kotagede in the year of 1978.

In 2010, I counted fifty-one mosques existing in Kotagede. That means another forty new mosques have been built after 1978. In addition, there are forty-eight *musholla* and *langgar* for daily prayers.[5] Except for some, these places for Muslim prayers are under the management of the the Muhammadiyah leadership of Kotagede. I obtained a booklet issued in 2003 by the Special Section on Mosque Affairs within the Council of Missionary and Propagation (Majelis Tabligh & Da'wah Khusus Seksi Kemasjidan). It drew up a list of *khotib* (sermon givers) to be sent to forty-seven mosques in the region from the central leadership of Kotagede Branch of the Muhammadiyah in rotation. At each of those mosques, a *takmir* — committee for management

---

5. Data KUA Kecamatan Kotagede 2006; *Monografi Desa Jagalan 2007*.

FIGURE 9.2

A neighbourhood mosque, Masjid Baiturrahman, in Kampung Selokraman.

— is organized by the local Muhammadiyah members. On Fridays, all the mosques are reportedly well attended by men who come for the collective noon prayers.

Idul Fitri and Idul Adha

On the two annual occasions of Islamic festivities, Idul Fitri and Idul Adha, mass prayers are held under the auspices of the Muhammadiyah in the open sports field of Karang, which has a space of one hectare.[6] The *khotib* for these occasions are usually invited from outside Kotagede. According to the Muhammadiyah leadership, the number of people joining in the mass

---

6. At the time of my first field stay in 1970–72, the *sholat ied* was held on the field in Giwangan, where the Muhammadiyah's technical high school, STM, is built now.

prayers on these occasions is increasing year by year. In fact, I witnessed the scene of open mass prayer in Karang on the occasion of Idul Adha on 28 November 2009. This spacious sports field was then filled with men, boys, women and girls — up to the side streets — estimated at more than 10,000 people. (See Figure 9.3.)

The practice of *zakat fitrah* (religious tax), one of the obligatory pillars for Muslims, has been an area where the efforts for its reform by the Muhammadiyah movement were well advanced (see p. 103). I have failed to obtain data on the practice of *zakat fitrah* collection and distribution in recent years. But, I assume that the practice has become more systematic and effective since the 1970–72 period.[7] So is *korban* (sacrifice), as shall be mentioned later in this chapter.

In addition to Friday and *ied* prayers, a number of *pengajian* are given regularly by the Muhammadiyah branch by its activists or outside lecturers in mosques, *musholla* and other public meeting places. The branch leadership of the Muhammadiyah itself gives the *pengajian ahad pagi* (Sunday morning lectures) regularly on every Sunday morning from 5.30 a.m. to 6.30 a.m. at the Al-Huda Mosque in Jagalan. The *pengajian* started in 1986 at another mosque, which was damaged by the 2006 earthquake. It was then moved to the present Al-Huda Mosque and has continued since without interruption. Each *pengajian* is attended by approximately 350 men and women on average.

---

7. At the time of my first field work in Kotagede, 1970–72, *zakat fitrah* was collected annually just before Idul Fitri from the "able families" at the fixed amounts of rice per their members and distributed to the "poor and needy" on the eve of Idul Fitri. (See Figures 5.8 and 5.9.) Accurate records of the collection and distribution of rice were made by the smallest units of the practice, i.e. committees formed at the level of hamlet (RT/*dukuh*) consisting mostly of Muhammadiyah members and others. It was unclear then whether the Muhammadiyah was engaged in the collection of *zakat* levied on the basis of one's wealth and assets. At present (2010), Kotagede branch of the Muhammadiyah does not seem to be involved in the collection/distribution of *zakat* in spite of the fact that *zakat* practice has been legalized nationally. For example, the 2005 annual report of the branch conference only lists *zakat fitrah* (and *korban*) as an item of its activity whereas its financial report includes an income of *zakat/infaq* amounting only to Rp7,844,000 (approximately US$784). The latter seems to be too small as an amount resulting from serious organizational efforts. At present, perhaps, an independent institution may be handling *zakat* collection. At any rate, empirical research is called for to investigate actual situations concerning *zakat* and *zakat fitrah* in Kotagede today.

The Achievements of the Muhammadiyah

FIGURE 9.3

Sholat ied during Idul Adha at Karang.

Another large-scale *pengajian* given regularly by the Muhammadiyah activists is the one held in Gedung Da'wah Al-Qur'an in Selokraman. It is held every Tuesday morning (hence named *pengajian Selasa pagi*) from 5.30 a.m. to 6.30 a.m., attended by approximately 250 men and women on average.

Also, there is another large-scale *pengajian* organized by the Kotagede branch of PDHI (Persaudaraan Djama'ah Haji Indonesia), an organization of Hajj returnees, most of whom are Muhammadiyah members and sympathizers. This is also held regularly on every Wednesday morning (*pengajian Rabu pagi*) from 5.30 a.m. to 6.30 a.m. at Gedung PDHI near the Gajah Wong River. (See Figures 9.4 to 9.6.)

Other than those *pengajian* open to public, there are numerous *pengajian* held by the Muhammadiyah sub-branches and autonomous organizations like 'Aisyiyah (women), Nasyiatul 'Aisyiyah (young women), Pemuda Muhammadiyah (youngmen), AMM (Angkatan Muda Muhammadiyah, an umbrella organization for young boys and girls), and FOKOPA (Forum Koordenasi Pengajian Anak, or Forum for Coordination of Pengajian for Children). There are also smaller groups of *pengajian* including the one specializing in the study of a particular text of Hadith held at Silver Mosque

FIGURE 9.4

PDHI Building — a *pengajian* in session.

The Achievements of the Muhammadiyah

FIGURE 9.5

PDHI Hall — former pilgrims association conducting regular *pengajian*.

FIGURE 9.6

Pengajian at PDHI Hall. The speaker is K.H. Hisyam Syafi'i of Pondok Pesantren Ibnu Qayim, Berbah, Seleman.

every Monday evening. An observer is quoted to have said, "There seems to be no single day passes without having *pengajian* somewhere in Kotagede."⁸

I have attended four of the regular weekly meetings and one large-scale annual meeting in celebration of the Islamic New Year, 1 Muharram, during my recent stay in Kotagede. All regular weekly meetings are well attended by men and women — most of them middle-aged to advance aged. The topics of lecture vary but mostly on religious/ritual or contemporary ethical and social themes. For example, the one held in Gedung Da'wah Al-Qur'an dealt with the proper way of treating a dead body (*jenazah*).⁹ Another speaker there took up the topic of "Ten Threats Causing the Destruction of Morality". Those speakers are mostly local and familiar faces to the audience, but sometimes renowned lecturers are invited from outside. The audience is always responsive, returning laughter and cries of approval or denial to the jokes and the punch lines presented by speakers. The atmosphere is always informal and friendly, sometimes allowing questions and answers. Glasses of tea and snacks are served for participants, and they donate a sum of cash. The number of participants can be counted rather accurately by the number of tea glasses used and packages of snacks distributed. A meeting on average is attended by 200 to 300 people. So, every week at least one thousand people attend and listen to religious propagation by Muhammadiyah speakers.

At the annual mass *pengajian* held in the Great Mosque of Mataram for the Islamic New Year of 1430, Dr Amien Rais (Former National Chairman of the Muhammadiyah and now a prominent statesman) was invited to speak (see Figure 9.7). The audience was so large that one thousand sets of glasses of tea and snacks were reportedly not enough.

The participants of these *pengajian* are mostly Muhammmdiyah members and sympathizers, but not always so. I met a pensioned gentleman who used to work in a Japanese company. He attends a number of *pengajian* held by the Muhammadiyah at different venues, but also the ones held by PKS and even MMI (Jihadist) outside Kotagede. He says that he wants to personally compare what speakers from different groups are talking. Meanwhile, NU

---

8. Agus Suryantoro, "Kilas Balik Kotagede 1992" [Flashback on Kotagede, 1992], *Brosur Lebaran*, No. 30, 1412H/1992M, p. 29. The author describes the Muhammadiyah as a "social organization of super-majority in Kotagede Region" then (p. 30).
9. The speaker mentioned the recent funeral of President Soeharto and mildly criticized that the burial of the body was delayed and the tomb was decorated both unnecessarily.

FIGURE 9.7

Dr Amien Rais in a *pengajian* at the Great Mosque.

members gather for daily, Friday and *ied* prayers at the mosques attached to their *pesantren*.

The *pengajian* is the vehicle for the Muhammadiyah movement where its central message of *"amar maruf nahi munkar"* (urge people to virtuous conduct and restrain them from evil deeds) is directly delivered to its audience. Thus far, the Muhammadiyah's communications in terms of its content and style seem to be well received by both the speakers and the audiences. The Muhammadiyah's élan for *pengajian* thus still seems strong.

THE MUHAMMADIYAH SCHOOLS

Another pillar of the Muhammadiyah movement is school education. From the beginning, the movement strived to establish and manage schools where modern secular subjects are taught alongside Islamic religious subjects, as we have seen in Chapter 4. This course of action has been maintained and further developed over the past forty years. As of the school year 2006–07, the following schools were in operation under the management of the Council for Primary and Secondary Education of the Kotagede Branch of the Muhammadiyah: 5 SDs (Sekolah Dasar or elementary school); 1 SMP (Sekolah Menengah Pertama or junior high school); 1 SMU (Sekolah Menengah Umum or general senior high school, sometimes expressed as SMA, or Sekolah Menengah Atas); and 1 SMK (Sekolah Menengah Kejujuran or vocational senior high school). The 'Aisyiyah has established 13 TKs (Taman Kanak-Kanak or kindergartens) at various neighbourhoods in Kotagede. The schools have varying degrees of "success" as far as the number of intakes of children and students is concerned. (See Table 9.2.)

These Muhammadiyah schools have their own long histories individually, some going back to the very beginning of the Muhammadiyah in Kotagede such as SD Bodon. The school made a modest start in 1924 using a private house owned by Haji Masjhudi as its first class room.[10] After moving from one *pendhapa* to another, the school obtained a permanent place to operate in Silver Mosque in the 1940s. Then, it finally settled down at the present location, which is in a house owned by the Atmosudigdo family, one of the former "merchant kings", in Bodon, Jagalan. Many teachers in the pre-war time were unpaid or paid only a nominal honorarium. After the war

TABLE 9.2
Muhammadiyah Schools in Kotagede, 2004–07

No.	Names of Schools	Number of Enrolment of Pupils and Students by Academic Year			Remarks
		2004–05	2005–06	2006–07	
1	SD Kleco 1 & 3	409	435	494	Joint management
2	SD Kleco 2	62	61	—	No data for 2006/2007
3	SD Purbayan	125	147	—	No data for 2006/2007
4	SD Bodon	458	486	487	
5	SMP MUH 7	606	584	553	
6	SMU MUH 4	474	386	312	
7	SMK MUH 3	1,251	1,137	1,239	
8	13 Kindergartens	325	842	931	Managed by 'Aisyiyah

Source: Laporan Kegiatan (Report on Activities), Pimpinan Cabang The Muhammadiyah Kotagede [Branch leadership of the Muhammadiyah Kotagede], Kota Yogyakarta, 2007, p. 9.

---

10. *Profil Sekolah* [Profile of School]: *SD Muhammadiyah Bodon* (Bodon: Jagalan, Banguntapan, Bantul, n.d. [2004?]).

and the revolution, the Government of the Republic of Indonesia began subsidizing private schools including the Muhammadiyah ones. The SD Bodon also started to obtain government assistance in 1951. The 1950s and 1960s were difficult years for the Muhammadiyah schools because of the competition with government schools whose teachers were dominantly PKI members or sympathizers. At that time, many Muhammadiyah school teachers were graduates of the Muhammadiyah's teachers training high schools in Yogyakarta — Madrasah Mu' allimin (for boys) and Mu' allimat (for girls). Some college students from the Muhammadiyah families also taught there voluntarily.

It was just before the G30S Affair in August 1965 that a junior high school in Kotagede under the management of the Muhammadiyah, a forerunner of the SMP Muhammadiyah Yogyakarta 7, began receiving an increasing number of students who had finished Muhammadiyah elementary schools. But it took some time and a good amount of hard work as well as the devotion of a number of individuals to run the school.[11]

FIGURE 9.8

Inner yard of SMP Muhammadiyah Yogyakarta 7.

---

11. *The Exquisite of MUTU: Sejarah SMP Muhammadiyah 7 Yogyakarta dari Masa ke Masa* [The Exquisite of MUTU: A History of SMP Muhammadiyah 7 Yogyakarta from Age to Age], n.d.[2005?]. Also, personal communication with Drs Wahzary Wardaya, who taught at the school in 1969–78.

After 1965, with the change of national ideological tide to anti-communism and with the official emphasis on religious education, the Muhammadiyah schools made continuous steady development, increasing the enrolment of pupils and students locally as well as nationally.

In 1978, a senior high school, SMA Muhammadiyah Yogyakarta 4, was established in the complex of Silver Mosque to provide continuous Muhammadiyah education for SMP graduates. Since the mid-1980s, thanks to high demand for school education and government assistance for private schools, especially for Islamic schools, Muhammadiyah schools in Kotagede flourished in the 1980s and 1990s. Meanwhile, a large amount of donation of private lands or *wakaf* to the Muhammadiyah schools and other religious facilities provided a solid material foundation for them. (More details on *wakaf* shall be discussed later.)

In spite of generally favourable environment after 1965, SMP Muhammadiyah Yogyakarta 7 (nicknamed MUTU, a short for Muhammadiyah Tujuh [7]; *mutu* also means high quality) experienced a long, tedious history through the 1970s as mentioned above. This was mostly because of uncertainty in securing teaching staff and difficulty in finding a permanent location.

Since 1981, however, the school has been well established in Purbayan. The Kridoharsoyo family, who had previously resided in the area, provided SMP 7 with a large plot of land. Drs Koesnaeni (b. 1924), a member of the family, and sole inheritor of the land, decided on this deal. After having studied in Japan during and after World War II, he worked for the Central Government in Jakarta for a number of years. He and his Japanese wife, Machiko-san, are still residing in Jakarta. When his brother asked if he was interested in helping the Muhammadiyah school in their native town, he answered positively. After negotiating with the Muhammadiyah Kotagede, he agreed to transfer the right to use his ancestral land of 2,700 square metres to the latter. This made a solid start for SMP Muhammadiyah 7 to grow rapidly since then. In 2010, the school is reputed to be one of the best among the Muhammadiyah junior high schools in the Yogyakarta region.

The kind gesture of Drs Koesnaeni in assisting the development of a Muhammadiyah school attracts our special attention. Instead of giving up the land to the school totally (*wakaf*), he still retain the ownership. In his own words, the deal was made as follows:

> I don't like the idea [of *wakaf*]. For the consequences will be that our relationship with Kotagede will be finished if the land is given to the Muhammadiyah. We will own nothing there any more. We need to keep our relationship with Kotagede because our ancestors are buried there. You may not worry about what happens after you die, but I do. My children

can still go to Kotagede. That was the first reason. The second reason is that if we finish our relationship, no more business with Kotagede. I don't want this because the school still needs our help. A number of students are receiving scholarships from us. I gave the Muhammadiyah the right to use (*hak pakai*) the land forever until my *keturunan* (descendants) think otherwise. ... So, the deal was made.[12]

Thus, in order to keep his relationship with the school alive, Drs Koesnaeni is providing a number of scholarships annually to needy talented students in the school. His brother has also donated a set of *gamelan* to the school. Here, we can see an interesting pattern of "*pulang kampung*" (returning to the native community) of city folks, keeping ongoing relationships with their rural home area. Drs Koesnaeni and his wife, Machiko-san, are hoping that their children will continue their ties with Kotagede in the future.[13]

Among those Muhammadiyah schools under the management of the Kotagede Muhammadiyah, the most competitive in terms of its performance vis-à-vis similar schools in Yogyakarta is the SMK (senior high school for vocational training) in Giwangan, just outside Kotagede. The school was built in 1987 on a large plot of land, which was formerly used for drying crops and as a space for mass prayers during Idul Fitri and Idul Adha for the Kotagede Muhammadiyah. The land of about 3,000 square metres was purchased in the name of the Kotagede Muhammadiyah through the funds prepared by H. Syamsuhadi and H. Muhammad Chirzin, both top leaders of the Muhammadiyah Kotagede Branch.[14] The land where the school is situated is now widened to 18,810 square metres, thanks to additional contributions. The late Haji Ismail reportedly provided initial funds for the construction of the school buildings, now occupying a floor space of 9,827 square metres. He was a native of Kotagede and the owner of a shop, Terang Bulan, the largest batik shop on Malioboro Street in Yogyakarta today. The school is located on the main street connecting Yogyakarta city and rural hinterlands in the south. It has attracted a large number of students for its eight courses of specialization: mechanics for automobile, technologies for machines, welding, audio-visual instruments, electricity, architectural designing, wood works, and computer and networking. Many graduates have easily found employment

---

12. Interview with Drs Koesnaeni and Mrs Machiko Koesnaeni in Jakarta, 17 February 2008.
13. Ibid.
14. Most of the funds seem to have derived from the family of Haji Zubair. Personal communication from Drs. A. Charris Zubair.

FIGURE 9.9

Students and a teacher at SMK Muhammadiyah Yogyakarta 3.

after graduation. Also, a significant proportion of graduates reportedly advance to tertiary education at such prestigious institutions as Institut Teknologi Bandung, Universiti Gadjah Madah and Surabaya Institute of Technology (SIT). The SMK Muhammadiyah 3, Giwangan, has thus made a very rapid growth over the past twenty years and now is considered as one of the best vocational high schools in the Special Region of Yogyakarta.[15]

In spite of the past steady growth, the Muhammadiyah schools are facing increasing competition from other schools in recent years. The general situation of schools in Kecamatan Kotagede is shown in Table 9.3.

In terms of the number of pupils and teachers, Muhammadiyah elementary schools are overwhelmed by the government schools. However, they are still relatively well established in the midst of neighbourhoods where the Muhammadiyah's influence is strong. In those neighbourhoods, kindergartens

---

15. *Proposal Pengembangan Gedung Baru* [Proposal for the Construction of New Building], SMK Muhammadiyah 3 Yogyakarta, n.d. [2007]. Also, interview with the School Master, Drs Sutrisno, on 18 January 2008.

TABLE 9.3
Schools in Kecamatan Kotagede, 2007

No	Name of School	Number of Schools	Number of Pupils/ Students	Number of Teachers	Number of Classrooms	Remarks
1	SD Negeri/Inpres	15	3,052	199	108	Government
2	SD Swasta Umum	1	118	6	6	Private, general
3	SD Swasta Islam	4	672	50	24	Muhammadiyah
4	SMP Negeri	1	674	32	26	Government
5	SMP Swasta Umum	1	33	16	3	Private
6	SMP Swasta Islam	1	553	80	23	Muhammadiyah
7	SMU Negeri	1	776	44	30	Government
8	SMU Swasta Islam	1	254	34	10	Muhammadiyah
9	ST Swasta Umum	1	278	15	6	Academy, private, on environment

Notes: SD = elementary school, SMP = junior high school, SMU = senior high school, ST = tertiary education.
Source: *Data Monografi Kecamatan 2007.*

under the management of 'Aisyiyah are growing rather rapidly. Also, such primary schools as the SD Muhammadiyah at Bodon, which is well known historically, continue to attract parents even from rural hinterlands to send their children.

Meanwhile, government schools are more competitive than before, thanks to improvements in buildings, facilities and quality of teachers. Nowadays, the Muhammadiyah primary schools can no longer claim to be leading in terms of general quality. Besides, there is a financial factor, which makes some Kotagede parents hesitant in sending their children to the Muhammadiyah schools.

The financial factor is relatively high entrance fees required as an initial contribution to the school buildings. Reportedly, Rp3 million (approximately US$300) is required as entrance fee. Because of this requirement, a "stigma has developed that the Muhammadiyah schools are exclusive and elitist", serving economically privileged people only.[16] Those parents who are not economically well-off simply avoid the Muhammadiyah schools altogether.

---

16. "Sekolah Muhammadiyah Mahal?" [Are the Muhammadiyah schools expensive?], *Brosur Lebaran*, No. 48, 1430H/2009M, pp. 13–24.

Meanwhile, there is another tendency for those who are economically sufficient to avoid the Muhammadiyah schools in Kotagede. It seems rather reasonable to send the children to better private schools in the City of Yogyakarta which are all similarly expensive. These problems are keenly felt by the Muhammadiyah school managers, school committees as well as by the Muhammadiyah branch leadership since the number of applicants for its secondary schools is declining recently. They have attempted various measures to solve declining enrolments.

One measure taken by the SD Muhammadiyah at Kleco is a special discount of school fees and graded subsidies for the children from those families designated as "Gakin", a short from of "Keluarga Miskin" (poor family). Gakin is an official designation by the local government for families eligible for various subsidies. It is reported that about 30 per cent of the school's pupils are classified as Gakin.[17] The SMP Muhammadiyah 7 has also instituted scholarships for students from economically less privileged families including the scholarships from Drs Koesnaeni. Also introduced for those schools is the scheme of "Anak Asuh" (cared child), the coverage of school fees by 'Aisyiyah donors, and the payment of school fees and contributions by instalment. The children from Muhammadiyah families are given priority. Efforts to erase the stigma of exclusiveness and elitism recently labelled upon the Muhammadiyah schools have just begun. It will need some time to see the results.

Another challenge facing the Muhammadiyah schools is coming from the Islamist schools. PKS activists have established a number of schools, which are generally called "Sekolah IT" ("Islam Terpadu", meaning integrally Islamic). In these schools, Islamization of all subject matters is attempted including extra-curricular activities. The teaching methods employed at those schools somehow resemble the American educational TV programme, *Sesame Street*, with a sweet atmosphere and the use of humour. IT schools are said to be posing real threats to the Muhammadiyah schools in terms of quality. Their threats are most keenly felt at the level of kindergartens in new residential areas. PKS' TK IT (kindergartens with Islamic integrity) offers a longer stay for children at TK until 2.00 p.m. whereas 'Aisyiyah TKs are in operation

---

17. Ibid., p. 23. The problem of the poor will be discussed later.

until 12.00 noon. Working mothers prefer to send their children to TK IT for the convenience rather than for ideological affinity.[18]

IQRO' AND "QURANIC KINDERGARTEN"

Kotagede is known as the centre of a new method of learning the recitation of the Qur'an, known as "Iqro'". The method was initiated and promoted by two key persons, H. As'ad Humam and Jazir Asp. Both of them emerged from the Muhammadiyah circles, but the movement of Iqro' is independent and has no organizational relationship with Muhammadiyah.[19]

Pak As (as the late H. As'ad Humam was affectionately known) was born in 1933 as a second generation Muhammadiyah family of H. Humam Siradj, a successful businessman in Selokraman. Pak As went to the SD Muhammadiyah Kleco and then to Mu'allimin, and SMP Negeri in Ngawi, East Java. He came back to Yogyakarta and entered the Teachers' Training School (SGA) Muhammadiyah. In 1963, he was struck by a disease that calcified his backbones, which had him hospitalized for one and a half years and handicapped for life. He stopped formal education then but was able to continue receiving lessons from many people around him including his father, a teacher at SD Kleco and a popular preacher (*muballigh*). Pak As sought religious instructions not only from the Muhammadiyah environments but also from NU ones: he spent two years at Pesantren Al-Munawir, Krapyak, well-known for the excellence in teaching the recitation of the Qur'an. Meanwhile, Pak As was very active with other Muhammadiyah members in organizing *pengajian* for small children in and around Kotagede. While doing so, he was not satisfied with the traditional method of learning the recitation of the Qur'an, i.e. Bagdhadiyah, which usually required two to three years to master.

---

18. See Sri Puji Lestari, "Taman Kanak-Kanak Islam Terpadu, Sebuah Pilihan: Studi Kasus di Taman Kanak-Kanak Islam Terpadu Kotagede Yogyakarta" [Intensive Islamic Kindergartens, An Alternative: Case Study at Intensive Kindergarten, Kotagede, Yogyakarta], Masters thesis, Faculty of Cultural Sciences, Gadjah Mada University, 2003.
19. As'ad Humam, "Pengajian Anak-Anak dan TKA-TPA: Lembaga Pendidikan Non-Formal Yang Sangat Vital Dalam Mengantarkan Anak Menuju Generasi Yang Islami" [Propagation for Children and Quar'anic Kindergarten and Qur'anic Garden for Pupils: Non-Formal Educational Institution Vital for Leading Children to an Islamic Generation], *Brosur Lebaran*, No. 33, 1415H/1995M, pp. 62–68.

FIGURE 9.10

Qur'an kindergarten — a teacher tutoring children to recite the Qur'an.

In 1983, Pak As and his team organized Tadarus AMM (Young Generation's Team of Masdjid and Musholla for Group Recitation of the Qur'an) with the cooperation of young colleagues, mostly students, headed by Jazir Asp. Jazir was a student activist in the anti-Soeharto movement in the late 1970s. He was arrested by the authorities and was imprisoned for a few years. After his release from prison, he and his former comrades decided to take up a "cultural approach" towards the establishment by nurturing social forces for reform on the basis of Islam rather than attempting a frontal political attack again. A number of Jazir's friends joined Pak As's team. Through the network of student organizations, a number of young female students were recruited into the AMM movement as Qur'anic teachers for pre-school children. The training of those young teachers became the job of Pak Jumanuddin, younger brother of Pak As and an active Muhammadiyah member.

In 1982, the Department of Religious Affairs decided to start the campaign for the creation of a "Qur'anic Generation" to eradicate "illiteracy in reading and writing the Qur'an". Thus, political and social environments for Team Tadarus AMM became favourable. In 1988, the first TK Al-Qur'an (Kindergarten for learning the Qur'an) was opened in Kotagede with the official approval from the regional office of Department of Religious Affairs. Since then, the TK Al-Qur'an spread to other parts of the Yogyakarta Region, and also to other parts of the country. The booklets of the Iqro' texts written by Pak As started to be published with accompanying cassette tapes and were distributed in large numbers to various parts of Indonesia.[20] (See Figures 9.11 and 9.12.)

FIGURE 9.11

Iqro' textbook by K.H. As'ad Humam.

---

20. *Buku Iqro': Cara Cepat Belajar Membaca Al-Qur'an* [Iqro' Book: Quick Method for Learning to Recite the Qur'an], As'ad Humam, AMM (Angkatan Muda Masjid Musholla or Youth Generation of Mosques and Musholla), [Kotagede, n.d., many printings].

FIGURE 9.12

Iqro' textbooks in the printing plant of Team Tadarus AMM.

Soon, the new Iqro' methodology (Metode Iqro') became known not only in the country but also in Singapore, Malaysia and Brunei. Since the textbook was copyrighted, its sale nationally and internationally has brought a significant amount of income for the Team Tadarus AMM. On the basis of this income, a general meeting hall for *pengajian* and social gatherings (Gedung Dakwah Al-Qur'an AMM Kotagede) was built in Selokraman and has been frequently used. (See Figures 9.13 to 9.15.)

Within a span of ten years from the late 1980s, TK Al-Qur'an for preschool children, TP (Taman Pelajar or, lit., Pupils Garden) Al-Qur'an for primary school children and high school students, and also classes for adults were established all over in Indonesia. The Department of Religious Affairs started to promote the Festival Anak Saleh Indonesia (Indonesian Festival of Pious Children) since 1995, and this policy accelerated significantly the spread of Iqro' methodology and TK/TP Al-Qur'an nationally.

FIGURE 9.13

Front view of AMM Meeting Hall.

The success of the AMM Kotagede was a case of intricate interactions between Islamic social forces critical of the Soeharto's regime and the latter's efforts to co-opt the former. For example, teachers at the TK Al-Qur'an were exclusively female college and university graduate. AMM absorbed a large

FIGURE 9.14

Pak Jazir speaking at a *pengajian* in the AMM Meeting Hall. Photograph of AMM's founder, As'ad Humam, is on the wall.

FIGURE 9.15

A *pengajian* in session at AMM Meeting Hall.

amount of energy from the student movement, which was generally critical of the establishment. Their male counterpart also busied themselves with "cultural approach" of Islamization. Meanwhile, a generation of young children who had learned to recite the Qur'an fluently came to age during the 2000s. Many of them are said to have "stayed on" within the Muhammadiyah circles from which the AMM movement originated. However, many also went to the PKS circles, and some to NU. Overall, the TK Al-Qur'an movement with the Iqro' methodology has enhanced the tendency of deepening Islamization in Indonesian society. It is to be seen whether the increased literacy in the Qur'an is also deepening the substantive understanding of the contents of the messages in application to the social context of contemporary Indonesia.

PKU VS. PUSKESMAS: COMPETITION AND COMPLEMENT IN HEALTH CARE

As mentioned above, the Muhammadiyah's clinic, PKU, is no longer an exclusively modern medical institution in Kotagede. The role of PKU in diminishing the influence of unscientific superstitions around illnesses and child birth has also become insignificant with the progress of school education and the increasing role of the government institution PUSKESMAS in public health. Since the 1990s, the PUSKESMAS has emerged as the most popular centre of medical services for the local community. Recent statistics as shown in Table 9.4 indicate this point:

TABLE 9.4
Patients Visiting PKU and PUSKESMAS, January–June 2007

No	Institution	No. of Patients
1	PKU Muhammadiyah	7,368
2	PUSKESMAS	25,003

Source: Monografi Kecamatan Kotagede 2007, p. 19.

The popularity of PUSKESMAS is obvious. Therefore, the PKU Muhammadiyah has been specializing as a hospital for the delivery of babies and maternity and childcare (*Rumah Sakit Khusus Ibu dan Anak*). PKU's public clinic is still in operation, covering general practice, pediatrics, dentistry, circumcision, and family planning. Pupils and students of the Muhammadiyah schools, who are covered by the Muhammadiyah's insurance system, are also given regular check-ups and immunization at PKU. It is to be seen whether PKU can continue with its complementary role vis-à-vis PUSKESMAS in the future.

WAKAF: THE FOUNDATION FOR THE MUHAMMADIYAH'S INSTITUTIONAL STRENGTH

According to Islamic law, one can give up permanently the private ownership of mobile as well as immobile property for the use of the common good, most often for religious purposes. This is called *wakaf* (*waqf*). *Wakaf* is regarded as *amal jariah* (ever-lasting good deed), which assure heavenly reward for the donor in his/her afterlife. In Kotagede, a number of extensive plots of lands have been donated for the construction of buildings for the purpose of religion, education and social welfare. These include mosques, *musholla*, *langgar*, schools, kindergartens, a clinic and a hospital, a radio station and the office of the Muhammadiyah branch.

According to Drs Mardjuki, who is in charge of *wakaf* affairs for the Kotagede branch of the Muhammadiyah, the procedure to make a plot of land into *wakaf* is as follows: the status of privately owned land is converted to *wakaf* according to Islamic law. This is done simply by the declaration of the intention of the owner with the witness of two adult men.[21] In addition, to make it legally effective according to the national law of the Republic of Indonesia, the following procedure is required. First, the owner has to possess the certificate of land ownership. For this, usually one has go through the offices of all administrative units including RT, RW, and Kelurahan/Desa in order to secure their approval. Then, the person obtains a certificate from the KUA (Office of Religious Affairs at the Kecamatan level) stating that the land is donated as *wakaf* according to Islamic law and also that a certain body is designated to manage it in the future. The certificate is then taken to the National Land Agency (BPN or Badan Pertanahan Nasional) to be registered as *wakaf*. Upon completion of this procedure, the land is to be used permanently for the declared purpose of donation under the management of the Muhammadiyah.

The total *wakaf* lands managed by the Kotagede branch of the Muhammadiyah today amounts to 36,055 square metres consisting of 89 plots,

---

21. Interview with Drs Mardjuki on 6 January 2008. He was born in 1966 in Purbayan, Kotagede, went to the Muhammadiyah schools in Kotagede, and then to IAIN SK. He was involved in the legal process of *wakaf* land for the Muhammadiyah branch of Kotagede since 1979 even though he had no special knowledge on the matter. He had to learn all about *wakaf* until he became an expert on *wakaf*. His assistance is now sought by other branches of the Muhammadiyah in the Yogyakarta region as well.

according to the list prepared by Drs Mardjuki.[22] A shorter list of relatively large plots of lands selected from the original is presented in Table 9.5.

TABLE 9.5
List of Major Wakaf Lands Managed by the Muhammadiyah Kotagede

No	Purpose/Location	Land Area (sq. m)	Donor
1	Gedung Serbaguna/Alun-Alun Selatan	436	H. Suprapt
2	TK Al-Qur'an/Alun-Alun Utara	446	H. Jumanuddin
3	TK Al-Qur'an/Alun-Alun Utara	234	H. As'ad Humam
4	Masjid Baiturrahman/Alun-Alun Utara	291	Drs. H. Nur Barie
5	Musholla Selokraman/Alun-Alun Utara	278	Ny. A. Sayuti
6	SMP Muhammadiyah 7/Purbayan	680	Ny. Musrifah
7	Masjid Al-Makmur & TK/Mutihan	746	Hj. Hadimulyono & H.Karsoutomo
8	TK ABA Celanan/Jagalan	750	Ny. Sajiman Yazid
9	Musholla/TK ABA/Basen	1,065	H. Masjhudi
10	PKU/Basen	1,042	H. Masjhudi
11	Gedung Serbaguna/Basen	344	Ny. Hardjosudarmo
12	Masjid Mustaqim/Basen	566	Hj. Pawirosarjono
13	Masjid Perak/Prenggan	2,078	Dja'far Amir
14	Masjid Nur Hasani/Prenggan	380	H. Masrof Anwar
15	Masjid Muada bin Jabal/Prenggan	529	H. As'ad Humam
16	TK ABA Mesjid Perak/Prenggan	658	Ny. Suhartinah Pawirosarjono
17	PDHI & Musholla Himatus Sholihin/Prenggan	760	Hartosuharjo
18	Masjid Al-Fatah/Rejowinangun	284	Ny. Bandiyah
19	TK ABA/Rejowinangun	249	Drs. Darwin Harsono
20	TK 'Aisyiyah/Pilahan	1,113	H. Zubaidi
21	SD Muh. Kleco 2 & Masjid Baitul Qokhar	2,287	Syroj Cs
22	SMK Muhammadiyah 3/Giwangan	4,135	H. Syamsuhadi & Muh. Chirzin
23	Sub-total 1–22	19,351	
24	67 Plots of Other *Wakaf* & Purchased Lands	16,704	
25	Grand Total of 89 plots	36,055	

Note: Gedung Serbaguna = multi-purpose meeting hall.
Source: See note 21, this chapter.

---

22. *Majelis Wakaf* dan Kehartabendaan PCM Kotagede, Laporan Pelaksanaan Program Kerja dalam Raker 2007 (Council of *Wakaf* and Property, Branch Leadership of the Muhammadiyah Kotagede, Working Report for the Annual Meeting 2007) [typescript prepared by Drs Mardjuki].

Further, I have broken down the original total of 89 plots of land according to the purpose of donation as follows: (1) 30 for mosques, 15 for *musholla*, and 3 for *langgar* — a sub-total of 48 plots for the place of prayers; (2) 17 for TK (kindergartens) and 16 for schools — a sub-total of 33 plots for education; (3) 2 plots for PKU (clinic and maternity and childcare hospital); and (4) the rest for general meeting halls, the Muhammadiyah Branch Office, a dormitory, etc. *Wakaf* lands for mosques included a historic one — the Silver Mosque whose land of 840 sq. metres was donated by Dja'far Amir, one of the founding members of the Kotagede Muhammadiyah. Also, we find the name of H. Masjhudi, the first branch head of the Muhammadiyah Kotagede who donated 1,065 sq. metres of land for Musholla and TK Basen and another 1,042 sq. metres for PKU in the pre-war time.

According to Drs Mardjuki, the Dutch colonial government did not recognize the status of *wakaf*. So, the land intended for *wakaf* then had to

FIGURE 9.16

Drs. Mardjuki with a bundle of *wakaf* documents in Kotagede.

be registered in a private name.[23] *Wakaf* is now legally effective following the current national laws and regulations. However, it took a long time and much tedious work for Drs Mardjuki to convert all these privately registered lands into legally effective *wakaf* lands. In many instances the original certificates of land ownership were lost or the inheritors of a plot were scattered over various parts of Indonesia.[24]

In the list, we find the name of Mrs Sajiman Yazid, a descendant of the merchant king Atmosudigdo. Her land is made as a *wakaf* for a TK in Celanan, Desa Jagalan. The lands for TK Al-Qur'an in Alun-Alun Utara, which has become the national centre of Iqra' movement today since the 1980s, was donated by two members from the Humam family, H. As'ad Humam and H. Jumanuddin.

Wakaf properties under the Muhammadiyah management have provided a solid institutional basis for its activities. The enormous increase of *wakaf* lands and *wakaf*-based institutions in Kotagede can be said as an exact reflection of the growth of the Muhammadiyah itself in the town. So, we can say on the basis of this hard evidence that the Muhammadiyah has grown enormously over the past forty years.

Yet, the very fact of this "enormous growth" of the Muhammadiyah, reflected in the increase of *wakaf*-based institutions, invites a few critical questions. One observer of the Muhammadiyah in Kotagede stated sarcastically: "If someone who has no previous knowledge of the Muhammadiyah at all comes into the town of Kotagede and notices a large number of buildings bearing the sign of the Muhammadiyah, the person may think that the Muhammadiyah is a big business conglomerate owning a large number franchised shops." This comment somehow hits the mark. The Muhammadiyah today has grown to be a huge organization locally as well as nationally. The burden of administering a huge organization like this consumes much energy and funds from the members. The officers of the organization seem to be occupied to a considerable extent just to maintain those facilities as hardware and institutions on them as software.

---

23. Perhaps this is the reason why I regarded Haji Masjhudi to be one of the richest people in the town in 1971 for those lands were registered as his personal property according to the format of Letter C, the official document on landownership then.
24. Interview with Drs Mardjuki, 6 January 2008.

Perhaps, this is one of the reasons for the Muhammadiyah in Kotagede, as elsewhere, starting to be criticized as experiencing stagnation from the early 1980s. However, it should be understood that this stagnation came not in spite of but rather because of the enormity of the organizational growth of the Muhammadiyah thus far achieved.

More analytically, the history of *wakaf* lands in Kotagede seems to invite a critical question on the economic basis of the Muhammadiyah movement. As is well known, the Muhammadiyah movement in Kotagede was initiated by young *ulama* supported by prosperous business people during the 1910s and 1920s. It was just after the time when the Yogyakarta region underwent an administrative reform according to the framework of the "Ethical Policy" (see Chapter 2). The appanage (office land) system, which supported the status of Kotagede as royal heirloom, was abolished. However, the class differentiation in terms of resident's relationship to the land seems to have remained basically the same from the pre-reform period.

In relation to the matter of *wakaf*, I would like to hypothesize that many of the lands donated for *wakaf* in recent decades were derived from those lands that were owned by the privileged townspeople prior to the reform. As we have already seen, there existed strict demarcations among the townspeople in terms of their relationship to land (see p. 26 above). The court officials (*abdi dalem jurukunci*) were given *lungguh* (homestead and office land) whereas "free citizens" (*kuli kenceng*) owned house and land privately. Orang Kalang who seemed to be outside this hierarchy also occupied a large amount of land privately. It seems obvious that some of the descendants of court officials, *kuli kenceng*, and Orang Kalang had owned a large portion of the lands that had been converted to *wakaf* in recent decades. If this observation is correct, the Muhammadiyah movement was literally supported by the people of the "haves".

Besides inherited lands, some individuals seem to have acquired land owing to success in business in more recent years and have contributed it as *wakaf*. At any rate, it is irrefutable that the Muhammadiyah movement took a great advantage in building its material foundation over several decades of its development because of a large amount of inherited and acquired lands availed for *wakaf* from among its members and supporters.

10

INTERNAL DYNAMICS OF THE MUHAMMADIYAH MOVEMENT

THREE GENERATIONS OF LEADERSHIP

Over the period of forty years (1970–2010) that I have observed on the Muhammadiyah movement in Kotagede, I have witnessed three generations of leadership emerge. The first generation was that of Haji Masjhudi (1888–1972), the "founding fathers". They were mostly from the families of *ulama*, or wealthy merchants and industrialists. They were educated at traditional *pesantren* first but became critical of it later. They also became critical of Javanese Islam (*kejawen*) embodied by the Mataram Sultanate and advocated its purification and reform. They led the Muhammadiyah movement through the "*tiga zaman*" (three ages, i.e. the periods of Dutch, Japanese, and Independent Indonesia), 1920s to 1950s. (See Chapters 3 to 5.)

The second generation was mostly from the families of the founding fathers. Their leadership almost paralleled the presidency of General Soeharto (r.1966–98) for the nation. Typical of this second generation was Bashori Anwar (1933–2006) (Figure 10.1), who occupied the chairmanship of the Kotagede Branch of Muhammadiyah for four five-year terms from 1970 to 1990.

After a transitional zig-zagging for fifteen years from 1990 to 2005, the branch leadership of the Kotagede Muhammadiyah is now in the hands of the third generation represented by its current chairman Kaharuddin Noor

FIGURE 10.1

Pak Bashori and wife showing their little fingers after voting at the 2004 presidential election.

(b. 1963). He is no longer from the "elite families" of the town. He is the son of a tailor well known for his skills but modest in lifestyle. His chairmanship indicates that the centre of gravity of the Muhammadiyah leadership in the town has moved to the new educated middle class. In this chapter, I shall examine these generational transitions and their implications for the local Muhammadiyah movement.

THE SECOND GENERATION OF THE MUHAMMADIYAH LEADERSHIP

Most of the members of the second generation of the Muhammadiyah leadership in Kotagede were born in the families of the Muhammadiyah founders. They were also mostly the direct products of the Muhammadiyah's "internal breeding". In other words, they were the first products of the Muhammadiyah's educational system. Many of them went to the Muhammadiyah's local primary school, then to its teachers' training high schools, Mu'allimin (for boys) or

Mu'allimat (for girls), in Yogyakarta. After graduation, some were sent out to other areas for missionary work. Some came back to settle down in Kotagede and became active in the Muhammadiyah movement while engaging in local trade or industry. They were from the "old middle class" in the traditional sector of society, who formed the core of the Muhammadiyah establishment in Kotagede for approximately the next two decades, 1970 to 1990.

During the following brief period of transition from 1990 to 2005, the Muhammadiyah in Kotagede was led by relatively younger members of the second generation of the establishment. From 2005, the leadership has moved to the post-Reformasi phase, recruiting mostly from the third generation. They were mostly college educated, having worked in the modern sector of society. A clear generational turnover is now under way since then.

PAK BASHORI: A TYPICAL SECOND GENERATION LEADER

A typical person in the category of the second generation was the late Bashori Anwar (1933–2006). He was the son of Haji Anwar Rofi'i, one of the founders of the Muhammadiyah in Kotagede. He went to the Muhammadiyah primary school in Bodon, then to the Mu'allimin boarding school up to its senior high level. He came home to marry Praptini, with whom he had six children. All of them became active in the Muhammadiyah including their second son, Khoiruddin, who later became prominent as Rector of Muhammadiyah University, Yogyakarta, and, their third son, Sholehuddin, as Lurah (Village Head) of Jagalan. Bashori himself engaged in trade, keeping a general store for textile, clothes and other daily necessities on the main street of Kotagede while occupying the branch chairmanship of the Muhammadiyah for four periods from 1970 to 1990. He was a rather reserved person even though he was always welcoming visitors who came to ask for his advice. Other than the Muhammadiyah, he was also actively involved in the affairs of the neighbourhood association and cooperated well with the local government. He was urged to serve as a city or provincial level of officer for the Muhammadiyah organization several times. However, he declined by saying, "Basically, I just want to manage Kotagede matters only (*Pokoke tak ngurusi Kotagede wae*)." He was "Kotagede-minded" all through his life.[1]

---

1. "Biografi: H. Bashori Anwar", *Brosur Lebaran*, No. 47, 1429H/2008M, pp. 60–67.

Pak Bashori was a representative leader of the Orde Baru generation who contributed to the enormous growth of the Muhammadiyah through the period. He and his colleagues succeeded in spreading religious lectures (*pengajian*) to every corner of Kotagede. He was a regular speaker for the special *pengajian* of the P2A (Proyek Pembinaan Agama, or Project for Religious Guidance) of the local government designed for the "rehabilitation" of ex-G30S/PKI people (see Chapter 9). During his tenure, the Muhammadiyah increased its number of mosques, *musholla*, kindergartens (TK) and schools (SD, SMP, SMA and even SMK).

A contemporaneous leader of the Pemuda (Youth) Muhammadiyah, Habib Chirzin, stated in an article entitled "Bettering Kotagede Community through the Muhammadiyah" in *Brosur Lebaran* of 1974 that the Muhammadiyah's task was to contribute voluntarily to the improvement of Kotagede in real terms.[2] That was Pak Bashori's aim too. All through the period of the leadership of Bashori Anwar, the Muhammadiyah's relationship with the local government was cordial, providing its cooperation in terms of anti-communist propagation, its support for the government's development programmes without posing a political threat. In fact, the leadership of the Muhammadiyah was more respected than local civil, military, and police authorities by the townspeople. The government side often had to consult with the Muhammadiyah leaders when important projects were to be carried out. The framework for the fundamental direction and organizational structure of the Muhammadiyah was well established during this period.

AN OPPOSITION NIPPED IN THE BUD

At the beginning of this period, however, there seems to have emerged considerable resistance form among the younger generation against taking accommodative stance vis-à-vis the New Order regime. The crucial issue was the Soeharto government's rejection of the rehabilitation of the Masyumi Party. Before the banning of the party by Soekarno in 1960, it commanded the support of almost 40 per cent of the townspeople, while another 40 per cent supported the PKI. (See pp. 123–25.) At the beginning of the New Order, a majority of young activists among the Muhammadiyah in Kotagede

---

2. Habib Chirzin, "Meng-Khoirokan Ummat di Kotagede melalui Muhammadiyah", *Brosur Lebaran*, No. 12, 1394H/1974M, pp. 23–25, 41–43. He mentioned the presence of six kindergartens, seven primary schools, one junior high schools, PKU hospital and clinic, a number of mosques, *mosholla* and *langgar*, and a meeting hall and a library as the achievements of Muhammadiyah.

seem to have demanded the boycotting of the 1971 general election unless the Masyumi party participated. In spite of this resistance, the core of the Muhammadiyah leadership including Pak Bashori decided to support the Parmusi (Partai Muslimin Indonesia), an inheritor of Masyumi without its senior leaders whose political rehabilitation was prevented by Soeharto. The conflict was so tense that *Brosur Lebaran* No. 10 for the year 1392H/1972M was threatened to cease publication because of non-cooperation from young activists. The older generation eventually contained this youthful revolt. But, a number of young activists became inactive so that, reportedly, those who remained with the Muhammadiyah leadership dwindled drastically in number. In fact, Habib Chirzin (see p. 309 for his biography), son of a former Muhammadiyah chairman Pak Chirzin, was called home from Pesantren Modern Gontor to engage in the repair work. Historically, the implications of this conflict for the subsequent course that the Muhammadiyah had actually taken remain to be studied further.[3] That might have been one of the deep causes of the "stagnation" faced by the Muhammadiyah during the 1980s.

IBU UMANAH AND IBU MARDI: TYPICAL 'AISYIYAH LEADERS

It may be useful to introduce the profiles of two typical 'Aisyiyah leaders, Hajah Umanah Rofi'ie[4] (b.1937) and Ibu Mardi (1920–2001), to illustrate the social milieu of the women's organization paralleling its male counterpart.

Hj. Umanah was born in Joyopranan to the family of H. Jawadi Rofi'ie, a prosperous batik industrialist. She was educated fully at the Muhammadiyah schools, starting from kindergarten, primary school in Bodon, and Mu'allimat in Yogyakarta. At the age of seventeen and when still in school, she was

---

3. See Sugiyanto, "Angkatan Muda Merubah Pandangan" [The young generation changes its view], *Brosur Lebaran*, No. 11, 1393H/1973M, pp. 13–17, 32–33. See also a memoir by the central actor then, Habib Chirzin, "Brosur, kenangan dan harapan" [Brosur, memories and hopes], *Brosur Lebaran*, No. 25, 1407H/1987M, pp. 47–50, and a brief mentioning of this conflict by Mustofa W. Hasyim, "Diskontinuitas dan stagnasi seharusnya tidak perlu terjadi" [Discontinuity and stagnation does not have to happen], *Brosur Lebaran*, No. 29, 1411H/1991M, p. 12.
4. *Buku Kenangan 50 Tahun Perkawinan H. Hajid Mutohar dan Hj. Umanah Rofi'i* [Commemoration book for the 50 years of marriage between H. Hajid Mutohar and Hj. Umanah Rofi'i], 22 Desember 1954–22 Desember 2004, UMAHA Family, Kotagede, Yogyakarta [n.d.].

married to H. Hajid Mutohar (1930–2000) of Selokraman. He was also from a Muhammadiyah family — he went to a local Muhammadiyah primary school, then to the secondary school at Madrasah Ma'had Islamy, and finally to the Faculty of Social and Political Sciences, Gadjah Mada University. He joined the Republican Army during the War of Independence and achieved the rank of Second Lieutenant. After the military service, he went back to his family business, engaged in batik production and others, while serving as an officer for the veterans' association. For the next eighteen years, the couple had thirteen children (eight boys and five girls). Since the mid-1970s, Hj. Umanah became socially active in 'Aisyiyah, and she repeatedly elected to the top leadership of its Kotagede branch during 1985–2000. She also served the Kotagede branch of the veterans' wives association as its head continuously since 1975 to 1995. Meanwhile, H. Hajid and Hj. Umanah brought up their children with the motto of *Sesuk gedhe pinter ngaji, pinter sekolahan lan pinter nyambut gawe* (you should grow up to be good at religion, wise at school, and skilled in work). With their parents' guidance, all the children have obtained *Sarjana* (S1, or equivalent to a Bachelor's degree) or higher

FIGURE 10.2

Ibu Hj. Umanah Rofi'ie, an 'Aisyiyah leader.

academic degrees. Seven have S1, five obtained S2 (equivalent to a Master's degree) from leading institutions such as UGM, UI, UNAIR, and one of them a Ph.D. from the United States. Six of them run their own businesses, two work with the central government, one in the local government, one in a private bank, and one teaches at a university. Of their twelve spouses, seven have S1 degrees, two doctoral degrees (one Ph.D. from the United States and another from UI). Four of the spouses are engaged in their own businesses, two work with private companies, one in government banking, one in the local government, and one teaches at a university. Hj. Umanah received the title of "Exemplary Mother" (*Ibu Teladan*) from the BP4 (Counselling Body for Marriage and Family Affairs),[5] Special Province of Yogyakarta, in 2003. As of 2004, she is enjoying life as a grandmother of twenty-six grandchildren, although her husband, H. Hajid, passed away in 2000. Out of her thirteen children, only three remain in Kotagede.

She can indeed be regarded as a typical 'Aisyiyah lady for the period of the New Order in terms of her role as a wife of a veteran, of the ways she brought up her children, and of her own activities as a businesswoman and as a leader in women's organizations.

Besides Ibu Umanah, another pioneering 'Aisyiyah leader, Ibu Mardi Siswoyo[6] (1920–2001), should be mentioned here. She was less privileged in socio-economic terms than Ibu Umanah but equally well respected by many women for her dedication to formal as well as informal education. She was born to a modest family in Selokraman in 1920, and went to the Muhammadiyah primary school in Kleco, and then to the Mu'allimat in Yogyakarta. Upon graduation, she was sent to Kudus, an old town on the north coast of Java, for missionary work by the Yogyakarta HQ of 'Aisyiyah. She taught at SD Muhammadiyah at Besito in the morning and then at Madrasah Tsanawiyah in the afternoon. She was also active in the 'Aisyiyah organization in Kudus. She was married to Pak Murohar in 1942, but he died three years later without having any children with Ibu Mardi. She returned to Kotagede in 1955 and was married to Pak Mardi Siswoyo, who had lost his wife a couple years before. Pak Mardi had four children from his previous marriage, and Ibu Mardi became their stepmother.

---

5. For a glimpse into the working of this body, see "Divorce Counseling at BP4" in Hisako Nakamura, *Divorce in Java: A Study of the Dissolution of Marriage among Javanese Muslims* (Yogyakarta: Gadjah Mada University Press, 1983), pp. 82–94.
6. "Sosok, Badia'ah Mardi Siswoyo" [Figure of Badia'ah Mardi Siswoyo], *Brosur Lebaran*, No. 30, 1412H/1992M, pp. 46–48.

In Kotagede, she was actively involved in the establishment of the 'Aisyiyah kindergarten at Musholla Basen in 1958, which was the first 'Aisyiyah kindergarten in the town and she became its first teacher. She also joined the BP4 as one of the advisers in 1962. In 1967, she was appointed as Mistress of Dormitory for Midwives at PKU, Yogyakarata, and also taught religion at the 'Aisyiyah's school for student midwives. She assumed the role of a mother to her four stepchildren as well as a number of students at the 'Aisyiyah school and its dormitory. After almost thirty years of service for the HQ of the 'Aisyiyah in Yogyakarta, she returned to Kotagede in 1995, and helped the *pengajian* via Radio PTDI, Kota Perak. With her soft motherly voice, her advice on air in Javanese was very popular. She passed away in 2001 at the age of eighty-one. One of her stepchildren is Suhardjo MS, a teacher at SMP Muhammadiyah 7, who became Chairman of the Kotagede Branch of the Muhammadiyah in 2000–05. Ibu Mardi represented those men and women who have dedicated their whole life for the promotion of education in the Muhammadiyah circles.

At the national level, the period during which Pak Bashori, Ibu Umanah, and Ibu Mardi were active in the Muhammadiyah and the 'Aisyiyah corresponded with the time of the leadership of K.H. A.R. Fakhruddin (1968–1990). His leadership was characterized by accommodation to Soeharto's New Order, cultural adaptation to local constituency, gradualism in reform, and avoidance of political partisanship. His amiable personality was accompanied by splendid skills in communicating with rather less educated folks in the Javanese language via local idioms and humour.[7] His leadership led to a spread of the Muhammadiyah's influence into lower social strata than before. Similar styles of communication were observed among the Muhammadiyah leaders of Kotagede during the corresponding period. For example, Pak Bashori Anwar, Ibu Umanah and Ibu Mardi were all eloquent speakers in the refined Javanese language.

CRITICISM AGAINST COMPLACENCY AND STAGNATION

As early as the early 1980s, serious criticism against complacency and stagnation of the Muhammadiyah movement began to be heard from within

---

7. See, for example, his speech quoted in Chapter 6, pp. 189–90 above.

the organization. The most frequently pointed out issue was insensitivity of the Muhammadiyah leadership vis-à-vis a number of social problems arising from rapid social change and also the very slow rate of generational turnover in the leadership. Transition to the next generation of leadership had been urged but the resistance was still strong. The move was finally set in motion in the 1990s. The process of the transition and the internal dynamics of the Muhammadiyah through this process may be observed by examining a list of the major topics for the annual publication of *Brosur Lebaran*.

Brosur Lebaran has been published every year just before Idul Fitri since the mid-1960s by AMM (Angkatan Muda Muhammadiyah or Young Generation of the Muhammadiyah) — a coordinating body of the youth organizations of the Muhammadiyah movement, i.e. Pemuda Muhammadiyah (young men), Nasyiatul 'Aisyiyah (young women), and Ikatan Remaja Muhammadiyah (school boys and girls). The contents of *Brosur Lebaran* have reflected both continuity and change in the Muhammadiyah movement over time. The special topics selected each year seem to have represented the urgent matters faced by the young activists of the Muhammadiyah. Also, the editors of *Brosur* have been trying to make it as a forum in which an objective picture of Kotagede could be presented, and discussions could be held on how the Muhammadiyah should relate to it. In other words, they have been trying to employ an objective approach to look at the historical and contemporary

FIGURE 10.3

Front covers of *Brosur Lebaran* 1991, 2006 and 2009.

social reality of Kotagede as the starting point for the formulation of strategy for the Muhammadiyah movement in the town.

A list of topics covered by the available volumes of *Brosur Lebaran* between 1980 and 1995 is presented in Table 10.1.

In the 1980 issue, with the headline "Uncertainty of the Future", the editorial began with the following statement: "What can be promised for the present generation of the youth as to their future? Uncertainty."[8] The editor then listed a number of social vices that appeared among the younger generation of Kotagede since 1975 until 1980 as the reflection of uncertainty. The article listed the following: "premarital sex and shotgun wedding, alcohol consumption and display of stupidity in public, and the use of narcotics."[9]

In the same issue, Bachrun Nawawi, an Australian-educated community development worker raised the question of the preparedness of the Muhammadiyah leaders as social reformers (for more on his life history, see later pp. 304–306). He asked a bitter question as follows: "Are the Muhammadiyah and its autonomous organizations really prepared to become social reformers? Are they not just going along easy without considering seriously social problems

TABLE 10.1
List of Major Topics of Brosur Lebaran, 1980–95

No.	Year M/H	Topics of Special Issues and Major Articles
18	1980/1400	Uncertainty of the future. Environmental problems. Arts. Social problems.
19	1981/1401	Our portrait. Developing Kotagede. Who are the reformers? Javanese culture.
20	1982/1402	Impact of Social Organization Law. Social change. Life of the homeless.
21	1983/1403	Erosion of religiousity. Javanese Islam. Appearance of red-light areas. Job opportunity for youth.
22	1984/1404	History of the struggle of Muhammadiyah. Leadership needs to be straightened up. Monopoly of Muhammadiyah is lost. Regeneration of leadership is needed. Emergence of "Bapak Muda and Ibu Muda".
27	1989/1409	Kotagede is changing. What's wrong with it?
29	1991/1411	Reflection on our contemporary stagnation. Carrying out propagation through arts.
30	1992/1412	Our generation in the era of "parabola".
33	1995/1415	Our people are leading the nation — really?

---

8. *Brosur Lebaran*, No. 18, 1400H/1980M, p. 1.
9. Ibid., p. 2.

facing Kotagede? Are they not separated from the reality of Kotagede and losing the position of house owner in their own house?"[10] Many among the younger generation apparently started to share Bachrun's fear that the Muhammadiyah was losing its vitality and relevance.

Five years later in 1985, a contributor stated more explicitly: "a large part of the Muhammadiyah leadership is composed of people who lack higher education. This affects the range of their thinking to be limited. ... [M]eanwhile, society has gone much further to the fore so that the leaders are left behind. ... The Muhammadiyah seems to be just staying on stagnant water at present — not going forward but not going backward, either. ... Because of the appearance of a number of non-Muhammadiyah social institutions, ... the Muhammadiyah may soon be left behind by the community."[11]

In the same volume, in an article entitled "Leadership that requires straightening-up", Bachrun Nawawi acknowledged that the Muhammadiyah has lost its monopoly in the area of education and health care, and proposed that a systematic data gathering and the formulation of long-term strategy were needed with the replacement of leadership by younger generation.[12] Siti Waringah, an active leader of the Nasyiatul 'Aisyiyah also wrote, "The Muhammadiyah and its autonomous organizations are experiencing regression. Or, to be said as experiencing stagnation. Its members, even its officers, are losing loyalty towards the organization. ... For some officers, the Muhammadiyah schools are just temporary places where they can get reserved seats."[13]

In response to those criticisms and demands for the change of leadership, a senior Muhammadiyah officer replied: "The growth of young people is expected. But, it should not mean that the old ones are stagnant in activities. They should still be playing roles and not to be marginalized."[14] Apparently, no significant change in the direction or composition of the branch leadership was visible for the next several years.

---

10. Bachrun Nawawi, "Masalah Sosial Kotagede dan Pemecahannya" [Social problems in Kotagede and their solutions], *Brosur Lebaran*, No. 18, 1400H/1980M, pp. 41–43.
11. Edi Wahyono, "Tantangan Muhammadiyah Cabang Kotagede, lain dulu lain sekarang" [Challenges of Muhammadiyah Branch of Kotagede, different past and different present], *Brosur Lebaran*, No. 22, 1404H/1984M, p. 16.
12. Ibid., pp. 17–18.
13. Ibid., p. 21.
14. Syamsuhadi, B "Berjuang melawan akhlak [*sic*]" [Struggle against character], *Brosur Lebaran*, No. 22, 1404H/1984M, pp. 19–20.

It was in the *Brosur Lebaran*, No. 29 for 1411H/1991M that the issue of stagnation was tackled squarely again. The volume had a special title, "Reflection on our stoppage today", and it reported on the results of the discussion joined by a number of Muhammadiyah activists, young and old, and male and female. The discussion was motivated by a realization felt by many of them that the Muhammadiyah movement in Kotagede was "experiencing discontinuity or even a stagnation from the period of 1980s to the 1990s."[15] This time, internal debate among the Muhammadiyah activists seems to have been quite heated.

It may be interesting to mention here that a criticism against my view on Muhammadiyah appeared in this special issue of *Brosur Lebaran* in the context of evaluating its performance.[16] The criticism was presented by Khoiruddin Bashori. As mentioned above, he is son of the late Bashori Anwar, a long-time chairman of the Kotagede branch of the Muhammadiyah. Khoiruddin himself obtained BA, MA and PhD from Gadjah Mada University in psychology and became a professor at the Muhammadiyah University of Yogyakarta, occupying its rector's position in 2003–08. He is one of the most distinguished intellectuals among the Muhammadiyah leaders at the national level at present.

Professor Khoiruddin made a comment on my paper presented at a conference in Australia in 1980.[17] Quoting from this 1980 paper of mine in an article entitled, "Manajemen Perubahan di Kotagede" [Management of Change in Kotagede], he commented that my paper was an example of excessive optimism for the Muhammadiyah. The excerpt quoted by Khoiruddin from my paper reads in its English original as follows:

> Since Muhammadiyah has been capable of formulating and implementing a series of social reforms on the basis of Islamic teachings concretely, steadily and continuously over generations, it is likely that it will meet successfully the challenge of novel social conditions at present and in the future.[18]

---

15. From the editorial of *Brosur Lebaran*, No. 22, 1404H/1984M.
16. Khoiruddin Bashori, "Manajemen Perubahan di Kotagede" [Management of Changes in Kotagede], *Brosur Lebaran*, No. 29, 1411H/1991M, pp. 27–29.
17. Mitsuo Nakamura, "The Reformist Ideology of Muhammadiyah", in *Indonesia: The Making of a Culture*, edited by James J. Fox et al., Research School of Pacific Studies, The Australian National University, 1980, pp. 273–86. The paper was a summary of my PhD dissertation, which was to be published later in 1983.
18. Ibid.

His point of criticism was as follows:

> [But,] can the statement by Nakamura still be showing its validity at present? In the context of Kotagede today, it is felt to be showing an excessive optimism of Nakamura. Why? Because Kotagede as a *santri* town and one of the "pockets" of the Muhammadiyah, which used to be very active and dynamic, is now felt to be lifeless. Moreover, according to the friends of *Brosur*, there occurred recently discontinuity in the process of transferring religious values from the preceding generation to the continuing generation so as to be causing stagnation in the dynamism of religious movement among the younger generation of this place.[19]

By referring to my paper of 1980, which was based on fieldwork in 1970–72, as an optimistic overestimation, Professor Khoiruddin contrasted the stagnant state of the Muhammadiyah movement in Kotagede in the early 1990s as "lifeless". I feel his critical comment on my observation is a bit anachronistic since the dynamism of Muhammadiyah in the early 1970s under the leadership of his father was quite impressive. Indeed, it was so impressive that I was unable to foresee the possibility of stagnation in the movement later on.

Setting aside my personal lament, I must acknowledge here his straightforwardness in admitting the depression of the Muhammadiyah movement in Kotagede. He then proposed the necessity of having a methodology to identify the causes of the slump via empirical research and to formulate a strategy to overcome them. Unfortunately, his proposal in the *Brosur* presented an abstract framework only. Even after the open debate of 1991, neither himself nor anyone else among the Muhammadiyah activists, especially those who studied social sciences, undertook objective research on the causes of the stagnation and the generational gap. His proposal for formulating a methodology of "management of change in Kotagede" remained as an unfinished homework.

Meanwhile, at the level of the national leadership, generational takeover occurred from K.H. A.R. Fakhruddin to Dr Basyir Azhar in 1990, and then to Dr Amien Rais in 1994. Amien Rais started to raise vocal criticism of President Soeharto for corruption and mismanagement of national resources, and demanded regeneration of the nation's leadership and a broad reform for its democratization. The Muhammadiyah movement was getting into a commotion nationally.

---

19. Khoiruddin, ibid., p. 27.

Yet, the stagnation continued at the local level of Kotagede. As late as the year 2000, *Brosur Lebaran* still carried explicit complaints of a young activist as follows: "There is a gap of leadership between the old and young generations. This is caused by the fact that there was no chance given for the coming generation. The Branch leadership of the Kotagede Muhammadiyah for the past three periods is occupied by the generation of Bashori Anwar, Yatiman Syafi'i, and Syamsuhadi. Many of those in the following generation have not come up, and thus the gap developed."[20] However, a meaningful change of leadership had to wait for another five years.

LEADERSHIP CHANGE

For the next five years from 2000, a senior person of Suhardjo MS (b. 1937, step-son of Ibu Mardi mentioned above) occupied the chairmanship of the Kotagede branch of the Muhammadiyah. Then, a significant generational turnover occurred in 2005. In order to take a look at the transition of leadership to the younger generations of the Muhammadiyah in Kotagede, it may be useful to present again a list of major topics of *Brosur Lebaran* from 2000 to 2008.[21]

From Table 10.2, it may be felt that younger generations of the Muhammadiyah activists have been getting increasingly impatient in pursuit of "really real Muhammadiyah" against the background of the unsatisfactory "reality of Muhammadiyah".

Personal Background of New Leaders of the Muhammadiyah

In 2005, prior to the branch conferences of the Muhammadiyah and the 'Aisyiyah, both organizations produced lists of candidates for the election of the top leadership of the each organization. Apparently, there occurred a significant change in the personal background of new leadership, especially in education and occupation, compared to the older leadership. Details on the lists are summarized in the Tables 10.3 and 10.4.

---

20. Article based upon interview with Akhid Widi Rahmanto, Branch Chairman of the Pemuda Muhammadiyah, "Opini dan harapan kinerja Pimpinan Cabang Muhammadiyah Kotagede" [Opinions and hopes for the performance of Muhammadiyah branch leadership of Kotagede], *Brosur Lebaran*, No. 39, 1421H/2000M, pp. 51–52.
21. Unfortunately, the issues of *Brosur Lebaran* during the turbulent years of the mid-to late 1990s, i.e. Nos. 31, 32, 35, 36, and 37 were not available to me.

TABLE 10.2
List of Major Topics of *Brosur Lebaran*, 2000–08

No.	Year M/H	Topics of Special Issues and Major Articles
38	2000/1420	Visiting history for the future of Kotagede. Festival Kotagede '99
39	2000/1421	The classic face of Kotagede. Human behaviour in Kotagede from ethical viewpoint.
40	2001/1422	Kotagede flooded by lottery gambling. Opening polemic on Festival Koategede
41	2002/1423	We want Kotagede clean from vices. Heritage of Mataram.
42	2003/1424	Learning from democracy: General elections. Propagation through culture.
43	2004/1425	The reality of Muhammadiyah and really real Muhammadiyah. "Minamata" in Kotagede?
44	2005/1426	It is no time to remain silent any longer (against PKS).
45	2006/1427	Post-earthquake recovery of Kotagede
46	2007/1428	10% national value-added tax chokes folk industry of silver in Kotagede.
47	2008/1429	MBA (Marriage by Accident) — moral degradation of our youths. When Muhammadiyah politicizes.

TABLE 10.3
Personal Background of Candidates for the Branch Leadership of the Muhammadiyah, Kotagede, 2005–10

(1) Age

No.	Age (year)	Total (person)	%
1	<30	1	1.9
2	30–40	8	15.7
3	40–50	16	31.4
4	50–60	15	29.4
5	60<	11	21.6
	Average	49.98 years old	

(2) Place of Birth

No.	Place of Birth	Total (person)	%
1	Yogyakarta	34	66.7
2	Kab. Bantul	11	21.7
3	Other Kab. in DIY	1	1.9
4	Other Region in Java	2	3.9
5	Outside Java	3	5.8
	TOTAL	51	100

TABLE 10.3 — *continued*

(3) Occupation

No.	Occupation	Total (person)	%
1	Teacher/*Dosen* Government	6	11.8
2	Teacher/*Dosen* Private	9	17.6
3	Business	9	17.6
4	Employee Private	12	23.6
5	Government employee/pensioner	13	25.5
6	Other	2	3.9
	TOTAL	51	100

(4) Level of Education

No.	Level of Education	Total (person)	%
1	Higher Education	40	78.5
2	Senior High School	7	13.7
3	Junior High School	1	1.9
4	Other	3	5.9
	TOTAL	51	100

(5) Institution of Higher Education

No.	Institution of Higher Education	Total (person)	%
1	UGM	1	2.5
2	IAIN / UIN	8	20
3	IKIP YOGYA / UNY	7	17.5
4	UII	4	10
5	UMY	5	12.5
6	Other	15	37.5
	TOTAL	40	100

Note: Dosen = teacher at institute of higher education
UGM = Gadjah Mada University; IAIN = State Institute of Islamic Studies; UIN = State Islamic University; IKIP Yogya/UNY = Institute of Education and Pedagogical Sciences; UNY = National University of Yogyakarta; UII = Indonesian University of Islam; UMY = University of Muhammadiyah Yogyakarta.
The table is not about the elected leaders but about candidates for election. Therefore, the profile of the actually elected leadership is a bit older and less well educated than the average listed in the table (same can be said of the 'Aisyiyah). Yet, the information contained in the table seems to be useful to understand the social attributes of the Muhammadiyah leadership as a whole.
Source: Data for the working conference of Kotagede Branch of Muhammadiyah, 2005.

First of all, the average age of fifty years indicates that some of the older generations were still difficult to be replaced among the Muhammadiyah leaders. But the fact that Kaharuddin Noor (b.1963) was eventually elected to take over the chairmanship from the incumbent Suhardjo MS (b. 1937) indicates that there were substantial efforts to bring in a generational renewal in the top leadership. Secondly, an overwhelming majority of them were born in Kotagede (including the Bantul area), i.e. 44 out of 51, or 88.4 per cent. They are literally the sons of Kotagede. In terms of occupation, those engaged in education — government and private — occupy 29.4 per cent of the total, followed by 25.5 per cent of government employees and their pensioners. There are 23.6 per cent of the total working as employees at private businesses, and 17.6 per cent as independent business people. As a whole, those employed in the private sector amount to 58.8 per cent, a majority, whereas 37.3 per cent in the government sector including pensioners.

A significant change from the past generations is found in the level of education. It was clear that many of the previous generation had graduated from the senior high school level of the Mu'allimin and its equivalent. Now this pattern is no longer dominant, occupying only 13.7 per cent. Meanwhile, college graduates occupy an overwhelming percentage of 78.5 per cent. Among

FIGURE 10.4

Pak Kaharuddin (front left) and Pak Natsir (right) in a *pengajian* at the Grear Mosque.

college graduates, the largest group is those from the IAIN SK (now UIN, or State Islamic University, Sunan Kalidjaga), a leading national institution of higher education in modern Islamic studies. The former national teachers training college, the IKIP Yogyakarta (now UNY, or Yogyakarta State University) comes at the second place with 17.5 per cent. Gadjah Mada University (UGM), one of the most prestigious state universities in Indonesia today, has only one graduate. Those graduates of government institutions are followed by graduates from private institutions: 12 per cent of the University of Muhammadiyah, Yogyakarta (UMY) and 10 per cent from the Islamic University of Indonesia (UII) — the oldest private university of the Republic of Indonesia. Those college graduates with *Sarjana* degrees include four individuals holding S2 (Master) or equivalent degrees.

Personal Background of 'Aisyiyah Leaders

Let us turn our attention to the top leadership of the women's organization, the 'Aisyiyah. Their personal backgrounds have been summarized in Table 10.4.

It should be noted that the women leaders are more than seven years older than their male counterpart in average. This is perhaps because they came to be active in the organization at an older age than their male counterparts because of their duties as mother and wife. In the above case of Ibu Umanah, she took a leadership position in the 'Aisyiyah at the age of 48 after her youngest child finished primary school. Their birthplaces are also limited to the Kotagede region (81.13 per cent) suggesting the frequent practice of endogamy among the Muhammadiyah families. In terms of occupation, the category of businesswomen is dominant at 37.74 per cent indicating the prominent female role in local economy. It is significant that the category of government employees and their pensioners, mostly former schoolteachers, occupies the second largest position of 26.41 per cent, and if added by their counterpart in higher education, the percentage becomes 32.07 per cent. Those who take care of household affairs only as mere "housewife" are a minority at 16.98 per cent.

Of the education, those who had received higher education occupy the largest category of 37.74 per cent, senior high graduates at 32.07 per cent and junior high 15.09 per cent.[22] So, the level of education of the 'Aisyiyah leaders is getting higher, catching up with that of their male counterpart.

---

22. Unfortunately, there is no information available concerning the specific institutions from which those individuals have graduated.

TABLE 10.4
Personal Background of Candidates for the Branch Leadership of the 'Aisyiyah, Kotagede, 2005–10

(1) Age

No.	Age (year)	Total (person)	%
1	40–50	6	11.32
2	50–60	27	50.95
3	60<	14	26.41
4	No information	6	11.32
	Average	57.19 years old	

(2) Place of Birth

No.	Place of Birth	Total (person)	%
1	Yogyakarta	32	60.38
2	Kab. Bantul	11	20.75
3	Other Kab. in DIY	1	1.89
4	Other region in Java	2	3.77
5	Outside Java	1	1.89
6	No information	6	11.32
	TOTAL	53	100

(3) Occupation

No.	Occupation	Total (person)	%
1	Teacher/*Dosen* Government	3	5.66
2	Business	20	37.74
3	Employee Private	1	1.89
4	Government Employee/Pensioner	14	26.41
5	Housewife	9	16.98
6	No information	6	11.32
	TOTAL	53	100

(4) Level of Education

No.	Level of Education	Total (person)	%
1	Higher education	20	37.74
2	Senior High School	17	32.07
3	Junior High School	8	15.09
4	Elementary School	1	1.89
5	Other	1	1.89
5	No information	6	11.32
	TOTAL	53	100

Note: Again, the following data are not for the actual leadership but for its candidates. Therefore, there are some biases for a more conservative side in terms age, education, etc. But, they will be enough to give a general picture of 'Aisyiyah leadership.
Source: Data for the working conference of the 'Aisyiyah, 2005.

SOCIAL DIMENSIONS OF THE NEW LEADERSHIP

As mentioned above, since the early 1990s, the third generation of the Muhammadiyah leaders has finally come to fore in Kotagede. Tables 10.3 and 10.4 show more recent data on them. They are mostly college graduates, many from IAIN but also many others from the institutions of secular higher education. In terms of occupation, they include a number of government employees and private office workers. The number of large business people (entrepreneur or *wiraswasta*) among them has shrunk compared to that of older generation in 1971, i.e. from 23.5 per cent to 17.6 per cent in 2005. Also in the 1971 data on the Muhammadiyah members, 68.6 per cent belonged to the two categories of private sector, i.e. "entrepreneurs" as well as "craftsmen, small trader and workers" in contrast to 12.8 per cent of "officials and professionals". In 2005, 58.8 per cent are in the private sector whereas 37.3 per cent in the government sector. In the overall occupational composition, therefore, the government sector is increasing significantly compared to the private one even in this town of Kotagede known to be a

FIGURE 10.5

2009 annual conference of Kotagede branch of Muhammadiyah at Yogyakarta City Hall.

town of traders and craftsmen. Meanwhile, an old pattern of the core leaders of the Muhammadiyah being *ulama*-cum-entrepreneurs is disappearing swiftly. Instead of independent *ulama*, university teachers are emerging as intellectual leaders of the Muhammadiyah movement even at the local level. It is obvious that a sort of "upgrading" of religious learning from the senior high level of the Mu'allimin to the level of higher education, or even to the level of postgraduate education, at the IAIN/UIN has occurred among the top leaders of the local Muhammadiyah. Besides those, another group of them have graduated from secular institutions of higher education, and some continue to teach there. Those people are beginning to bring in the approaches of secular social science and humanities into the activities of the movement. In addition, the contribution from the expertise in natural sciences, technology, and civil engineering has started to be felt in the movement.

THE GENERAL MEMBERSHIP OF MUHAMMADIYAH

I have failed to obtain reliable data on the general membership of Kotagede branch of the Muhammadiyah, which can be compared to the 1971 data (see pp. 134–43). This is because of the very simple fact that the branch office has no current data on the membership. Reportedly, the old system of manually writing in the membership book and the issuance of membership card thereupon has ceased to be practised some time ago. In its place, the Muhammadiyah organization as a whole introduced a new system of registration of membership via computer with the issuance of a serial number of national membership. Now almost all members of the Kotagede branch of the Muhammadiyah seem to possess their membership cards (or at least the membership numbers, NBM). In theory, that situation should have made available the exact information on the branch membership at any time. However, in practise, somehow the branch leaders are unable to retrieve the information from the central office. Therefore, there is no reliable information on the current branch membership.

Accordingly, I had to make an estimate on the number of individuals belonging to the Kotagede branch of the Muhammadiyah and its associate organizations. I have used two sources for that. One is the result of the recent election. As we have seen before, in the most recent election of the Yogyakarta City Council, those two political parties, PAN and PPP, which are most likely to have received support from the Muhammadiyah members and its sympathizers have actually obtained about 5,000 votes from Kecamatan Kotagede. Of course, the actual members of Muhammdiyah must be much less than this. Meanwhile, there was an "Apel Akbar" (Grand Roll Call) and a following parade organized by the AMM of the Muhammadiyah on Sunday, 27 January 2007 when I was in the town. It was a show of force by the grand family of the Muhammadiyah. The official target for the number of people to be mobilized was 1,500. However, I counted more people than that — around 2,000 participating in the rally and the parade. So, in conclusion, the number of individuals belonging to the Muhammadiyah and its associate organizations is estimated to be at least at 3,000 for the entire Kotagede.

If this estimation is not so remote from the reality, then the general membership of the Muhammadiyah family has grown more than twice as much as that of 980 individuals (adult male only) in 1972 (see p. 135). Meanwhile, the entire population has grown twice from roughly 17,000 to 35,000 (see Table 8.1).

There is no exact information covering the social attributes of the general Muhammadiyah members. I can only express my impressions that its coverage has widened greatly to include the lower middle-class, and even the poor. It is expected that the branch leadership will undertake a survey on social characteristics of the general membership in order to grasp exact information on its own so that appropriate planning can be done for the management of the organization.

REFORMING REFORMISTS: LIFE HISTORY OF BACHRUN NAWAWI

To illustrate innovative trends among the new generation of Muhammadiyah leaders, a biography of Bachrun Nawawi is presented here. He was born in 1944 from father, Kyai Nawawi, a preacher at Masjid Perak (Silver Mosque),[23] and mother, a trader of clothes at the Yogyakarta market of Bringhardjo. When he was a third-year student in psychology at Gadjah Mada University, he obtained a scholarship to study at the University of Western Australia, receiving a diploma in education. Back in Yogyakarta, he was employed by the Foster Parents Program (FPP) and sent to Bantul and Gunung Kidul as a field worker. FPP then assigned him to work in Africa as director of community development for more than eight years. Upon his return, he was sent to work in Sumbawa, NTT Barat, to direct a community development programme until 1996. He then quit the FPP job. Considering the importance of marriage and family, he came home to settle down in Kotagede for good. He purchased rice fields of 3,000 square metres in Bantul, harvests from which would have been enough to support his family's livelihood. Then, with the advent of Reformasi, he

---

23. Kyai Nawawi was the author of its history, see Nawawi Daman (1957) in Bibliography.

FIGURE 10.6

Pak Bachrun Nawawi (left) at the 2009 annual conference of Kotagede branch of Muhammadiyah.

joined the PAN and was elected to the Provincial Council of Yogyakarta via the 1999 elections. But, soon he was disappointed with party politics, which was, according to him, full of egoism and pursuit of personal gains. He stopped his involvement in politics after 2004 and has since been concentrating on Muhammadiyah matters.[24]

He became very critical of the local leadership of the Muhammadiyah as early as the beginning of the 1980s, pointing out that it was insensitive to ongoing social change while just enjoying a comfortable monopoly of the public space created by the eradication of Communists and Left-Nationalists after 1965.[25] Several years later, he warned that the Muhammadiyah's monopoly

---

24. Interview on 3 January 2008.
25. Interview on 3 January 2008. Also see, Bachrun Nawawi, "Masalah sosial Kotagede dan pemecahannya" [Social problems in Kotagede and their solutions], *Brosur Lebaran*, No. 18, 1400H/1980M, pp. 37–43, and "Siapa mau jadi pembaharu?" [Who wants to become a reformer?], *Brosur Lebaran*, No. 19, 1401H/1981M, pp. 61–65.

in education and health care was being threatened by the appearance of non-Muhammadiyah private schools and government's PUSKESMAS health service centres. He then proposed to formulate concrete measures to keep the competitiveness of the Muhammadiyah in those areas. He urged the Muhammadiyah to set up a special task force to collect data and design long-term programmes, which could respond to the consequences of ongoing social change. He also emphasized the need for regeneration of the Muhammadiyah leadership by younger generation to overcome stagnation, but he was unable to obtain support from the members.[26] His criticisms seemed to have encountered a persistent resistance from the older generation until the advent of Reformasi in the late 1990s. Since then, he has received stronger support from the younger generation. In fact, he received the largest number of votes for the election of chairman at the branch conference of the Muhammadiyah in 2005, but its selection committee decided to pick Kaharuddin, perhaps because of his age (61 years old then). Instead, Bachrun was elected to its advisory board along with Ahmad Charris Zubair.[27] The present leadership of the Kotagede branch of the Muhammadiyah is largely composed of those individuals who are responsive to Bachrun's ideas. It is to be seen how soon and to what extent the Kotagede Muhammadiyah will be modified in the direction suggested by Bachrun Nawawi, Charris Zubair and other former critics.

KAHARUDDIN NOOR: A YOUNGER LEADER

The chairman actually selected to lead the Kotagede branch of the Muhammadiyah for the period 2006–10 was Kaharuddin Noor (b.1963), who has been a Muhammadiyah activist since his childhood in Kotagede.[28] His father, Wazir Noor, was a tailor who excelled in sewing batik shirts, with a high reputation among local customers. He was also a long-time activist of the Muhammadiyah at the sub-branch level. Kaharuddin attended

---

26. Bachrun Nawawi, "Kepemimpinan yang perlu dibenahi" [Leadership that needs to be straightened up] (interviewed by M. Setiawan and Hamid Nuri, written by Erwito Wibowo), *Brosur Lebaran*, No. 22, 1404H/1984M, pp. 17–18.
27. Interview on 3 January 2008.
28. Interview on 29 November 2009.

Muhammadiyah schools in Kotagede, and then to the IAIN SK (State Institute of Islamic Studies, Sunan Kalidjaga) in Yogyakarta. Having obtained a *Sarjana* (BA) degree, he was employed by the Department of Religious Affairs and assigned to work in Kulon Progo, a *kabupaten* southwest of the *kabupaten* Bantul, and other places until he was called back to an office of the Department in the city of Yogyakarta in 1990.

All through his campus and office life, he was actively engaged in the organization of the Muhammadiyah including a post at its city-level leadership. Unlike most of his predecessors, he was not from the "elite families" of the town, from which most of the top leaders of the Muhammadiyah branch had thus far been selected. In that, he broke the tradition and came closer to reflect a majority of the membership today, which had shifted from the upper-middle to the middle and lower-middle social strata of the town. With the start of new leadership under Kaharuddin, a number of improvements have already been initiated. One of them is the strengthening of the Council for Research and Development. Objective data gathering is expected to begin on the membership of the Muhammadiyah and related organizations so that its action programmes could be formulated with more realistic goals.

FACING COMMON SOCIETAL PROBLEMS

With the increasing significance of the Muhammadiyah as a social force in the local community, a number of its members have become involved in local administration. In fact, the mayor of Yogyakarta city is now a Muhammadiyah member and so are several heads of *kelurahans* and RWs in Kotagede. This situation requires the Muhammadiyah to clarify its position on a number of societal problems arising from rapid transformation of the town's life. They include worsening traffic jams and congestion of the market, air pollution from ever-increasing automobiles, and the possible pollution of underground water because of the use of certain chemicals and rare metal in the processing of silver and other metals (i.e. the danger of so-called "Minamata disease" in Kotagede), smoking in public, especially among juveniles, increase in vices and moral decay including prostitution, gambling, alcoholism, MBA ("marriage by accident") (see Table 10.2 above).

Some Islamic leaders justify "direct action" to prevent those vices in terms of Qur'anic junction of *amar maruf nahi munkar* ("urging good deeds and preventing evil deeds", Qur'an 3:104). According to their interpretation, the command of *nahi munkar* ("preventing evil deeds") obligates Muslims to undertake "direct action" against those sinful actors in case the government is incapable of preventing them.[29] The mainstream of Muhammadiyah, however, advocates "friendly persuasion", and avoiding violence.[30]

At any rate, the Muslim community is called to present its policy alternatives to contribute to the promotion of the "common good" in society, and the Muhammadiyah is expected to take up initiatives to do so.

PROSPECTS FOR NEW LEADERSHIP

With a considerable time lag from the generational takeover of national leadership, the branch leadership of the Muhammadiyah in Kotagede finally achieved a significant rejuvenation at its 2005 conference as we have seen above. Bachrun Nawawi, who had long been insisting on the turnover of leadership by younger generation, was now made an adviser to the branch leadership. So was A. Charris Zubair as a member of the advisory board. Erwito Wibowo, the culture man, was also included in the branch leadership to head the Culture and Sports Council. Newly elected Chairman Kaharuddin Noor is, as mentioned above, not from among the "elite families" of the Muhammadiyah but from an "ordinary" family.

Activities of the "Cultural Muhammadiyah" outside the formal organization of the Muhammadiyah, such as the grouping around Saleh Udden (Sholehuddin) and Natsier in Yayasan Kanthil, and Charris and Erwito in PUSDOK, are getting energized. Here we find obvious and positive efforts for fruitful rapprochement between Islam and local cultural tradition. As pointed out by Muhadjir Darwin, alongside the trend of Islamization, which has been going on for several decades, a new counter or parallel trend of Javanization has been developing within the Muhammadiyah itself.[31] *Shalawatan* (prayers in melody) has become a standard item in the repertory of the Muhammadiyah's school activities. Gamelan performance is also often employed as a standard introduction into the Muhammadiyah's cultural event. Performance of *wayang kulit* or *wayang wong* is sometimes sponsored by the Muhammadiyah itself as an organization or privately by its members. As we

---

29. Yazir, "Aksi Bukan Program Pokok" [Action is not the principal programme], *Brosur Lebaran*, No. 43, 1423H/2002M, pp. 19–22.
30. Interview with Syafi'i Yatiman, 31 December 2007.
31. Muhadjir Darwin,"Dinamika Kultur Urban Kotagede: Islamisasi vs. Jawanisasi" [Cultural Dynamics in Urban Kotagede: Islamization vs. Javanisation], *Brosur Lebaran*, No. 46, 1428H/2007M, pp. 41–44.

FIGURE 10.7

Drs. Habib Chirzin speaking at a discussion on epistemology in April 2011.

shall see later in Chapter 12, these dialectic interactions between Islam and local culture have culminated in Festival Kotagede '99.

Another explicit feature of the Muhammadiyah Kotagede is a continuing input of national and international perspectives by those who are active on those horizons. Habib Chirzin (b.1949), who originated as a Pemuda Muhammadiyah leader in Kotagede, has become well known on the national and international stages. Among others, he served as a member of the KOMNASHAM (National Commission of Human Rights), 2002–07, and has also been active internationally as one of the founding members of the AMAN (Asian Muslim Action Network) and other regional and global organizations. He is a vocal advocate of interfaith dialog and pluralism in the post-Reformasi era. Darwis Khudori, who obtained a doctoral degree from Sorbonne, is living and teaching in France now. As a specialist in architecture and urban planning, he has been directly involved in the local efforts to recover and preserve the "urban heritage" in Kotagede after the destruction by the 2006 earthquake.[32] Muhadjir Darwin (b.1953) quoted above, who also originated from Kotagede, has received a PhD from the University of Southern California. He is living outside Kotagede at a northern edge of the city of Yogyakarta and heading one of the prestigious research institutions at Gadjah Mada University, i.e., Centre for Population and Policy Studies. He is a specialist on gender and reproductive rights, and has been involved in the formation of Southeast Asian as well as Asian-Pacific networks for those who are concerned with social sciences and medicine, especially with health and reproductive rights.[33] He strongly advocates the reinterpretation of Islamic teachings in the context of contemporary social ethics. For example, he urged the Muslim community of Kotagede in his *khutbah* (sermon) delivered on the occasion of Idul Adha 1428H/2007M to engage in *"korban sosial"* (social sacrifice) in which the faithful is expected to make productive investment in social business for the common good.[34]

Perhaps more importantly in a long run, a significant number of children of those individuals among the third generation of the Muhammadiyah are growing up and educated in cross-cultural environments and naturally adapting themselves to global horizons. It is expected that they will soon be making substantial contributions to the development of Kotagede community, if not directly to the Muhammadiyah, in the new age of globalization.

As we have seen above, those individuals who were young and critical a couple of decades ago are now becoming the generation of "Bapak" and "Ibu" themselves. Their participation in the leadership of the local Muhammadiyah seems to be bringing it into a new stage of maturity. Now the ability of the new leadership to reinvigorate a century-old organization is tested. Will their initiatives be accepted and implemented at local level? The future of the Muhammadiyah in Kotagede depends largely on this reinvigoration.

---

32. Darwis Khudori, "Membangun Kembali Kotagede" [Building back Kotagede], *Brosur Lebaran*, No. 45, 1427H/2006M, pp. 73–79.
33. Muhadjir Darwin, *Negara dan Perumpuan: Reorientasi Kebijakan Publik* [The State and Women: Reorientation of Public Policy] (Yogyakarta: Media Wacana, 2005).
34. Muhadjir Darwin, "Korban Sosial Sebagai Nilai Budaya Baru Untuk Mengatasi Problema Bangsa" [social sacrifice as a new cultural value to overcome national problems], Khutbah Idul Adha 10 Dzulhijah 1428 Hijiriyah.

11

CHALLENGES FACING THE MUHAMMADIYAH

In the context of enormous social changes since the 1970s described in Chapter 8 — urbanization, diversification and globalization — the Muhammadiyah in Kotagede is faced with major challenges such as pluralism, "culture of poverty", and "poverty of culture". Also, the Muhammadiyah Kotagede is operating in the national context of post-Reformasi situation, which is impacted by democratization and decentralization. The future development of the Muhammadiyah movement will be dependent upon the results of how it deals with those challenges and make positive social contributions in the ever-changing environment.

THE CHALLENGE OF PLURALISM AND DEMOCRACY

Nationally, since the official acceptance of Pancasila as the basic framework of the state in the 1985 national congress, the Muhammadiyah has made it clear that it would not seek to establish an Islamic state but to endeavour to realize an Islamic society. Its current statute states that its aim is to realize an "excellent society" (*masyarakat utama*) according to the teachings of Islam. The concept of "excellent society" seems to imply two aspects: the Muhammadiyah itself and Indonesian society at large. The logic of the Muhammadiyah movement is to seek an excellent society for Indonesia at large through the excellence of the Muhammadiyah. In this context, the term "*utama*" (excellent) reminds us of the Budi Utomo (Excellent Work) — an organization formed by the Javanese youths as the first move for nationalist movement at the dawn of the twentieth century. K.H. Ahmad Dahlan, the founder of the Muhammadiyah, was, in fact, one of the original members of Budi Utomo. Moral connotation of the term "*utama*" is obvious. The Muhammadiyah strives to uplift individual morality, by which to realize an ideal society.

Now the realistic task of the Muhammadiyah is to define its position and role in Indonesian society whose political underpinning (Constitution) is pluralism in terms of the Five Principles or Pancasila. The national motto has been Bhinneka Tunggal Ika (Unity in Diversity). Furthermore, the political reforms achieved through the post-Soeharto legislation have strengthened institutional framework for democracy.[1] In this situation, Muhammadiyah must show its excellence in cooperation as well as in competition with others. In other words, the basic reference point of the Muhammadiyah is not so much the Muslim community alone as the entire Indonesian society consisting of diverse cultures and religions. The implication of this national situation applies to the local context of Kotagede, too.

As we have seen above, now the dominance of the Muhammadiyah is gone from the public stage of the town. The Muhammadiyah has to show its prominence by contributing to the common interest of local community in which it is operating. In other words, the Muhammadiyah has to seek its excellence not self-righteously nor exclusively but in cooperation with other socio-cultural forces, Muslim as well as non-Muslim.

In this respect, Buya Syafi'i (Dr Ahmad Syafi'i Maarif), former National Chairman of Muhammadiyah, has contributed an instructive article to *Brosur Lebaran* of AMM, Muhammadiyah, Kotagede, as early as 1992. He has touched upon the theme of impending religious situation in the twenty-first century as follows:

> [A] Muslim may be living next door to an atheist or a believer of a different religion. I feel there should be nothing to block cooperation among the groups different in religion or worldview as far as worldly affairs are concerned. In other words, Islam can accept religious and cultural pluralism as sociological

---

1. See my paper, "Muhammadiyah faces the challenge of democracy", in *Muhammadiyah Menjemput Perubahan* [Muhammadiyah faces change], edited by Mukhaer Pakkanna and Nur Achmad (Jakarta: P3SE STIE Ahmad Dahlan & Penerbit Buku Kompas, 2005).

reality. With the shrinking of the world caused by the progress in information technology, attitudes of exclusivism must be regarded as a thing of past.[2]

The plurality in religion, culture and ethnicity as a basic social reality of the Indonesian nation state seems to be well accepted among the Muhammadiyah circles today. Moreover, there are some arguments to recognize this reality as "*Sunnatullah*" (God's law, i.e. natural law).[3] Accordingly, Muhammadiyah seems to be getting less reactive, or defensive, to the presence of non-Islamic groups among the same local community than before. Warnings against active missionary works by certain denominations of Christianity are still heard. Generally speaking, however, amiable relationship with other religious groups is sought from the Muhammadiyah side as well. This is the effect of the move developed at the national level among the representatives of major religious organizations in the post-Reformasi situation. They have been cooperating closely in the wake of religious and ethnic conflicts in the late 1990s. The personal initiative and dedication of Buya Syafi'i was instrumental to launch this move.

In Kotagede, as mentioned in Chapter 8, Kyai Abdul Muhaimin of NU started an initiative for interfaith dialog, and has attracted national as well as international attentions. At present, the local Muhammadiyah seems to be still hesitant to respond positively to his initiative. However, the challenge of pluralism is real and has to be faced squarely by Muhammadiyah leaders. The matter is not for Muslim community alone but for the entire local community in which non-Muhammadiyah Muslims, Christian Protestants and Catholics occupy a significant portion.

In this respect, a recent official document drafted by Saleh Udden (Sholehuddin), the village head of Jagalan, seems extremely significant. He came from an established family of the Muhammadiyah,[4] and has impeccable reputation as a pious Muslim. He has formulated the following statement in a decision taken by the Jagalan Council for Empowerment of Village Society, an official body for the consultation and formulation of policy at village level:

---

2. Ahmad Syafi'i Maarif, "Agama dan Permasalahannya di Abad XXI (Sebuah Perspektif Islam)" [Religion and its Problematics in the 21st Century (An Islamic Perspective)], *Brosur Lebaran*, No. 30, 1942H/1992M, p. 22.
3. "Konsep Dakwah Kultural Muhammadiyah: Sebuah Tinjauan Wawasan" [The Muhammadiyah's Concept of Cultural Propagation: A Survey of Opinions], *Brosur Lebaran*, No. 43, 1425H/2004M, pp. 9–14.
4. Son of Bashori Anwar, see p. 285 above.

The importance of religious aspect [in village life] does not mean primordialism [sic] in the form of a particular religion. It should mean that universally noble values followed by all religions be applied to everyday social interactions in the community.[5]

He is also known to have adopted the following traditional motto in Javanese for the management of his village: "*Ngesuhi deso sak kukuban.*" The motto roughly means "taking care of all elements in the village with heart".[6] It is true that he is appealing this point not as a Muhammadiyah leader but as a community leader. Therefore, whether his positive advocacy for pluralism will be accepted and honoured by the villagers including the members of Muhammadiyah should be seen in the future.

Another challenge facing the Muhammadiyah comes from within the Muslim community itself. That is the emergence of the PKS (Partai Keadilan Sejahtera or Prosperous Justice Party), which follows closely the ideology of Ihwanul Muslimin of the Middle East. The party has surfaced to the public political stage since the advent of Reformasi, enjoying the freedom of political expression and association. At the initial stage of its membership recruitment, the PKS (formerly PK or Partai Keadilan) took the strategy of infiltration into the established socio-religious organizations, among which the Muhammadiyah was the primary target. Thus, the PKS cells (*halaqah*) were formed in the Muhammadiyah youth and student groups, mosque committees, school and kindergarten managements, and even in a university under the Muhammadiyah's direct management in Yogyakarta.

According to the former chairman of the local Muhammadiyah, Yatiman Syafi'i, the PKS has brought serious damage to the Muhammadiyah by carving out a significant number of young activists to its organization. Unlike the Muhammadiyah members in such political parties as PAN, PPP, PDIP and Golkar, who do not bring in political differences to the Muhammadiyah activities, the PKS used the Muhammadiyah organization — members, facilities and resources — for its own political purposes.[7]

---

5. Lembaga Pemberdayaan Masyarakat Desa, "Desa Jagalan, Rencana Pembangunan Jangka Menegah, Tahun 2007–2011" [Mid-Term Development Plan, 2007–2011], p. 12.
6. This is also the title of a book edited by M. Jadul Maula, *Ngesuhi Deso Sak Kukuban* (Yogyakarya: LKiS, 2001). I owe Ahmad Charris Zubair for the translation of this Javanese expression into English. In an article in the book written by Jadul himself, Saleh Udden (Sholehuddin) appears as "Lokajaya"(see pp. 29–31).
7. Interview on 31 December 2007.

Having realized this parasitic nature of the PKS's strategy, the national leadership of the Muhammadiyah has decided to strictly forbid the PKS infiltration and the utilization of facilities owned by Muhammadiyah by the PKS.[8] Locally, the Muhammadiyah Kotagede branch has also begun an active anti-PKS campaign. An article entitled "It's time not to remain silent any longer!"[9] which appeared in *Brosur Lebaran* in 2006 expresses straightforward annoyance and anger at the PKS. (See Figure 10.3.)

Organizationally, this attitude seems to have been effective to eliminate the PKS members from the Muhammadiyah and has prevented its further infiltration. It seems, however, unavoidable for the Muhammadiyah to develop a fresher persuasiveness in ideology and a more active working style in order to attract back those young people whose hearts have swung to PKS. This will be ultimately an ideological competition.

The challenge of pluralism is basically the challenge of democratic values, which uphold the rights of the minority. Under the regime of President Soeharto, the Muhammadiyah was often asking and relying on the government control of Islamic as well as non-Islamic minority groups. Now that the intervention of government in the realm of individual conscience is prohibited constitutionally, *de jure* at least,[10] the Muhammadiyah is tasked to embody civic values in democracy as one of the largest civil society organizations in Indonesia.

THE PROBLEM OF POVERTY

Indonesia is still facing the problem of poverty after more than sixty years of its independence and after more than ten years of the 1997–98 Asian economic crisis. As a socio-religious movement aimed at the promotion of social welfare and social justice for the people of Indonesia, poverty alleviation has been one of the central tasks of the Muhammadiyah since its incipience until today. As we have seen before, the Muhammadiyah was started as a social movement of "the haves" in the town of Kotagede many decades ago. It has since widened its constituency to include the middle to lower social strata in recent decades. A new middle class with higher education and professional skills has emerged from relatively low-income families. This phenomenon has blurred the image of the Muhammadiyah as a group of "the haves". Yet, charitable activities in terms of Islamic framework to assist the poor and needy

---

8. Surat Keputusan Pimpinan Pusat Muhammadiyah No. 149/KEP/I.O/B/2006 [Decision by the Central Leadership of Muhammadiyah].
9. *Brosur Lebaran*, No. 45, 1427H/2006M, pp. 26–29.
10. This principle seems to be threatened in view of the more recent government dealing vis-à-vis the Ahmadiyah.

still constitutes as one of the pillars of the Muhammadiyah's social contribution. The Muhammadiyah continues to promote and develop further the collection and distribution of *zakat fitrah* at Idul Fitri and that of sacrificial animals at Idul Adha as religiously obligated action. Collections of money in terms of *infak* and *sadakah* are also conducted at various occasions. In addition, a number of programmes of *santunan* to assist the poor and needy directly have been implemented by the Muhammadiyah.[11] (See Figure 11.1.)

FIGURE 11.1

Free medical check-up of the aged by PKU Muhammadiyah.

---

11. I failed to obtain comprehensive data on current ZIS practice (*zakat, infak, sadakah*) conducted by the Kotagede branch of Muhammadiyah except for the information contained in its financial report for the year of 2007. As far as *infak* (occasional cash contribution) is concerned, it is reported that the Mumhammadiyah collected Rp11,240,000 at the mass prayer meeting held at Karang on Idul Adha 1427H (13 January 2007), Rp24,442,750 at that of Idul Fitri 1428H (13 October 2007), and Rp16,261,450 at that of Idul Adha 1948H (23 December 2007). All the amounts of money went into the treasury of Muhammadiyah as its income. *Source:* "Laporan Keuangan Pimpinan Cabang Muhammadiyah" [Financial Report of the Branch Leadership of Muhammadiayah], Augustus 2006–Februari 2007.

Still, it is an undeniable social reality that poverty persists in the town as Table 11.1 indicates. The government has been conducting official surveys on the poor households since the "multi-dimensional crisis of 1997–98". These surveys are meant to obtain data to determine the target population of poverty alleviation measure, called "Raskin" (a short for "*beras miskin*", meaning "rice for the poor") (Figure 11.2). Table 11.1 presents the most recent statistics on the households eligible for receiving "Raskin" in the town of Kotagede.

FIGURE 11.2

An advertisement for RASKIN.

TABLE 11.1
Poor People and Poor Household Heads (HH) in Kotagede

No.	Kelurahan/Desa	(A) Total Population	(B) No. of Poor People	B/A in %	(C) Total No. of HH	(D) No. of Poor HH	D/C in %
1	Rejowinangun	12,233	2,119	17.32	2,612	529	20.25
2	Prenggan	11,484	2,361	20.55	2,701	716	26.5
3	Purbayan	9,704	2,940	30.3	2,063	735	35.62
4	Jagalan	3,465	500	14.43	867	?	?
5	Total	36,886	7,920	21.47	8,243	?	?

Source: Data Monografi Desa Jagalan, 2007; Data Monografi Kecamatan Kotagede, 2007.

Table 11.1 shows an astonishing degree of persistent poverty in Kotagede. The poor in Kelurahan Purbayan is reaching 30 per cent of the entire residents and 35 per cent of all the households, i.e. more than one household out of three is poor. Rejowinangun, an area for former farmers and new residents, shows a relatively lower percentage for the poor whereas the old settled area of Jagalan the lowest.

Table 11.1 indicates the fact that 20 to 30 per cent of the townspeople in Kotagede are depending day to day on government subsidies in the form of rice. The reader may refer to Appendix II in which data on the average daily income of Kotagedeans in 1972 is presented. The data indicates the reality of abject poverty — an average per capita cash income of Rp38 a day, or an equivalent of US$0.10 at that time. That was barely enough to purchase 1 kg of rice per day for a family then.

The situation has not improved significantly as far as the poor are concerned. According to the website of BPS (Central Bureau of Statistics), there were 585,800 individuals below the officially set poverty line of Rp211,978 income per month out of approximately 3.5 million people as the total population of DIY in 2008. The percentage of the poor, i.e. those below the poverty line, becomes 17.23 per cent. Those eligible for Raskin are supposed to receive 156 kg of rice per person a year at the reduced price of Rp1,600 per kg (the market price of the same kind of rice is Rp5,000 per kg).

Meanwhile, the officially set level of minimum wage for the DIY as of the year 2009 was Rp745,694 per month, which was an equivalent of approximately US$70 per month or US$2.30 day. In nominal terms, if this figure is compared to average per capita cash income of Kotagedeans in 1972, it has arisen more than twenty times. As mentioned above, the average daily income in 1972 was a little less than US$0.10 or Rp35 per day according to my own survey. When calculated against the price of rice, which was Rp32–35 per kg in 1972, the daily income then was approximately equal to the money needed for purchasing 1 kg of rice. In 2010, per capita income according to the official minimum wage of US$2.30 a day (approximately Rp2,300) enables one to purchase approximately only 0.46 kg of rice in the market, or less than half of the amount in 1972. With the government subsidy, the poor are able to obtain Raskin at the price of Rp1,600 per kg. Then, the amount of rice thus purchased becomes barely equal to that of 1972. This shows that the Raskin Programme is an extremely substantial subsidy for the poor to survive.[12]

The persistent poverty in Kotagede seems to be related to the source of livelihood, or the occupation of the townspeople. For that, Table 11.2 on the occupational composition of the townspeople seems to be useful. Unfortunately, data are available only from Kecamatan Kotagede for I was unable to find equivalent data from the Bantul part of Kotagede.

An outstanding feature of Table 11.2 is the enormity of those who belong to the social category of so-called *wong cilik*, or "small people". They are those engaged in small trade (*pedagang, bakul*) or daily labourers in industry (*buruh*

TABLE 11.2
Population by Occupation, Kecamatan Kotagede, 2007

No.	Occupation	N	%
1	Small trader	6,104	33.08
2	Worker in industry	5,219	28.29
3	Worker in construction	2,088	11.32
4	Transportation	1,758	9.53
5	Government employee	1,553	8.42
6	Cottage Industry/Artisan	577	3.13
7	Pensioner (civil & military)	463	2.5
8	Farmer/Peasant	286	1.55
9	Animal Husbandry	206	1.12
10	ABRI (Armed Forces)	165	0.89
11	Business, medium/large	31	0.17
	Total	18,450	100

Source: Data Monografi Kecamatan Kotagede, 2007.

---

12. I appreciate the help of Professor Kano Hiroyoshi of Tokyo University for providing information on the rice for poor programme and the minimum wage level in Yogyakarta.

industri), construction (*buruh bangunan*), and transportation (*angkutan*). The sub-total of the number of individuals in this category amounts to 15,169, or 82.22 per cent of the total number of individuals, 18,450.

The entry of *pedagang* (small traders without shops) may include not only petty traders (*bakul*) without permanent places for trade, but also relatively successful traders having sales lots in the market of Kotagede, or that of Yogyakarta, or elsewhere. Also, the entry of *angkutan* (transportation) may include independent taxi drivers owning their own cars as well as mere *becak* (trickshaw) pedalists who own nothing but are hired daily. Even so, the dominance of the combined percentage of about 40 per cent for the entries of *buruh industri* and *buruh bangunan* is amazing. Reportedly, those workers are usually employed for short periods when there are work to be done and paid wages daily or weekly without any official social securities.

It was reported that a large number of skilled and semi-skilled labourers in silver and other cottage industries in town have lost their jobs because of the 2006 earthquake. They have become daily *buruh bangunan* (construction workers) employed temporarily for the removal of debris and for the work

FIGURE 11.3

A vegetable vendor (*bakul*) in Kotagede market.

for repair/reconstruction of damaged buildings. Perhaps, the above figures reflect this temporary situation. However, it is difficult to imagine these people finding more stable jobs when the "reconstruction boom" of the post-earthquake (*pasca gempa*) is over.

Silver handicraft industry (*kerajinan perak*), which used to be almost a synonym of Kotagede, is in drastic decline since the economic crisis of 1997–98. The price of imported silver alloy increased from Rp3,000 to Rp4,000 per gram.[13] Kotagede products have been experiencing fierce competition with foreign products from China, Thailand, Malaysia and other neighbouring countries. Besides, domestic competitors have been emerging from the rural hinterlands of Kotagede, such as Wonosari and Plered, where wages for labourers are much cheaper.[14]

The cooperative of silver industrialists (KP3Y or Koperasi Pengusaha Produksi Perak Yogyakarta) is still in operation, with an office and sales counter on the main street of Kotagede. It also has a sales section in the well-known Sarinah department store in Jakarta. The number of member industrialists in 2007 was 98, a decrease of 4 from 102 in the previous year. (In 1971, there were 117 members. See Chapter 5). For the year 2006, the transaction of raw material was totally impossible because of the weak market situation and the imposition of 10 per cent value added tax by the government. The substantial income of the KP3Y was only obtained from the sales of the products previously displayed in Sarinah at the amount of Rp47 million (approximately US$4,700).[15]

Competitions with imported products are getting very fierce. Besides, the earthquake of 27 May 2006 not only caused extensive damage to the office and the sales counter of the KP3Y in Kotagede, but also created a complete stoppage of business for a while. After the earthquake, the number of foreign tourists visiting Kotagede and purchasing silver products has shrunk drastically. Relatively good business is enjoyed by only two giant enterprises, each occupying two strategic locations at the entrances to the town, one from the north and the other from the west. Those shops are in contract with tourist agencies, which bring in tourists by bus. Tourists on foot rarely come to visit silver shops located in the centre of the town. However, a small number of enterprising industrialists are now using websites and e-mails to

---

13. "PPN 10% Mencekik Pengrajin Perak Kotagede" [10% Value added tax is choking the silver folk industry], *Brosur Lebaran*, No. 46, 1428H/2007M, pp. 22–26.
14. Ibid., p. 24.
15. From the 2007 annual report of KP3Y.

solicit direct transactions from overseas. All in all, Kotagede is threatened to lose its position as the traditional centre of the silver handicraft industry. Effective means to attend to this tendency are urgently needed.[16]

Consequences of the decline of the silver industry impacted upon the workers' situation drastically, too. It is roughly estimated that, among approximately 2,000 silverwork artisans (*tukang*) and labourers (*buruh*) who existed before the economic crisis and the earthquake, about 30 per cent switched their jobs to daily labour, as construction worker, small traders, or pedicab drivers; of those who are staying on, 40 per cent are now engaged in production of other metal work such as copper and brass.[17] The enormity of the number of day labourers and small traders in the previous statistics is very much likely to be the reflection of this economic change.

The reality of the economic situation of Kotagede may be learned from another statistics prepared by the office of Kecamatan Kotagede. That is on the business enterprises (*perusahaan/usaha*) and their employees. The breakdown of employees by the kind of business is presented in Table 11.3. It shows more explicitly the dominance of industrial workers in employment. Industries, from home and small scale to large ones totalling at 608, are employing 4,813 individuals, or 60.71 per cent of the total of 7,926 employees

TABLE 11.3
Business Enterprises (*Perusahaan/Usaha*) and their Employees in Kecamatan Kotagede, 2007

No.	Business Enterprise	N	%	No. of employees	%
1	Large Industry	5	0.42	2,245	28.33
4	Medium Industry	26	2.2	522	6.56
2	Small Industry	294	24.84	1,150	14.51
3	Home Industry	283	23.9	896	11.31
5	Hotel	5	0.42	34	0.43
6	Food Stall	76	6.42	237	2.99
7	Restaurant	3	0.25	48	0.61
8	Trasportation	476	40.2	2,716	34.27
9	Others	16	1.35	78	0.99
	Total	1,184	100	7,926	100

Source: Data Monografi Kecamatan Kotagede, 2007.

---

16. Interview with the officers of KP3Y on 12 January 2008.
17. *Brosur Lebaran*, No. 46, 1428H/2007M, p. 23.

in Kecamatan Kotagede.[18] Among the rest of the employed people, a total of 2,716 individuals, or 34.27 per cent, are working in the transportation business. The location of Kotagede, at the centre of a hub of roads connecting the rural hinterlands and the city of Yogyakarta, seems to be contributing the prominence of those people working in the area of transportation.

All in all, it is indeed difficult not to admit the reality that Kotagede today has become a town flooded by low-income *buruh* (workers) and *bakul* (petty traders), instead of the town of proud independent *tukang* (artisans) and enlightened affluent *juragan* (business owners, entrepreneurs) it once was.[19]

Yet, on the surface, a tour through the main streets of the town may give an impression of thriving economic life. Among others, the jostling crowd around the Kotagede market on every thirty-fifth day cycle of Legi-cum-Sunday — coming with all sorts of means of transportation — is producing an incredible scene: a huge number of people rushing there to buy and sell, i.e. spending money! In addition, let me present a list of new features of the town in addition to traditional silverwork shops and general stores — they are observable as a reflection of recent changes in the local economy and lifestyle: three branches of big banks; one micro-credit bank; three automobile garages and sales shops; one motorbike shop; seven large general stores and mini-markets; six Muslim/Muslimah dress shops and boutiques; two AC sales and service stations; two large photo studios with video shooting service; one huge catering service factory with a shopfront; a station for fresh cow milk; six shops for traditional and modern cakes and snacks; two gyms for exercise (especially for women); and two Internet stations. The town is rapidly "modernizing" if it is looked at from the main streets only. However, the bulk of the poor townspeople are living in the neighbourhoods behind those rows of "modern buildings" there.

---

18. There is an apparent difference between this figure of 7,926 individuals and that of Table 11.2, i.e. 18,450 individuals as the total number of employees. The gap of 10,524 individuals is perhaps caused by the fact that they are working outside the categories of "formal business", which is captured by official statistics. I have not asked about this gap at the Kecamatan Office. This point, however, is to be explored in future.
19. Rosyad Saleh, Secretary of the Central Leadership of the Muhammadiyah, gave a *khutbah* at Idul Fitri of 1427H/2007M held in Karang, Kotagede, in which he emphasized the urgency of alleviating poverty as one of the obligations of the Muslim community. *Brosur Lebaran*, No. 46, p. 100.

OVERCOMING THE "CULTURE OF POVERTY"

One of the serious challenges facing the Muhammadiyah is, then, how to deal with poverty and the socio-economic structure underlying it. It seems high time for the Muhammadiyah to begin reviewing and assessing its achievements thus far attained in this area. They have been resulted mostly in terms of fulfilling religious obligations (*ibadah*) such as *zakat*, *infak*, *sadakah* and *korban*, and voluntary action of *wakaf* (donation of property) and *santunan* (giving gift and service). It is one thing to evaluate these acts in terms of the expression of religious piety and devotion. It is, however, another to look at them in terms of how they have contributed in reforming the socio-economic structure of local community for the benefit of the poor. They are to be reviewed not only in terms of the religious commitments of the actors but also from the viewpoint of actual effects of those activities, which might or might not have improved the life of the target population. To put it simply, the Muhammadiyah is expected to evaluate to what extent and in what ways the movement has contributed to the alleviation of poverty in the town.

It seems obvious that poverty has been structural. Recent history has significant relevance for these consequences. Demands for the improvement of wages and working conditions of the poor workers, mostly represented by the PKI and SOBSI previously, have been blocked for so long due to the absence of social forces engaged in such advocacy in their place. Those social forces that might have represented the demands of workers have not grown in the town since the PKI and SOBSI were removed from the public scene in 1965. Any slight attempt to improve the plight of the poor since then, except those from the government side, was feared and labelled as a sign of PKI's revival.[20] Recent attempt to organize a silver workers association, Paguyuban Perak Kotagede, seems to be having difficulty because of internal competition.[21] Perhaps it is high time for the local Muhammadiyah to consider whether it can and should take up the role of labour advocacy since it has an impeccable reputation of anti-Communist stance.[22]

Moreover, poverty has been cultural, too. As is well known, there is a concept of "culture of poverty", coined by an American anthropologist

---

20. For the incident of "Workers Accuse" in Festival Kotagede 2000, see pp. 347–48.
21. *Brosur Lebaran*, No. 46, p. 26.
22. One may recall the murder of Marsinah in 1993, a Nasyiatul 'Aisyiyah labour activist in a watch factory of East Java, who was kidnapped and killed by a gang hired by her employer.

who studied the poor families in Mexico City.[23] He observed that a culture of poverty, i.e. ways of life that make the poor content with poverty, was persistently reproduced over generations. Lacking the means of improving one's plight structurally, many of the poor gave up the hope for a better life itself. It seems that a parallel situation has obtained in Kotagede in particular and among the Javanese urban poor in general. Perhaps, the traditional Javanese value of *nrimo* (accepting one's fate as God given, or fatalism) may be working here.

Also, dependence on the "goodwill" of the haves — a business boss or a rich neighbour — has been only available strategy to survive day-to-day for the poor. The widespread practice of giving out *santunan* (gift, ex. *sembako*) and services (medical check up, etc.) free of charge by the haves seems to be reproducing this pattern constantly. Government as well as political parties, social organizations as well as private individuals are engaged in this practice. "Raskin" (rice for the poor) by the government is the most typical of these.

It should be reviewed whether these acts of "goodwill" (of the haves) are actually contributing to the empowerment of the poor so that they become able to help themselves, or that they are merely prolonging and reproducing their dependency. For example, one catering factory/shop in Kotagede is reportedly distributing 5,000 free kits of *sembako* every three months. On the occasion, a long queue is formed leading to the shop — a situation requiring police control. The practice is received by the townspeople with praise, envy, and criticism. Yet, no serious attempts have thus far been made to evaluate the case and other similar practices in socio-economic terms.

Another concrete case in point is the practice of "Anak Asuh", which has been promoted by the 'Aisyiyah members for many years. According to this scheme, they contribute a certain amount of money regularly to the school committees of the Muhammadiyah. The committees select the needy but academically promising pupils and students as the recipient of the subsidy for their school fees. The donor is reportedly notified of whom she is assisting while the recipient parent/child is kept from knowing the identity of the donor. This practice is providing assistance to approximately 300 pupils and students in Kotagede annually at present.[24]

The practice seems to have been welcomed by the poor of the town and contributed to create their support for the Muhammadiyah and the 'Aisyiyah. Seemingly, however, there has been no attempt at all at evaluating this practice

---

23. Oscar Lewis, *Five Families: Mexican Case Studies in the Culture of Poverty* (New York: Basic Books, 1959).
24. Annual Report of the 'Aisyiyah, 2007.

from the viewpoint of assessing its actual effectiveness in alleviating poverty or accelerating upward social mobility among the townspeople. For example, there has been no follow-up survey to trace the academic performance and social achievements (upward social mobility) of the recipients of the Anak Asuh subsidies.

Generally, it is recognized that large-scale scholarship programmes are quite effective in changing the structure of income distribution in a society. Therefore, in addition to the expressive value of the Anak Asuh programme as a venue for religious commitment, the social effectiveness, or instrumental value, of the programme should become the focus of attention for the Muhammadiyah and 'Aisyiyah. This might be a challenge for the Muhammadiyah movement not only in Kotagede but at the national level as well since similar schemes are reportedly practised widely.

Besides such direct charitable projects as Anak Asuh, there was an attempt at improving occupational skills by a group of the Muhammadiyah activists in the northeastern part of the town.[25] This project was also motivated to create unity between students and workers in the area through a series of activities in addition to routine *pengajian* and concomitant *arisan* (rotary mutual crediting). Between the years 1977–82, Muhammadiyah youths there set up a *"pondok ketrampiran"* (training camp) to provide courses in typewriting, English conversation, silk-screening (*sablon*), and machine sewing to the locals. Unfortunately, this project was discontinued mainly because of the departure of its central figure, Darwis Khudori, for study overseas.

BMT An Ni'mah: Growing Micro-Financing

The most recent attempt to help the poor is a scheme of micro-financing. As a section of the Economic and Business Council of Kotagede Muhammadiyah, the office of the BMT An Ni'mah Syariah has been in operation at the western edge of the Kotagede market since the beginning of 2007. The office is engaged in a number of activities, mostly aimed at assisting petty traders (*bakul*) in and around the market. The office provides Islamic micro-financing (*mudhorobah*, *musyarokah* and *murobahah*) and savings, as well as the use of the office space as a prayer room (*musholla*), WC, *wartel* (telephone and fax), parking for bicycles and motorbikes, and storage of merchandise.

Drs. Asngari Jakfar (b.1944), who is a retiree of the Department of Labour and Transmigration, has been managing the micro-financing office. He was a student of the Faculty of Economics, Gadjah Mada University and an activist of

---

25. "Senja di Kotagede Tenggara" [Sunset in Southeastern Kotagede], *Brosur Lebaran*, No. 27, 1409H/1989M, pp. 24–25.

Pemuda Muhammadiyah when I first met him in 1970. After living in Jakarta for many years and working for the Department, he and his wife are now back home in Kotagede. With a stable life as a government pensioner, Drs. Asngari is dedicating his time, energy and expertise to the micro-financing scheme (Figure 11.4). The scheme is now an integral part of the Muhammadiyah's official operation in the town. The Muhammadiyah branch provided initial capital for the scheme. Then, small amounts of money are credited out to the clients on the basis of personal intimacy and trustworthiness without requiring collateral. Most of the clients chose the method of repayment on the basis of profit sharing (*mudhorobah*). In other words, this scheme is an operation of Syariah banking on a small scale. I have just made a brief observation on the transaction at the office of this programme, a place where the studio of PTDI (Muhammadiyah's FM radio station) used to be located. The office was busy enough from the early morning (open from 3.00 a.m. to 11.00 p.m.) since, in addition to the office of micro-financing (open 7.00 a.m. to 11.00 a.m. daily and 5.00 p.m. to 7.30 p.m. on Monday, Thursday, and Saturday), there was a large space to keep merchandise overnight and to park bicycles and motorbikes during the daytime for a small fee.

FIGURE 11.4

Drs. Asngari Jakfar, a leader for micro-financing.

Drs. Asngari seemed to be happy with the increasing popularity of the office. In 2007, the total amount of commercial turnover (*omset*) of the BMT An Ni'mah was Rp285,752,000 (approximately US$28,575),[26] more than three-fold increase from the previous year's Rp87,932,000 (approximately US$8,793). Total amount of credit (*piutang*) provided for the clients was Rp111,162,900, (approximately US$11,116) whereas the total amount of savings (*simpanan*) was Rp168,399,242 (approximately US$16,839). Total amount of contribution from January 2006 to February 2008 by the BMT office to the account of the Muhammadiyah amounted to Rp6,860,000 (approximately US$686). This perhaps comes mostly from various fees paid to the office.[27]

Those figures may seem rather small to observers from the Western countries or from Japan. But, recalling the fact that the official poverty line was just Rp211,978 (approximately US$21) per month for the Yogyakarta Special Region in 2010, the first year operation of the BMT Muhammadiyah in Kotagede can be said as having made a significant start. It is expected that an objective assessment of the scheme be made by specialists in microfinancing in order to evaluate actual effectiveness of the scheme in alleviating the poverty in the town.[28]

PHQK: Promoting "Social Business"

Pusat Hewan Qurban Kotagede (PHQK, or Kotagede Centre for Sacrifice Animal)[29] is a "social business" initiated by the Muhammadiyah sub-branch of Prenggan.

---

26. Based on my estimated rate of Rp10,000 = US$1.
27. Those figures are taken from the report of Majelis Ekonomi dan Kewirausahaan PCM Kotagede (Economic and Business Council of the Branch Leadership of the Muhammadiyah Kotagede) signed by Drs. H. Asngari Djakfar, MBA, on 31 December 2007.
28. The BMT like the one in Kotagede is now becoming part of the standard operation of the Muhammadiyah movement nationally. It is expected that its centennial congress of 2010 in Yogyakarta will produce an official assessment on the operation.
29. For an earlier history of the centre, see "Sejarah PPHQ: Pusat Pengadaan Hewan Qurban AMM Kotagede" [History of PPHQ: Centre for the Provision of Sacrificial Animals, AMM, Kotagede], *Brosur Lebaran*, No. 39, 1421H/2000M, pp. 53–57.

Under the scheme, the centre purchases sacrificial animals (goats and cows) from animal markets at a low price a few weeks before Idul Adha, and keeps and feeds them in stables until the day before the festive day. Meanwhile prospective buyers pre-order the animals, which are then delivered to the buyers one day before Idul Adha (see Figures 11.5 and 11.6).

The entire operation is executed by a committee consisting of a few senior managers and a number of young workers of the Muhammadiyah sub-branch of Prenggan. Local Muhammadiyah members provide a space for the stables and feeding grounds, vehicles for transportation, and an office with necessary equipment including a computer set, a whiteboard and furniture. Through such an operation, in 2007 the committee was able to earn a net profit of Rp36,370,550 (approximately US$3,637), being the difference between the income of Rp380,450,000 (sales of 21 cows and 322 goats) and the expenditure of Rp344,079,450. The expenditure included wages for the youths who were responsible for the caring and distribution of the animals.[30]

The significance of the PHQK is multiple. First of all, it has brought economic rationalization into the Idul Adha ritual of animal sacrifice. The

FIGURE 11.5

PPHQ Market for Sacrificial Animals.

---

30. "Evaluasi (Evaluation): PHQ Kotagede, Muhammadiyah Prenggan 2007", 2 January 2008 (typescript).

Sacrificial animals at PPHQ.

rationalization is beneficial to the *sohibul* (donor or buyer of the animals), the committee officers and workers, and the recipients of the meat. The donor purchases the animal at a reasonable price without having to go through the hustle of bargaining at the market, so the value of the donor's money is maximized. As a result, the meat of the animal can be distributed more widely and the quantity of meat can be increased for the recipients. Also the operation has generated substantial monetary rewards for the officers and workers — managers as well as young field workers engaged in the operation. In addition, the operation has provided opportunities for the training of youths in entrepreneurship as well as for cadre recruitment and financial contribution to the Muhammadiyah sub-branch. The operation lasts only for a short period of several weeks between Idul Fitri and Idul Adha every year, but it has proven to be a valuable experience for those young activists who have participated in the operation.

All in all, various efforts have been made to deal with the problem of poverty. The centennial anniversary of the Muhammadiyah this year may be an appropriate occasion to take stock of those efforts and evaluate them carefully. On the basis of evaluation, it is hoped that the Muhammadiyah movement ventures into a new strategy to tackle the real cause of structural poverty.

OVERCOMING THE "POVERTY OF CULTURE"

"Dryness" in Culture

Now let us turn our attention to another type of poverty. It is a fact that the Muhammadiyah has been labelled as experiencing a "poverty of culture". This term refers to the often-mentioned situation in which the past success of the Muhammadiyah in "purifying" the worldview and practice of Javanese Muslim from *kejawen* has impoverished their culture to the extent of almost drying it up. The word "dry" or *kering* is often heard to depict the situation.

Kejawén vs. Muhammadiyah

Kejawen (ke-jawi-en) literally means Javanese-ness. The term refers to a variety of things in use. During the late Dutch colonial period, its narrow use was to refer to the four principalities in Central Java, in whose territories no private Dutch land ownership was allowed. Also narrowly, *kejawen* meant Javanese cultural elements individually as well as collectively, most of which were derived from pre-Islamic period. More broadly, the term also referred to traditional Islam in Java, in which religious beliefs and practices deriving from indigenous, Hindu-Buddhist and Islamic elements were amalgamated. The latter often contained prayers to invoke souls of the dead, including those of Mataram royal ancestries, and Hindu-derived deities as well as local spirits and deities. More often than not, as media to communicate with those spiritual beings, trance, séance, magic, sorcery, and meditation were resorted. Modern reformist Islamic movements — Muhammadiyah most actively among them — attacked syncretic *kejawén* of this brand as heretical.

Muhammadiyah regarded it as containing un-Islamic polytheistic elements of TBC, i.e. *takhayul, bid'ah,* and *churafat [khurafat]* (myths, deviant innovations, and superstitions). TBC is also an acronym for tuberculosis — one of the most feared contagious diseases of the day. Muhammadiyah deliberately borrowed the term to give a negative image to *kejawen*. Meanwhile, there developed self-conscious non- and anti-Islamic religious expressions of Javanese-ness in the form of sects and associations, some of them calling themselves *kejawen* but some other of them *kebathinan*. Recently, Muhammadiyah has revised its position vis-à-vis local cultures, especially Javanese one, in order to revitalize and make effective its propagation among the *abangan* segment of population: so *kejawen* should not be rejected wholly. *Shalawatan, mocopat, wayang kulit, wayang orang, karawitan,* and even *kethoprak* are not only acceptable but also encouraged depending on contents. The negative connotation of *kejawen* is waning now among Muhammadiyah circles.

In fact, what has been developing is a continuous dialectic between the persistent vitality of local culture and the Muhammadiyah movement. It is true that, to a great extent, the influence of *kejawen* in the areas of *iman* (credo) and *ibadah* (ritual) has receded. First of all, what I have described as the "cult of royal glorification" (see Foreword to the First Edition) has almost gone. Those are the beliefs and practices centring about the mystical power of the Mataram royalty believed to be resided in its ancestral graves. It has disappeared from the pillars of religious life of the majority of Kotagedeans today. Its residue is still visible, but is practised mostly by visitors from outside rather than by locals.[31] (See Figures 11.7 and 11.8.) The concept of *tauhid* promoted by Muhammadiyah has excluded the royal ancestries from the realm of deity. Also, such rituals as the commemoration of the dead on the seventh, tenth, hundredth and thousandth days have been regarded as *bid'ah* (unfounded innovation in terms of the Qur'an and Hadith), and have almost disappeared among Muhammadiyah circles. So are the traditional Muslim rituals of *yasinan* and *tahlilan*.[32] Meanwhile, the questionable area has been such traditional genres of cultural and artistic expressions as *mocopat, wayang kulit, wayang wong, srandhul, campursari, keroncong,* and *kethoprak*.[33]

However, there have been persistent critical views as to the relationship of Islam with such items of local culture as mentioned above among the members of the Kotagede branch of the Muhammadiyah. They regarded almost all traditional practices performed around the Royal Cemetery of Mataram as *bid'ah*. Also they regarded the Royal Cemetery complex itself as the source of TBC among the townspeople. So, as we have seen before in Chapter 4, the immediate target of Muhammadiyah's attack was the Royal Cemetery complex itself and those practices of TBC there in the pre-war time.

---

31. See a *Sarjana* thesis by Masayu Nurul Ana entitled, "Ziarah dalam Kebudayaan Jawa: Ziarah di Kompleks Makam Raja-Raja Mataram, Kotagede, Yogyakarta" [Pilgrimage in Javanese Culture: Pilgrimage to Mataram Royal Cemetery Complex in Kotagede, Yogyakarta], Faculty of Cultural Science, Gadjah Mada University, 2002.
32. *Yasinan* is the melodic group recitation of the Surah Yasin of the Qur'an to commemorate the dead. *Tahlilan* is repeated group recitation of the Muslim confession of faith to pray for the soul of the dead.
33. *Mocopat (macapat)* is the recitation of the rhymed Javanese verses. *Wayang kulit* is shadow play with one-dimensional leather puppets. *Wayang wong = wayang* played by actual people instead of puppets. *Srandhul* is a version of *kethoprak* with spontaneous dialogues between actors and the audience. *Campursari* is gamelan music. *Keroncong* is a modern folk music with a strong influence of Portuguese music. *Kethoprak* is folk drama mostly of historical episodes.

BOX 10
The Enshrined Turtle

The yellow turtle, named Kyai Dudo, which was the master of the Siliran Spring in the complex of Royal Cemetery (see p. 10), was dead for some time but now is enshrined as a stone statue located beneath the graves of Senapati and his family. With an altar to burn incense, the stone turtle signifies the fact that *kejawen* practice of this kind is still continued around the complex especially for visitors from outside.

Politicization of Culture

Prior to the so-called G30S/PKI Affairs, the PKI and its front organizations (Lekra, Pemuda Rakyat and Gerwani) were extremely active in mobilizing local cultural and artistic activities. Culture and politics were totally mixed up, then. So, after the Affairs, the Muhammadiyah's stance of anti-TBC cum anti-*kejawén* received a sort of political legitimacy. A local observer described the situation as follows:

> The period of PKI's victory (*zaman kejayaan* PKI) was a time for the victory of *kethoprak* (folk drama), too. Every hamlet had an amateur *kethoprak* troupe. There were even a couple of popular commercial ones based in Kotagede. They were almost all engaged in PKI's political propaganda or supporting Soekarno's campaign for Manipolusdek. The Muhammadiyah was not discouraged, however. Its youths organized a modern drama troupe and it was pretty popular, too. PNI activists were not silent, either. A number of *keroncong* bands [modern folk songs imbued with foreign, especially Portuguese, elements] were formed and also popular. So, the cultural situation in the town was very lively (*ramai*). The G30S/PKI Affairs changed this situation overnight. PKI and leftist PNI were gone. The town became sober. Cultural activities in general became subsided for some time until about the time for the first general elections by New Order in 1971.

FIGURE 11.7

Inner yard of the Royal Cemetery.

> Then, Golkar started to revive cultural groups, *kethoprak*, *wayangan*, dancing, etc., for campaign attractions. Others followed.[34]

Politicization of cultural activities had thus left deep stigmas: the associations of *kethoprak* with the PKI, *keroncong* with the PNI, and modern drama with the Masyumi/Muhammadiyah persisted for a long time after 1965. Among others, the rigid stance of anti-TBC taken by the mainstream of the Muhammadiyah seemed to have worked to create an association that traditional cultural and artistic activities were all anti-Islamic by nature and suspect of the residue of the PKI. Thus, an over-killing of local culture in terms of anti-TBC, being added by political elimination of cultural activities associated with the PKI, worked against the positive appreciation of traditional culture among the Muhammadiyah circles. Thus the traditional culture was impoverished.

---

34. Interview with Ahmad Charris Zubair on 2 January 2008.

Aspiration for Local Culture

However, efforts to make room for local cultural expressions in the Muhammadiyah have been attempted by the younger generation a number of times. These efforts have been reflected in the list of *Brosur Lebaran* topics as follows: as early as in the 1977 issue, there was an article written by Khadi Raharjo reviewing the central role of drama in relation to other genres of culture and arts, with an expectation for its revival in Kotagede.[35] In the following year, Darwis Khudori, a student of architecture and already a well-known writer then, wrote a short essay entitled "Why should there be arts?" The answer he gave himself was very radical and universal, "Because they are arising from basic human nature (*fitrah*)."[36] A few years later, Mustofa W. Hasyim (b.1954), an aspiring journalist and a novelist then, made an attempt at "grasping cultural atmosphere of Kotagede," and concluded that there was a good amount of cultural and artistic potentials to be developed in Kotagede.[37]

Then, Ahmad Charris Zubair (b.1952), a young scholar of ethics at Gadjah Mada University at that time, wrote an article entitled "Philosophy of Javanese People in Kotagede"[38] on the basis of his *Sarjana* thesis[39] submitted to UGM. In the article and the thesis, he emphasized the point that Islam is an integral part of *kejawen*, i.e. traditional Javanese worldview and customs, transmitted over generations in Kotagede: the Muhammadiyah has brought a new concern for business, rationality, and social activism upon it. Charris stressed the point that the open conflict between *kejawen* and Islam was a political product arising from one particular phase of history while the two have been well integrated within Javanese Muslim individuals in Kotagede.[40]

---

35. "Kegiatan apresiasi seni dan hubunganya dengan seni drama" [Activities appreciating arts and their relationship with drama), *Brosur Lebaran*, No. 15, 1397H/1977M, pp. 30–34, 53–56.
36. "Kenapa mesti seni?" [Why should there be arts?], *Brosur Lebaran*, No. 16, 1398H/1978M, pp. 23–27.
37. "Menangkapi suasana kesenian di Kotagede", *Brosur Lenaran*, No. 18, 1396/1980, pp. 32–36.
38. "Filsafatnya orang Jawa di Kotagede", *Brosur Lebaran*, No. 19, 1401H/1981M, pp. 71-79.
39. "Islam dan Kejawen di Masyarakat Kotagede" [Islam and *kejawén* in Kotagede society], Skripsi Sarjana, Fakultas Filsafat, UGM, 1979.
40. "Catatan tentang masyarakat Kotagede" [Notes on Kotagede Society], *Brosur Lebaran*, No. 21, 1403H/1983M, pp. 6–12.

Erwito Wibowo (b.1958), a poet and an organizer of cultural activities, joined the editors of *Brosur Lebaran* since 1984, and endeavoured continuously to cover local culture and arts in its publication.

It was, however, not until 1995 the relevance of local culture for Islam became appreciated officially and positively among the Muhammadiyah circles. In that year, a national conference of the Majelis Tarjih (Council for Theological and Legal Deliberation) held in Aceh opened up a discussion on Islam and local culture. Charris from Kotagede joined the conference and presented a paper.[41]

In parallel to this development, a section to handle cultural and artistic activities was set up in the branch leadership of the Muhammadiyah Kotagede. With an urgent cry, "The Muhammadiyah can no longer look at culture with only one eye!", the *Brosur* editors interviewed the new head of the section on culture, Dr Samija, a teaching staff at the IKIP (National Teachers Training College) in Yogyakarta.[42] He acknowledged the potential of local arts and cultural expressions as media of propagation (*dakwah*). But, he stressed the need to identify and distinguish those cultural and artistic phenomena, which were violating the essence of Islam from others that were not: Then the latter should be "Islamized" through systematic "social engineering (*rekayasa sosial*), which would take a long time".[43]

Further on, the forty-fourth national congress of Muhammadiyah held in Jakarta in 2000 adopted a guideline for Islamic life for the members, in which culture and arts were mentioned as the ways to make human beings feel refinement and beauty, a way to approach the Highest Being.[44]

However, in Kotagede, every time an attempt at the appreciation of local culture was made, it was met with stiff resistance, or negative sanction, by

---

41. "Kebudayaan dan kesenian dalam perspektif Islam", makalah pada Musyawarah Nasional Tarjih Muhammadiyah XXIII di Banda Aceh, 1995 ("Culture and Arts in Islamic Perspectives", paper presented at the National Meeting of Deliberation, Muhammadiyah XXXIII, Banda Aceh, 1995).
42. "Menyeret dakwah budaya, mengiring masyarakat modern" [Dragging in cultural propagation, joining modern society], *Brosur Lebaran*, No. 30, 1412 H/1992M, pp. 38–41.
43. Ibid., p. 39.
44. See M. Thoyibi, Yayah Khisbiyah and Abdullah Aly, eds., *Sinergi Agama & Budaya Lokal: Dialektika Muhammadiyah dan Seni Lokal* [Synergy of Religion and Local Culture: Dialectics between the Muhammadiyah and Local Culture] (Surakarta: Muhammadiyah University Press, 2003), pp. 3–4.

some leaders of the older generation in the Muhammadiyah. Their argument went as follows: Methods of propagation via local cultural means like *wayang* was a thing of the past. Purification of traditional Islam has greatly succeeded generations ago in Kotagede. So much so that it is no longer necessary to employ traditional media for propagation in the modern contexts. "No need to return to the days of Sunan Kalijaga!"— reportedly, an elder leader almost shouted down the voice of the youth.[45] Meanwhile, there was another argument

FIGURE 11.8

Still asking for help from the spirit of Senapati in 2008.

---

45. Cf. "Konsep Dakwah Kultural Muhammadiyah: Sebuah Tinjauan Wawasan" [The Muhammadiyah's Concept of Cultural Propagation — a survey of opinions], *Brosur Lebaran*, No. 43, 1425H/2004M, p. 12.

coming from the opposite direction to contain the demand of the youth, saying that purification of *tauhid* was still the central task of the Muhammadiyah since the practices of TBC were persistently going on in the local society, especially around the Royal Cemetery of Mataram Sultanate. Moreover, the recent flood of external culture of permissiveness and consumerism through the various media, such as television, VCDs and Internet, has increased the urgency for the renewed efforts for the Muhammadiyah's propagation for purification. Emergent vices of prostitution, alcoholism, narcotics, and free sex among the Kotagede youths have increased the need for strong counter measures by the Muhammadiyah.

Eventually, the younger generation's aspiration for the enhancement of local culture and arts crystallized into the formation of a group called PUSDOK (Pusat Studi dan Dokumentasi Kotagede, or Centre for Research and Documentation in Kotagede). PUSDOK was established in 1989 by Ahmad Charris Zubair, a third generation of the Muhammadiyah founder's family (son of Haji Zubair and grandson of Haji Muchsin), and Ahmad Noor Arief (son of Yatiman Syafi'i, former Chairman of Muhammadiyah Kotagede). Members of the centre include Shinta Waringah (a neighbour of Charris, a non-Muhammadiyah), Darwis Khudori (cousin of Charris), Erwito Wibowo, Mustofa W. Hasyim, M. Natsir (son of Muhammad Chirzin, former Chairman of Muhammadiyah Kotagede). (See Figure 11.9.)

The PUSDOK started with a modest purpose of "collecting data on Kotagede". After a long inactivity, however, with the advent of Reformasi in 1998, it was revitalized as "Pusat Studi, Dokumentasi, dan Pengembangan Budaya Kotagede", i.e. Centre for Research, Documentation and Development of Culture in Kotagede. The Centre started active projects for the collection of historical documents and photographs, cultural, industrial and household artefacts, the conservation of socio-cultural environment (historical remains and traditional architecture), and organizing groups for the development of cultural activities. In 1999, PUSDOK contributed to the revitalization of local culture and arts by playing a central role in organizing the Festival Kotagede (FK). The details of FK shall be discussed later in Chapter 12.

Another organization, Yayasan Kanthil (Kanthil Foundation) was established in 2000 with the urgently felt need for empowering local culture and arts in Kotagede for the promotion of tourism as well as for preserving the town as a "Cultural Heritage District" (*kawasan cagar budaya*). The founders and core activists of the Kanthil Foundation included Saleh Udden (Sholehuddin, Village Head of Jagalan, son of H. Bashori Anwar, Chairman of Muhammadiyah Kotagede), above-mentioned M. Natsir and Shinta (the last two withdrew from PUSDOK for Kanthil), and a number of young people.

FIGURE 11.9

Drs. Charris Zubair and the PUSDOK panel; a two-storey old *langgar* behind him.

As described above, activists in both PUSDOK and Yayasan Kanthil were mostly from the established Muhammadiyah families and used to be actively engaged in its student or youth organizations. However, over time, they started to distance themselves from the mainstream of the local Muhammadiyah or were rather "marginalized" from it. Yet, they themselves were convinced that they embodied the original spirit of the Muhammadiyah movement, i.e. *ijtihad* (independent thinking) and *tajdid* (reform). So, they were often called, and call themselves, the "Cultural Muhammadiyah" in contrast to the "Structural Muhammadiyah", i.e. its elected officers.

In fact, those individuals in the category of the "Cultural Muhammadiyah" were a cutting edge for the Muhammadiyah movement in a broad sense.

They were facing positively new challenges and seeking fresh responses with the spirit of independent thinking and reform. Their activities were to be culminated into the Festival Kotagede in 1999 and then into the post-earthquake efforts for cultural recovery and preservation as we shall see in Chapters 12 and 13.

BOX 11
The Fall of a Banyan Tree

When I visited Kotagede for the first time in 1970, there stood a pair of banyan trees in the entrance yard of the Great Mosque of Mataram leading to the Royal Cemetery of the dynasty. According to a local legend, the older tree, *waringin sepuh*, was planted by a Javanese saint, Sunan Kalijaga, to foretell the establishment of the Mataram Kingdom with Kotagede as its first capital. Presumably, the tree was more than 400 years old in 1970. I heard no particular story as to the origin of the younger one. But, together with the older one, both had grown imposingly very high then, and they had been sources of many traditions emphasizing the mystical powers of the Royal Cemetery as mentioned in Chapter 2. They had been part and parcel of the *kejawen* culture in Kotagede. However, when I revisited the town in the early 1990s, the younger one had long gone and there was only a huge hole left in the ground. I requested an explanation for the fall of the tree from a Muhammadiyah man with college education. He said that the cause of the death of the younger tree was chemical and biological: the people living in the yard next to the tree were careless about letting the wastewater from their kitchen and bathroom to flow into the roots of the tree. The roots of the tree were thus weakened by this habit and eventually could not stand its weight when hit by a strong wind. The older tree, which had no houses nearby was not affected. The people of Kotagede including this person seemed to be no longer making any supernatural fuss about the fall of the banyan tree. This might be an indication of the success of Muhammadiyah in demystifying *kejawen*.

12

FESTIVAL KOTAGEDE
Conflict and Integration

THE BEGINNING: SUCCESS OF FESTIVAL KOTAGEDE 99

Efforts for the revitalization of local culture and arts have been realized in a series of community events called the Festival Kotagede (FK) held in 1999, 2000, and 2002. Those events have reflected internal dynamics within the local community in which the Muhammadiyah has occupied a significant position. The Muhammadiyah as an organization did not participate in the events. But, it became an informal stakeholder since its members were divided into two opposing groups — one group promoted the festival while the other criticized some of the programmes of the FKs. The events have given serious and meaningful lessons to the Muhammadiyah in terms of its relationship with local culture and arts in particular and its overall relationship with the diversifying local community.

Furthermore, the events were extremely significant in many ways beyond local context. From a national perspective, FK seems to be inseparable from the nationwide atmosphere of the Reformasi. Certainly, the removal of President Soeharto from the top of the power structure opened up a Pandora's box including culture: freedom of cultural expression went hand in hand with the guarantee of political freedom. PAN, PDI-P, Golkar, PKB, and other political groups were now free to express sub-cultures of their own respective constituencies in election campaigns. Also, with the advancement of regional autonomy, the provincial and municipal governments of Yogyakarta have become more active in promoting tourism on their own initiatives than before. International attention and cooperation has also become much wider and more active than before as indicated by the funding provided by the World Bank. Those factors all worked in favour of the FK. In a sense, the FK was a local celebration and appreciation of the Reformasi.

Therefore, it is understandable that two serious studies have already been made on FK, one by a university student[1] native of Kotagede and the other, by an experienced outside observer.[2] *Brosur Lebaran* has also taken up the events on several times.[3] I shall rely on these sources when describing and discussing the events.

The actual beginning of the FK was made by the meeting of two actions: (1) an inventory of local cultural and artistic activities taken by Erwito Wibowo in 1999[4] and (2) the offer of a small grant from the World Bank for the promotion of local culture. Erwito's list prepared at the request of the Cultural Division of the Yogyakarta Provincial Government provided solid evidence that Kotagede had the potential of holding such events. On the basis of this inventory, cultural and artistic activities were now not only officially recognized as common asset of the town but also moved out of its narrow environments as attractions for the Independence Day celebration held in local neighbourhoods or as the residue of the Kraton tradition. The basis for FK as a much wider public event was thus founded.

---

1. Nur Cahyati Wahyuni, "'Kotagede Ewuh': Festival Kotagede dan Identitas Kultural" ['Kotagede Prepares a Party', Festival Kotagede and Cultural Identity], a *Sarjana* thesis in anthropology, Faculty of Cultural Studies, Universitas Gadjah Mada, 2005.
2. M. Jadul Maula, "The Moving Equilibrium: Kultur Jawa, Muhammadiyah, Buruh Gugat di dalam Festival Kotagede 2000" [The Moving Equilibrium: Javanese culture, Muhammadiyah and Workers' Demand in Festival Kotagede 2000], in *Ngesuhi Deso Sak Kukuban*, by M. Jadul Maula (Yogyakarya: LKiS, 2001), pp. 3–39.
3. "Agenda Kotagede: Festival Kotagede '99", *Brosur Lebaran*, No. 38, 1420H/2000M, pp. 62–63. "Membuka Frame Festival Kotagede di Tengah Polemik Pemikiran" [Opening the Frame of Festival Kotagede in the midst of polemic of thoughts], *Brosur Lebaran*, No. 40, 1422H/2001M, pp. 29–39.
4. Erwito Wibowo, "Peta Potensi Seni Tradisional di Kotagede" [Map of Traditional Arts in Kotagede], *Brosur Lebaran*, No. 38, 1420H/2000M, pp. 72–77. "Kelompok Kesenian Srandul, Purba Budaya Bumen, Pimpinan Basis

Even though the grant from the World Bank was small, it gave an impetus to launch a new challenging project. The meeting of the two factors was sufficient to mobilize further action locally. A committee was formed around PUSDOK, which called for wider participation through official channels of Kecamatan and RW. The committee consisted of members from PUSDOK, YHS (Yogyakarta Heritage Society), YRSMI (Yayasan Seni Rupa Mataram Indonesia, Foundation for Expressive Arts of Mataram, Indonesia), Dinas Pariwisata Kota Yogyakarta (Tourism Division of Yogyakarta Municipal Government), FOKOPA (Forum for Coordination of Childrens' Pengajian), ASITA (Association of the Indonesian Tour and Travel Agency), and representatives of local artist groups. Instead of assisting various groups individually, the committee decided to have a period of joint events of cultural activities and artistic performances during 26–29 August 1999, and named it Festival Kotagede (FK) 99.

Let me quote from *Brosur Lebaran*, No. 38, a full passage describing the actual events of FK 99 as follows:

> "People of Yogyakarta, please be careful when you are passing Kotagede on 28 August! For Kotagede will be to-o-o-tally ja-a-a-mmed." Such was the pattern of a spot announcement *à la* Festival Kotagede. The spot message was broadcast over radio a few days before the opening of Festival Kotagede. The message was enough to hypnotize Wong Yogya [Yogyakarta folks]. Moreover, the echo of Festival Kotagede '99 was bounced to all corners of the motherland through the dailies *Republika*, *KR* [*Kedaulatan Rakyat*, Yogyakarta], *Bernas* [*Berita Nasional*, Yogyakarta], *Solo Pos*, and other print media.
>
> Eventually, the "threat" of the committee did prove to be true.
>
> Towards the evening of 28 August 1999, traffic jam all through Jalan Kemasan, around Pasar Kotagede, and front of Wisma Proyodranan began to emerge. Stages for shows began to be constructed and food stalls started to appear. Mothers (*ibu-ibu*) displayed all sorts of foods and snacks individually or in the name of groups along the side streets. Old women (*mbok-mbok*) began to arrive from outside Kotagede on foot carrying baskets

---

Hargito" [Srandul Art Group — Purba Budaya in Bumen under the leadership of Basis Hargito], *Brosur Lebaran*, No. 39, 1421H/2000M, pp. 68–70, and "Profil Wayang Thinklung Ki Cermo Supardi Mujihartono, Kampung Karangduren" [Profile of Wayang Thingklung by Ki Cermo Supardi Mujihartono in Kampung Karangduren], ibid., pp. 70–71.

on the back. They started to spread their special merchandise like fatty sate (*sate gajih*), shelled peanuts (*kacang kulit*), marinaded tofu (*tahu bacem*), rice cake (*jadah*), sweet sticky rice cake (*wajik*) and other snacks at places they regarded as strategic.

Such was the situation: towards the night, it was already obvious that Kotagede was becoming totally jammed. After the Isya' [evening prayer], the flow of people from the direction of Yogyakarta increased rapidly, flooding the streets of Kotagede. At about 8.00 p.m., on the stage in front of Pacak Suji [Monument for the Crowning of Sultan Hamengku Buwono IX at the northeastern corner of Pasar Kotagede], a group of *gamelan* musicians combined from Mutihan, Singosaren, and Purbayan welcomed with rhythmic sounds of zither (*siteran*) invited guests and crowded visitors milling in front of the stage. When the music was over, such was the opening of Festival Kotagede 99 with the lighting of torches by a number of people representing various elements within the community.

Meanwhile, almost at the same time the opening ceremony was going on, there started a *kethoprak* for children with a play of Joko Tinkir in Wisma Proyodranan. In Wisma Proyodranan itself the activities of Festival Kotagede 99 had already begun since 26 August 1999 with the exhibition of objects by artists organized into YSRMI.

From Proyodranan, we jumped to the northernmost stage, to be exact, in the Housing Complex of Balekembang, Pilahan, where *wayang kulit* was performed. Just a slight move to the south then, on the street of Jalan Kemasan in front of the pawnshop, the stream of Yogyakarta folks swarmed crowdedly to see what was displayed before them. In the yard of a pawnshop, in advance of the performance of band and music by Joglo-Jagonya Sawung Jabo, there performed dances by children and tambourines by a group from Jejeran, Bantul. More walk to the south, the stage of Patalan was presenting the traditional art of Sekaran Campur Babad Djawi, being intervened by the recitation of verses whose contents were specifically narrating history and the greatness of Mataram kings.

From Patalan, we moved near Apotek Citra. At a stage prepared by the residents of Paseko (Pasegan, Sokowaten and Keboan), all through the night, a parade of band performances continued until their total exhaustion. The audience clapped and whistled every time a singer ended a song.

Walking a short distance again to the south, to be exact in front of Nufa's Silver, Pekaten, there was a setting designed by the use of the cement bags and sufficient lighting. *Wayang humor* held here, which became the mainstay of the stage at Pekaten, was capable of making the audience who jammed around the stage roar with laughter. Also similar things were presented on the stage in front of Pacak Suji. The art of *srandhul* with familiar dialogues and frequent fresh gags indeed made the audience doubled up with laughter many times.

From the front of Pacak Suji, we walked to the west, and stopped exactly at the north of Babon Anim. There the visitors were shown films by BKKBN (National Family Planning Agency). In addition to BKKBN, LSPPA (Institute of Research and Development for Women) set up a screen at the south of Pasar to show a film for children, *Golden Cucumber*. Children and adults in the audience sat quietly on the ground to enjoy this old story.

And, finally we came to stop at the stage of *wayang thingklung* in the parking lot of general store, PENI. The master puppeteer from Kampung Karangduren showed his expertise by utilizing his mouth in place of a set of *gamelan*.

When the show of *wayang thinklung* was over, the streets of Kotagede returned to quietness. The long work that was engaged by a number of elements from the community like PUSDOK, YHS, FOKOPA, AMM, YSRMI, Cagar Budaya (Cultural Heritage) and certainly the support from the townspeople of Kotagede made a brilliant incision in history in order to develop culture and arts for the future of Kotagede. Hopefully, Festival Kotagede 99 shall not be the last. Hopefully, not just to stop by.[5]

The above reportage conveys well the enthusiasm and excitement generated by the FK 99 among the townspeople as well as visitors from outside. It was a *sukses* in many accounts: revitalization of local culture, promotion of tourism, active participation of the townspeople, especially the youth and local artists, an occasion for extra income for *ibu-ibu* and *mbok-mbok*, and, above all, a good time for a great number of people.

The atmosphere of FK 99 was, reportedly, very different from similar events held during the New Order era. At that time, on Independence Day of 17 August, Rukun Kampungs (RK) held various events of "Pitulasan" (Tujuhbelasan, The Seventeenth [of August]) including cultural and artistic performances, sports tournaments, some games, parades, etc. However, they lacked spontaneity since the RKs were obligated by the local government to participate. The occasions were used by the authorities — military, police and civil — to indoctrinate the local population along New Order government policies. FK 99 was free from such government pressure.

However, some local artistes expressed dissatisfaction when FK 99 was over.[6] They felt that their representation in it was not sufficient. Meanwhile, YRSMI was regarded not so oriented to represent Kotagede. In fact, those shortcomings did not impair the process of the FK 99 while it was going

---

5. "Agenda Kotagede", pp. 62–63.
6. Nur Cahyati Wahyuni, "Kotagede Ewuh", pp. 57–58.

on. Yet, the dissatisfaction foretold a new direction the festival was taking: the more genuine local participation, or the more authentic expression of identity as Kotagedeans.[7]

FK 2000: DEMOCRACY, SCHISM AND HARMONY

The Yayasan Kanthil came forward alongside PUSDOK to take up the initiative in preparing the FK 2000 in the following year. Kanthil's basic strategy was explicitly to make local artistes a central actor of the entire operation:

> A fundamental matter which became the guideline of its action was that the people of Kotagede ("Wong Kotagede") were the owners of local culture and arts so that they knew well by themselves how their conditions were and what was indeed needed. The Festival Kotagede was therefore developed in a different concept from similar agendas in various places, e.g. "of the people, by the people, and for the people".[8]

A steering committee with twenty-three members was formed.

Yet, there was another stakeholder that was interested in making use of cultural resources of Kotagede — the tourism division of the government. It was planning to have a cultural festival of Kotagede through the Kecamatan administration with the title of "Exhibition of the Potentials in Culture and Arts of Kecamatan (Gelar Potensi Seni dan Budaya Kecamatan)".[9] Overlapping programmes and conflicts were bound to happen. Meanwhile, among some senior members of the local Muhammadiyah developed a strong criticism that the FK was reviving all sorts of TBC (myths, innovation and superstition) that once had been regarded as expelled from the public scene of Kotagede. Those Muhammadiyah seniors seemed to have been waiting for a chance to strike back.[10]

The repertory of the FK held in 2000 was much wider and richer than the previous one, including (1) an informal discussion meeting (*sarasehan*) on the development of tourism, (2) a number of artistic performances on an open stage, and (3) a carnival (parade) of cultural exhibitions. On 2 September 2000, sixteen Rukun Wargas constructed stages facing the main

---

7. Ibid., p. 58.
8. Ibid., pp. 58–59.
9. Ibid., p. 59.
10. *Brosur Lebaran*, No. 40, 1422H/2001M, p. 31.

streets — performances included *kethoprak*, *wayang thingklung*, *shalawatan*, *geguritan* (recitation of Javanese poems), *mocopatan*, *campursari*, folk music of *keroncong* and modern band music. *Wayang kulit* was held on a central stage set in the front yard of the Great Mosque of Mataram. The carnival, which was the most prized presentation by the committee, was participated by twenty units. Those included a group of the old boys of the HW (Hizbul Wathan or Muhammadiyah's Boy Scouts), a number of drum bands from the Muhammadiyah schools, parades of jeeps and antique cars, a number of exhibitions on historical episodes of the Mataram kingdom, and a unit entitled *Buruh Gugat* (Workers Accuse) on the contemporary plight of workers in the silver industry (see Figure 12.1). Also there were a group of *shalawatan* as well as a unit for religious harmony. Also included in the repertory of FK 2000 were traditional games for children, contest of children's pictures and clay figures, contest of the sketches of Kotagede, *jathilan* (dancing on fake horse), a festival of roasted corn, and film shows. The entire programme lasted for a month through September 2000.

As mentioned above, the mode of popular participation in FK 2000 was explicitly "democratic", expressed in the slogan: "Festival Kotagede of, by and

FIGURE 12.1

The Plight of Handicraft Workers in Kotagede.
Source: Courtesy of Pak M. Natsir.

for the people" (*Festival Kotagede dari rakyat, oleh rakyat dan untuk rakyat*).[11] Compared to FK 99, participation in the preparation and presentation of cultural activities and artistic performances at the grassroots level for FK 2000 was much deeper and wider. The entire townspeople felt that they were truly engaged in the preparation of FK 2000. Thus, the banners of "Kotagede Ewuh" (Kotagede Prepares a Party) spread across the main streets aptly expressed the atmosphere of the town. There developed unprecedented communal joyfulness and emotional solidarity across religious, ideological, political, cultural, generational, and geographic barriers. Everybody was excited to join in and execute the festival. The town became one in excitement. A great success!

Yet, as suggested earlier, the wider the participation of stakeholders, the more complex the dynamics of the FK. Latent schisms emerged in various ways. Although those antagonisms were not open during the process of the FK itself, they did impress their marks upon the course of history in Kotagede.

The cleavages developed in a number of ways: vertically, the one between the rich business owners (*juragan*) vs. the poor workers (*buruh*) expressed by a unit in the carnival entitled "Workers Accuse" (*Buruh Gugat*). Perhaps, this was a public expression of the dissatisfaction of the silver industry workers against low wages and poor working conditions for the first time since the G30S/PKI Affairs. (See Figure 12.1.) A segment of the townspeople reacted to this show of complaints as a "revival of PKI". Reportedly, the *jurangan* of the firm whose workers had braved this protest got angry and declared that he would stop contributing to the FK.

Another schism developed horizontally along cultural lines. As mentioned above, conservative elements in the older generation of the Muhammadiyah leadership in Kotagede seemed to be quite unhappy about the emergence of the "Cultural Muhammadiyah" who promoted the FK. "The FK was regarded as revitalizing the disease of TBC (myths, deviant innovation, and superstition) by the use of culture like *jaelangkung*.[12] (See Figure 12.2.) Still more, some units participated in the cultural carnival taking up stories from the old times of the Mataram Kingdom with the burning of incense."[13]

---

11. Nur Cahyati Wahyuni, "Kotagede Ewuh", p. 59.
12. Séance performed via straw men made of bamboo and kitchen utensils like rice scooper. In fact, the FK committee eventually decided against its actual performance. The straw men were used just as symbolic decoration of the main stage of FK. Nur Cahyati Wahyuni, "Kotagede Ewuh", p. 66. Interview with A. Charris Zubair, 28 November 2009.
13. *Brosur Lebaran*, No. 40, ibid., p. 31.

FIGURE 12.2

Jaelangkung (straw men) at Festival Kotagede 2000.
Source: Courtesy of Pak M. Natsir.

Without having an official meeting of the Branch leadership or having a direct inquiry with the FK committee, one of the senior leaders of the Kotagede Muhammadiyah produced a letter criticizing the FK for the inclusion of *jaelangkung* and *jathilan* in the programme and distributed it to all the mosques to be read at Friday prayers and *pengajians*. The letter appealed: "Behaviour which concerns or plays with *setan* [satan, devil] is a kind of *syirik* [polytheism]. For example, the performance of *jaelangkung* as well as *jathilan* are like that. They have been seen in the Festival Kotagede. For that, all the people in the community, let us tighten up our waist belt and remove every behaviour comprising polytheism appearing in the FK!"[14]

Since *jaelangkung* was not performed actually (the straw men were used as a decoration only), nothing more happened. *Jathilan* was performed by children without trance. But, the incident ensued a long period of controversy among

---

14. Ibid., p. 32.

the Muhammadiyah members. To the best of my knowledge, there has been no official decision taken by the Kotagede branch of the Muhammadiyah as to its attitudes towards the FK. An informal consensus among the members now seems to be that the Muhammadiyah should support and get involved in the FK but the selection of programmes should be done carefully.[15]

Another dimension in which a sort of conflict developed was the FK's relationship with the government. As mentioned above, the Division of Culture and Tourism of the municipal government of Yogyakarta planned to organize "The Exhibition of Cultural Potentials of Kotagede" and invited the FK committee to join with a suggestion of funding. As it turned out, the government's intention was to place FK under its control. Therefore, the FK committee rejected the government's approach. YRSMI and some other groups and individuals joined the government's project. Eventually, the two series of artistic performances and cultural activities were held almost at the same time in Kotagede. According to a report, however, the government programmes — an exhibition of paintings, performances of *kethoprak, srandhul, shalawatan, keroncong*, etc. with the distribution of *sembako* (nine items of daily necessities) — were less popular than the FK's counterparts because of their rather exclusive outlook.[16] After all, the existence of a parallel government's version of the FK seemed to have stimulated the "people's" FK to be truly independent and to endeavour to make the FK "of, by and for the people".

FK 2002: DIVIDED AGAIN

The success of FK 2000 had a long echo. There was a move from the government to provide a budget for another FK in the year 2002. Most importantly, a number of artistes and performers wanted to have another occasion to present their performances. Also, the general public was favourable to have a good time again. So, a new committee was formed by the Yayasan Kanthil. Eventually, FK 2002 was executed between 23 September and 2 October in a much smaller scale than FK 2000 because of a number of reasons. Again, there was the presentation of a competing Kecamatan government's programme in cooperation with a private radio station. That event was named "Gebyar Pesta Rakyat Merdeka" (Exhibition of People's

---

15. "Membuka Frame Festival Kotagede di Tengah Polemik Pemikiran" [Opening the Frame of Festival Kotagede in the Midst of Polemic of Thoughts], *Brosur Lebaran*, No. 40, 1422H/2001M, pp. 29–39.
16. Nur Cahyati Wahyuni, "Kotagede Ewuh", pp. 67–69.

Festival for Independence) and held in the soccer field of Karang without the involvement of the FK committee. With sufficient funding, the Kecamatan government prepared programmes similar to those which had been earlier developed by the FK.

A number of RWs were reluctant to join the FK 2002 because of the lack of funds to construct open stages. The committee itself experienced deficiency of active members for various reasons. Eventually, there were only nine stages constructed for the FK 2002. A new programme of Pedicab Racing presented by the Association of Pedicab Drivers certainly generated popular enthusiasm. But, an overall impression was that the FK 2002 was extremely scaled down compared to the previous ones.

IMPLICATIONS OF "*KOTAGEDE EWUH*"

In spite of some negative reactions to the FK like the ones concerning the *Buruh Gugat* and *jaelangkung*, majority of the townspeople seemed to have enjoyed FK 99 and FK 2000. It was also obvious that "Kotagede folks" (*wong Kotagede*) enjoyed them not so much passively as the audience but rather actively as participants. The slogan of "Kotagede Ewuh" (Kotagede Prepares a Party) seemed apt to reflect the situation. "Ewuh" in Javanese referred to a situation in which the entire community participated in the preparation of occasions such as weddings, circumcisions, commemorations of the dead, or community events like a village clean-up (*bersih desa*). On these occasions, all the neighbours come out to help one another. It is a show of communal solidarity. In the case of the FK, not only the artistes and performers participated in the FK, but a large proportion of the town's population became the supporters and audience.

Meanwhile, Jadul as an outside observer presented a rather different perspective into the FK.[17] On the basis of his observation on FK 2000, he criticized my 1983 book on two accounts. One is that my assessment of the Muhammadiyah's success in eliminating *kejawen* elements was shallow. The other was that I was underestimating latent class conflicts in the silver industry. He stated as follows:

> In the broad line of a complex encounter which has lasted all through the 20th century, history has thus far recorded that the leadership of the Muhammadiyah carrying the religious views of modernist Islam has faced against two prime competitors in Kotagede. The first was against

---

17. M. Jadul Maula, "The Moving Equilibrium".

the group of *kejawen* in the field of culture via seizure of the initiatives in the management of rituals at the Great Mosque of Mataram and via desacralization of the Royal Graves. The second was against the supporters of PKI in the political and economic areas, which was fought out in the competition for recruiting members and controlling the KP3Y (Production Cooperative of Silverwork Enterprises of Yogyakarta). For the first two decades of the New Order rule, 1970s–1980s, the Muhammmadiyah was successful in occupying a hegemonic position in several fields of social life in Kotagede, evidenced by the public image held until today concerning Kotagede that it is a Muhammadiyah town.[18]

And, Jadul continued that my book was published in 1983 as if to "naturalize" and "normalize" this seemingly static situation under the hegemony of the Muhammadiyah. In fact, Jadul suggested, the situation was only a temporary state within the process of a "moving equilibrium" as the title of his paper expressed.

I fully agree with his characterization of the situation in the 1970s and 1980s, as I have done myself in the earlier chapters, in that the Muhammadiyah did establish hegemony in cultural as well as social and political areas in the national and local contexts that favoured its development. If I were to be criticized for "naturalizing" and "normalizing" the static situation, I must admit that the local hegemony of the Muhammadiyah at that time in cooperation with government authorities was so thorough that, perhaps, any signs of conflicts were smoothed out quickly. Or, at least, I was unable to discern any open antagonism. This was also partly because I was doing my research under an extremely restricted condition and unable to deal with any conflict situation. As mentioned above (p. 238, note 15), any academic research to be undertaken by Indonesian or foreign scholars during the Soeharto rule was not allowed to touch upon any social phenomenon related to SARA (*suku, agama, ras dan antar golongan*, or ethnicity, religion, race and inter-group relationship). Every research proposal was carefully scrutinized by national intelligence agencies, and any of it with the "smell" of SARA was rejected. I was not allowed to meddle with any conflictive situations even academically.

So, officially, I was not doing research on Islam, the Muhammadiyah or *kejawen* at all. I was just studying "traditional patterns of Javanese urban culture and society" — the title of my research proposal submitted to Indonesian authorities. In spite of the fact that the Muhammadiyah was not the topic for my field research initially, I began to feel in the field that its feature as a

---

18. Ibid., p. 38.

genuine voluntary association of individuals with high levels of independence, honesty, discipline, and dedication to the cause of reforming traditional Islam and modernizing society should be worth taking up as a topic of dissertation. I thought that I should convey to the wider public the fact that such a civil voluntary movement based upon Islamic faith did exist in contemporary Indonesia and was transforming local society. I believe I have done the job with my dissertation and its eventual publication.

As to both the vitality of *kejawen*, which endured the onslaught of the Muhammadiyah, as well as a sort of "class conflict" popping up in and around the silver industry in Kotagede, I feel we need more detailed studies than mine or Jadul's. For the resurgence of *kejawen* elements in recent years, especially those seen in the repertory of the FK, is not a simple replication or revival of them from the period prior to the dominance of the Muhammadiyah. As I see it, for example, those beliefs and rituals related to what I have called "the cult of royal glorification" are not reviving now. This is because the roots of the cult were struck down first by the Dutch reform of abolishing the appanage system in the 1910s, then by the attack of Muhammadiyah youths in the 1930s, and finally by the democratization and desacralization of the Yogyakarta Sultanate by Sultan Hamengku Buwono IX himself after Independence.[19] So, what is recovering now is a repertory of popular traditional cultural performances of dancing, *gamelan* music, *wayang, kethoprak, mocopat, shalawatan*, etc. Most interestingly, those are enjoyed not only by older people for their nostalgic value but by younger people with a genuine enthusiasm for their artistic and entertaining values. So much so that the revival of *kejawen* in this sense was promoted by those individuals of the "Cultural Muhammadiyah", who appreciated culture and arts not so much as a mere means of religious propagation (*dakwah*) but as an expression of God-given human nature (*fitrah*).[20] So, the conflict over the FK was not a challenge of *kejawén* upon the Muhammadiyah. It was a spiritual battle within the Muhammadiyah itself between pro-*kejawen* and contra-*kejawen*.

In general, Mas Jadul seems to be a bit anachronistic like Professor Khoiruddin (pp. 294–95 above.) He is falling into a tendency of evaluating the situation in the early 1970s I have described in my old book through a framework of analysis for the post-Reformasi social dynamics. During the 1970s,

---

19. Selosoemardjan, *Social Change in Jogjakarta* (Ithaca: Cornell University Press, 1962). See especially Chapter 6, "Jogjakarta since Independence".
20. Cf. Darwis Khudori's essay, in *Brosur Lebaran*, No. 18, 1400H/1980M, pp. 32–36.

as mentioned before, any social cleavage, cultural or economic, was strictly sealed off. Certainly, Reformasi broke all these taboos and, as a result, all sorts of latent conflicts surfaced. To me, however, the most significant aspect of the FK is not so much as an arena of conflicts as suggested by Jadul's observation, but rather as the emergence of a "communitas" in Victor Turner's sense for social integration. The FKs evidenced that Kotagede residents were desiring and capable of creating a culturally integrated community cutting across religious differences even though it was a momentary experience. Laughter and happiness filled the community during the period of the festivity. And reportedly, even the notorious show of the *Buruh Gugat* was received by the audience in a humorous way. Certainly, the show was not simply laughed away but rather laughed in by the audience as the acknowledgement of a fragment of the bitter local reality of Kotagede.[21]

It was through their participation in the FKs that the townspeople expressed their identity as "*Wong Kotagede*" (People of Kotagede). Ahamad Charris Zubair, one of the organizers of the FK, evaluated it as a vehicle to promote the communal harmony as follows: "Through these activities, the community is able to present forward its cultural potentials. More importantly, these activities as joyful ones can keep conflicts away from appearing in the community. As a result, a peaceful and calm atmosphere can develop in the community." Charris regards the FK as occupying a strategic position in enhancing pluralism in the community:

> My view after the FK 2000 is that it would be much better if it could involve all the elements in the community. Not just one organization or group which is active in social cultural activities only. But, also the Muhammadiyah and NU's Pondok Pesantren Nurul Ummah, and Ma'had Islamy, too. All the elements from whichever social strata should be involved. So much so that all could present themselves commonly and develop the commonness.[22]

Meanwhile, the government authorities learned anew that traditional culture and arts as well as historical heritage (urban landscape and architecture) in Kotagede were extremely valuable resources for the development of a tourist industry. Such was the situation in Kotagede on the eve of the fatal 27 May 2006 earthquake.

---

21. Cf. Nur Cahyati Wahyuni, "Kotagede Ewuh", pp. 110–11.
22. *Brosur Lebaran*, No. 40, pp. 37–38.

13

THE MAY 2006 EARTHQUAKE AND RECONSTRUCTION OF KOTAGEDE

At 5.55 a.m. on 27 May 2006, an earthquake of 5.9 Richter scale hit the Special Region of Yogyakarta and the Province of Central Java. All the four *kelurahans* of the Kotagede area were affected. Destruction of buildings and human casualties in those *kelurahans* are shown in Table 13.1.

According to government statistics, those who were killed by the earthquake amounted to 6,234, and 36,147 were injured. Of the five

TABLE 13.1
Damage and Victims of 2006 Earthquake in Kotagede

No.	Kelurahan/Desa	Destruction of Buildings			Human Casualties	
		Light	Moderate	Heavy	Dead	Injured
1	Jagalan		245	478	7	8
2	Purbayan	548	353	225	2	2
3	Prenggan	582	433	275	9	
4	Rejowinangun	315	342	252	11	
5	Total	1,445	1,373	1,230	29	10

Source: "Recovery Pasca Gempa Bumi di Kotagede" [Post-Earthquake Recovery in Kotagede], *Brosur Lebaran*, No. 45, 1427H/2006M, pp. 30–39.

kabupatens in Yogyakarta, Bantul was the hardest hit. Desa Jagalan, located within the Kabupaten Bantul, suffered most in terms of the destruction of old buildings. Almost 80 per cent of the houses, totalling some 900, in Jagalan were severely damaged including a number of traditional structures of *joglo* and *limasan*. Also, public buildings including government offices, schools, mosques and prayer houses suffered extensive and serious destruction. In the Kecamatan of Kotagede, the damage was lighter, but 3,325 or 56 per cent of the total 5,932 buildings suffered various degrees of destruction.[1] Reportedly, those who died were mostly those who ran out of their houses and were crushed by falling high walls, which are typical features of old neighbourhoods in Kotagede. (See Figure 13.1.)

The post-earthquake processes of rescue, recovery and reconstruction brought a number of social, economic, religious, and cultural implications for the townspeople of Kotagede. From the social aspect, solidarity among neighbours was enhanced when they had to live together in temporary shelters and also while jointly working in the removal of debris and reconstructing houses. Economically, many lost or suffered damages to their properties — houses,

FIGURE 13.1

Professor A. Kahar Mudzakkir's house damaged by the 2006 earthquake. The outer brick walls (now replaced by bamboo fences) and library (the right front wing of the building) are gone.

---

1. *Brosur Lebaran*, No. 45, 1427H/2006M.

shops, and workshops. Most of those engaged in home industry like silver and other metalwork lost their businesses or jobs temporarily or permanently (Figure 13.2). Government and non-government agencies including foreign aid agencies performed immediate rescue works. Subsidies from the government became quite significant for the residents to survive day-to-day as well as to restart and recover their normal lives. The religious implication was that attendance in daily and Friday prayers at mosques and *musholla* increased to a significant degree, at least temporarily.

As far as the Muhammadiyah was concerned, the substantial medical assistance provided by the PKU clinic in Kotagede to the injured and sick was widely appreciated. Also, the Kotagede branch of the Muhammadiyah established a Pos Komand (POSKO, or Command Post). They organized and sent rescue work teams immediately to the hardest hit areas in the neighbouring Plered region. This was done before official assistance was provided by the government and international aid agencies.

FIGURE 13.2

A silver shop damaged by the 2006 earthquake. The inner *pendhapa* is used in place of the destroyed front part.

Mosques, *musholla* and schools under the Muhammadiyah's management in Kotagede suffered extensively (see Figure 13.3). Among others, its historic elementary schools in Bodon and Kleco were almost completely destroyed. However, they received substantial grants from overseas aid agencies to reconstruct and rebuild far better buildings than before.[2] (See Figure 8.10.)

A long-term consequence of the earthquake was the rise in consciousness towards recovering and preserving historical heritage of the town on the part of local governments as well as among a considerable segment of the townspeople. In addition to the traditional buildings and urban landscapes around the Royal Cemetery complex including the Great Mosque of Mataram, a number of old houses privately owned were damaged. The urgency of recovery, reconstruction and preservation of those structures were keenly felt because many owners were financially incapable of doing that.

FIGURE 13.3

The left wing of the Silver Mosque damaged by the 2006 earthquake.

---

2. "Recovery Pasca Gempa Bumi" [Post-Earthquake Recovery in Kotagede], *Brosur Lebaran*, No. 45, 1427H/2006M.

By declaring the establishment of the Kotagede Heritage District, M. Natsir of the Kanthil Foundation took the initiative to appeal to domestic and international donors and partners for cooperation. Darwis Khudori sent his passionate support for this from France.[3] Those efforts culminated in the formation of a new institution called Organisasi Pengelola Kawasan Pusaka Kotagede (OPKP, or Organization for the Management of Kotagede Heritage District). A series of substantial projects have begun, and it is now going on to repair, reconstruct and preserve old buildings, thanks to international and domestic contributions including from Siemens and Gadjah Mada University. (See Figure 13.4.)

FIGURE 13.4

Pamphlets of Kanthil Foundation.

---

3. "Membangun Kembali Kotagede" [Rebuilding Kotagede], *Brosur Lebaran*, No. 45, 1427H/2006M, pp. 73–79.

Public concern has been heightened, too, for the tourist industry to be the mainstay of the town's long-term reconstruction and development programme after the disaster. So much so that efforts for the preservation of traditional architecture, folk industry, local culture and arts are carried out by a number of agencies, among which OPKP is the most active. At present, activities like Rambling Through Kotagede and Living Museum are undertaken intermittently by OPKP and PUSDOK, attracting both domestic and overseas visitors.[4]

More specifically, the Kotagede branch of the Muhammadiyah is proposing a programme called Kampung Wisata Muhammadiyah (Sightseeing Tour of Muhammadiyah Neighbourhoods) to be held during the national congress celebrating the centennial birth year of the Muhammadiyah in July 2010. This might develop into a larger and long-term programme to promote sightseeing tours of neighbourhoods related to the early history of the Muhammadiyah in Yogyakarta. This covers the 3Ks — Kauman, Karangkajen, and Kotagede — and Nitikan.[5]

Apparently, the 2006 earthquake became a catalyst for the stakeholders concerned with the reconstruction and future development of the town to come together and cooperate. It is to be observed how the Muhammadiyah should behave in this new environment of community development. That will be a topic for future research.

---

4. The following websites carry a number of photographs of historical sites and street scenes in Kotagede: <http://www.virtualtourist.com/travel/Asia/Indonesia/Kotagede-1215906/TravelGuide-Kotagede.html>, <http://www.yogyes.com/en/yogyakarta-tourism-object/historic-and-heritage-sight/kotagede/>.
5. Erwito Wibowo, "Kampung Wisata Muhammadiyah Kotagede: Sebuah Gagasan" [Muhammadiyah Neighborhood Tourism in Kotagede: An Idea], *Brosur Lebaran*, No. 46, 1428H/2007M, pp. 82–85.

14

CONCLUDING REMARKS
Future of the Muhammadiyah

As concluding remarks for my observations on the history of the Muhammadiyah in Kotagede from 1972 to 2010, I shall present a review of a number of aspects concerning the achievements of the movement during the period and challenges it currently faces. On the basis of those reviews, I shall discuss the future of the movement.

BACKGROUND FOR THE SUCCESS OF THE MUHAMMADIYAH

The success of the Muhammadiyah in propagation and institution-building occurred mostly during the 1970s and 1980s. One of the objective conditions for this was the drastic change in national political situation after the G30S/PKI Affairs. The military led by General Soeharto took a firm anti-PKI stance, and engaged in violent suppression and persecution of PKI members and supporters. They were removed from the public stage forcibly. In Kotagede, the Muhammadiyah activists took initiatives to arrest and hand them over to the military.

In the aftermath of the G30S/PKI Affairs, the Communists were not only banished as political rebels but also designated as atheists who were antagonistic to Pancasila, the founding philosophy of the nation. Then, religions — the officially recognized ones — were utilized as a means to subjugate and brainwash ex-PKI members and supporters ideologically. For those people, the declaration of affiliation with one of those religions and the participation in religious activities provided a way of survival. In many areas outside Kotagede, this practice seemed to have benefitted Protestant and Catholic churches, which welcomed new converts from the ex-PKI members and supporters. In Kotagede where the number of Christians was negligible, it brought a favourable result for the Muhammadiyah. The local Muhammadiyah branch was actively engaged in propagating for ex-PKI members and sympathizers in cooperation with the government authorities, and thus expanded its influence in the ex-PKI neighbourhoods. In this way, the Muhammadiyah "won" the decades-long confrontation with the PKI and benefitted from the victory. In other words, the Muhammadiyah overwhelmed the PKI after the G30S Affairs not so much through ideological debates but through the coercive situation where few other choices were allowed for the ex-PKI people than to submit to the life-or-death pressure.

As we have seen in the Box 9 (pp. 239–41), there are still several hundred individuals who are officially registered as "Ex-Tapol" at present. To what extent has the brainwashing via the Muhammadiyah's propagation been effective in making them recant their past and "Islamize" them? How are they behaving in the post-Reformasi situation of democratization? Are they, and their descendants, not bouncing back to the previous stance of radical social protest? Are they not becoming a social force of their own because of their common fate and suffering? These are some of the questions I wanted to pursue anew in the field but so far have failed to do. I wish I could take up the task in the near future since their orientation might be impacting on the ideological constellation of the town for generations to come. I urge my colleagues to take up this topic for research, too. It is also my feeling that the Muhammadiyah movement will have to make an honest review of its confrontation with the PKI in history in order to learn objective lessons from the past and reassert its moral leadership among the townspeople.

THE MUHAMMADIYAH AND THE SOEHARTO GOVERNMENT

It was true that the New Order government tried to contain the political revival of the Masyumi from within the Muhammadiyah circles, and that policy affected the local political scene in Kotagede as well. (See Chapter 6.) Facing

Concluding Remarks

this pressure, a sharp antagonism developed among the local Muhammadiyah activists. It was between those individuals who hoped for the rehabilitation of Masyumi as a political party participating in the coming general elections and the mainstream leadership of the Muhammadiyah, which accepted the compromise of forming the Parmusi (Partai Muslimin Indonesia) as an unofficial inheritor of the Masyumi's tradition. The anti-mainstream group, mostly youths, was eventually silenced and marginalized before the general elections of 1971. (See pp. 286–87 above).

Thereafter, so long as the Muhammadiyah kept its activities to religious propagation, education and social welfare, the local government authorities did not intervene, and rather welcomed its active participation in the anti-atheist cum anti-communist campaigns.

As we have seen above, the anti-communism and pro-religion paradigm of the New Order regime provided a favourable environment for the development of the Muhammadiyah at the grassroots. Also, the regime's broad strategy for the modernization of the Indonesian nation was, to some extent and in many areas, in parallel with the basic orientation of the Muhammadiyah, which pursued "progress" (*kemajuan*) and "reform" (*tajdid*). Actual policies of the Soeharto government, however, were not necessarily beneficial to the Muhammadiyah. Dictatorial developmentalism of Soeharto, which welcomed Western capitals and relied on the dominance of Chinese oligarchs in economy, threatened the strengths of indigenous business people who made up a considerable social basis for the Muhammadiyah and other Islamic movements. The government policies sometimes invited a strong opposition from those Islamic forces as seen in the case of an aborted bill for national marriage law in 1973–74. However, in balance, the Muhammadiyah's stance vis-à-vis the government was that of loyal yet critical partner, and thus it continued to secure public space to manoeuvre throughout the New Order regime. This pattern was observed in Kotagede as well.

The attitude of the Muhammadiyah, which was rather cautiously self-defensive and reactive vis-à-vis the government, was nurtured throughout the New Order era. This stance seems to continue into the post-Reformasi situation. Nationally, the Muhammadiyah's fundamental goal of an "excellent society" remains abstract, lacking a clear image and a persuasive road map to attain it. Meanwhile, its top leaders seem to be so often busying themselves in elitist bargaining with the power holders. It is my observation that the Muhammadiyah activists and supporters at the grass-roots level are expecting a more proactive stance from the central leadership and a clearer guidance to direct their day-to-day activities in longer and wider perspectives.

STAGNATION OF THE MUHAMMADIYAH LEADERSHIP

As presented in Chapter 10, the leadership of the Muhammadiyah in Kotagede began to be criticized as failing to respond effectively to social changes and failing to make smooth generational takeover to renew itself. As a result, the movement fell into stagnation by the late 1980s. As we have already seen, causes of the stagnation were discussed from various viewpoints. (See Chapter 10.) In my view, however, one important aspect seems to be missing so far from the discussion: that is, the very fact that the success itself has brought stagnation. My observation is that the Muhammadiyah, especially its leaderships at various levels, became stagnant and failed to renew themselves because of its very success, i.e. the enormous growth in its organization and expansion of its institutions in the 1970s and 1980s. This included educational and social welfare institutions under its management. A number of cadres were assigned to new organizational duties and the management of those institutions, which absorbed a large amount of energies from them. Thus, former volunteers became *pegawai*, i.e., paid office workers: a sort of bureaucratization was inevitable. I believe that was one of the main causes of stagnancy.

Meanwhile, few innovative efforts were attempted to alter the strategy or organizational behaviour of the Muhammadiyah under the established leadership. It was content with the success, and everything was routinized while few attempts were made for innovation. This was perhaps partly because of the incumbent leaders' fear for the intervention by external forces. So, the old familiar faces continue to be re-elected to the leadership. This tendency seemed to have become stronger after the Social Organization Law became effective in 1984. Thus, Pak A.R. stayed on at the top of the organization for more than twenty years. So did Pak Bashori Anwar in Kotagede. It was "safer" to do so under the New Order.

If my observation is not missing the mark, it is obvious that the organizational and institutional expansion of the Muhammadiyah has brought it a huge asset as well as a serious liability. How to solve this dilemma? As I see it, the necessary condition is the reinvigoration of voluntarism to conquer mannerism, and the sufficient condition is the acquisition of skills and technology for modern organizational management.

CRITICISM FROM THE YOUNGER GENERATION

As we have seen from the pages of *Brosur Lebaran*, the younger generation's criticisms on the discontinuity and stagnation of the local Muhammadiyah leadership became stronger year after year towards the late 1980s and early 1990s. However, those criticisms were not accumulating enough. Perhaps this was simply because the criticisms were mostly coming from younger individuals who had just finished tertiary education or were still undergoing it. After graduation, many of them left Kotagede for employment elsewhere. Thus the "steam" for criticism did not accumulate into an explosive stage. I assume this was the main reason why a decisive leadership change in Kotagede was so delayed until 2005, well after the fall of the Soeharto regime.

This inaction, however, seemed to have cost the Kotagede Muhammadiyah dearly since a significant number of potential cadres for the future generation of its leadership distanced themselves from the organization. Many withdrew to concentrate on their family businesses or on their occupational duties. Some of them chose to become active in other organizations in Kotagede, including Team Tadarus AMM, Ma'had Islamy, FM radio stations, PUSDOK, and even in PKS (Partai Keadilan Sejahtera) later. Some of the young activists left Kotagede altogether, perhaps in dismay. As a result, the same individuals and those who are similar to them kept the leadership position of the Kotagede Muhammadiyah for decades. Thus, the stagnation remained and the generation gap widened.

Finally, a delayed leadership change took place in 2005. Meanwhile, the external situation for the Muhammadiyah changed significantly over time. It was apparent that its "monopoly" or "dominance" in the public space was gone. The Muhammadiyah had to admit the reality of diversity. A new type of leadership, internally consolidating and externally embracing, was required. The situation called for activists who had learned to work together with heterogeneous people of other faiths for the pursuit of a common good. In fact, those individuals who had been marginalized in the Muhammadiyah movement previously had much experience on working in a pluralistic situation. It was natural for those individuals to be invited to join the official leadership positions after 2005. But, they are ageing now. So, a great deal of effort to recruit younger cadres is needed. To attract them, however, it seems that organizational loyalty to the Muhammadiyah alone is insufficient in the contemporary situation of multiplying attractions and distractions. Intellectual stimulation, spiritual satisfaction and concrete achievements seem necessary. For this, the style of the Muhammadiyah activities will have to approach that of certain NGOs or NPOs with definite action programmes, or to join them in common action.

REFORMASI, POLITICS, AND THE MUHAMMADIYAH

An immediate result of the democratization of Indonesian polity since the fall of the Soeharto regime was the formation of new political parties at the local level. The mainstream of the branch leadership of the Muhammadiyah in Kotagede went along with the central and provincial leadership and decided to support the establishment of the branch of Partai Amanat Nasional (PAN). A significant number of Muhammadiyah cadres, especially the middle-aged to younger ones, were spared for the launching of the newly formed party. Meanwhile, a sizeable minority of the Muhammadiyah activists continued to support a well-established politician from Partai Persatuan Pembangunan (PPP) instead of the PAN. Besides, a number of young activists were secretly recruited to Partai Keadilan (PK) since the late 1990s and grew visible through the 1999 and 2004 elections. With the 2009 general and presidential elections, PKS emerged as one of the largest parties at the local and national levels. Also, a small number of Muhammadiyah activists together with those from different backgrounds formed a local branch of Partai Demokrat (PD) for the 2004 and 2009 elections. Surprisingly, the PD obtained a significant number of votes for its legislative candidates and for the presidential ticket of SBY-Boediono in 2009.

Thus, the Muhammadiyah has become a common hunting ground for a number of political parties to recruit cadres in the post-Reformasi period, and was weakened in terms of its own manpower. However, it is certain that an overall effect of the introduction of party politics at the grassroots level in Kotagede has been positive in that popular participation in politics has been promoted in that way. Meanwhile, for the Muhammadiyah, it led to an emergence of explicit differences in political views and interests among its own cadres, ordinary members and supporters. Therefore, the organizational activities and the feeling of solidarity among the Muhammadiyah circles were inevitably destined to become lower during the election campaign periods. However, by maintaining political neutrality and "equal distance" to all parties as directed by the central leadership, the Kotagede Muhammadiyah was spared serious internal splits arising from the involvement in party politics. In the end, solidarity as a "Big Family of the Muhammadiyah" (*Keluarga Besar Muhammadiyah*) was re-established when the elections were over.

However, there was an exception in the case of the PKS people. Parasitic and subversive activities of the PKS cadres prior to their surfacing to the public scene left feelings of hostilities among the Muhammadiyah circles vis-à-vis the PKS. Overcoming these feelings for the sake of a wider solidarity of Muslim community and of the entire society as common citizens of Kotagede would become a challenge for the local Muhammadiyah.

All in all, separating as well as coordinating the relationships between the Muhammadiyah and political parties will continue to be a difficult task for the organization. The lessons learnt will be an important contribution to the development of civic culture at the grassroots level, not for the Muhammadiyah alone but also for the entire community.

FESTIVAL KOTAGEDE: JUBILATION AND FRUSTRATION

As described in Chapter 12, Festival Kotagede (FK) was initiated in 1999 by several individuals including those of the "Cultural Muhammadiyah". They had been critical of the "Structural Muhammadiyah" and kept a distance from of it. They had pursued their own strategy to reinvigorate the local community culturally and took up their own initiatives to revive local cultural and artistic activities in the openness of the post-Reformasi situation. Thus, the FK was launched. Through the FK, they played the role of a new solidarity maker for the local community.

As we have seen above, the FK was carried out as an occasion for the Kotagedeans to celebrate and enjoy the fruits of the Reformasi in spontaneous ways. Yet, the involvement of the Muhammadiyah in the FK was ambiguous. No official discussion or decision was held in the Muhammadiyah organization on the first FK of 1999. In reality, the FK created an unprecedented level of participation and enthusiasm from a wide range of the townspeople. Its success led to the FK 2000 being held with much more extensive participation from a number of neighbourhoods in Kotagede, with more enriched presentations and performances. Yet, a sharp opposition came up from a few individuals in the branch leadership of the Muhammadiyah against the inclusion of *jaelangkung* and *jathilan*, Javanese folk art and performances often involving séance and trance. Also, some businesspeople from the silver handicraft industry felt offended by the *Buruh Gugat* item in the parade, which expressed the labourers' protest against their plight of low wages and long workings hours.

To sum up, the FKs created a great amount of jubilation among the townspeople on the one hand, but also left various kinds of hostilities and frustration in certain groups and individuals on the other. The scale of the annual FK declined drastically since 2002, and it seemed to have dwindled down further. The FK had ceased to be held before the 2006 earthquake. No initiatives are seen to revive it after that.

In my view, the behaviour of the local Muhammadiyah leadership — inaction rather than action from the beginning and all through the process of the FKs — indicated its weakness or incapacity in the area dealing with the matter of secular "common good" (*maslaha*) for the local community. Perhaps, the point of reference for many of the Muhammadiyah leaders in evaluating the FK's significance was still solely in terms of benefitting or not for "the *ummat* Islam" or even for the "*ummat* Muhammadiyah" in a narrower sense. The common interest or happiness of the general Kotagede population with its heterogeneity now — inclusive of Muslims and non-Muslims — did not seem to have come into the framework of their evaluation. So, many of them only focused their attention on the matter of "TBC", i.e. *jaelangkung* and *jathilan*, while the matter of overall societal significance of the FK was not appreciated.

Meanwhile, it is apparent that the Muhammadiyah's "official" stance vis-à-vis local culture has drastically changed recently. Cultural and artistic attractions presented at its centennial anniversary congress in Yogyakarta in July 2010 were a parade of appreciation for the richness of local cultures including the Javanese one. The national chairman of the Muhammadiyah and the mayor of Yogyakarta, a Muhammadiyah man, took part in a *kethoprak* show as a part of popular attraction!

It is my observation that the debate on the FKs still has a long and profound echo among the Muhammadiyah circles in Kotagede. In the near future, after a series of serious discussions, the initiative for the revival of the Festival Kotagede and for active participation in it may come from the local Muhammadiyah leadership itself. Then, it will signal a decisive turnaround of the stance of the Muhammadiyah in Kotagede vis-à-vis local cultural traditions.

THE CHALLENGE OF THE "COMMON GOOD"

It is also my feeling that the Kotagede Muhammadiyah has been taking similar attitudes of inaction or indifference when it was confronted with other wider societal problems beyond the immediate concern of the *ummat* Islam or the *ummat* Muhammadiyah in religious terms. In fact, those problems have been attracting serious concerns from young activists of the Muhammadiyah as exemplified by many of the topics taken up in the past *Brosur Lebaran*. They have included such problems as traffic jams, air and water pollution, disorderly garbage dumping, poor management of the market, economic burden of compulsory education, tax on the silver handicraft industry, unemployment among youths, school drop-outs, abject working conditions of labourers in small industries, increase in crimes and moral decay, preservation of historic heritage, and the need for long-term city planning for the town.

Young activists seemed to have considered those problems as acute societal problems, but seemingly they have failed for them to be taken up in the action programme of the Muhammadiyah. Perhaps, the branch leadership may have assumed an approach of lobbying behind the scene vis-à-vis concerned parties to deal with some of those problems. However, their efforts have not surfaced nor brought visible results.

More importantly and fundamentally, as mentioned above, such inaction of the Muhammadiyah seems to indicate the weakness or incapacity of its commitment to act on behalf of the "common good" of the community if those societal problems are not directly concerned with religious matters.

At the level of national discourse, the Muhammadiyah does refer to the contribution of the association (*persyarikatan*) of the Muhammadiyah to the common interest of the entire nation. The leadership states that it seeks to uplift the nation to the level of superior civilization (*peradaban utama*) through the excellence of the Muhammadiyah (*keunggulan Muhammadiyah*) — that is the slogan frequently heard these days.

However, in a concrete local case like the community-wide event of the FK, the official attitude of the Muhammadiyah was ambiguous, if not antagonistic, to say the least. How to encounter the opportunity of community-wide event like the FK seems to be still a challenge to be worked out by the Muhammadiyah. The incorporation of the "Cultural Muhammadiyah" people in the composition of the new leadership formed at the 2009 conference of the Kotagede branch of the Muhammadiyah would open up the ways for fruitful discussions and policy making concerning the "common good" of the community in the future. Also, the approach of Pak Saleh Udden, village head of Jagalan, pushing forward the "universally noble values" in order to consolidate pluralism in the everyday life of the townspeople, invites our continuous attention.

LOVE FOR KOTAGEDE

One thing that explicitly stood out while I was examining the back issues of *Brosur Lebaran* was the expression of love and emotional attachment to the town of Kotagede by the young contributors. The contents of every issue of *Brosur Lebaran* — editorials and columns by editors, articles and essays, short stories and poems, even routine reports of the activities of youth groups — in other words, almost the entire substance of the writings contain deep concern and affection to the town of Kotagede where the contributors were born and raised. (See, for example, the poem "Coming home" on p. 216.) It is undeniably clear that young Muhammadiyah activists are strongly committed to the happiness and welfare of the townspeople and the prosperity of the community.

This has been especially so after the 2006 earthquake. Their participation in the immediate rescue and recovery works was quite significant. Also, the air of increasing urgency for the preservation of historic heritage has become very much obvious by now. To that effect, the Kanthil Foundation and PUSDOK are developing extensive activities by involving a number of young people to promote the preservation of historic buildings and local cultural items, including food and traditional cakes, and organizing local tours for visitors and tourists to enjoy these via "rambling through *kampung*".

The affection towards the town and the concern for the welfare of the townspeople were also observed at a parade, Pawai Ta'aruf, held by AMM on 27 January 2008. It was participated by a group of young boys on bicycles under the banner of Hizbul Wathan (Muhammadiyah's Boy Scouts). The boys carried placards which showed exactly their concern for "common good" as mentioned above. These included various slogans for environmental preservation, anti-air pollution, anti-water pollution, anti-greenhouse gas effects, and even anti-smoking.

I have also learned that a group of students from the Muhammadiyah junior high school 7 in Purbayan received a prize from a U.S. foundation in an international contest for civic education in 2007. The students produced a report and policy recommendation for the enhancement of the silver handicraft industry in Kotagede. For winning the contest, this group of students and their teacher was invited to Washington, D.C., to join high school students from other countries who also won the contest.

These are random examples, but they seem to be sufficient to indicate the intensity of the "love for Kotagede" felt by the young people and their potential energy and readiness to dedicate themselves to the cause of the "common good" of the community. I am anticipating that those trends will be channelled well into the grown-ups of the Kotagede Muhammadiyah soon. I am also hopeful that those young people would be prepared to take the entire Kotagede society as their reference point and be willing to compete and cooperate with others from different social streams and religious beliefs in their common efforts for community development.

CONCERN FOR THE POOR

It is my observation that the Muhammadiyah's concern for the plight of the poor and for the necessity of solving the problem of poverty have been heightened via the forty-sixth and centennial anniversary congress of the Muhammadiyah held in Yogyakarta in July 2010. It has become often heard recently — in the *pengajian* of the Muhammadiyah or in its publications

— the relevant injunction in the Qur'an, i.e. Surah Al Ma'un.[1] The verse titled "Charity" urges humane concern and assistance for the poor and the orphaned, i.e. the socially weak and suffering, as a pious act of devotion to God. Reportedly, the verse provided a strong motivation and justification for K.H. Ahmad Dahlan to launch the PKO (Penolong Kesengsaraan Oemum, now PKU, Assistance for the Relief of Public Suffering) as an integral part of the Muhammadiyah movement in the 1920s. Perhaps, a review of the current PKU system, which has grown to be a robust bureaucracy itself, may be necessary to bring about its overhaul at the national and local levels to revive and reconstruct it as a genuine channel for Islamic philanthropy.

THE FUTURE OF THE MUHAMMADIYAH

Inertia of the success of the Muhammadiyah in the past century may soon be lost or will even become a bureaucratic burden to overshadow its future. To pursue significant progress further in the twenty-first century, the Muhammadiyah seems to need a revitalization of the entire movement, to the extent or even more of vigour, steadfastness and a clear vision exemplified by its founder, K.H. Ahmad Dahlan.[2] The key to success, according to my field observation, may be found by focussing attention to the branch and sub-branch levels. There, local cadres and ordinary members are engaged in a series of new experiments for the common good of society, still being inspired by the pristine model of K.H. Ahmad Dahlan but adapting to changing social situation. If and when a sufficient degree of innovativeness and a vital new élan is accumulating at those grassroots levels and if and when the leaderships above them are responsive enough to recognize and promote those orthogenetic developments with a long-term perspective and a clear national strategy, the further progress of the Muhammadiyah may be assured.

---

1. "In the Name of God, the Merciful, the Compassionate. Hast thou seen him who cries lies to the Doom? That is he who repulses the orphan and urges not the feeding of the needy. So woe to those that pray and are heedless of their prayers, to those who make display and refuse charity." *The Koran Intepreted*, Sura CVII, "Charity", translated by Arthur J. Aberry (New York: Macmillan, 1979 [1955]), p. 351.
2. Cf. *Sang Pencerah* [The Enlightener], by Akmal Nasery Basral (Jakarta: Mizan Pustaka, 2010) is a historical novel based upon a film scenario of the same title depicting the life of K.H. Ahmad Dahlan. It describes vividly the brightening episodes of his figure and action.

POSTSCRIPT TO PART II

Here I would like to indulge in a bit of personal reminiscences to put my original work into perspective. I shall be doing so by acknowledging the help of several individuals who assisted or encouraged me in writing my dissertation and the subsequent "Banyan Tree" book in various ways. I would also like to thank those people who have helped me to undertake a brief but fruitful fieldwork for revisiting Kotagede, December 2008 to February 2009.

My initial as well as official research topic before visiting Indonesia for the first time was on the social history of indigenous Javanese urban society. I intended to replicate and test Clifford Geertz's work on the social history of a Javanese town of "Modjokuto" in a more appropriate location. I felt that Geertz's "Modjokuto" was too shallow in its history and marginal to the centre of Javanese civilization. The town of Pare, which is the real name of "Modjokuto", was in fact a young frontier town just emerged since the mid-nineteenth century, thanks to the growth of sugar and tobacco cultivation. It was inappropriate, according to my view, to be taken as a sample for representing the traditional urban ways of Javanese life. I was planning to conduct fieldwork in Kotagede and Klaten, following Professor Selosoemardjan's suggestion, to compare "old and new" urban communities in inner Central Java.

Kotagede was thought to be a natural choice to study traditional urbanism in Java. The town appeared in history as the initial capital of the Islamized Mataram Kingdom in the late sixteenth century and has continued to maintain its physical and cultural identity until the modern times. The town was much older than Yogyakarta and Surakarta, the capitals of the two principalities tracing their history back to 1755 when the Mataram Kingdom split into two, and then four. Meanwhile, Klaten was somewhat comparable to "Modjokuto" as a new frontier town, developed with the imposition of the Culture System by the Dutch authorities in rural Central Java. However, I had to abandon the plan to do fieldwork in Klaten in the end because the data gathering in Kotagede consumed the entire time (and funds) allowed for me.

It was in the course of doing general ethnographic fieldwork in Kotagede that my attention started to turn to the religious life of the townspeople. For, until the early twentieth century, the entire society was ordered to sustain the authority and power of the Surakarta Susuhunate and Yogyakarta Sultanate religiously in the framework of Javanese Islam, or *kejawen*. Then, I encountered the Muhammadiyah, a movement for rationalization, enlightenment and modernization supported by the indigenous bourgeoisie. I began to realize gradually the significance of the movement in transforming the social, political, and cultural make-up of the town. As a result, I did collect a relatively large amount of data on the movement. And, the more did I learn about it, the stronger did my interest grow on it. Indeed, there occurred a shift of my attention in the field, i.e. from studying social history and general ethnography of the town to putting emphasis on the religious life of the townspeople and its transformation promoted by the Muhammadiyah movement. But, I was not quite sure yet whether I should take up the Muhammadiyah as the topic of my dissertation even after leaving Kotagede for Ithaca in 1972. For, I had a good amount of data on many other aspects of the town as well.[1]

It was after having arrived back at Cornell that I finally decided to arrange and analyse my data along the development of the Muhammadiyah in the local context. For this, David Penny of the Australian National University (ANU), who was visiting Cornell then, gave me a decisive advice: "You have sufficient data to write up ten dissertations, Mitsuo. But, you can and should write only one. So, what is your choice and what is your thesis?" I chose to deal with the Muhammadiyah and present, as my thesis, the point that Islam had been a deep-rooted living faith and the Muhammadiyah was growing stronger in the town via reforming it. Looking back, I deeply appreciate Dr Penny's advice.

Before completing my dissertation, I had to leave for Adelaide to start teaching there in 1974. There I finished writing my dissertation and sent it to Cornell University. It was accepted in 1976.

After that, I had to endure a sort of "intellectual isolation" for some time because of my decision to take up the Muhammadiyah as my dissertation topic. At that time, in the social sciences as well as in the area studies in the West, research topic on Islam was unpopular. Generally speaking, not only Islam but also other world religions were all regarded as waning according to the prevailing "modernization = secularization" theory. For Indonesia in particular, many American colleagues of my generation were abandoning or

---

1. In fact, Professor Dr Muhadjir Darwin, one of my research assistants in Kotagede in 1970–72, confided in a seminar at the UGM which he organized for me in February 2008: "We [Nakamura's research assistants] were all unaware that Pak Nakamura was preparing a dissertation on the Muhammadiyah!"

avoiding Islam as research topic.[2] Under the New Order of General Soeharto, Islam was regarded as diminishing in significance politically as well as culturally. Instead, *kebatinan*, Javanese mysticism favoured by Soeharto himself, became "fashionable" as research topic and deemed relatively easy to get funded if one joined this academic bandwagon. My experience in Kotagede, however, prevented me from going along with the trend.

At the end of 1975, I was invited by Pak Selo to join the PLPIIS (Social Science Research Training Station) attached to the Faculty of Social Sciences, the University of Indonesia, Jakarta, as its research associate. I accepted the invitation since the position seemed to offer a golden opportunity to enter the centre of intellectual life in Indonesia. Indeed in Jakarta, I started to get acquainted with a number of prominent social scientists of Indonesia including Pak Koko (Soedjatmoko), Pak Kun (Koentjaraningrat), Pak Harsya (Harsya Bachtiar), and Pak Sayogyo. Also, I had numerous opportunities to join lively discussions held among young intellectuals basing themselves at the LP3ES with the journal, *Prisma*, as their medium of public communication. There, I also got to know a group of young Muslim intellectuals pursuing "an inclusive, contextual and forward looking Islam" (Aswab Mahasin's wording) including Dawam Rahardjo, Djohan Effendi, Nurcholish Madjid, and Abdurrahman Wahid (Gus Dur). These acquaintances gave me an assurance for the appropriateness of my thesis that "Islam is a vital living faith" in the contemporary Indonesian society. Among them, it was Gus Dur who appreciated my dissertation explicitly. Moreover, he invited me to widen my coverage of Islam by observing the Nahdlatul Ulama at first hand as well[3] in addition to studying the Muhammadiyah.

Back in Australia in 1977, I started to revise my dissertation for publication while staying at the ANU as a visiting fellow. Anthony John's pioneering efforts to take up Islam seriously, by combining area studies and Islamic studies, were a sure guide for my project. Meanwhile, from the middle towards the

---

2. A political scientist specialized in studying Indonesian Islam gave up his career to become a lawyer. Another became a government consultant in foreign relations. Also there was one who became an intelligent officer of a major Western government.
3. Upon his invitation, I attended the National Congress of the NU. My observation thus obtained has yielded a report, "The Radical Traditionalism of the Nahdlatul Ulama in Indonesia: A Personal Account of Its 26th National Congress, June 1979, Semarang", *Tonan Ajia Kenkyu* (Southeast Asian Studies, CSEAS, Kyoto University), 19, no. 2 (1981).

end of 1970s, Islam began to attract Western public attention because of the OPEC's oil embargo and the eruption of a Shiite revolution in Iran in 1979. A sudden surge of "experts" on Islamic affairs occurred in the Western world with numerous publications. I was afraid that my dissertation, if published, might be buried in the piles of those instant works. My hesitation for its publication was greatly lessened when I was given a comment on my dissertation by an Indonesian student whom I met in Canberra: "Pak Nakamura, I do thank for your work as a Muslim since you have taken Islam seriously as a living faith of a vast number of my countrymen before the advent of the 'oil shock'." After an unsuccessful attempt for its publication in Australia, Gadjah Mada University Press under the directorship of Pak Koesoemanto accepted my dissertation for publication. He also agreed with me to solicit a foreword from Professor Mukti Ali.

I presented my findings in the book with a thesis that Islam *à la* Muhammadiyah was a dynamic force transforming the traditional *kejawen* socio-cultural complex at least in "my" town. So, Islamization was ongoing. On the basis of my observation, I have even predicted that the kind of Islam promoted by the Muhammadiyah would be gaining an increasing support from the general population of the town. I believe that my prediction was basically correct in that the Muhammadiyah kept growing during the last few decades of the twentieth century.

What I had underestimated in retrospect, however, was the persistence of *kejawen* cultural elements among the townspeople even including the Muhammadiyah members themselves. I did emphasize in my dissertation a general point that the Javaneseness and Islam were inseparably amalgamated in the Muhammadiyah of Kotagede in the field of ethical values, and that there obtained a fine case of the fusion of ethics deriving from a universal religion and a local value system expressed in vernacular languages. Yet, I left out untouched the cultural and artistic spheres. In fact, I did observe in the field the persistence of *kejawen* cultural expressions like *mocopat, wayang kulit, wayang wong, kethoprak, campursari, jathilan* and so forth. But, I was noticing those performances mainly on political occasions including Independence Day celebrations and the campaigns for General Elections of 1971. Then, the local government (military, police and civil administration = Golkar) often sponsored those, partly utilizing ex-PKI cultural talents to attract townspeople in countering the Parmusi campaigns. So, I perceived the phenomenon as a case of political control and mobilization of *kejawen* by the New Order authorities. I was not appreciating their genuine cultural values. In other words, I was not able to understand fully the continuity deep-rooted in history between *kejawen* and the modernist Muhammadiyah.

On the other hand, my anthropological observation in the field did not miss the fact that puritan piety of the Muhammadiyah did not exclude necessarily the mystical dimension of Muslim life like the performance of voluntary prayers (*doa* and *zikir*, in addition to *sholat*) and the recitation of the Qur'an (*wirid*) often done in the middle of the night or early in the morning.[4] The more did I learn about local spiritual life, the richer it became.[5]

It is interesting to note that my emphasis on the transformative effect of Islamization by the Muhammadiyah on the townspeople presented in my dissertation has irritated some of the local Muslim intellectuals within the Muhammadiyah circles. They seemed to have felt that my observations were "too simplistic to be true". I believe that Achmad Charris Zubair's *Sarjana* thesis on *kejawen* and Islam[6] presented to the UGM in 1979 was, in a sense, a subtle criticism and correction of my dissertation. He attracted our attention to the fruitful fusion of the three elements, i.e. *kejawen*, modernist Islam and entrepreneurial rationalism among the Kotagedeans. I was in a sense very happy with Charris's thesis since my imperfect work has given him a stimulus to correct and complement it from the "native's viewpoint". I believe such an intellectual interaction between a foreign researcher and a local scholar improves and enriches our ethnographic knowledge and mutual understanding.

While working at the PLPIIS, Jakarta, I had several opportunities to talk with Soemarsaid Moertono, who had produced a seminal work on the Javanese state and statecraft.[7] I offered my criticism of his work saying that it was too much slanted towards the Javanese concept of power *à la* Ben Anderson at the expense of belittling the aspects of the later Mataram kingdom being a Muslim polity. For example, I raised the important position of Penghulu at the Palace as the highest spiritual adviser to Raja and his judicial authority as

---

4. Mitsuo Nakamura, "Sufi Elements in Muhammadiyah? Notes from Field Observation", *Prisma* Vol. IX, No. 8, (Jakarta: LP3ES, 1980).
5. Mitsuo Nakamura, "The Cultural and Religious Identity of Javanese Muslims: The Case of Muhammadiyah", *Prisma* (English), No. 31 (Jakarta: LP3ES, 1984).
6. Ahmad Charris Zubair, "Tinjauan tentang nilai-nilai Islam dan *kejawen* sebagai sumber gagasan dari pola hidup sosio-filosofis masyarakat Kotagede". Skripsi Sarjana, Fakultas Filsafat, Universitas Gadjah Mada, Yogyakarta, 1979.
7. Soemarsaid Moertono, *State and Statecraft in Old Java: A Study of the Later Mataram Period, 16th to 19th Century* (Ithaca: Modern Indonesia Project, Southeast Asia Program, Cornell University, 1981 [1968]).

the head of religious court (*srambi*), in which Islamic laws were employed to judge. In short, I said to Pak Moertono, "Virtually, no detail was presented in your work on the presence and the role of *abdi dalem putihan* (court religious officials) as an integral part of the Islamized Javanese polity." He admitted that he himself regretted the bias. He said he would try to rectify it some time and encouraged me to pursue the topic. But, he was gone before undertaking the job by himself.

I was aware that I lacked appropriate research tools (classical Javanese) to follow the suggestion of Pak Moertono. So, I was very much delighted when Pak Zaini Ahmad Nuh, who was a high-ranking officer in the Department of Religious Affairs and himself a descendant of a *Penghulu* in West Java, pointed out this oversight in Western Indonesian studies. He mentioned this point first in his introduction to the Indonesian translation of Daniel Lev's *Islamic Courts in Indonesia*, and then more fully in a booklet entitled *Sebuah Perspektip Sejarah Lembaga Islam di Indonesia*.[8]

My wife Hisako did fieldwork, too, on divorce while we were in Kotagede, 1970–1972. She employed an unobtrusive method to collect and analyse the contents of the local records on divorce kept at the office of KUA (*naib*, subordinate of *Penghulu*) and the recorded tapes of conversations between counsellors and clients who came with marital problems to the office of BP4. The result of her study indicated that Islamic law (*syari'ah*) has long been employed in the areas of marriage and divorce in Javanese society, whereas many aspects of them have also long been perceived as *adat* (customary law) by a number of Western scholars including Hildred Geertz.[9] Hisako submitted her research findings as a Master's thesis to the Australian National University in 1982. Gus Dur assumed the role of external examiner of Hisako's thesis. He also contributed a substantial foreword to the published version of Hisako's thesis by saying that it "deserves praise for the pioneering achievements". According to him, Hisako's work revealed that "many practices in the dissolution of marriage find their origins or counterparts in Islamic law although they have been deemed by students of Indonesia as 'customary'."[10] He then asserted: "In essence, this work's message should be taken seriously:

---

8. Published by Al-Ma'arif in Bandung, 1980.
9. Hildred Geertz, *The Javanese Family: A Study of Kinship and Socialization* (New York: Free Press of Glencoe, 1961).
10. Abdurrahman Wahid, "Foreword" to Hisako Nakamura, *Divorce in Java: A Study of the Dissolution of Marriage among Javanese Muslims* (Yogyakarta: Gadjah Mada University Press, 1983).

it is impossible to separate completely Indonesian from Islamic studies."[11] Besides the academic significance of its own as appreciated by Gus Dur, Hisako's work and mine complemented each other in emphasizing the depth of indigenization of Islam in Javanese society.

Another person to be mentioned is Rex Mortimer. During the recess of a conference in Australia in 1979, I massaged him as he was complaining of severe backaches. He passed away a few months later because of cancer. While massaging, I told him of my dissatisfaction with his monumental work on the post-Independence PKI.[12] For me, it had contained tantalizingly little information on the PKI's ideological and political relationships with Islam and the Islamic forces. He admitted the shortcomings and urged his younger colleagues including me to fill the gap. Herbert Feith was another person who showed a genuine humane concern for the Islam/PKI conflict. Every time I met him, he raised the subject and urged me to pursue it. The history of antagonism between the PKI and the Islamic forces, especially its local realities escalating to the mass killings of 1965–66, has been largely left in the dark even until the present post-Reformasi era.[13] A short reportage I have included in this book (see Box 9: Ex-Tapol (Political Prisoners)) is my small effort to fill the "will" of these two senior colleagues of mine. For this, I must express my appreciation to the late Pak Djumairy of Kotagede, who entrusted me a dossier recording the list of arrestees by the Pasukan Senopati he led during the months of October 1965 to January 1966. I hope that the piece of information would become a step to help open the "forbidden pages" in the local history of Kotagede — once a stronghold of the PKI.

In the United States, in 1980–81, Hisako and I were indebted, among others, to two scholars of Islamic studies: Professor William A. Graham, Dean of Harvard Divinity School, who helped our entry to the circles of Harvard's Islamic studies, and Professor Wilfred Cantwell Smith, with whom Hisako and I were fortunate indeed to have had a chance to attend his lectures given during his final year at Harvard and to have been given an opportunity for a sort of "tutoring" from him. The year at Cambridge widened our perspective

---

11. Ibid. Unfortunately, Gus Dur's foreword was eliminated for unknown reasons from the second printing of Hisako's book, also bearing a changed title of *Javanese Divorce*, and from its Indonesian version, *Perceraian Orang Jawa* (Jakarta: Gadjah Mada University Press, 1983).
12. Rex Mortimer, *Indonesia Communism under Sukarno: Ideology and Politics, 1959–65* (Ithaca: Cornell University Press, 1974).
13. In Indonesia, publications on the topic are still banned at present.

to locate modern Islam in Indonesia in a worldwide context, and gave me a final push to complete the draft of my book (Part I of this book).

Finally, let me mention the most incisive and decisive critique of Clifford Geertz's work that I have ever heard. Pak Koko (Soedjatmoko) gave it in a seminar held at the LP3ES in 1978. He stated: "The approach taken by Geertz was completely wrong. Think about a situation in which it was applied to the US field. Say, you visit and conduct fieldwork in a small country town in the Midwest. You interview some townspeople including a butcher, a corn farmer, an employee at a gas station, a teacher at a primary school, a Boy Scouts leader, a Catholic Father, a minister of a Baptist church so forth, and then, on the basis of those interviews, produce a book presenting that 'this is the American religion'. American readers will get angry. For such an approach will result in ignoring totally the historical depth of religion in American civilization — its richness in theology and thoughts, the complex structures of the church organizations, etc. Geertz has done something exactly like that for Java. I criticized him personally, but he would not listen."[14] Pak Koko's criticism expressed mine so beautifully. I became more boldly critical of Geertz after having heard those words uttered by one of "the Best and the Brightest" of the contemporary Indonesian intellectuals. Pak Koko passed away in late 1989 while joining a seminar chaired by Amien Rais at the UGM.

To conclude this post-postscript, I would like to mention a number of individuals who have contributed to the completion of the present work. Pak Rosyad Saleh, General Secretary, and Pak Haedar Nashir, Chairman, of the Central Leadership Board of the Muhammadiyah who invited me to undertake a "revisiting" research in Kotagede, December 2007 to February 2008. Pak Jumanuddin and Ibu Siti, and their daughter Ibu Amanah and her husband Yusron Asrofie, who hosted Hisako and me during our "revisit" to Kotagede as before. Of course, the cooperation given to me from the Kotagede branch of the Muhammadiyah and the 'Aisyiyah was indispensable and most valuable for my latest fieldwork. There are so many individuals who assisted me that it is difficult to mention all their names. I would just list up the following people as their "representatives": Former and current chairmen of the Muhammadiyah branch of Kotagede, Pak Yatiman Syafi'i and Pak Kaharuddin Noor, its leaders — Pak Ahmad Charris Zubair, Pak Bachrun Nawawi, Pak Asngari Dja'far, Pak Mardjuki, and the officers and

---

14. Mitsuo Nakamura, "Koko Tsuiso" [Memory of Koko], *Nampo-bunka* (Tenri Bulletin of South Asian Studies), Tenri Nampo Bunka Kenkyukai, Vol. 18 (November 1991): 281–86 (in Japanese).

activists of the branch and the sub-branches; from the 'Aisyiyah circles, Ibu Ummah and Ibu Nilawati, and the branch officers and activists; among the Muhammadiyah schools, Pak Sutrisno of SMK 3, Pak Selamet Fauzin of SMP 4, and the teachers of SMA 7 including its "old-hand", Pak Wahzary Wardoyo, and the teachers of SD Bodon; Andhi Kurniawan, a young Muhammadiyah activist, who helped me as research assistant during my last revisit earns special thanks of mine. A PAN politician from Kotagede, Pak Arief Noor Hartanto, was instrumental in acquainting me with the City and Provincial governments of Yogyakarta.

Outside the Muhammadiyah of Kotagede, I would like to thank the following institutions and individuals for their kind cooperation and assistance: The Offices of Kecamatan and KUA Kotagede, Kl. Rejowinagun, Kl. Prenggan, and Kl. Purbayan; the Office of Desa Jagalan; K.H. Abdul Muhaimin of Pondok Pesantren Nurul Ummahat, Pak Rudy Pesik of Rumah Pesik, Pak Muhadjir Darwin and Pak Pande of the UGM, Pak Habib Chirzin of AMAN, and Pak Koesnaeni and his wife, Machiko-san, of Jakarta.

I am also deeply honoured and grateful to have a foreword from Professor Merle C. Ricklefs, undoubtedly the most authoritative historian of modern Indonesia, to this book — an attempt at micro-history and ethnographic sketches of the Muhammadiyah movement in Kotagede over the past one hundred years.

Last but not least, I express my apologies and appreciation for the trust and forbearance given to me by Mrs Triena Ong and Ms Rahilah Yusuf of the Publications Unit of the Institute of Southeast Asian Studies, Singapore. They have waited warmly for the slow progress of my work in revising and enlarging my old "Banyan Tree" book into the present shape.

Mitsuo Nakamura
Ito, Japan
March 2011

BIBLIOGRAPHY

Aardrijskundig. *Aardrijkskundig en statistisch woordenboek van Nederlandsch Indie.* Amsterdam, 1869.

Abdurrahman Wahid. *Bunga Rampai Pesantren: Kumpulan Karya Tulis Abdurrahman Wahid.* Jakarta: Dharma Bhakti, 1979.

———. "Foreword". In *Divorce in Java: A Study of the Dissolution of Marriage among Javanese Muslims,* by Hisako Nakamura. Yogyakarta: Gadjah Mada University Press, 1983.

Adam. L. "Geschiedkundige anteekeningen omtrent de Residentie Madioen, IV. Restanten van Kalangs". *Djawa* XVIII (1938): 103–107.

Agus Suryantoro. "Kilas balik Kotagede 1992" [A flashback on Kotagede 1992]. *Brosur Lebaran,* no. 30, 1412H/1992M, pp. 28–32.

Ajip Rosidi. "Snouck Hurgronje dan H. Hasan Mustapha". *KOMPAS,* 22 October 2004.

Akhid Widi Rahmanto. "Opini dan harapan kinerja Pimpinan Cabang Muhammadiyah Kotagede" [Opinions and hopes for the performance of Muhammadiyah branch leadership of Kotagede]. *Brosur Lebaran,* No. 39, 1421H/2000M, pp. 51–52.

Alfian. "Islamic Modernism in Indonesian Politics: The Muhammadijah Movement during the Dutch Period (1912–1942)". Unpublished Ph.D. dissertation, University of Wisconsin, 1969.

———. *Muhammadiyah: The Political Behaviour of a Muslim Modernist Organization under Dutch Colonialism.* Yogyakarta: Gadjah Mada University Press, 1989.

Amir Hamzah Wirjosukarto. *Pembaharuan pendidikan dan pengadjaran Islam jang diselenggarakan oleh pergerakan Muhammadijah.* Jogjakarta, 1962.

Anderson, Benedict R.O'G. *Mythology and the Tolerance of the Javanese.* Ithaca: Modern Indonesia Project, Southeast Asia Program, Cornell University, 1965.

———. "The languages of Indonesian politics". *Indonesia,* No. 1 (April 1966): 89–116.

———. "The idea of power in Javanese culture". In *Culture and Politics in Indonesia,* edited by Claire Holt et al. Ithaca: Cornell University Press, 1972*a*.

———. *Java in a Time of Revolution: Occupation and Resistance 1944–1946.* Ithaca: Cornell University Press, 1972*b*.

Arberry, Arthur J. *The Koran Interpreted.* 2 vols. London: George Allen and Unwin, 1955.

As'ad Humam. "Pengajian Anak-Anak dan TKA-TPA: Lembaga Pendidikan Non-Formal Yang Sangat Vital Dalam Mengantarkan Anak Menuju Generasi Yang Islami" [Propagation for Children and Quar'anic Kindergarten and Qur'anic

Garden for Pupils: Non-Formal Educational Institution Vital for Leading Children to an Islamic Generation]. *Brosur Lebaran*, No. 33, 1415H/1995M, pp. 62–68.

———. *Buku Iqro': Cara Cepat Belajar Membaca Al-Qur'an* [Iqro' Book: Quick Method for Learning to Recite the Qur'an]. Kotagede: AMM, various years.

Bachrun Nawawi. "Masalah Sosial Kotagede dan Pemecahannya" [Social problems in Kotagede and their solutions]. *Brosur Lebaran*, No. 18, 1400H/1980M, pp. 37–43.

———. "Siapa mau jadi pembaharu?" [Who wants to become a reformer?]. *Brosur Lebaran*, No. 19, 1401H/1981M, pp. 61–65.

———. "Kepemimpinan yang perlu dibenahi" [Leadership that needs to be straightened up]. Interviewed by M. Setiawan and Hamid Nuri, written by Erwito Wibowo. *Brosur Lebaran*, No. 22, 1404H/1984M, pp. 17–18.

Bambang Sumantri, H. "Orsos Muhammadiyah" [The Muhammadiyah as Social Organization]. *Brosur Lebaran*, No. 46, 1428H/2007M, pp. 29–30.

Bani Mukmin (Descendants of Mukmin). *Silsilah Bani Mukmin dan Anggaran Rumah Tangga*. Kotagede, Jogjakarta, 1954.

Benda, Harry J. *The Crescent and the Rising Sun: Indonesian Islam under the Japanese Occupation, 1942–1945*. The Hague: W. van Hoeve, 1958.

———."Continuity and Change in Indonesia Islam". *Asian and African Studies* (Jerusalem) I (1965): 123–38.

———. "South-East Asian Islam in the Twentieth Century". In *The Cambridge History of Islam*, edited by P.M. Holt et al., vol. 2A, pp. 182–207. Cambridge: Cambridge University Press, 1970.

Berg, C.C. "Indonesia". In *Whither Islam? A Survey of Modern Movements in the Moslem World*, edited by H.R.A. Gibb, pp. 237–311. London: Victor Gollangz, 1932.

Bevervoorde, W.F. Engelbert van. "Monografie der Solosche Enclaves Pasargede en Imagiri". Unpublished manuscript, 1905.

Boland, B.J. *The Struggle of Islam in Modern Indonesia*. Verhandelingen van het Koninklijk Institute voor Taal-, Land- en Volkenkunde. No. 59. The Hague: Martinus Nijhoff, 1971.

Bousquet, G.H. *A French View of the Netherlands Indies*. London and New York: Oxford University Press, 1940.

Brosur Lebaran, No. 18, 1400H/1980M, p. 1.

———, No. 27, 1409H/1989M. "Senja di Kotagede Tenggara" [Sunset in Southeastern Kotagede], pp. 24–25.

———, No. 29, 1411H/1991M. "Diskontinuitas dan stagnasi: Cermin kemacetan kita dewasa ini" [Discontinuity and stagnation: Reflection of our stoppage at present time], p. 15.

———, No. 30, 1412 H/1992M. "Menyeret dakwah budaya, mengiring masyarakat modern" [Dragging in cultural propagation, joining modern society], pp. 38–41.

———, No. 30, 1412H/1992M. "Sosok, Badia'ah Mardi Siswoyo" [Figure of Badia'ah Mardi Siswoyo], pp. 46–48.

———, No. 38, 1420H/2000M. "Agenda Kotagede: Festival Kotagede '99" pp. 62–63.

———, No. 39, 1421H/2000M. "Sejarah PPHQ: Pusat Pengadaan Hewan Qurban AMM Kotagede" [History of PPHQ: Centre for the Provision of Sacrificial Animals, AMM, Kotagede], pp. 53–57.

———, No. 40, 1422H/2001H. "Membuka Frame Festival Kotagede di Tengah Polemik Pemikiran" [Opening the Frame of Festival Kotagede in the Midst of Polemic of Thoughts], pp. 29–39.

———, No. 43, 1425H/2004M. "Konsep Dakwah Kultural Muhammadiyah: Sebuah Tinjauan Wawasan" [The Muhammadiyah's Concept of Cultural Propagation: A Survey of Opinions], pp. 9–14.

———, No. 45, 1427H/2006M. "Recovery Pasca Gempa Bumi" [Post-Earthquake Recovery in Kotagede].

———, No. 45, 1427H/2006M. "Saatnya Untuk Tidak Tinggal Diam!" [It's time not to remain silent any longer!], pp. 26–29.

———, No. 45, 1427H/2006M. "Membangun Kembali Kotagede" [Rebuilding Kotagede], pp. 73–79.

———, No. 46, 1428H/2007M. "PPN 10% Mencekik Pengrajin Perak Kotagede" [10% Value added tax is choking the silver folk industry], pp. 22–26.

———, No. 47, 1429H/2008M. "Biografi: H. Bashori Anwar", pp. 60–67.

———, No. 48, 1430H/2009M. "Sekolah Muhammadiyah Mahal?" [Are the Muhammadiyah schools expensive?], pp. 13–24.

Buku Kenangan 50 Tahun Perkawinan H. Hajid Mutohar dan Hj. Umanah Rofi'i [Commemoration Book for the 50 years of marriage between H. Hajid Mutohar and Hj. Umanah Rofi'i], 22 Desember 1954 – 22 Desember 2004. Kotagede: UMAHA Family, [n.d.].

Burger. *The Structural Changes in Javanese Society: The Supra-Village Sphere.* Ithaca: Modern Indonesian Project, Southeast Asia Program, Cornell University, 1956.

Carey, Peter. "Javanese histories of Dipanegara: The Buku Kedhung Kebo, its authorship and historical importance". *Bijdragen tot de taal-, land- en volkenkunde, Koninklijk Institute voor Taal-, Land- en Volkenkunde*, vol. 130 (1974a): 259–88.

———. *The cultural ecology of early nineteenth century Java.* Occasional Paper No. 24. Singapore: Institute of Southeast Asian Studies, 1974b.

Castles, Lance. *Religion, Politics, and Economic Behavior in Java: The Kudus Cigarette Industry.* New Haven: Cultural Report Series No. 15, Southeast Asia Studies, Yale University. 1967.

Charris Zubair, Ahmad. "Tinjauan tentang nilai-nilai Islam dan *kejawen* sebagai sumber gagasan dari pola hidup sosio-filosofis masyarakat Kotagede". Skripsi Sarjana, Fakultas Filsafat, Universitas Gadjah Mada, Yogyakarta, 1979.

———. *Brosur Lebaran*, No. 18, 1400H/1980M, pp. 37–38.

———. "Filsafatnya orang Jawa di Kotagede" [Philosophy of Javanese People in Kotagede]. *Brosur Lebaran,* No. 19, 1401H/1981M, pp. 71–79.

———. "Catatan tentang masyarakat Kotagede" [Notes on Kotagede Society]. *Brosur Lebaran,* No. 21, 1403H/1983M, pp. 6–12.

———. "Kebudayaan dan kesenian dalam perspektif Islam". [Culture and Arts in Islamic Perspectives]. Paper presented at the National Meeting of Deliberation, Muhammadiyah XXXIII, Banda Aceh, 1995.

Darwis Khudori. "Kenapa mesti seni?" (Why should there be arts?). *Brosur Lebaran,* No. 16, 1398H/1978M, pp. 23–27.

———. *Brosur Lebaran,* No. 18, 1400H/1980M, pp. 32–36.

———. *Orang-Orang Kotagede.* Yogyakarta: Yayasan Bentang Budaya, 2000.

———. "Membangun Kembali Kotagede" [Building back Kotagede]. *Brosur Lebaran,* No. 45, 1427H/2006M, pp. 73–79.

Dawam Rahardjo, M. "Kehidupan pemuda santri: Penglihatan dari jendela pesantren di Pabelan". In *Pemuda dan Perubahan Sosial,* edited by Taufik Abdullah, pp. 90–112. Jakarta: LP3ES, 1974.

———, ed. *Pesantren dan Pembaharuan.* Jakarta: LP3ES, 1974.

Deliar Noer. "Masjumi: Its organization, ideology, and political role in Indonesia". M.A. thesis, Cornell University, 1960.

———. *The Modernist Muslim Movement in Indonesia, 1900–1942.* East Asian Historical Monographs. London and Kuala Lumpur: Oxford University Press, 1973.

Dewey, Alice G. *Peasant Marketing in Java.* New York: Free Press of Glencoe, 1962.

Dingemans, L.F. *Gegevens over Djokjakarta,* n.p. [Jogjakarta], 1925.

———. *Gegevens over Djokjakarta,* n.p. [Jogjakarta], 1926*a*.

———. *Gegevens over Djokjakarta,* n.p. [Jogjakarta], 1926*b*.

Drewes, G.W.J. "Indonesia: Mysticism and Activism". In *Unity and Variety in Muslim Civilization,* edited by G.E. von Grunebaum. Chichago: University of Chicago Press, 1955.

———. "New light on the coming of Islam to Indonesia". *Bijdragen tot de taal-, land- en volkenkunde, Koninklijk Institute voor Taal-, Land- en Volkenkunde,* vol. 122 (1966): 433–59.

———. "Javanese poems dealing with or attributed to the Saint Bonan". *Bijdragen tot de taal-, land- en volkenkunde, Koninklijk Institute voor Taal-, Land- en Volkenkunde,* vol. 124 (1968): 209–37.

———. *The Admonitions of Seh Bari. A 16th century Javanese Muslim text attributed to the Saint Bonan,* re-edited and translated with an introduction. Blibliotheca Indonesia, No. 4. Koninklijk Institute voor Taal-, Land- en Volkenkunde. The Hague: Martinus Nijhoff, 1969.

———. *An Early Javanese Code of Muslim Ethics.* Bibliotheca Indonesia, No. 18. Koninklijk Instituut voor Taal-, Land- en Volkenkunde. The Hague: Martinus Nijhoff, 1978.

Echols, John M. and Hassan Shadily. An *Indonesian-English Dictionary.* 2nd ed. Ithaca: Cornell University Press, 1963.

Edi Wahyono. "Tantangan Muhammadiyah Cabang Kotagede, lain dulu lain sekarang" [Challenges of Muhammadiyah Branch of Kotagede, different past and different present]. *Brosur Lebaran,* No. 22, 1404H/1984M, p. 16.

E.N.O.I. *Encyclopaedie van Nederlandsch Oost-Indie.* Leiden: Brill; The Hague: Martinus Nijhoff, 1917–39.

Encyclopaedia of Islam. Leiden: Brill; London: Luzac, 1934.

Erwito Wibowo. "Pasar Kotagede 1960–1965". *Brosur Lebaran,* No. 33, 1415H/1995M, pp. 122–30.

———. "Peta Potensi Seni Tradisional di Kotagede" [Map of Traditional Arts in Kotagede]. *Brosur Lebaran,* No. 38, 1420H/2000M, pp. 72–77.

———. "Kelompok Kesenian Srandul, Purba Budaya Bumen, Pimpinan Basis Hargito" [Srandul Art Group — Purba Budaya in Bumen under the leadership of Basis Hargito]. *Brosur Lebaran,* No. 39, 1421H/2000M, pp. 68–70.

———. "Profil Wayang Thinklung Ki Cermo Supardi Mujihartono, Kampung Karangduren" [Profile of Wayang Thingklung by Ki Cermo Supardi Mujihartono in Kampung Karangduren]. *Brosur Lebaran,* No. 39, 1421H/2000M, pp. 70–71.

———. "Kampung Wisata Muhammadiyah Kotagede: Sebuah Gagasan" [Muhammadiyah Neighborhood Tourism in Kotagede: An Idea]. *Brosur Lebaran,* No. 46, 1428H/2007M, pp. 82–85.

"Evaluasi [Evaluation]: PHQ Kotagede, Muhammadiyah Prenggan 2007", typescript, 2 January 2008.

Fakhruddin Hadi, ST. "Pusat Pengembangan Budaya Kotagede" [Centre for the Cultural Development of Kotagede]. Thesis submitted to the Department of Architecture, Faculty of Engineering, Gadjah Mada University, 2004.

———. "Tahun 2012 Ibukota Dunia Pindah ke Kotagede" [By 2012, World Capital Will Move to Kotagede]. *Brosur Lebaran,* No. 44, 1426H/2005M, pp. 112–15.

Faried Ma'ruf, H.M. "Analisa achlaq dalam perkembangan Muharnmadijah". *Almanak Muhammadijah,* ke-XXII (1381/1382H; 1961/62M): 5–23.

Fathurahman, M. "Smurawtnya lalulintas di Kotagede" [Traffic congestions in Kotagede]. *Brosur Lebaran,* no. 43, 1425H/2004M, p. 3.

Federspiel, Howard M. *Persatuan Islam: Islamic Reform in Twentieth Century Indonesia.* Ithaca: Modern Indonesia Project, Southeast Asia Program, Cornell University, 1970.

Geertz, Clifford. *The Social Context of Economic Change: An Indonesian Case Study.* Center for International Studies, Massachusetts Institute of Technology, 1956.

———. *The Religion of Java.* New York: Free Press of Glencoe, 1960.

———. *Peddlers and Princes: Social Change and Economic Modernization in Two Indonesian Towns.* Chicago: University of Chicago Press, 1963*a*.

———. *Agricultural Involution: The Process of Ecological Change in Indonesia.* Berkeley: University of California Press, 1963*b*.

———. *The Social History of an Indonesian Town.* Cambridge, MA: M.I.T. Press, 1965.

———. "Religion as a cultural system". In *Anthropological Approaches to the Study of Religion,* edited by Michael Banton. ASA Monograph No. 3, pp. 1–46. London: Tavistock, 1966.

———. *Islam Observed: Religious Development in Morocco and Indonesia.* New Haven: Yale University Press, 1968.

Geertz, Hildred. *The Javanese Family: A Study of Kinship and Socialization.* New York: Free Press of Glencoe, 1961.

Graaf, H.J., de. *De regering van Panembahan Senapati Ingalaga.* Verhandelingen van het Koninklijk Instituut voor Taal-, Land-en Volkenkunde. Deel XIII. The Hague: Martinus Nijhoff, 1954.

———. *De regering van Sultan Agung, Vorst van Mataram 1646–1677.* Verhandelingen van het Koninklijk Institute voor Taal-Land-en Volkenkunde. Deel XXXIII. The Hague: Martinus Nijhoff, 1958.

———. *De regering van Sunan Mangku-Rat I Tagal-Wangi, Vorst van Mataram 1646–1677.* Verhandelingen van het Koninklijk Instituut voor Taal-, Land-en Volkenkunde. Deel XXXIII. The Hague: Martinus Nijhoff, 1961.

———. *De regering van Sunan Mangku-Rat I Tegal-Wangi, Vorst van Mataram 1646–1677. II. Opstand en Ondergang.* Verhandelingen van het Koninklijk Institute voor Taal-, Land-en Volkenkunde. Deel XXXIX. The Hague: Martinus Nijhoff, 1962.

———. "South-East Asian Islam to the Sixteenth Century". In *The Cambridge History of Islam,* edited by P.M. Holt et al., vol. 2A, pp. 123–54. Cambridge: Cambridge University Press, 1970.

Groneman, J. *De Garebeg te Ngajogjakarta.* Koninklijke Institute voor de Taal-, Land-en Volkenkunde van Nederlandsch-Indie. The Hague: Martinus Nijhoff, 1895.

Habib Chirzin. "Meng-Khoirokan Ummat di Kotagede melalui Muhammadiyah". *Brosur Lebaran,* No. 12, 1394H/1974M, pp. 23–25, 41–43.

———. "Brosur, Kenangan dan Harapan" [Brochure, memories and hopes]. *Brosur Lebaran,* No. 25, 1407H/1987M, pp. 47–50.

Harahap, Parada. *Indonesia Sekarang.* Djakarta: Bulan Bintang, 1952.

Hardjono, S.K. "Perkembangan Muhammadijah di Kotagede". *Brosur Lebaran,* 1389H/1969M, pp. 27–30.

Harsya, Bachtiar. "The Religion of Java: A commentary". *Majalah Ilmu-Ilmu Sastra Indonesia* V (January 1973): 48–85.

Hazim Abdullah Umar, M. "Kedudukan dan peranan 'Kaum rois' di masyarakat Kecamatan Pleret Kabupaten Bantul". Skripsi Sarjana Ilmu Ushuluddin, Fakultas Ushuluddin, Institut Agama Islam Negeri, Sunan Kalijaga, Yogyakarta, 1977.

Hoesein Djajadiningrat, P.A. "Islam in Indonesia". In *Islam, the Straight Path: Islam interpreted by Muslims,* edited by Kenneth W. Morgan. New York: The Ronald Press. 1958.

Indonesia, Kementerian Penerangan. *Republik Indonesia, Daerah Istimewa Jogjakarta.* Djakarta, n.d. [1953–54].

Jadul Maula, M. *Ngesuhi Deso Sak Kukuban.* Yogyakarya: LKiS, 2001.

———. "The Moving Equilibrium: Kultur Jawa, Muhammadiyah, Buruh Gugat di dalam Festival Kotagede 2000" [The Moving Equilibrium: Javanese Culture, Muhammadiyah and Workers' Demand in Festival Kotagede 2000], pp. 3–39. In *Ngesuhi Deso Sak Kukuban,* by M. Jadul Maula. Yogyakarya: LKiS, 2001.

Jay, Robert R. *Religion and Politics in Rural Central Java.* Cultural Report Series No. 12. New Haven: Southeast Asia Studies, Yale University, 1963.

Jazir Asp. See Yazir.

Johns, A.H. *The Gift Addressed to the Spirit of the Prophet.* Canberra: The Australian National University, 1965.

———. "Islam in Southeast Asia: Reflections and new directions". *Indonesia,* No. 19 (April 1975): 33–56.

———. "From coastal settlement to Islamic school and city: Islamization in Sumatra, the Malay Peninsula and Java". In *Indonesia: The Making of a Culture,* edited by James J. Fox, pp. 163–82. Canberra: Research School of Pacific Studies, The Australian Natinonal University, 1980.

Junus Anis, M. *Riwayat Hidup K.H.A. Dahlan dan Perjuangannya.* Yogyakarta: Pusat Pimpinan Muhammadijah, 1962.

Junus, Mahmud. *Sedjarah Pendidikan Islam di Indonesia.* Jakarta: Pustaka Muhammadijah, 1960.

Kang Iping. "Trah Bani Fesbuk" [Facebook Kinship]. *Brosur Lebaran,* No. 48, 1430H/2009M, pp. 47–48.

Kat Angelino, P., de. *Batikrapport.* 3 vols. Publicatie No. 6 van het Kantoor van Arbeid. Weltvreden: Landsdrukkerij, 1930.

Kedaulatan Rakyat [Rakjat]. Daily newspaper. Yogyakarta.

Kessler, Clive S. "Islam, society and political behaviour: Some comparative implications of the Malay case". *British Journal of Sociology* XXIII, No. 1 (March 1972): 33–50.

Khadi Raharjo. "Kegiatan apresiasi seni dan hubunganya dengan seni drama" [Activities appreciating arts and their relationship with drama]. *Brosur Lebaran,* No. 15, 1397H/1977M, pp. 30–34, 53–56.

Khoiruddin Bashori. "Manajemen Perubahan di Kotagede" [Management of Changes in Kotagede]. *Brosur Lebaran,* No. 29, 1411H/1991M, pp. 27–29.

Koentjaraningrat, R.M. "The Javanese of South Central Java". In *Social Structure in Southeast Asia,* edited by George Peter Murdock, pp. 88–115. Viking Fund Publications in Anthropology. Chicago: Quadrangle, 1960.

———, ed. *Villages in Indonesia.* Ithaca: Cornell University Press, 1967.

Koloniale Tentoonstelling Semarang. 2 vols. Semarang, n.d. [1914?].

Kumar, Ann. "Dipanegara (1787?–1855)". *Indonesia,* No. 13 (April 1972), pp. 69–118.

———. "Javanese court society and politics in the late eighteenth century: The record of a lady soldier. Part I: The religious, social, and economic life of the court". *Indonesia,* No. 29 (April 1980*a*), pp. 1–46.

———. "Javanese court society and politics in the late eighteenth century: The record of a lady soldier. Part II: Political developments: The courts and the company, 1784–1791". *Indonesia,* No. 30 (October 1980*b*).

Kusudyarsono. "The royal cemetery in Kotagede". *Welcome to Jogja,* vol. 1, no. 7 (October 1970).

Kwantes, R.C., ed. *De ontwikkeling van de nationalistische beweging in Nederlandsch-Indie.* (Estestuk, 1912-medio 1923). Groningen: H.D. Tjeenk Willink, 1975.

"Laporan Keuangan Pimpinan Cabang Muhammadiyah" [Financial Report of the Branch Leadership of Muhammadiayah], August 2006–February 2007.

"Lapuran Tahunan 2006 KP3Y (Koperasi Produksi Pengusaha Perak Yogyakarta)" [2006 Annual Report of KP3Y (Production Cooperative of Silverwork Enterprises, Yogyakarta)].

Legge, John D. *Indonesia.* 3rd ed. Sydney: Prentice-Hall of Australia, 1980.

Lev, Daniel S. *Islamic Courts In Indonesia: A Study in the Political Bases of Islamic Institutions.* Berkeley: University of California Press, 1972.

Lewis, Oscar. *Five Families: Mexican Case Studies in the Culture of Poverty.* New York: Basic Books, 1959.

Majul, C.A. "The divine-human encounter in Islam". Unpublished manuscript. Ithaca, 1974.

Mailrapport. (Report to the Governor-General of the Netherland East Indies.)

Mahfoeld, M.A. "Islam dan politiek peperintahan negeri". *Almanak Moehammadijah,* Tahoen Hidjrah 1352, Bagian Taman Poestaka, Pengoeroes Besar Moehammadijah, Djokjakarta, 1933, pp. 123–48.

Mansoer, K.H. Mas. "Kjahi Hadji Ahmad Dahlan" (disoesoen oleh Anwar Rasjid). *Adil,* No. 3, September1938.

———. *Risalah Tauhid dan Sjirik.* Peneleh: Surabaja, n.d.

Martohastono, R.L. *Riwajat Pasarejan Mataram.* Kotagede, Djogjakarta, n.d. [195?].

Masa Kini. Daily newspaper. Yogyakarta.

Masayu Nurul Ana. "Ziarah dalam Kebudayaan Jawa: Ziarah di Kompleks Makam Raja-Raja Mataram, Kotagede, Yogyakarta" [Pilgrimage in Javanese Culture: Pilgrimage to Mataram Royal Cemetery Complex in Kotagede, Yogyakarta]. *Sarjana* thesis, Faculty of Cultural Science, Gadjah Mada University, 2002.

McVey, Ruth T. *The Rise of Indonesian Communism.* Ithaca: Cornell University Press, 1965.

———."Islam explained: Review article". *Pacific Affairs,* vol. 54 (Summer 1981): 260–87.

Mertju Suar. Daily newspaper. Yogyakarta.

Milone, Pauline Dublin. *Urban Areas in Indonesia: Administrative and Census Concepts.* Research Series, No. 10. Institute of International Studies. Berkeley: University of California, 1966.

Moertono, Soemarsaid. *State and Statecraft in Old Java: A Study of the Later Mataram Period; 16th to 19th Century*. Ithaca: Modern Indonesia Project, Southeast Asia Program, Cornell University, 1968.
Monografi Desa Jagalan 2007.
Monografi Kecamatan Kotagede 2000.
Monografi Kecamatan Kotagede 2007.
Monografi Kelurahan Prenggan 2007.
Mook, H.J., van. "Koeta Gede". *Koloniaal Tijdschrift* XV (1926*a*): 353–400.
———. "Nieuw Koeta Gede". *Koloniaal Tijdschrift* XV (1926*b*): 561–603.
———. "Kuta Gede". In *The Indonesian Town: Studies in Urban Sociology*, edited by W.F. Wertheim, pp. 275–331. The Hague: W. van Hoeve, 1958.
———. *Kuta Gede*. Diterdjemahkan dengan pengawasan Dewan Redaksi dengan kata pengantar oleh Harsja W. Bachtiar. Djakarta: Bhratara, 1972. [Indonesian translation of van Mook 1926*a*].
Mortimer, Rex. *Indonesia Communism under Sukarno: Ideology and Politics, 1959-1965*. Ithaca: Cornell University Press, 1974.
Muhadjir Darwin. *Negara dan Perumpuan: Reorientasi Kebijakan Publik* [The State and Women: Reorientation of Public Policy]. Yogyakarta: Media Wacana, 2005.
———. "Korban Sosial Sebagai Nilai Budaya Baru Untuk Mengatasi Problema Bangsa" [Social Sacrifice as a new cultural value to overcome naitonal problems]. Khutbah Idul Adha 10 Dzulhijah 1428 Hijiriyah. [Idul Adha Sermon, 2007].
———. "Dinamika Kultur Urban Kotagede: Islamisasi vs. Jawanisasi" [Cultural Dynamics in Urban Kotagede: Islamization vs. Javanization]. *Brosur Lebaran*, No. 46, 1428H/2007M, pp. 41–44.
Muhammad Kamal Hassan. *Muslim Intellectual Responses to "New Order" Modernization of Indonesia*. Kuala Lumpur: Dewan Bahasa dan Pustaka, Kementerian Pengajaran Malaysia, 1980.
Muhammadiyah [Moehammadijah]. *Verslag Moehammadijah di Hindia-Timoer*. Tahun Ke X (Januari-Desember). Djokjakarta: Pengoeroes Besar Moehammadijah, 1923.
———. *Peringatan Congres Moehammadijah Ke XXI*. [Jogjakarta]: Hoofdbestuur Moehammadijah Hindia-Timoer, 1932.
———. *Almanak Moehamadijah Ke X* (Tahoen Hidjrah 1352). Djokjakarta: Pengoeroes Besar Moehammadijah, Bahagian Taman Poestaka, 1933/34.
———. *Boeah Congres Moehammadijah Seperempat Abad*. Djokjakarta: Hoffdcomite Congres Moehammadijah, 1936.
———. *Boeah Congres Akbar Moehammadijah*. Djokjakarta: Hoofdcomite Congres, 1937.
———. *Boeah Congres Akbar Moehammadijah*. Djokjakarta: Hoofdcomite Congres, 1938*a*.
———. *Statuten dan Qa'idah Moehammadijah* (Lampiran Boekoe Congres Ke-23 [1935]). Djokjakarta: Hoofdcomite Congres Moehammadijah, 1938*b*.

―――. *Buku Peringatan 40th Muhammadijah.* Pusat Panitia Perajaan 40 tahun berdirinya Perserikatan Muhammadijah, Djakarta, 1952*a*.

―――. *Suara Muhammadijah* (Mendjelang Peringatan 40 Tahun Muhammadijah) XXXIII, no. 27 (November1952*b*).

―――. *Buah Keputusan Mu'tamar Muhammdijah Ke-34 di Djokjakarta.* Panitia Mu'tamar Muhammadijah ke-34, Djokjakarta, 1960.

―――. *Almanak Muhammadijah,* Ke-XXI, 1380/1H, 1960/61.

―――. *Almanak Muhammadijah,* Ke-XXII, 1381H, 1961/62.

―――. *Pemberesan dan Penjelesaian: Mu'tamar Muhammadijah Ke-35 Setengah Abad di Djakarta.* Jogjakarta: Panitia Pusat Mu'tamar Muhammadijah, 1962.

―――. *Muhammadijah Membangun: Prasaran dalam Mu'tamar Muhammadijah Ke-36 di Bandung.* Jogjakarta: Pimpinan Pusat Muhammadijah, 1965.

―――. *Anggaran Dasar dan Anggaran Rumah Tangga Muhammadijah* (Keputusan Sidang Tanwir 1966 di Bandung dan Keputusan Sidang Tanwir 1967 di Jogjakarta). Jogjakarta: Pimpinan Pusat Muhammadijah, 1967.

―――. *A Shorter Introduction to Muhammadijah.* Jakarta and Yogyakarta: Central Leadership of Muhammadiyah, 1979.

Mukti Ali, Abdul. "The Muhammadijah movement: A bibliographical introduction". M.A. thesis, McGill University, 1957.

Mulder, N. *Mysticism and Everyday Life in Contemporary Java: Cultural persistance and Change.* Singapore: University of Singapore Press, 1978.

Mustofa W. Hasyim. "Menangkapi suasana kesenian di Kotagede" [Grasping cultural atmosphere of Kotagede]. *Brosur Lenaran,* No. 18, 1396H/1980M, pp. 32–36.

―――. "Diskontinuitas dan stagnasi seharusnya tidak perlu terjadi" [Discontinuity and stagnation does not have to happen]. *Brosur Lebaran,* No. 29, 1411H/1991M, p. 12.

―――. "Interogasi". In *Bayi-Bayi Bersayap.* Jakarta: Progres, 2003.

Nagazumi, Akira. *The Origin and the Earlier Years of the Budi Utomo, 1908–1918.* Tokyo: Institute of Developing Economies, 1972.

Nakamura, Hisako. "A study of the dissolution of marriage among Javanese Muslims". M.A. thesis, The Australian National University, Canberra, 1981.

―――. "Divorce Counseling at BP4". In *Divorce in Java: A Study of the Dissolution of Marriage among Javanese Muslims,* pp. 82–94. Yogyakarta: Gadjah Mada University Press, 1983.

Nakamura, Mitsuo. "Masalah Gerakan Islam di Kotagede". *Brosur Lebaran,* No. 9, 1391H/1971M, 1971, pp. 51–57.

―――. "Professor Haji [Abdul] Kahar Muzakkir and the development of the Muslim reformist movement in Indonesia". In *Religion and Social Ethos in Indonesia,* edited by Benedict R.O'G Anderson, Mitsuo Nakamura, and Mohammad Slamet, pp. 1–20. Melbourne: Centre of Southeast Asian Studies, Monash University, 1977.

―――. "The reformist ideology of the Muhammadiyah". In *Indonesia: The Making of a Culture,* edited by James J. Fox, pp. 273–86. Canberra: Research School of Pacific Studies, The Australian National University, 1980.

———. "Sufi Elements in Muhammadiyah? Notes from Field Observation". *Prisma* IX, no. 8 (1980). LP3ES, 1980

———. "The radical traditionalism of the Nahdlatul Ulama in Indonesia: A personal account of its 26th national congress, June 1979, Semarang". *Tonan Ajia Kenkyu* (Southeast Asian Studies), vol. 19, no. 2 (September 1981), The Center for Southeast Asian Studies, Kyoto University, pp. 187–204.

———. *Bulan Sabit Muncul dari Balik Pohon Bringin: Studi tentang Pergerakan Muhammadiyah di Kotagede, Yogyakarta,* translated by Yusron Asrofie. Yogyakarta: Gadjah Mada University Press, 1983.

———. "The Cultural and Religious Identity of Javanese Muslims: The Case of Muhammadiyah". *Prisma,* no. 31 (Jakarta: LP3ES, 1984).

———. "Koko Tsuiso" [Memory of Koko]. *Nampo-Bunka* (Tenri Bulletin of South Asian Studies), Tenri Nampo Bunka Kenkyukai, Vol. 18 (November 1991): 281–86 (in Japanese).

———. "Muhammadiyah faces the challenge of democracy". In *Muhammadiyah Menjemput Perubahan* [Muhammadiyah faces change], edited by Mukhaer Pakkanna and Nur Achmad. Jakarta: P3SE STIE Ahmad Dahlan & Penerbit Buku Kompas, 2005.

Nasery Basral, Akmal. *Sang Pencerah* [The Enlightener]. Jakarta: Mizan Pustaka, 2010.

Nawawi Daman, Mo. *Riwajat Mesdjid Perak Kotagede.* Kotagede: Muhammadijah Bagian Tabligh, 1957.

Nishihara, Masashi. *Golkar and the Indonesian Elections of 1971.* Ithaca: Modern Indonesian Project, Southeast Asia Program, Cornell University. 1972.

Nizar Chirzin, Muhammad. "Biography K.H. Amir". *Brosur Lebaran,* No. 7, 1389H/1969M, pp. 14–19.

Nur Cahyati Wahyuni. "'Kotagede Ewuh': Festival Kotagede dan Identitas Kultural" ['Kotagede Prepares a Party', Festival Kotagede and Cultural Identity]. *Sarjana* thesis in anthropology, Faculty of Cultural Studies, Gadjah Mada University, 2005.

O'Malley, William J. "Indonesia in the Great Depression: A study of East Sumatra and Jogjakarta in the 1930s". Unpublished Ph.D. dissertation, Cornell University, 1977.

Osamu Shudan Shireibu. *Zen Jawa Kaikyo Jokyo Chosasho.* Djakarta: Gunseikanbu, 1943.

Palmier, Leslie H. "Modern Islam in Indonesia: The Muhammadiyah after Independence". *Pacific Affairs* XXVII, no. 3 (September 1954): 255–63.

Peacock, James L. *Purifying the Faith: The Muhammadiyah Movement in Indonesian Islam.* Menlo Park, California: Benjamin/ Cummings, 1978*a*.

———. *Muslim Puritans: Reformist Psychology in Southeast Asian Islam.* Berkeley: University of California Press, 1978*b*.

Penny, D.H. and M. Singarimbun. *Population and Poverty in Rural Java: Some Economic Arithmetics from Srihardjo*. Ithaca: Dept of Agricultural Economics, Cornell University, 1973.

Pigeaud, Theodore G.Th. "Vorstenlandsche Garebeg's". *Djawa,* vol. 12, no. 1, (1932): 24–31.

———. *Javaans-NederlandsHandwoordenboek*. Groningen and Batavia: Wolters, 1938.

——— and H.J. de Graaf. *Islamic States in Java 1500–1700*. Eight Dutch books and articles by Dr. H.J. de Graaf as summarized by Theodore G.Th. Pigeaud. Verhandelingen van het Koninklijk Institut voor Taal-, Land- en Volkenkunde, no. 70. The Hague: Martinus Nijhoff, 1976.

Pijper, G.F. *Studien over de geschiedenis van de Islam in Indonesia 1900–1950*. Leiden: Brill, 1977.

Pranoto Hadi. "Spintas tentang ekologi sosial di Kotagede" [Briefing on social ecology of Kotagede]. *Brosur Lebaran,* no. 17, 1399H/1979M, pp. 34–35, 50.

Price, Susan K. "Pekajangan: Religion, textile production and social organization in a Javanese village". M.A. thesis, The Australian National University, Canberra, 1977.

Pringgodigdo, A.K. *Sedjarah Pergerakan Rakjat Indonesia*. 3rd ed. Jakarta: Pustaka Rakyat, 1950.

Profil Sekolah [Profile of School]: *SD Muhammadiyah Bodon*. Bodon: Jagalan, Banguntapan, Bantul, n.d. [2004?].

Proposal Pengembangan Gedung Baru [Proposal for the construction of New Building]. SMK Muhammadiyah 3 Yogyakarta, n.d. [2007].

Raffles, Sir Thomas Stamford. *The History of Java,* with an Introduction by John Bastin. Kuala Lumpur and New York: Oxford University Press, 1817 [1965].

Rasjidi, H.M. *Islam dan Kebatinan*. Jakarta: Bulan Bintang, 1967.

———. *Mengapa Aku Tetap Memeluk Agama Islam*. Jakarta: Hudaya, 1968.

Revianto Budi Santosa. *Kotagede: Life between Walls*. Photography by Bambang Tri Atmojo. Jakarta: PT Gramedia Pustaka Utama, 2007.

Ricklefs, Merle Calvin. *Jogjakarta under Sultan Mangkubumi, 1749–1792: A History of the Division of Java*. London: Oxford University Press, 1974*a*.

———. "Dipanegara's early inspirational experience". *Bijdragen tot de taal-, landen volkenkunde, Koninklijk Institute voor Taal-, Land- en Volkenkunde,* vol. 130 (1974*b*): 227–58.

———. "Six centuries of Islamization in Java". In *Conversion to Islam,* edited by Nehemia Levtzion, pp. 100–28. New York and London: Holms and Meier, 1979.

———. *Polarising Javanese Society: Islamic and Other Visions c. 1830–1930*. Singapore: Singapore University Press; Honolulu: University of Hawai'i Press; Leiden: KITLV Press, 2007.

———. *Islamisation and Its Opponents in Java: A Political, Social, Cultural and Religious History, c. 1930 to the Present*. Singapore: NUS Press; Honolulu: University of Hawai'i Press, 2012.

Robson, S.O. "Java at the crossroads: Aspects of Javanese cultural history in the 14th and 15th centuries". *Bijdragen tot de taal-, land- en volkenkunde, Koninklijk Institute voor Taal-, Land- en Volkenkunde,* vol. 137 (1981): 259–92.
Roff, William R. *The Origins of Malay Nationalism.* New Haven: Yale University Press, 1967.
———. "Indonesian and Malay students in Cairo in the 1920s". *Indonesia,* no. 9 (April 1970*a*): 73–87.
———. "South-East Asian Islam in the Nineteenth Century". In *The Cambridge History of Islam,* edited by P.M. Holt et al., vol. 2A, pp. 155–81. Cambridge: Cambridge University Press, 1970*b*.
Rouffaer, G.P. "Vorstenlanden". *Adatrechtbundels* XXXIV, serie C, no. 81 (1931[1905]).
Samson, Allan. "Islam in Indonesian Politics". *Asian Survey,* vol. 8, no. 13 (1968).
Samudja Asjari. *Kedudukan Kjaji di Pondok Pesantren.* Skripsi Sardjana, Fakultas Sastra dan Budaya, Universitas Gadjah Mada, Yogyakarta, 1967.
Sartono Kartodirdjo. *The Peasant's Revolt of Banten in 1888: Its Conditions, Course and Sequel. A Case Study of Social Movements in Indonesia.* [The Hague: Nederlandsch Boek-en Steen-drukkerij v/H Smits.] 1966.
———. "Agrarian radicalism in Java: Its setting and development". In *Culture and Politics in Indonesia,* edited by Claire Holt et al., pp. 71–125. Ithaca: Cornell University Press, 1972.
Schrieke, B. *Indonesian Sosciological Studies.* 2nd ed. 2 vols. The Hague: W. van Hoeve, 1966.
Selosoemardjan. *Social Changes in Jogjakarta.* Ithaca: Cornell University Press, 1962.
Setyobudi, I. "Dunya yang paradoks: Pandangan petani tentang posisi diri dalam tata ruang kota (Kasus Pilahan Lor di Kotagede, Yogyakarta)" [A paradoxical world: Farmers' view on themselves in an urban space — The case on North Pilahan, Kotagede Yogyakarta]. Faculty of Cultural Studies, Gadjah Mada University, 1997.
Siegel, James T. The Rope of God. Berkeley: University of California Press. 1969.
Sisten, Peter H.W. *Industrial Development of the Netherlands Indies.* Bulletin No. 2 of the Netherlands and Netherland Indies Council of the Institute of Pacific Relations. Director of Industrial Division, Dept of Economic Affairs, Batavia, n.d. [1942?].
Smith, Wilfred Cantwell. *Islam in Modern History.* Princeton: Princeton University Press, 1957.
Snouck Hurgronje, Christian. *Mekka in the Latter Part of the 19th Century: Daily Life, Customs and Learning of the Moslims of the East-Indian Archipelago,* translated by J.H. Monahan. Leiden: Brill, 1931.
Soebardi, S. "Santri religious elements in the Rook of Tjentini". *Bijdragen tot de taal-, land- en volkenkunde, Koninklijk Institute voor Taal-, Land- en Volkenkunde,* vol. 127 (1971): 331–50.

———. *The Book of Cabolek.* Bibliotheca Indoensia, no. 10, Koninklijk Instituut voor Taal-, Land- en Volkenkunde. The Hague: Martinus Nijhoff, 1975.

Soedjono Tirtokoesoemo, R. *De Garebegs in het Sultanaat Jogjakarta.* Jogjakarta: H. Buning, 1931.

Soejatno. "Revolution and social tensions in Surakarta 1945–1950", translated by Benedict Anderson. *Indonesia,* no. 17 (April 1974): 99–111.

Soemarsaid Moertono. *State and Statecraft in Old Java: A Study of the Later Mataram Period, 16th to 19th Century.* Ithaca: Modern Indonesia Project, Southeast Asia Program, Cornell University, 1981 [1968].

Soepomo Poedjosoedarmo. "Javanese speech levels". *Indonesia,* no. 6 (1968): 54–81.

Solichin Salam. *K.H. Ahmad Dahlan: Tjita-tjita dan Perdjuangannja.* Jakarta: Depot Pengadjaran Muhammadijah, 1962.

———. *K.H. Hasjim Asj'ari, Ulama Besar Indonesia.* Jakarta: Djajamurni, 1963*a.*

———. *K.H. Ahmad Dahlan, Reformer Islam Indonesia.* Jakarta: Djajamurni, 1963*b.*

———. *Muhammadijah dan Kebangunan Islam di Indonesia.* Jakarta: Mega, 1965.

———. *Muhammadijah di Pekadjangan.* Jakarta: Iqbal, 1968.

Sosrosoegondo, R. "Kjahi Hadji Achmad Dahlan. Bapa dan pendiri Muhammadijah". *Adil,* June–November 1938.

Sri Puji Lestari. "Taman Kanak-Kanak Islam Terpadu, Sebuah Pilihan: Studi Kasus di Taman Kanak-Kanak Islam Terpadu Kotagede Yogyakarta" [Integrally Islamic Kindergarten — An Alternative: Case Study at Integrally Islamic Kindergarten, Kotagede, Yogyakarta]. *Sarjana* thesis, Faculty of Cultural Sciences, Gadjah Mada University, 2003.

Statuten Centraale Paduinders Vereniging di Djokjakarta. Jogjakarta, 1921.

Statuten dan Qa'idah Moehammadijah (Lampiran Boekoe Congres Ke-23 [1935]). Djokjakarta: Hoofdcomite Congres Moehammadijah, 1938*b.*

Steenbrink, Karel Adriaan. "Pesantren, madrasah, sekolah: Recente ontwikkelingen in indonesisch islamonderricht". Doctoral dissertation. Katholieke Universiteit te Nijmegen, 1974.

Stutterheim, W.F. "De Kalangs op het spoor?". *Kofoniaal Tijdschrift* XXIV (1935): 97–105.

Sudjoko Prasodjo et al. *Profil Pesantren: Laporan Hasil Penelitian Pesantren Al-Falak dan Delapan Pesantren Lain di Bogor.* Jakarta: LP3ES, 1974.

Sugiyanto. "Angkatan Muda Merubah Pandangan" [The young generation changes its view]. *Brosur Lebaran,* No. 11, 1393H/1973M, pp. 13–17, 32–33.

Suranto Atmosaputro and Martin H. Hatch. "Serat Wedatama: A translation". *Indonesia,* no. 14 (October 1972): 157–81.

"Surat Keputusan Pimpinan Pusat Muhammadiyah, no. 149/KEP/I.O./B/2006" [Decision by the Central Leadership of Muhammadiyah].

Sutherland, Heather, "The Priyayi". *Indonesia,* no. 19 (April 1975): 57–78.

Syafi'i Maarif, Ahmad. "Agama dan Permasalahannya di Abad XXI (Sebuah Perspektif Islam)" [Religion and Its Problematics in the 21st Century (An Islamic Perspective)]. *Brosur Lebaran,* No. 30, 1942H/1992M, p. 22.

Syamsuhadi, B. "Berjuang melawan akhlak" [Struggle against character]. *Brosur Lebaran,* No. 22, 1404H/1984M, pp. 19–20.

Taufik Abdullah. *Schools and Politics: The Kaum Muda Movement in West Sumatra (1927–1933).* Ithaca: Modern Indonesia Project, Southeast Asia Program, Cornell University, 1971.

Tedjo Soesilo. "Perkembangan perusahaan perak di Kotagede". Skripsi Sardjana Fakultas Sastra dan Budaya, Universitas Gadjah Mada, Yogyakarta, 1970.

The Exquisite of MUTU: Sejarah SMP Muhammadiyah 7 Yogyakarta dari Masa ke Masa [The Exquisite fo MUTU: A History of SMP Muhammadiyah 7 Yogyakarta from Age to Age], n.d. [2005?].

Thoyibi, M., Yayah Khisbiyah and Abdullah Aly, eds. *Sinergi Agama & Budaya Lokal: Dialektika Muhammadiyah dan Seni Lokal* [Synergy of Religion and Local Culture: Dialectics between the Muhammadiyah and Local Culture]. Surakarta: Muhammadiyah University Press, 2003.

Turner, Victor. *The Forest of Symbols: Aspects of Ndembu Ritual.* Ithaca: Cornell University Press, 1967.

———. *The Ritual Process: Structure and Anti-Structure.* Chicago: Aldine, 1969.

———. *Dramas, Fields, and Metaphors: Symbolic Action in Human Society.* Ithaca and London: Cornell University Press, 1974.

van der Wal, S.L. *De opkomst van de nationalistische beweging in Nederlands-Indie.* Groningen: Wolters, 1967.

van Koningsveld, P. Sj. *Snouk Hurgronje dan Islam.* Jakarta: Girimukti Pusaka, 1989.

Van Niel, Robert. *The Emergence of the Modern Indonesian Elite.* The Hague and Bandung: W. van Hoeve, 1960.

Ward, K.E. *The Foundation of the Partai Muslimin Indonesia.* Ithaca: Modern Indonesia Project, Southeast Asia Program, Cornell University, 1970.

Wertheim, W.F., ed. *The Indonesian Town: Studies in Urban Sociology.* The Hague and Bandung: W. van Hoeve, 1958.

———. *Indonesian Society in Transition: A Study of Social Change.* 2nd and rev. ed. The Hague: W. van Hoeve, 1959.

Widjojo Nitisastro. *Population Trends in Indonesia.* Ithaca: Cornell University Press, 1970.

Yazir. "Aksi Bukan Program Pokok" [Action is not the principal programme]. *Brosur Lebaran,* No. 43, 1423H/2002M, pp. 19–22.

Zaini Ahmad Noeh, *Sebuah Perspektip Sejarah Lembaga Islam di Indonesia.* Bandung: Al-Ma'arif, 1980.

Zamakhsyari Dhofier. "The Pesantren Tradition: A Study of the Role of the Kyai in the Maintenance of the Traditional Ideology of Islam in Java". Unpublished Ph.D. dissertation, The Australian National University, Canberra, 1981.

GLOSSARY

abangan	literally, "red"; Javanese Muslim with syncretic beliefs, laxed in performing obligatory rituals; nominal Muslim
abdi dalem	royal servant, court official
abdi dalem jurukunci	court official in charge of upkeeping the Royal Cemetery complex in Kotagede (and elsewhere)
abdi dalem santri (putihan)	court religious official
adat	customs
akal	reason, rationality
akhérat	after-life
akhlak	moral character
alim	learned man in the Islamic teaching; singular of *ulama*
bakul	peddler
batik (bathik)	intricate wax-dyeing fabric
batin	inner self; internally
batos	Krama of *batin*
bekel	assistant to appanage holder *(patuh)*, tax collector
bid'a (bid'ah)	"innovation"; deviation from orthodoxy
buruh	semi-skilled or unskilled worker
dagang	trade; trader
dakwah (da'wah)	"invitation"; religious propagation, preaching
desa	rural village; rural
dhagelan	short comic with witty exchange of words, often with horseplay
dhalang	puppeteer of shadow play, *wayang*
dhukun	magical healer; diviner; medium
gadho-gadho	vegetable salad
gamelan	gong orchestra
gusti	Lord (capitalized for God, e.g. Gusti Allah = God, the Lord)
Hadith	records of the sayings and the deeds of the Prophet Muhammad; Traditions

Haji	title for a person who has performed the pilgrimage to Mecca; abbreviated as H.
hajj	pilgrimage to Mecca
halus (alus)	fine, refined, sophisticated; beautiful
hawa nafsu	lowly desire, lust
Idul Adha	annual festival of pilgrimage on the tenth day of the eleventh month of the Islamic calendar (Dulkijah); sacrificial animal (*Korban*) is slaughtered on this day (i.e., Hari Korban)
Idul Fitri	annual festival on the first day of the month of Syawal following the fasting month of Ramadhan; the biggest annual festival celebrated by Javanese Muslims; Lebaran
ijtihad	individual reasoning
ikhlas	pious, devoted to God; sincere
jaelangkung	straw man made of bamboo and kitchen utensils like rice scooper by which séance is performed
jathilan	dancing on two-dimensional horse figure often in trance
juragan	master of business firm or workshop
jurukunci	literally "key-keeper"; caretaker
kabupaten	regency
kalurahan (kelurahan)	administrative village; abbreviated as Kl.
kampung	urban neighbourhood or rural hamlet, abbreviated as Kp.
kasar	coarse, rude, unsophisticated; ugly
kasekten	mystical powers
kawula	slave, servant
kecamatan	sub-district
kejawen	Javanized syncretic Islam, Javanism
kemantren	old term for sub-district in the City of Yogyakarta; ward
kethoprak	folk drama popular in Central Java
ketib (khotib)	Friday sermon giver
khutbah	Friday sermon
Kl.	see *kalurahan*
korban	sacrifice, sacrificial animal
kota	town, city, urban
Kp.	see *kampung*

Krama	high speech level in Javanese
kramat	mystical powers; their locus, e.g., saint's grave
Kraton	court, royal palace
KUA	abbreviation of Kantor Urusan Agama, i.e., office of religious affairs
kuli kenceng	holder of house-compound (and farmland); villager with full rights and obligations
Kyai	title for learned man in Islam, *alim/ulama*, often the head of pondok pesantren; abbreviated as K.
lahir	external self; externally
langgar	prayer house for daily prayers
lungguh	appanage; office land for village official
lurah	chief; village chief
Masyumi (Masjumi)	abbreviation of Madjelis Sjuro Muslimin Indonesia Consultative Council of Indonesian Muslims, 1943–45; the so-named political party, 1945–60
masjid (mesjid)	mosque
Mu'allimat	Muhammadiyah's high school (for girls) for the training of religious teachers
Mu'allimin	Muhammadiyah's high school (for boys) for the training of religious teachers
muballigh	Islamic missionary, propagandist
musholla	prayer house
Nahdlatul Ulama	abbreviated as NU; "Renaissance of Ulama", association of Islamic scholars adhering to the four schools of Islamic jurisprudence — Shafi'is, Malikis, Hanbalis and Hanafis
Ngoko	low speech level in Javanese
NU	*see* Nahdlatul Ulama
pamrih	personal interest, egoism
PAN	Partai Amanat Nasional (National Mandate Party); formed in 1998, headed by Amein Rais and supported mostly by Muhammadiyah people
Parmusi	Partai Muslimin Indonesia (Indonesian Muslim Party); successor to Masyumi Party after its rehabilitation was blocked by Soeharto in 1968
pasar	market
Pasareyan	Royal Cemetery in Kotagede (and elsewhere)
patuh	appanage holder
PDI	Partai Demokrasi Indonesia (Indonesian Democratic

	Party); formed by the fusion of PNI, other secular nationalist parties, and Christian parties in 1973
PDIP	Partai Demokrasi Indonesia Perjuangan (Indonesian Democratic party of Struggle); successor to PDI under the leadership of Megawati Soekarnopoetri, daughter of Soekarno
pegawai	official; office worker
pegawai negeri	government official
pendhapa, pendopo	open reception hall in the traditional Javanese house plan
pengajian	learning the Qur'anic recitation; religious lecture; (*pengaosan* in Javanese Krama)
penghulu	head of religious officials at regency level
pesantren	Islamic school with fully boarding students (*santri*)
PKB	Partai Kebangkitan Bangsa (National Awakening Party); formed in 1998 by Abdurrahman Wahid (Gus Dur) and supported by the NU people
PKI	Partai Komunis Indonesia (Indonesian Communist Party)
PKS	Partai Keadilan Sejahtera (Prosperous Justice Party); formerly PK (Partai Keadilan, or Justice Party), formed in 1998 by Islamist *ulama* and activists
PKU (PKO)	Originally acronym for Penolong Kesengsaraan Umum (Oemum), meaning "relief of public suffering", a department in Muhammadiyah dedicated for social welfare and charitable activities, like clinics, hospitals, delivery houses, orphanages, houses for elder people and the poor, etc. Actual words for the acronym have changed over time; currently, PKU stands for Pembina Kesejahteraan Ummat (Service for Community Welfare)
PNI	Partai Nasional Indonesia (Indonesian Nationalist Party), constituency of Sukarno, fused into PDI in 1973
pondok	alternative or supplementary term for *pesantren* above, e.g., *pondok pesantren*
PPP	Partai Persatuan Pembangunan (United Development Party); formed by the fusion of all Islamic parties including NU Party and Parmusi in 1973
priyayi	aristocrat, court official

puasa	fasting
PUSKESMAS	Pusat Kesehatan Masyarakat, community health centre, government facility for public health and medical care set up at sub-district level
putihan	literally, "white"; pious Muslim, *santri*
R.K.	*see* Rukun Kampung
rukun Islam	five pillars of Muslim, i.e., Confession of Faith, daily prayers, fasting, payment of religious taxes, and pilgrimage to Mecca
Rukun Kampung	abbreviated as R.K.; neighbourhood association, lower semi-official unit of urban administration
santri	student in *pesantren*; pious Muslim
Sarekat Islam	abbreviated as S.I.; Islamic Union established in Surakarta in 1911
shalawatan	melodious prayers recited in group
SOBSI	Sentral Organisasi Buruh Seluruh Indonesia (All Indonesia Workers Organisation Centre); PKI-led federation of trade unions, banned after G30S/PKI Affairs in 1965
Syariah	Islamic law
tajdid	reform pursued by the Muhammadiyah movement
tarekat	Muslim devotional order, Sufi brotherhood
TBC	acronym for *takhayul, bid'ah,* and *churafat* [*khurafat*] (myths, deviant innovation, and superstition), one of the targets of Muhammadiyah's reform movement
tukang	craftsman, artisan
ulama	Islamic scholar or teacher; plural of *alim*
Ummat Islam	the community of the faithful; Muslim Community
wakaf (waqf)	permanent and irrevocable donation of properties (land, building, valuables including cash) for the benefit of the common good (*maslahah*) of Muslim community
wayang	puppet shadow play
wong cilik	"little people", common people
zakat	one of the five prescribed obligations of Muslims to pay "religious tax" due annually on 2.5 per cent of disposable income; currently a number of bodies including the LAZISMU of Muhammadiyh are legally authorized to collect zakat and utilize the funds for the common good (*maslahah*) of Muslim community

zakat fitrah — alms contributed by "able families" in the form of rice (2.5 kg of basic or principal food per member of family) on the eve of Idul Fitri and distributed directly to the poor and needy in the neighbourhood before the prayer of Idul Fitri is performed

APPENDICES

APPENDIX I

HOUSE-COMPOUND HOLDERS IN KOTAGEDE BY OCCUPATION AND VILLAGE (1922)

Occupation	Administrative Village (Kalurahan)									
	Prenggan		Basen		Sayangan[a]		Mutihan[b]		Total	
	N	%	N	%	N	%	N	%	N	%
I. "Royal servants"[c] Public offices and professions	27	8.5	15	7.3	34	9.1	15	8.5	91	8.5
Sub-total	27	8.5	15	7.3	34	9.1	15	8.5	91	8.5
II. "Wealthier inhabitants"[c]										
1. Wholesale trade in cloth, etc.	61	19.1	15	7.3	43	11.4	1	0.6	120	11.2
2. Trade in working of precious metals and jewelry	56	17.5	7	3.5	25	6.7	3	1.7	91	8.5
Sub-total	117	36.6	22	10.8	68	18.1	4	2.3	211	19.7
III. "Craftsmen and lesser traders"[c]										
1. Batik-making, cloth-dying, cloth-printing	58	18.2	40	19.6	100	26.7	22	12.6	220	20.5
2. Copper and brass-working	46	14.4	23	11.3	35	9.3	12	6.9	116	10.8
3. Various handicrafts (smiths, carpenters, horn-workers, tailors, brick-makers, etc.)	20	6.3	67	32.8	46	12.3	17	9.7	150	14.0
4. Retail and *toko* trade[d]	14	4.4	24	11.8	57	15.2	13	7.4	108	10.0
5. Trade in foodstuffs	28	8.8	9	4.4	33	8.8	14	8.0	84	7.8
Sub-total	166	52.1	163	79.9	271	72.3	78	44.6	678	63.1
IV. "Day-labourers and peasants"[c]										
1. Agriculture	1	0.3	2	1.0	—	—	73	41.7	76	7.1
2. Unskilled labour	8	2.5	2	1.0	2	0.5	5	2.9	17	1.6
Sub-total	9	2.8	4	2.0	2	0.5	78	44.6	93	8.7
TOTAL	319	100.0	204	100.0	375	100.0	175	100.0	1,073	100.0

Notes:
(a) R.K. Alun-Alun at present (1972).
(b) R.K. Purbayan at present (1972).
(c) The wording of the four major categories follows van Mook's (1958).
(d) Small shops.
Source: van Mook (1926a, p. 363; 1958, p. 289).

APPENDIX II

OCCUPATION AND INCOME IN KOTAGEDE, 1972: A RESULT OF SAMPLE HOUSEHOLD SURVEY

In March–April 1972, with the help of four local assistants I administered an intensive survey of 60 households, a 2 per cent sample of the total households of 2,892 in the urban area of Kotagede. The area comprised of four Neighbourhood Associations (R.K.), Alun-Alun, Prenggan, Basen and Purbayan, all belonging to the Ward (Kemantren) of Kotagede Yoggyakarta, the City of Yogyakarta (Kota Madya Yogyakarta); a hamlet *(dukuh)* of Joyopranan belonging to the Village of Singosaren (Kl. Singosaren); and one entire administrative village of Kl. Jagalan, both belonging to the District of Kotagede Surakarta (Kecamatan Kotagede Surakarta) of the Regency of Bantul (Kabupaten Bantul) (see Figure 2.1).

Out of the 60 households *(rumah tangga)* selected randomly from the records of the 1972 national census, 56 households heads *(kepala somah)* were interviewed. The survey covered a number of items including household composition, occupation, education, language, religious and political affiliation, marital history, occupational history, property and income. A thorough statistical analysis of the survey results has yet to be done. But I have obtained a result of a preliminary analysis of the data concerning the occupation and income of the sample as follows:

OCCUPATIONAL COMPOSITION

The 56 sample households had 276 individuals in total, of whom 100 has cash-earnings occupations. The occupations of these cash-earners are categorized and corresponding figures obtained as follows:

Table App. II.1
Occupational Composition

Occupation	N	%
I. Professionals	10	10.0
II. Entrepreneurs	13	13.0
III. Craftsmen, small traders, workers	77	77.0
IV. Others	0	0
Total	100	100.0

The category of "professionals" included 2 active and 3 retired government officials *(pegawai negeri)*, 1 hamlet chief *(kepala dukuh)*, 2 teachers, and 2 private firm clerks *(pegawai swasta)*. In the category of "entrepreneurs", 6 were *pengusaha* (lit., entrepreneurs, i.e., factory or workshop owner/managers) and 7 *dagang* (large traders). In the third category, 18 were craftsmen and artisans *(tukang)*, of which silversmiths *(tukang perak)* were the largest group with 10 individuals. Small traders were 23 in total, including 18 peddlers *(bakul)* and 3 *warung* (small foodstall) keepers. Also in the third category there were 32 semi-skilled and unskilled workers *(buruh)*, in which 14 *penjahit* (lit., "sewers", or assistants to master tailors) formed the single largest group while the rest were mostly assistants to craftsmen/artisans. There were also 4 farm workers *(buruh tani)* in the third category, but in the entire sample there were no owner-farmers *(tani)* at all.

INCOME

The daily incomes of the 100 cash-earning individuals were distributed as follows:

Table App. II.2
Daily Cash Income

Income in rupiahs	N	%
50 and less	42	42.0
51–100	33	33.0
101–150	8	8.0
151–200	9	9.0
201 and more	6	6.0
No information	2	2.0
Total	100	100.0

At the time of the survey (March–April 1972), the price of medium quality rice *(beras)* at the Kotagede market ranged from Rp32 to Rp35 per kilogram, and the official exchange rate of Indonesian rupiah was Rp415 to US$1.

The percentage of the individuals whose daily cash income was less than 100 rupiahs amounted to 75 per cent of the total sample. The lowest cash earner was a bamboo artisan *(tukang bambu)* who earned only Rp10 a day. The highest daily income of Rp1,300 was made by a batik entrepreneur.

Statistically, the mean of the incomes for a cash-earning individual was Rp108 and the median Rp73 a day. Per household cash income including non-cash-earning members was Rp189 a day: an average household had 4.93 persons of whom 1.78 persons were cash-earning. Per capita cash income including non-cash-earning persons averaged at Rp38 a day, i.e., a little less than 10 cents in the U.S. dollar or rice equivalent of slightly more than 1 kilogram per person.

INDEX

A
abangan, xxxiv, xxviin, xxix, 14, 16–17, 46, 91, 102, 118n, 119, 148–51, 153, 169, 185, 198, 206–207, 331
abangan-santri-priyayi trichotomy, 148
abdi dalem, xxxiv, 15, 110, 113, 118, 133, 173
  jurukunci, 15, 17, 30, 33, 35, 61, 133
  karya, 40, 43
  putihan, 15
  santri, 15, 51–56
Abduh, Muhammad, xxv, 91
Abdul Aziz, K.H., 89
Abdul Kahar Mudzakkir, 40, 79–80, 92, 95–96, 123, 143, 356
Abdul Muhaimin, Haji, 237, 313
Abdul Mukti, K.H., 89
Abu Amar, K.H., 89
Achmad, Nur, 312n
Adam, L., 44n
adat, 39
  Islam, 35, 49, 90, 109, 118
  -*isti-adat,* 34, 37
adipati, 26
Administration, 10, 16n, 21, 26, 32, 47–49, 56, 133
  Dutch, 172
Administrative Kotagede, 221, 224
Administrative re-designation, 221–25
Administrative reforms, 11, 33, 45, 133, 282
  impact of, 46–50
Ahmad Dahlan, K.H. *See* Dahlan, Kyai Haji Ahmad

Ahmad Syafi'i Maarif (Buya Syafi'i), 312–13
'Aisyiyah, 176, 260, 264
  kindergarten, 290
  leaders, 287–90, personal background of, 300–301
akal, 152n
akhérat, 178–79, 201
akhlak, 180, 185, 188–89, 205
Al-Fatihah, 162, 177
Alfian, 5n, 52n, 67, 73n
Al-Huda Mosque, 256, 258
Al-Ikhlas, 198
alim, 79n, 83–84, 86–88, 91, 187
  see also *ulama*
Ali, Mukti, xxxvii
Alimin, 62, 75
Allah, 20, 27, 49, 54, 163n, 201
Allahu Akbar, 161–63
Alun-Alun, R.K., 22, 24, 28, 57, 84, 89–90, 117, 126, 135–36, 221, 256
  Lor, 31
  Utara, 281
alus vs. kasar, 186–91
Aly, Abdullah, 336n
amal jariah, 278
AMAN (Asian Muslim Action Network), 309
Amangkurat Amral, 19
amar maruf nahi munkar, 263
Ambarawa, 170
Amir, Dja'far, 280
Amir, Kyai, 8n, 80, 85–92, 94, 111–13, 123, 143, 170
AMM Kotagede. *See* Angkatan

Muda Muhammadiyah (AMM) Kotagede
AMM, Team Tadarus, 272–73
  Meeting Hall, 275–76
Anak Asuh, 270, 325–26
Anderson, Benedict R.O'G. (Ben Amderson), xxvii, 35n, 65n, 97n, 167, 188, 376
Angkatan Muda Muhammadiyah (AMM) Kotagede, 224n, 260, 345
anti-air pollution, 370
anti-Communism, 253
anti-Communist
  campaigns, 363
  Muslim, 238n
  propagation, 286
anti-greenhouse gas effects, 370
anti-smoking, 370
anti-Sukarno campaign in Jakarta, 171
anti-water pollution, 370
Anwar, Bashori H., 144, 283, 285–86, 296, 338, 364
apem, 35
Apotek Citra, 344
Arief, Ahmad Noor, 338
arisan, 326
As'ad Humam, K.H. (Pak As), 271, 273, 281
Asngari Djakfar, H., 327, 328n
Association of the Indonesian Tour and Travel Agency (ASITA), 343
Asy'ari, Pak (pseud. name), 175–84, 187–88, 198, 201
ati kang wening, 36
Atmosudigdo, Mas, 80–81, 91, 95, 132, 264, 281
Atmosudigdo, Rasjidi, 96
Azhar, Basyir, 295

B
babad, 173–74
Babon Anim, 345

Bachrun Nawawi, 304–306, 308
Badan Keamanan Rakyat, 170
Bagdhadiyah, 271
Bahuwinangun, 61, 81, 132, 248
Bakar, Haji, 101
bakul, 93, 134, 140–41, 319–20, 323, 326
Bambang Sumantri, H., 245n
Bani Mukmin, 79–80, 142–43
Bantul, 18, 22, 79, 146, 222, 224, 255, 304, 307, 319, 344, 356
banyan tree, 17, 24, 340
Basen, R.K., 24, 57, 83, 126, 135–36, 221, 240
Bashori Anwar, Pak, 144
Basis Hargito, 343n
Batavia, 58, 74
batik, 42–43, 52, 57–58, 79–80, 84, 104, 131–32, 146, 267
  jaman, 58
batin (batos), 168, 179
  lahir vs., 183–86
Bayi-Bayi Bersayap, 254n
becak, 320
bedhug, 33–34
bekel, 21, 26, 28, 32, 40, 46–48, 73, 169, 172
Benda, Harry J., 4n, 6n, 121, 166
Beras Miskin (Raskin), 317–19, 325
Berg, C.C., 7
Berita Nasional, 343
bersih desa, 351
bersih linkungan, 240
besek, 173
Bevervoorde, van, 9–11, 31–33, 42–43, 57, 125
Bhinneka Tunggal Ika, 312
Bishop, Gordon, 249
BKKBN (National Family Planning Agency), 345
black hole in history, 253–54
black market, 125, 132
BMT an Ni'mah, 326–28

Bodon, 255–56, 264, 269, 358
Boharen, 79, 90
Boland, B.J., xxi–xxii, 6n
Bousquet, G.H., 99, 101
Boven Digul, 77, 124
brasswork, 132
Bringhardjo (market), 176, 304
Brosur Lebaran, 291–93, 296, 312, 335–36, 342, 343, 364, 368–69
  topics of, 292, 297
Brunei, 247, 274
BTI, 240
Buddhist, 235
budi pekerti, 188
Budi Utomo, 52, 53, 56, 63, 312
bupati, 31, 40, 47
bureaucracy, xxxi
Burger, D.H., 14
buruh, 130–31, 134, 140–41, 146, 239, 322–23
  bangunan, 320
  industri, 319
  jahit, 130, 141
  juragan vs., 348
  perak, 143
Buruh Gugat (Workers Accuse), 347–48, 351, 354

C

Cairo, 80, 91, 95–96
campursari, 332, 347
Castles, Lance, 6n, 14
Celanan, 281
centennial birth year, 360
Centraale Padvinders Vereniging, 68
charity, 371
charms, 35
Charris Zubair, Ahmad, 267n, 306, 308, 314n, 335, 338–39, 354
children's education, 143–51
Chinese, 14, 42, 63, 235
Chirzin, Habib, 286, 287, 309
Chirzin, H. Muhammad, 144, 267

Christianity, 313
Christianization, xxx
Christians, 236
  Catholic churches, 362
  Catholics, 236, 313
  Protestants, 313
Cirebon, 58
civil servants, 120, 133
civil voluntary movement, 353
clinics, xxvi, xxxi, 5, 7, 93–103, 167, 286n
Colonial Fair, 84
commercial spirit, 63
communication
  in Kotagede, 229–30
  between Muhammadiyah people, 189–90
Communism, 71, 76–77
Communist, 62, 71, 75, 124, 139, 150, 171, 185, 189, 253, 361
community, 277, 341, 369–70
  development, 360
  development programme, 304
  religious, 119, 122, 154
Confession of Faith, 178, 180, 198
Constitutional Assembly, 120
copperware, 40, 43
Cornell University, xxvi, 373
cotton goods, 42–43, 79
Coup of October 1, 125
craftsman, 73, 93, 109, 130, 134, 139–40, 142, 150–51
craftsmen, xxxiv, xxxiii, 13–15, 21, 40–41, 43, 57–58, 71, 104, 106, 302
Crown Prince, 32
cult of royal glorification, 7, 10, 13, 28
Cultural Heritage District, 338, 345
Cultural Kotagede, 224
Cultural Muhammadiyah, 339–40, 348, 353, 367, 369
cultural proselytization, xxiii–xxvi

culture
  local, 335–41
  politicization of, 333–34
  of poverty, 324–40

D
dagang, 134
Dahlan, Kyai Haji Ahmad, xxv, 51–56, 52n, 62, 66–67, 75, 80, 86, 90, 172, 312, 371
dakwah (da'wah), 254–63, 336, 353
dalem, 249–50
Danuredjan, 79, 88
Darwin, Pak & Bu, 143–48
Darwis Khudori, 254, 309, 326, 335, 338, 359
de Kat Angelino, P., 58
Deliar Noer, 5n, 120n
democracy, xxx, xxxi, 346–50
  challenge of, 311–15
democratization, 353, 362, 365
Department of Religious Affairs, 8, 83, 86, 272, 274, 307
desacralization, 353
Desa Jagalan, 222, 224, 227, 230, 236, 247, 281, 356
Desa Mutihan, 222, 224
Desa Singosaren, 222
devotion, religious, 119, 122
dhagelan, 188, 202
dhalang, 195
dhawuh, 182
dhukun, 37, 101, 109, 168
Dingemans, L.F., 13n, 74–75
Dipanegara War, 79
diversity in politics, 237–45
divorce counseling, 289n
Djumairy Martodikoro, 169n
djumbuhing kawulo-gusti, 182
Dondongan, 37
Drewes, G.W.J., 4n, 198
Dulkijah, 31
Dutch
  authorities, 11, 13n, 56, 62, 67

colonial government, 46, 280
colonial rule, xxv, 6n, 121
East Indies Company, 14
Governor, 40
Governor-General, 32
dyewood, 43

E
earthquake, 227, 229, 354
  in Kotagede (2006), 355–60
economic impoverishment, post-war, 125–34
economy, xxxiii, 14, 40–42, 44–45, 57–58, 93, 104, 125, 130–32, 146, 300, 363
  of globalization, 245–46
  in Java, 6n
édan-édanan, 195
education, 232–34, 284, 298–300
  Muhammadiyah member's, 137–39
  and social welfare, xxv–xxvi
educational and social welfare institutions, 364
egalitarianism, 122
Egypt, 91
elections, 296, 303.
  in 1971, xxxv
  in 1999, 305, 366
  in 2004, 366
  in 2009, 366
  parliamentary and presidential, xxx
  see also general elections
electricity, 131, 228
emping, 176
entrepreneur, 14, 15, 42, 73, 104, 106, 109–10, 125–26, 131–32, 134, 139–43, 150, 153, 302
erfbezitter (house-compound holder), 26, 42
Erwito Wibowo, 254n, 308, 336, 338, 342, 360n
Ethical Policy, 46, 97, 282
ethnicity, growing diversity in, 234–37

European, 14, 43
  plantation, 41
"excellent society", 311, 363
ex-PKI people, 254
Ex-Tapol (Political Prisoners), 239–41

F
Facebook, 230
Fakhruddin, Kyai Haji A.R., 96, 165, 187–93, 290, 295
fakir miskin, 103, 199
Fathurahman, M., 232n
Fekih, K.H., 89
Festival Anak Saleh Indonesia, 274
Festival Kotagede (FK), 338, 340
  in 1999, 341–46
  in 2000, 346–50
  in 2002, 350–51
festive prayer (*sholat ied*), 155, 157–59, 161–63, 199
five-day cycle (Javanese calendar), 22, 146
"Followers of Muhammad", 5
Forum Koordenasi Pengajian Anak (FOKOPA, Forum for Coordination of Childrens' Pengajian), 260, 343, 345
Foster Parents Program (FPP), 304
France, 359
Friday prayers, 357

G
gadho-gadho vs. true Muslim, 168–80
Gadjah Mada University (UGM), xxi, 147, 268, 288, 294, 300, 304, 310, 324n, 335, 359
Gajah Wong River, 20, 22, 37, 43–45, 223, 228, 260
Gakin, 270
gambling, 28, 40, 195, 197, 204
gamelan, 31, 34, 46, 67, 195, 267, 308, 344–45, 353
Garebeg, 28
  Besar, 31

Maulud, 31
Puasa, 31
Gedongan, 221
Gedongkuning (Gedungkuning), 79, 221
Gedung Da'wah Al-Qur'an, 260, 262
Gedung PDHI, 260
Geertz, Clifford, xxxiv, xxi, xxvii, 6n, 14, 16, 17, 41n, 149, 152n, 166–67, 172, 181n, 183, 190–91, 198, 200, 207, 379
geguritan, 347
gemeenteraad, 48
general elections
  in 1955, 120, 123, 209
  in 1971, 135–36, 175, 209, 287, 363
  in 2009, 366
  Muslim's task in, 177, 201, 204
  problem of, 178
Gerindera, 243
Gerwani, 124
Giwangan, 257n, 267–68
globalization, xxix, xxx
  of economy, 245–46
  positive side of, 246–47
Goddess of the Southern Ocean, 32, 82
gold, 41, 43, 57, 61, 88, 130
goldsmith, 40, 73, 124, 141
Golkar, 136, 184–85, 237, 242–43, 314, 334, 341
Government, 11, 34, 61, 64, 73–74, 76, 89–90, 93–94, 97–99, 112, 119, 121, 123, 125–26, 128, 130, 132–34, 139, 147, 169, 232, 253, 285–86, 288, 315, 363
  agencies, 357
  Central, 266
  development programmes of, 286
  employees, 300
  local, 358
  offices, 356
  policies, 345

schools, 265, 268–69
statistics, 355
tourism of, 346, 350, 354
Graaf, H.J., 4n, 18n, 46
grand vizier, 26, 32, 47
Great Mosque, 38–39, 85–86, 109–10, 112, 118
　of Kotagede, 32, 103, 109, 168, 170
　of Mataram, 12, 20, 24, 34, 49, 109, 255, 262, 340, 347, 352, 358
　of the Sultan, 56
　Sultanate of Yogyakarta, xxv
　of Surakarta, 85
　of Yogyakarta, 52, 85
greeting, 162, 177, 189
Groneman, J., 31
G-30-S, 170–71, 265, 348
　Affairs, xxix, 333, 361–62
　Coup, 36n
　PKI, 238n, 239
guru ngaji, 65
Gusti, 182–83
　Allah, 111, 178–80

H

Hadith, xxv, xxxvi, 7, 65, 86, 88, 90–91, 98, 168, 189, 210, 260
haji, 56, 260
hajj, xxii, 31,
Hajid, Haji, 75–76, 89
Hajid Mutohar, H., 288
hakim, 89
hak pakai, 267
halal-bihalal, 187
halaqah, 314
Hamin, K.H., 89
handicraft, xxxiii, 14, 41–43, 58, 136
　industry, 367–68, 370
　in Kotagede, 347
Hani, Raden, 75–76
Hanura, 243

Harahap, Burhanuddin, 171
Harahap, Parada, 108
haram, 163
Hardjono, S.K., 9, 13, 68n
Hari Korban, 199
harmony, 346–50
Harsya Bakhtiar, 16
Hasjim Asj'ari, Kyai Haji, 87
Hasyim, Mustofa W., 254n, 335, 338
hawa nafsu, 168
　vs. *ikhlas*, 191–97
health care, 232–34, 277
Heiho (Auxiliary Forces), 143
High Javanese, 19–20, 22
HIK Muhammadiyah, 176
Himpunan Mahasiswa Islam (HMI), 148
Hindu-Balinese, 44
Hindu-Buddhist, 7, 331
Hindu-Javanese, 15, 206
Hiroyoshi Kano, 319n
historic heritage, 370
Hisyam Syafi'i, K.H., 261
Hizbullah, 122, 176
Hizbul Wathan (HW), 67–68, 109, 170, 347, 370
Hizbut Tahrir, 244
Hollandsch Inlandsche School (HIS), 89, 94, 98, 170
Holy City, 84n, 87–88
Holy Scriptures, 153, 205
Hoogere Inlandsche Kweekschool (HIK), 176
hospitals, 5, 93, 101, 200, 286n, xxvi, xxxi
H.O.S. Tjokroaminoto, 62
Humam Siradj, Haji, 271
HW. *See* Hizbul Wathan (HW)

I

IAIN SK (Insititut Agama Islam Negeri, Sunan Kalidjaga), 278n
ibadah (ibadat), 183, 324, 332

Idul Adha, 31, 155, 157–59, 199, 254, 257–63, 267, 316n, 329–30
Idul Fitri, 31, 82, 155–57, 254, 257–63, 258n, 267, 316, 323n, 330
ijtihad, 339
ikhlas, 113, 163, 168
   hawa nafsu vs., 191–97
   vs. pamrih, 198–207
ilmu agama, 149
imam, 162–63
iman, 332
Iman, K.H., 89
imitasi, 108, 130
Imogiri, 10, 19, 21–22, 35, 133
incense, 13, 36
indigo, 41
Indonesia, 265, 273–74, 277
   modern Islam in, 6n
   Muslims and Islam in, 121
   national economy of post-war, 131
   politics, 120
   post-colonial government of, 8
   Republican forces, 82
   revolution, 122
   society, 311–12
Indonesian Students Action Front (KAMI), 172
industry, xxxiii, 7, 10, 14, 20, 43, 84, 104, 108–109, 124, 128, 130, 143, 177, 285, 367–68, 370
   folk, 360
   silver, 353, 357
   tourist, 360
   workers in, 348
infak, 316, 324
infrastructure, 131, 228
Ingsun, 27, 178, 182
inlanders, 6n
Inlandsche dorpsgemeente, 46
"*Interogasi*", 254n
inviolability, 163
Iping, Kang, 230n

Iqro', 271–77
   Book, 273
   methodology, 274, 277
Iranian Islamic Revolution in 1979, xxvi
ironsmith, 40, 42
Islam, 210, 335
   culture of, xxvii
   defence of, 121–22
   importance of, 121
   in Java, 212, 331
   and local cultural tradition, 308
   modern, 166
   nationalism *vs.,* 244
   orthodox, xxvi, 208
   political forces of, 237
   reality of, 212
   religion of, xxvii, 154
   research on, 352
   ritual orthodoxy of, xxxiv
   and trade, xxxiv
   traditional, 337
Islam Terpadu (IT), 237, 270
Islamic
   Appeals Court, 89
   bureaucracy, 121
   calendar, 31
   Centre, 255
   civil society organization, 25
   Communism, 76
   community, 97n, 109–10
   globalism, xxviiin
   history, 99
   judicial system, 6n
   justice, 89
   law, 85, 88n, 278
   legal institutions, 210
   micro-financing, 326
   movements, xxxiii, 213
   New Year, 262
   obligations, 210
   orthodoxy, 15, 51
   philanthropy, 371

political party, 120, 209, 238, 243
reforms, xxi, xxxiii, 13, 91, 95
"revolution", 9
schools, 147, 266, 270
society, 208, 254
state, 120
studies, 212, 300
symbols, 122
teachings, 7, 40, 45n, 86, 172, 174, 185–86, 294, 310
traditional education, 65
Islamic University of Indonesia (UII), 123, 300
Islamization, xxxix, xxii, xxiv, 15, 17, 24, 209, 270, 277, 308, 362
of Java, 3–9
Ismail, Haji, 267
istana raja dagang, 248
Isya' prayer, 33–34, 344

J

Jadul Maula, M., 342n, 351–52
jaelangkung (straw men), 348–49, 351
Jagabaya, 47–48
Jagalan, 24, 136, 222–23, 229, 244, 248, 258, 264, 313, 356
Jakarta, 234, 239, 245, 266, 327
Jakarta Post, 250n
Ja'far, Pak (pseud. name), 123, 169–76, 185, 198–200
Jakfar, Asngari, 326–28
Jaksa, 63
Jalan Gedongkuning, 237
Jalan Kemasan, 343–44
Jalan Mondorakan, 224
jaman kethoprak, 125
Jamhari, Pak M., 144
Japan, 80, 85–86, 89
Japanese, 85–86, 89
  authorities, 121, 123
  Christian, 206
  government in Yogyakarta, 123
  Islamic policy, 121
  military government, 121
  occupation, 5, 120–21, 123, 128
  occupation Army, 143
  rulers, 121
  war, 121
jathilan, 347, 349
Java, xxxiii, 14, 67, 94, 97, 289
  Central, xxii, xxxiv, xxxv, xxxix, 3, 6, 10, 18, 41, 44, 58, 86, 88, 171, 208–10, 245, 355
  Central and East, 6n, 7, 45
  East, xxxv, 84, 86–87, 194, 209, 271, 324n
  Islam in, xxv, xxviii, xxxix, 212, 331
  Islamization of, 3–9
  re-Islamization, 208–11
  South Central, 170, 194
  West, 6n
Javaansche Padvinders Organisatie, 66
Java-based traditionalist Muslim party, 120
Javanese
  calender, 79
  "Chinese" (Pecina Jawa), 14
  culture, xxix, 166, 342n
  in ethnicity, 236
  folk art, 367
  Islam, xxxiii, xxxv, 208, 283
  language, 186, 290
  Muslims, xxv, 210
  ngelmu, 182
  principalities, 17, 21, 41, 46
  religious tradition in, 211
  student population in Cairo, 95
  town, 6, 9, 21
  traders, xxxiii, 13
  urban centre, 7, 95
Javanese Muslims, xxxvi
  religious communications among, 165–68
Javanization, xxiv, 308
Jawah community, 95, 98
Jay, Robert R., 6n

Jazir (Yazir) Asp, 271–72
Jejeran, 344
jenazah, 262
jewelry, 33, 41, 43, 57, 61, 88
jihad, 200
jihadist, 262
jimat (charms), 35
Jogjakarta (Yogyakarta), 221
joglo, 356
Joglo-Jagonya Sawung Jabo, 344
Johns, Anthony H., 3–4n
Jombang, 87, 89
Joyo News Service, 249
judicial system, Islamic, 6n
Jumanuddin, H., 272, 281, 379
Junus, Mahmud, 52n
juragan, 57, 104, 134, 140, 323
  vs. *buruh,* 348
juru ramal, 168
jurukunci, 21, 26–27, 33, 36, 44, 49–50, 133–34, 172

K
Kabupaten, 22, 24, 146, 177, 222, 224, 307
kacang kulit, 344
kadonyaan, 178, 201
kafir, 169, 179
Kahar Mudzakkir, Abdul, 80, 90, 92, 96
Kaharuddin Noor, 283, 306–308
Kahin, George, xxxv, 209
kain, 43
kakuwaosan, 49
Kalang
  family, 45
  group, 45
  people, 15, 42, 44–46, 57, 131
Kalurahan, 21, 24, 26, 47–49, 125–26, 133, 136, 173
KAMI (Indonesian Students Action Front), 172
Kamil, R., 52n

kamituwa, 47
kampil, 33
Kampung, 47, 136, 142–43
  Karangduren, 343n, 345
  of Kotagede, 169–71, 175–77
  Wisata Muhammadiyah, 360
Kanthil Foundation, 338, 359, 346, 350, 370
  pamphlets of, 359
Karang, 257, 259, 351
Karangkajen, 360
karawitan, 331
Karta, 19
Kartasura, 19–20
Kartodirdjo, Sartono, xli
kasar vs. alus, 186–91
kasektèn, 35, 40, 49, 206
kaum, 34, 47, 101–102, 103n
Kauman, 51–56, 67–68, 80, 89, 360
  of Kudus, 63
  Pijenan, 79
kawasan cagar budaya, 338
Kawasan Kotagede, 222–24
kawula, 178, 182–83
  -*gusti,* 182
kebayan, 47
Kecamatan Kotagede, 221, 224, 227, 229–30, 233–34, 236–37, 242, 319, 323
  employees in, 322
Kedaton, 22
Kedaulatan Rakyat (KR), 18, 343
Kediri, 58, 84
kedukuhan, 24
Kedungbánteng, 89
kejawen, 335, 340, 351–53
  vs. Muhammadiyah, 331–32
Kelompok Kesenian Srandul, 342n
Keluarga Miskin (Gakin), 270
Kelurahan, 221, 243, 355
Kelurahan Banguntapan, 222
Kelurahan of Prenggan, 221, 225, 236, 243

Kelurahan of Purbayan, 221, 243, 318
Kelurahan of Rejowinangun, 225–26, 243
Kelurahan Singosaren, 224
Kelurahan Wirokerten, 222
Kemantrean Kotagede, 224
Kemantren, 22, 133, 136–37, 184, 221, 255
Kemasan, 40, 228
kendil, 34
kenduren, 35
Keprabon, 89
Keputran, 83
kerajinan perak, 321
kerata-basa, 191
keroncong, 332–34, 332n, 347, 350
kerupuk, 168
kethoprak, 125, 194–97, 203–204, 331–34, 344, 347, 350, 353
Khisbiyah, Yayah, 336n
Khoiruddin Bashori, 290, 294–95, 353
khotib (ketib), 49, 52, 56, 85, 159, 162, 168–70, 256–57
khutbah, 159, 162, 168, 323n
kiblat, 52n
Ki Gede
  Mataram, 18–19
  Matarem, 19
Ki Hadjar Dewantoro, 62
Kitha Ageng, 20
Kleco, 270–71, 289, 358
knighthood, 206
Koentjaraningrat, 16
Koesnaeni, 266–67, 267n, 270
Koesoemanto, K.H., xxxiii
KOMNASHAM (National Commission of Human Rights), 309
konfeksi, 130
  workshop, 107
Kooperasi Produksi Pengusaha Perak Yogyakarta (KP3Y, KP3J), 124, 128–29, 143, 177, 321

korban, 159, 258, 324
Kotagede, xxix, 84, 125, 127–28, 251–52, 369–70
  Beatles in, 207
  cultural resources of, 346, 350, 354
  desa, 24–25, 135, 224, 227
  economy, 130–31, 322
  Great Mosque of, 168, 170
  growth of, 57–62
  kota, 24–25, 135–36, 140, 143, 148, 176, 224, 227
  market, 59, 320
  market on Legi, 230–31
  Muhammadiyah
    development, xxvi, 9–13
    paradoxes of Muhammadiyah in, 13–16
  people (folks) of, 173, 335, 340, 346, 351
  PKI influence in, 124
  political developments in, 123
  poor household heads in, 318, 319
  population, 368
  pre-Muhammadiyah Islam in, xxxiv
  region, 217–18
  silverwork industry in, 129
Kotagede Centre for Sacrifice Animal (PHQK), 328–30
Kotagede Ewuh, 348, 350n
  implications of, 351–54
Krama (Javanese), 167, 181
  Andhap, 181n
  Inggil, 181–82
kramat, 151
Krapyak, 271
kraton, 6, 18–19, 22, 71, 109, 149, 195, 342
Krida Mataram, 67
Kridoharsoyo, 266
kris, 41, 43
KUA (Kantor Urusan Agama), 34, 82, 141, 149, 197, 236, 240, 278
Kudus, 289

kuli kenceng, 26, 32, 42, 282
kumawula, 179
kuningan, 132
Kusudyarsono, 36n
Kutha Gedhe, 20
kuwalat, 35
Kwantes, R.C., 52n
Kweekschool, 56, 63, 176
kyai (kjaji, kyayi), 17, 66, 83, 174, 213, 237, 240
Kyai Amin, 86, 88
Kyai Baghowi, 79
Kyai Djalal Sajuthi, 86
Kyai Dudo, 333
Kyai Haji Masjhudi, 78, 88–89, 119
Kyai Ibrahim, 86, 96
Kyai Mahfudz, 84
Kyai Muhtaram, 84
Kyai Nawawi, 86
Kyai Sekati, 31
Kyai Sjafi'i, 79
Kyai Zainuddin, 84

L
labuhan, 32
lahir, 168, 179–80, 191
    vs. *batin*, 183–86
langgar, 7–8, 67, 111, 161, 185, 255–56, 278, 280
Lasykar Rakyat, 122
Later Mataram, 6–7, 10, 18–22, 31–32, 35–36, 40, 109, 195
Lawiyan, 63
leadership
    'Aisyiyah, personal background of, 300–301
    Muhammadiyah, 296-300
    prospects for, 308–10
    social dimensions of, 302–303
    stagnation of Muhammadiyah, 364
leatherwork, 40, 108
lebai, 34
Legge, John D., 4n
Legi, 22, 43, 230–31

Lekra (League of People's Culture), 125
Lembaga Pemberdayaan Masyarakat Desa, 314
Lestari, Sri Puji, 271
lingua franca, 95
Living Museum, 360
local culture, aspiration for, 335–40
Low Javanese, 20
LSPPA (Institute of Research and Development for Women), 345
ludruk, 194
lungguh, 21, 26, 133, 282
lurah, 27, 47–48, 88, 123, 285
lurah jurukunci, 26, 44, 133

M
Madiun, 58
madrasah, 89, 94, 237
Madrasah Mu'allimin, 265
Madya (Javanese), 181n, 182
magang, 50, 150
Magelang, 56
magersari, 26
Maghrib, 34, 91
Ma'had Islamy, 89, 94
    and PIRI, 147n
Mahasiswa Indonesia, 172
Mahfoeld, M.A., 120n
Mahfudz, Kyai Haji, 88
Mahkamah Islam Tinggi, 89
Mailrapport, 74, 98, 108
Majelis Mujahidin Indonesia (MMI), 244, 262
Majelis Tarjih, 89
Majelis Wakaf, 279n
Majul, C.A., 163n
Malacca, 88n, 95
Malay-Muslim world, 88n
Malaysia, 274
maleman, 32–33, 35, 109
ma-lima, 39
manca negara, 31
Mangkunegaran, 7, 20, 67

mantri kalang, 45
Mardi, Ibu, 287, 290
Mardihartoko, 66
Mardjuki, H., 278–80, 281n
market
   on Legi day, 230–31
   Royal Cemetery and, 18–25
Martohastono, 20
Mas (title), 26
Masa Kini, 9n
Masayu Nurul Ana, 332
Masjhudi, Haji (K.H.), 63, 67, 78–80, 82–86, 88–89, 91, 119, 123, 148–49, 264, 280–81, 283
Masjid (Mosque)
   Ageng Mataram, 24
   Al-Huda, 255
   Baiturrahman, 255, 257
   Mataram, 255
   Perak, 85, 89, 103, 113
Masjkur, K.H., 89
masyarakat utama, 311
Masyumi Party, 6n, 120–21, 123, 125, 139, 170–72, 286–87, 363
Mataram, 18–19, 36, 39, 49, 58, 68, 82, 227
   Great Mosque of, 340, 347, 352
   Kingdom, 19, 35, 227, 340, 348
   Sultanate, 338
Maulud, 31, 35
mausoleum, 19, 29, 36
Mawardi, K.H., 89
McVey, Ruth T., 73n, 77
Mecca, xxii, xxv, 33, 52, 56, 64n, 79–80, 84, 87–88, 91, 98, 161
merchant, 43–44, 57–58, 71, 80–81, 83, 88, 91, 94, 134, 140, 142
   king, 58, 61, 73, 80, 91, 132, 264, 281
   queen, 58
metalwork, 357
micro-financing, growing, 326–28
Middle Eastern Islamic reformism, 95

mikradan, 32
Minangkabau, 6n, 9n
minbar, 112, 162
Minister of Religious Affairs, 8n, 82
Mi'raj, 32
Misbach, Haji, 73n, 76
Mlangsen, 88
MMI (Majelis Mujahidin Indonesia), 244
mobile phones, 229–30
mocopat, (macapat), 331–32, 332n, 347, 353
modin, 101
Mojokerto, 88
Monggo chocolate firm, 247, 249–51
Mook, van, 10, 21n, 24, 26–27n, 35, 37, 46–48, 57–58, 61–62, 125–26, 140
mosques, 255–57, 357–58
Moving Equilibrium, The (Jadul), 351n, 352
Mranggen, 40
Mu'allimat, 94, 176–77, 265, 284–85, 287
Mu'allimin, 94, 170, 177, 271, 284–85, 299, 303
muballigh, 98n, 125, 167–68, 174, 183, 271
Muchsin, Haji, 80, 90, 94–95, 113, 115
Muhammad, Prophet, 7, 31, 53, 168–69, 174, 178
Muhammadiyah, 25, 35, 40, 47, 49, 121, 161, 219, 335–40
   and 'Aisyiyah, 287–90, 325–26
   background for success of, 361–62
   BMT, 328
   branches of, xxvi, 295, 302, 306
   Council for Primary and Secondary Education, 264
   Council for Research and Development, 307
   Council of Missionary and Propagation, 256

Index   419

children's education, 143–51
common challenge in, 368–69
complacence and stagnation,
  290–96
concept of *rezeki*, 152
concern for the poor, 370–71
criticism from younger generation,
  364–65
cultural, 339–40, 348, 353, 367,
  369
development of, xxxiii, 9–13
economic conduct, 152–53
entrepreneurs, 153
future of, 371
general membership of, 303–304
hard work and simple life, 143–51
hegemony of, 352
in Islamization of Java, 3–9
in Kotagede, 13–16, 123, 369–70
leadership of, 122, 154, 283–86,
  296–300, 364
PKU, 233, 316
poverty alleviation, 315
reformasi, politics and, 365–67
schools, 143, 147, 232–33, 263–71,
  306–307
and Soeharto government, 362–63
traders, 153
vs. kejawen, 331–32
wage-labourer, 153
Muhammadiyah Kotagede Branch,
  267, 280
Muhammadiyah members, 134–35
age and sex, 136–37
education, 137–39
geographic distribution, 135–36
occupational composition of,
  139–43
*Muhammadiyah Menjemput
  Perubahan*, 312
Muhammadiyah movement, xxii, xxvi,
  xxviii, 13n, 119, 125
Muharram, 262
Mudjono, Pak, 145

Mukmin, Bani, 79–80, 142
Mukmin, Haji, 91, 131–32, 142–43
Mukti Ali, Abdul, 5n, 8n, 82
Munawir, K.H., 86
Murohar, Pak, 289
musholla, 7, 83, 175, 255n, 256, 258,
  278, 280, 286, 326, 357–58
Musholla Basen, 290
Muslim
  community, 310, 314, 366
  gadho-gadho vs. true, 168–80
  leaders, 121, 125
  mass organizations, 122
  participation in Revolution, 122
  political forces, 120–21, 209
  population, xxxii
  in revolutionary politics, 121
Muso, 62, 75
musyrik, 173
Mutihan, 57, 344
Mutu, 265–66

N

nafkah, 151
nafsu (napsu), 180, 191
  mutma'innah, 191–92
Nagazumi, Akira, 52n, 63n
Nahdlatul Ulama (NU), xxv, xxiii, 87,
  120–23, 136, 236–37, 242, 313
Nakamura, Mitsuo, xxi, xxiv, xxxiii,
  xxxvi
Nasyiatul 'Aisyiyah, 148, 260
national awakening, 62
National Family Planning Agency,
  345
nationalism, 95, 99
  vs. Islam, 244
nationalist, xxiii
  movement, 9n, 97n
  parties, 243
National Land Agency, 278
National Marriage Law, 35, 209, 363
Natsir, M., 171, 338, 359
Nawawi, Kyai, 304

Netherlands, xxvi
  East Indies, 5, 80, 95
  Indies, 74
New Guinea, 95
New Order, xxi, 5, 15, 166, 171–72, 237–38, 286, 289–90, 345, 352, 362–64
Ngadiwinatan, 89
Ngawi, 271
Ngesuhi Deso Sak Kukuban (Jadul Maula), 314n, 342n
NGO, 247
Ngoko (Javanese), 20, 167–68, 181–82, 189–90, 195
  Madya, 181n
Ni'mah Syariah, 326–28
Nitikan, 360
Nizar Chirzin, Muhammad, 86n, 145
non-Islamic groups, 313
non-Muhammadiyah Muslims, 313
non-parliamentary extremism, 244
nrimo, 325
Nufa's Silver, 344
nyadranan, 32
Nyai Amir, 89
Nyai Chotidjah, 88
Nyai Loro Kidul, 32, 82

O
obong kalang, 44
occupation, population by, 319
Office of Religious Affairs (KUA), 34, 82, 89, 123
Old Banyan Tree, 20, 24, 35, 340
Old Kotagede, 227
O'Malley, William J., 21n, 41n
omong-omongan, 165, 190
Opak River, 22
opium, 13, 40, 63n
orang halus (ghosts), 75
Orang Hindia, 68
Orang Kalang, 282
Orang-Orang Kotagede, 254n

Orde Baru generation, 286
Organisasi Pengelola Kawasan Pusaka Kotagede (OPKP), 359–60
Organization for the Management of Kotagede Heritage District, 359
orphanages, xxvi, 5, 371
orthodox Islam, xxvi, 208
OSVIA (Training School for Native Administrators), 56

P
P2A (Proyek Pembinaan Agama), 253, 286
Pacak Suji, 344
Padvinders, 67
Paguyuban Perak Kotagede, 324
Pajang, 19
Pak A.R. *See* Fakhruddin, Kyai Haji A.R
Pak As. *See* As'ad Humam
Pakkanna, Mukhaer, 312
Pakualaman, 20–21, 68, 89, 133
palace guard, 61, 73
Palmier, Leslie H., 5n
Pamanahan Ki Gede Mataram, 18
pamong praja, 184–85
pamrih vs. ikhlas, 198–207
PAN (Partai Amanat Nasional), 241–44, 314, 341, 366
panakawan, 188
Pancasila, 311–12, 361
Pandéyan, 40
Pandora's box, xxix, 341
Panembahan Senapati, 19, 36–37, 109
panewu, 26
Pangeran Puger, 20
pangreh praja, 48, 50
para-military organizations, 121
parliamentary democracy, 120
Parmusi, 6n, 175, 177, 205, 209, 287, 363
Partai Demokrat, 242-44.
Partai Islam Indonesia (PII), 120

Partai Keadilan (PK), 314, 366
Partai Keadilan Sejahtera (PKS), xxiii, 237, 242–45, 262, 270, 314–15, 365–66
Partai Kebangkatan Bangsa (PKB), 242
Partai Komunis Indonesia (PKI), xxix, 62, 71, 73, 123–25, 128, 136, 139, 171, 186, 196–97, 238–41, 253, 265, 286, 324, 333–34, 348, 352, 361–62
Partai Muslimin Indonesia (Parmusi), 287
Partai Persatuan Pembangunan (PPP), 237–38, 242–44, 314, 366
Pasareyan, 19, 22, 109, 141, 149
   Mataram, 20
   Mosque, 109
Pasar Gede, 19–20, 43, 63–64, 64n
Pasar Kotagede, 343–44
Paseko, 344
Pasukan Pemuda Senopati, 171, 239
Patalan, 344
patuh, 21, 26, 47
PCM (Muhammadiyah Branch Leadership) Kotagede, 279n
PDHI. *See* Persaudaraan Djama'ah Haji Indonesia (PDHI)
PDI (Partai Demokrasi Indonesia), 237
PDIP (Partai Demokrasi Indonesia Perjuangan), 242–44, 314, 341
Peacock, James L., 194
Pecina Jawa, 14
pedagang, 83, 140, 319–20
Pedicab Racing, 351
pegawai, 93, 133–34, 140, 239, 364
   negeri, 133–34, 140
   swasta, 140
pegon, 90
Pekalongan, 58
pekarangan, 136, 227
Pekaten, 344

Pelajar Islam Indonesia (PII), 148
pembangunan, 219
Pemuda Muhammadiyah, 148, 260
Pemuda Rakyat (PR), 124, 239
pencak, 67, 171
pendhapa (pendopo), 45, 62, 74–75, 82, 93, 226–27, 264, 357
pengajian, 8, 55, 67, 85, 176–78, 180, 202, 244, 253–54, 256, 258, 260, 263, 271, 274, 276, 286, 299, 326, 349, 370
penggedhe, 134
penghulu, 27, 49, 54, 56, 89, 101, 103n, 113n, 118, 213
pengindung, 26
pengusaha, 140–41, 239
PENI, 345
People's Security Organization, 170
People's Union (Sarekat Rakyat), 73
perdikan, 27
Persatuan Islam (Persis), 6n
Persaudaraan Djama'ah Haji Indonesia (PDHI)
   Building, 260
   Hall, 261
perusahaan/usaha, 322
pesantren, 52, 65–66, 65n, 84, 98, 137, 176, 178, 237, 263, 283
   Tebuireng, 91
Pesantren Al-Munawir, 271
Pesantren Nurul Ummahat, 237
Pesik, Rudy, 247, 249n
Pigeaud, Theodore G.Th., 18n, 151, 191n
PII (Partai Islam Indonesia), 120, 148
Pilahan, 344
Pinalan, 221
Pitulasan, 345
Piyungan, 176
PKI, see Partai Komunis Indonesia
PKS, see Partai Keadilan Sejahtera
PKS' TK IT, 270
PKU, 101, 177, 233, 280, 286n, 290

clinic, 357
  vs. PUSKESMAS, 277
Plered, 321
pluralism, xxx, xxxi
  challenge of, 311–15
PNI (Partai Nasional Indonesia), 123, 171, 185, 237, 334
political choice, 237-44
political development
  in Kotagede, 123
  post-war, 120–25
political diversification, xxx
  consequences of, 244–45
political neutrality, 366
political prisoners, 239–41
politicization of culture, 333–34
politics, xxiii, xxx, xxxv, xxxvi, 46, 73–73n, 97, 100–101, 120–23, 180, 209–10, 352
  Indonesian, 167
  of reformist movements, 6n
polyclinic, 177
polytheism, 173, 349
Pondok, 52, 88
  Cepoko, 84
  Kanggotan, 84
  Krapyak, 86
  Magelang, 84
  Mojodari, 84
  Nganjuk, 84
  Punduh, 84
  Tebuireng, 87
  Termas, 84
  Wonokromo, 84
pondok ketrampiran, 326
population, 304, 345
  of Kotagede, 7, 28, 224–27, 368
  by occupation, 319
Pos Komand (POSKO), 357
post-Reformasi situation, xxix, xxx, 241–43, 313, 362–63, 367
post-war, 132
  economic impoverishment, 125–34
  political development, 120–25

poverty, xxiv, xxx
  of culture, 331–40
  culture of, 324–30
  problem of, 315–23
PPP (Partai Persatuan Pembangunan), 237–38, 242–44, 314, 366
PR (Pemuda Rakyat), 124, 239
prajurit kraton, 73
Pranoto Hadi, 224n
prayers
  Friday, 349
  houses, 356
  in Islam, 168, 177, 180, 190
pre-nationalism, 166
Prenggan, 24, 57, 83, 121, 126, 136, 225
  Syawalan meeting of, 187
presidential election
  in 2004, 284
  in 2009, 366
President Soeharto, 262n, 341
principalities, 6n, 7, 13n, 20–22, 31, 41–42, 46, 49, 61–62, 103–104, 113, 133
  courts, 10, 15
Pringgo Hastono, K.H., 144
priyayi, xxvii, xxxiv, 14, 16–17, 51–52, 56, 63, 83, 94, 118n, 119, 121, 126, 133–34, 149, 173–74, 185, 190, 195, 207
Progo River, 32
Project for Religious Guidance, 286
Prophet
  Ibrahim, 198–99
  Ismail, 199
  Muhammad, 31–32, 53, 168–69, 174, 178
Proposal Pengembangan Gedung Baru, 268
Protestant churches, 362
Protestantism, 166-67
Proyek Pembinaan Agama, 240, 286
pseudo-modernity, in Muhammadiyah, 167

Puasa, 31–33, 91, 109, 168, 183, 192
public buildings, 356
public infrastructure, 228
pulang kampung, 267
Purba Budaya Bumen, 342n
Purbayan, 136, 221, 227, 266, 278n, 344, 370
Purwokerto, 58
Purworejo, 86, 89
Pusat Hewan Qurban Kotagede (PHQK), 328–30
Pusat Studi dan Dokumentasi Kotagede (PUSDOK), 338–39, 343, 345–46, 360, 370
PUSKESMAS, 233–34
putihan, 16–17

Q

Qayim, Ibnu, 261
Queen Wilhelmina, 45
Qur'an, xxv, xxxvi, 7, 27, 53–54, 65, 67, 76, 84, 86, 89–90, 98, 102–103, 162, 168–69, 174–75, 177–78, 182, 198–200, 210, 271, 277, 371
Qur'anic Generation, 272
Qur'anic kindergarten, 271–77

R

Rabingulawal, 31
Raden (title), 26, 173–74
Raden Danudinoto, 75
Raden Reso, 75
Raden Sastrowidjono, 63
Raffles, Sir Thomas Stamford, 18–19, 44n
Raharjo, Khadi, 335
railroad, 41
Rais, Amien, 262–63, 295
raja dagang, 58, 61
Ramadhan, xxii, 31, 35, 187, 210
Rasjidi, H.M., 33–34, 63n, 80, 91, 96, 109, 187
Raskin (Beras Miskin), 317–19, 325

ratu dagang, 58
Red Cross Emergency Aid Centre, 247
Reformasi, 219, 241–43, 341
  movement, xxix
Reformist Islam, 166, 168, 172, 174
Regent, 31, 47
regional elections in 1957, 123
re-Islamization, xxvi, 4
  of Java, 208–11
Rejeb, 32
Rejowinangun, 221
rekayasa sosial, 336
religion
  growing diversity in, 234–37
  in Kotagede, 34
religious communications, among Javanese Muslims, 165–68
religious consciousness, 65, 122, 149, 200
religious devotion
  achievement of, 119
  expression of, 122
Religious Guidance Project, 253
religious lectures, 286
religious propagation, 254–63
religious taxes, 93, 258
Republican Army, 288
Republic of Indonesia (R.I.), 184, 265
Republika, 343
Resident, 40, 44–46, 74
  of Yogyakarta, 10, 13n
resurgence of Islam, xxvi
retail traders, 57–58
rezeki, 151–54
  in Muhammadiyah teaching, 152
R.I. *See* Republic of Indonesia
Riau Sultan, 88n
rice, 20, 22, 27, 33, 35, 43, 48, 66, 130–31, 143, 151, 156, 173, 179, 189, 224, 258n, 318–19
  in Central Java, 6
Ricklefs, Merle Calvin, 21n
Rida, Muhammad Rashid, xxv, 91
Ringin Tua, 22

Rinkes, 52n, 64n
ritual prayer, 155, 162–63
Riwajat Mesdjid Perak Kotagede (Nawawi), 110
R.K. (Rukun Kampung), 24, 84, 123, 125–26, 133, 136–37, 161, 176, 221, 345
Roff, William R., xxvii, xxviin, 4n, 88n
Rofi'ie, Hajah Umanah, 287–88
Rofi'i, Haji Anwar, 285
Rolls Royces, 45
rondha, 67
Royal Cemetery, 10, 15, 19–20, 22, 24, 27–28, 30, 32–37, 39–40, 43, 45, 49–50, 61, 133, 140, 332–34, 338, 340, 358
royal key-keepers, 15, 17, 33, 36, 61, 133, 140
royal servant, 15, 133, 173
RT (Rukun Tetangga), 221
rukun iman, 179, 183
rukun Islam, 135, 179, 183, 188, 205
Rukun Kampung (*See* R.K.)
Rukun Warga (RW), 221–22, 343, 351
  sixteen, 346
Rumah Pesik, 247
Rusdi, 79, 83
Ruwah, 32, 35
RW. *See* Rukun Warga (RW)

S

Saban, 32, 35
Sabillilah, 122
sabin, 179
sablon, 326
sadakah, 316, 324
Saleh, Rosyad, 323n
Saleh Udden, 313–14
Salim, Haji Agus, 9n
Samakan, 40
Samanhudi (Samanhoedi), 62, 86–88

Samudju Asjari, 65n
sangu, 179
santri, xxxiv, xxxix, xxviin, 14, 16–17, 20, 51–56, 87, 94, 102, 118–19, 149–50, 153, 169, 185, 189–90, 206–207, 295
santunan, 316, 324–25
SARA, 238n, 352
sarasehan, 346
Sarekat Islam (S.I.), 52–53, 56, 63–64, 166
Sarekat Islam Putih, 74
Sarekat Rakyat (S.R.), 73, 75–76
Sargedhe, 20
sarjana, 226n, 332n, 335, 342n
sarong, 83
Sartono Kartodirdjo, 16
sasrawungan ingkang saé, 165
sate gajih, 344
satrya, 206
Sayangan, 40, 57
Sayyid Shaykh, 87
Schrieke, B., 52n
scripturalist, 198
SD. *See* Sekolah Dasar (SD)
seafaring power, 6
second-class native school, 93
secularization, xxx
secular nationalists, 120–21
Seda-ing-Krapyak, 19
sega wudhuk, 35
Seinendan, 170, 176
Sekaten, 31
Sekolah Dasar (SD), 264
  Bodon, 265
  Kleco, 271
  Muhammadiyah, 270
Sekolah Islam Terpadu (IT), 270
Sekolah Menengah Atas (SMA), 264
  Muhammadiyah Yogyakarta 4, 266
Sekolah Menengah Kejujuran (SMK), 264
  Muhammadiyah Yogyakarta 3, 268

Index   425

Sekolah Menengah Pertama (SMP), 264
  Muhammadiyah, 290
  Muhammadiyah Yogyakarta 7, 265, 266, 270
  Negeri, 271
Sekolah Menengah Umum (SMU), 264
Seleman, 261
Selokraman, 86, 89, 111, 256, 260, 271, 274, 288–89
Selosoemardjan, 21n, 31, 41, 61, 133
Semarang, 41, 45, 58, 80, 170
Semaun, 62
sembahyang, 149
sembako, 325, 350
Senapati (Senopati), 19, 22, 35–37, 40
serakah, 169
sermon, 33, 52, 85, 111–12, 159, 162, 168, 170, 172, 174, 177, 199
sermon giver, 168–69
Sesame Street, 270
sesepuh, 124
setan, 349
Setyobudi, I., 226n
shahadat, 180
shalawatan, 331, 347, 350, 353
sholat, 155, 163n, 180, 197, 199
sholat ied, 155, 157–59, 163, 257n, 259
Shumuka, 90
S.I. (Sarekat Islam), 52–53, 56
Siam, 95
Siegel, James J., 152n, 162
Siemens, 359
Siliran, 18, 24, 35–36, 38
silver
  craftsman, 143
  industry, 33, 41, 57, 61, 103, 108, 320–22, 367–68, 370
  shop, 357
  -smith, 124, 130–31, 143
  -ware, 43, 105, 110, 113, 245–46
  -work, 103–104, 124, 128–30, 143
Silver Mosque, 85, 89, 103, 108–18, 255, 260, 264, 266, 280, 304, 358
Singapore, 87–88, 88n, 274
Singosaren, 24, 344
Siradj, K.H., 89
Siswoyo, Ibu Mardi, 289
siteran, 344
slametan, 28, 35, 173
slametan kekah, 34
slaughtering, 40
SMA. *See* Sekolah Menengah Atas (SMA)
SMK. *See* Sekolah Menengah Kejujuran (SMK)
SMP. *See* Sekolah Menengah Pertama (SMP)
SMU (Sekolah Menengah Umum), 264
Snouck Hurgronje, Christian, 92
SOBSI, 124, 240, 324
social business, promoting, 328–30
Social Organization Law, 364
social revolutions, 122
social welfare
  institutions, 364
  organization, xxiv
societal problems, 307–308
Soebardi, S., 4n
Soedjono Tirtokoesoemo, R., 31
Soeharto, xxi, 275, 295
Soeharto government, xxii, 286
  dictatorial developmentalism, 363
  and Muhammadiyah, 362–63
  political rehabilitation, 287
Soepomo Poedjosoedarmo, 181n
sohibul, 330
Solichin Salam, 9n
Solo Pos, 343
speech
  by Fakhruddin, Haji A.R, 188–93

level in Javanese, 180–83
   by Pak Asy'ari, 177–80
S.R. (Sarekat Rakyat), 73, 75–76
srambi, 33
srandhul, 332, 344, 350
stadsgemeente, 48
State Institute of Islamic Studies
   (IAIN), 82, 177
Statute of the Muhammadiyah, 53
straw men *(jaelangkung),* 348n
structural Muhammadiyah, 367
Stutterheim, W.F., 44n
sugar, 41
sugarcane, 22, 224
Sukarno's Guided Democracy, 120
Sultan Agung, 19, 44,
Sultan
   and Raja Muda, 88n
   of Yogyakarta, 26, 40, 51, 84, 113,
      133–34, 206,
Sultan Hamengku Buwono IX, 90,
   344, 353
Sultanate, 51, 56
   of Yogyakarta, xxv, 20–22, 56, 84
Sultan's Mosque, 52, 54
Sultan's treasury, 52
Sumatra, 9n
Sumatrans, 236
Sunan Kalijaga, 19, 24, 35, 82, 340
Sundanese, 236
Sunnatullah, 313
Surabaya, 41, 58, 234
Surabaya Institute of Technology
   (SIT), 268
Surakarta, 58, 73n, 94, 170–71
surban, 83
Suryantoro, Agus, 224n, 262n
Susuhunate of Surakarta, 20–22,
   26–28, 45, 47, 173
Sutherland, Heather, 14
Syamsuhadi, H., 267
Syarekatul Mubtadi (Association of
   Beginners), 7, 10, 64–67, 89, 93
Syariah, 88n, 152

Syawal, 31–32, 187
Syawalan, 92, 187–88
syirik, 349

T
tabligh, 176
tahlilan, 332
tahu bacem, 344
tahyul, 109
tajdid, 339
takbiran, 155–56
takhayul, bid'ah, and *churafat, see* TBC
takmir, 256
takwa, 179, 192
Taman Asuhan (TA), 237
Taman Kanak-Kanak (TK), 264
Taman Kanak-Kanak (TK) Al-Qur'an,
   272–73, 275, 277, 281
Taman Pelajar (TP), 274
tanah gaji, 149
tanah pusaka, 7, 20
taraweh, 33
tarekat, 65–66, 65n
tata-cara, 173, 181n
Taufik Abdullah, 6n
tauhid, 109, 173, 332, 338
TBC *(takhayul, bid'ah,* and *churafat),*
   331, 334, 338, 346, 348
Teachers' Training School (SGA), 271
Team Tadarus AMM, 272, 274
Tebuireng, 87, 91
Tedjo Soesilo, 40, 129–30
Tegalgendu, 37, 43–45, 57, 94, 131,
   221
television, 230
Terang Bulan, 267
terrorist attacks in Bali and Jakarta in
   2002–03, 245
textiles, 57–58, 80, 285
Thoyibi, M., 336n
Tinalan, 221
Tinkir, Joko, 344
tinsmith, 42
TK (Taman Kanak-Kanak), 264

tomb, 262n
tourism, 345
  of government, 346, 350, 354
TP (Taman Pelajar), 274
trade, xxxiii, 7, 10, 14, 42–43, 48, 130, 141, 176–77, 192, 285
  networks, 58, 88
trade union, 73, 124, 150, 171
traders, xxxiv, 13–14, 21, 41–42, 57–58, 63, 71, 79–80, 84, 91, 93, 125–26, 139–40, 142, 152n, 153, 176, 302
traditional administration, 26–40
traditional architecture, 356, 360
traditional economy, 40–46
trah/bani fesbuk, 230
transportation, 320
  in Kotagede, 230–32
Tujuhbelasan, 345
tukang, 73, 93, 134, 140–41, 239, 322–23
  amin-amin, 169
  emas, 73
  natah, 146
  penyu, 239
  perak, 104, 130, 143
Tulung Agung, 58
Turner, Victor, 155, 164
turtle, 18, 36
Twitter, 230

U
ulama, 17, 52, 76, 83–84, 88–89, 91–92, 282–83, 303
ulu-ulu, 47
Umanah, Ibu, 290, 300
ummat (ummah), 54, 97n, 103, 109, 122, 169, 178
  Islam, 74, 76, 97n, 154–64, 174, 199, 367–68
  Muhammadiyah, 367–68
Ummat Islam, 89
unemployment, 368
Unity in Diversity, 312

University of Muhammadiyah, Yogyakarta (UMY), 294, 300
upacara, 35
urban heritage, 309–10
urbanization, xxix
  buildings, 227
  communication, 229–30
  education and health care, 232–34
  growth of population, 224–27
  public infrastructure, 228
  transportation, 230–32

V
Volkstelling, 6n
voluntarism, 364

W
Wahzary Wardaya, 265n
wajik, 344
wakaf, 80, 93, 101, 187, 266, 278–82, 278n, 324
  documents, 280
  lands, 279, 282
Ward, K.E., 6n
Waringah, Siti 293
Waringah, Shinta, 338
waringin sepuh, 22, 35, 340
warnet (warung Internet), 230
War of Dipanegara, 21, 41
War of Independence, 288
wartel (warung telfon), 230, 326
warung, 43, 141, 195
Wates, 177
Watu
  Canteng, 22
  Gilang, 22
wax, 42–43
wayang, 46, 188, 195–96, 337, 353
  humor, 344
  kulit, 125, 194, 331–32, 332n, 344, 347
  orang, 331
  thingklung, 345, 347
  wong, 332

wedana, 40, 47
Wertheim, W.F., 71n, 166
Widjojo Nitisastro, 41n
Wira Tamtama, 68
Wirjosukarto, Amir Hamzah, 52n
Wisma Proyodranan, 343–44
witana, 36
WNI Keturunan, 234–36
wong
   cilik, 16, 28, 47–48, 134, 149, 195, 319
   Kalang (*See* Kalang People)
   Kotagede, 346, 351, 354
   Mataram (Mataram People), 58
   Yogya, 343
Wonokromo, 84, 89
Wonosari, 321
"Workers Accuse", 348
World Bank, 246, 342–43
World War I, 45, 64n, 84
World War II, xxxv, xxvi, 22, 84–85, 97, 197, 266

Y
yasinan, 332

Yayasan Kanthil *see* Kanthil Foundation
Yayasan Seni Rupa Mataram Indonesia (YSRMI), 343–45, 350
Yazid, Sajiman, 281
Yogyakarta, 127, 314
   city of, xxix, 7, 18, 22, 43, 45, 58, 74, 79, 84–85, 131, 133–34, 170, 218, 221, 224, 226, 228, 230, 235–36, 240, 242, 267, 270, 307, 323
   Cultural Division of, 342
   Japanese government in, 123
   Special Region of, 3, 6, 22, 133, 236, 268, 328, 355
   Sultan, 84, 113
   Sultanate, xxv, 45, 47, 51, 133, 353
Yogyakarta Heritage Society (YHS), 343, 345

Z
zakat, xxii, 168, 180, 185, 258n, 324
   fitrah, 34, 46, 93, 101, 103, 146, 156–57, 162, 254, 258, 316
zuhud, 169

About the Author

Mitsuo Nakamura is Professor Emeritus of Anthropology, Chiba University, Japan. After obtaining a Ph.D. from Cornell University, he has engaged in teaching and/or research at various institutions including University of Adelaide, University of Indonesia, The Australian National University, Harvard University, and Chiba University until his retirement from the latter in 1999. He has been, and still is, a close observer of the contemporary Islamic social movements in Indonesia, covering not only Muhammadiyah but also Nahdlatul Ulama and others. His recent "revisit" to Kotagede was his personal project to commemorate academically the centennial of Muhammadiyah, established in 1912.

www.ingramcontent.com/pod-product-compliance
Lightning Source LLC
Chambersburg PA
CBHW052048290426
44111CB00011B/1661